CHILTON'S Repair and Tune-Up Guide

Outboard Motors

30 Horsepower & Over

ILLUSTRATED

Prepared by the

Automotive Editorial Department

Chilton Book Company

401 Walnut Street
Philadelphia, Pa. 19106
215—WA 5-9111

managing editor **JOHN D. KELLY;** assistant managing editor **PETER J. MEYER;** editor **KERRY A. FREEMAN;** technical editors **Robert J. Brown, Philip A. Canal**

CHILTON BOOK COMPANY   PHILADELPHIA NEW YORK LONDON

Library of Congress Cataloging in Publication Data

Chilton Book Company.   Automotive Editorial Dept.
   Chilton's repair and tune-up guide: outboard motors,
30 horsepower & over.

   1. Outboard motors—Maintenance and repair.
I. Title.   II. Title: Repair and tune-up guide:
outboard motors, 30 horsepower & over.
VM348.C46   1973   623.87'23'4   72-11533
ISBN 0-8019-5722-2
ISBN 0-8019-5803-2 (pbk)

ACKNOWLEDGEMENTS

CHILTON BOOK COMPANY expresses appreciation to the following firms for their generous assistance and technical information:

BELK'S MARINE SUPPLY (MERCURY), *Holmes, Pennsylvania*

THE BOATING INDUSTRY ASSOCIATION, *Chicago, Illinois*

CHAMPION SPARK PLUG COMPANY, *Toledo, Ohio*

CHRYSLER OUTBOARD CORPORATION, *Hartford, Wisconsin*

J & J MARINA (JOHNSON), *Stone Harbor, New Jersey*

KIEKHAEFER MERCURY, *Fond du Lac, Wisconsin*

OUTBOARD MARINE CORPORATION (EVINRUDE), *Milwaukee,
Wisconsin*

OUTBOARD MARINE CORPORATION (JOHNSON), *Waukegan,
Illinois*
UNITED STATES COAST GUARD

The editorial content of this book has been compiled from au-
thoritative sources by skilled Automotive Editors. While every
effort is made to attain accuracy, the Publisher cannot be re-
sponsible for manufacturing changes, typographical errors, or
omissions.

Contents

1 · General Information and Maintenance

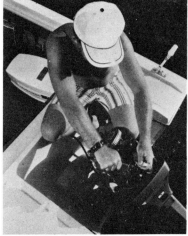

Introduction

This Repair and Tune-Up Guide is intended to contain the basic information necessary to repair and/or adjust the functioning systems of each specific outboard motor. Before attempting any service to your motor, it would be wise to read through the procedures and familiarize yourself with both the procedures and tools needed to complete the operation. A basic understanding of the operation of your motor will also aid in attempts to repair it. The use of special factory tools has been avoided wherever possible, although in some cases these tools are necessary. This book also assumes that the reader has at hand, a reasonable number of common tools and other equipment.

If you are in doubt concerning any operations in this book, consult either an authorized service facility or your owner's manual.

The operator of a boat should also read and become familiar with the Safety Afloat section of this book, which is contained in the Appendix. Familiarity with this section could save yours or someone else's life in an emergency.

Most outboards, given proper care, require little service other than periodic maintenance and adjustment. While common sense should dictate most normal maintenance, specific procedures are detailed for mid- and pre-season service and winterizing. Tune-up procedures and specific recommended maintenance are covered in the manufacturer's section. Specific procedures for removal, overhaul, and replacement of components is also covered in the manufacturer's section.

Most procedures in this book are recommended by the manufacturer or the Boating Industry Association. In some cases it was necessary to substitute more common tools for special factory tools; however, the usage of the special tool was kept in mind when selecting an alternate tool. If in doubt concerning the service of a motor, consult a dealer or, in minor cases, the factory authorized owner's manual.

Mounting the Motor on the Boat

Before buying a new or used outboard, it is wise to consult a dealer concerning the actual mounting dimensions and clearances. The following chart may help in determining whether a motor will fit a given transom.

NOTE: *This chart is taken from the Boating Industry Association's Marine*

Transom and Motor Well Dimensions

Motor HP	Transom Thickness Dimension A (in.)		Motor Clearance (in.) Dimension B	Cover Height (in.) Dimension C	Transom Height (Vertical) (in.) Dimension D		Cutout Length (in.) Dimension E ①
	Min	Max			Short Shaft	Long Shaft	
Under 5.5	1¼	1¾	14	18	14½–15	19½–20	21½
5.5–12	1⅜	1¾	17	22½	14½–15	19½–20	21½
12–61	1⅜	2	21	29	14½–15	19½–20	21½
61–91	1⅝	2¼	28	32½	——	19½–20	24
Over 91	1⅝	2¼	28	32½	——	19½–20	30

① If the transom cap strip extends more than ¹⁄₁₆ in. aft of the transom, the aft surface of the transom should be built up to bring the extension of the strip into tolerance.
As a safety measure, add 3 in. to Dimension E when the inboard section of the motor cutout is formed by the back of the seat.

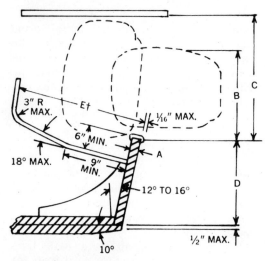

†The Fisher Pierce 55 H.P. requires an E dimension of 25 in.

Transom and motor well dimensions (© Boating Industry Association)

Service Manual of Recommended Practices and reproduced with the permission of the Boating Industry Association.
Most outboards, except very small models, have provision for bolting the motor to the transom. Large outboards use this method exclusively, while intermediate size models are equipped with bolt holes in the mounting bracket which serve as a safety feature, in addition the screw clamps on the mounting bracket.

Due to the weight involved with large outboards, installation is best left to a dealer, who is equipped with a hoist to handle the motor during installation. However, if a hoist or chainfall is available, the owner can satisfactorily mount the motor himself.

Usually the motor is mounted with the boat on the trailer, eliminating the possibility of the motor becoming submerged. Be sure that the boat is securely attached to the trailer, preferably by the bow winch line and serveral hold-down straps. Raise and support the front of the trailer so that the boat is on an even keel. Place jacks or cinder blocks with large timbers (4 in. x 4 in.) under the rear crossmember of the trailer to support the weight of the motor when it is lowered onto the transom. It is a good practice to use new thrubolts (preferably brass), nuts, and washers at the beginning of each season. Use the largest diameter bolt that will fit through the holes in the mounting bracket. It is also a good practice to install wood or rubber transom plates between the inside faces of the mounting bracket and the transom. These plates, available commercially, serve the dual purpose of acting as vibration dampers and protecting the transom.

Lift the motor (it is advisable to use the lifting ring available from the dealer) and carefully lower the motor onto the transom, aligning the bolt holes in the transom with those in the mounting bracket. *Do* not remove the lifting apparatus. If the motor is being installed for the first time, carefully center the motor on the transom. Carefully mark the locations of the bolt holes. Be sure that the motor rests with full weight on the transom.

NOTE: *If there is any doubt concerning placement of the motor on the transom, consult a dealer for special mounting instructions.*

Remove the motor from the transom and centerpunch, and drill the holes. Lower the motor onto the transom and securely fasten with thru-bolts and lockwashers. Be sure that the rear half of the mounting bracket rests flush against the transom. Tighten the screw clamps if provided.

If no bolt holes are provided on the mounting bracket, it is a good idea to install a safety chain, connected through an eye-bolt through the transom and attached to the motor.

NOTE: *It is not advisable to attach a safety chain to larger motors, since a motor which has vibrated loose could damage the transom.*

Be sure that the chain does not interfere with the steering gear. See the manufacturer's section for any specific mounting procedures.

General Care and Maintenance

Given proper care and maintenance, most outboard motors will reward the owner with years of reliable and relatively trouble free service. However, if abused, the condition of an outboard motor will quickly deteriorate. Following are suggestions which should help maintain the original condition of an outboard motor. Most outboard manufacturers also provide an owner's manual, which provides manufacturer's suggestions to properly maintain their outboards.

NOTE: *See the manufacturer's section for specific periodic maintenance. The following information ("Mid-Season Service," "Off-Season Service," and "Pre-Season Preparation") is taken from the Boating Industry Association's Marine Service Manual of Recommended Practices and reproduced with the permission of the Boating Industry Association.*

WARNING: *Disconnect the battery before servicing ignition (particularly CD) systems.*

OUTBOARD MOTOR MAINTENANCE

The following checks should be made in mid-season or every 50 hours.

1. Drain and flush the gearcase. Refill to correct level using manufacturer's recommended lubricant.

2. Remove and clean the fuel filter bowl. Replace the fuel bowl element. Always use new filter bowl gasket.

3. Clean and gap the spark plugs to recommended gap. Replace worn or burnt spark plugs. (Use new gaskets and torque plugs to manufacturer's recommendations.)

4. Check propeller for correct pitch. Replace if propeller is worn, chipped, or badly bent.

5. Lubricate all grease fittings, using manufacturer's recommended lubricant.

6. Check remote control box, cables, and wiring harness.

7. Check steering controls; lubricate mechanical steering.

8. Lubricate all carburetor and magneto linkages with manufacturer's recommended lubricant.

9. Adjust tension on magneto and/or generator drive belts.

10. Clean and coat the battery terminals with grease or special protective compound.

11. Check water pump and thermostat operation.

12. Check breaker points' condition and timing.

13. Check carburetor and ignition synchronization.

14. Check carburetor adjustment.

OFF-SEASON STORAGE

Operate the motor in a test tank, or on the boat, at part throttle with shift lever in neutral. Rapidly inject rust preventative oil (with pump type oil can) into carburetor air intake, or intakes, until the motor is smoking profusely. Stop the motor immediately to prevent burning oil out of the cylinders. This will lubricate and protect internal parts of the powerhead while motor is in storage. If motor was last operated in salt water, run it in fresh water before preparing it for storage.

1. Place the motor on a stand in the

normal upright position. Remove the motor cover.

2. Retard the throttle all the way and disconnect the spark plug leads. Manually rotate the motor flywheel several times to drain water from the water pump.

3. Drain the carburetor float chamber. Remove fuel filter bowl. Drain, clean, and replace the fuel filter element and gasket.

4. Clean and lubricate the electric starter drive mechanism.

5. Completely drain and clean the fuel tank.

6. Remove the propeller and check for condition and pitch. Clean and liberally lubricate the propeller shaft. Replace the propeller drive-pin if bent or worn. Replace the propeller using new cotter pin or tab-lock washer.

7. Drain and refill gearcase, using the manufacturer's recommended lubricant.

8. Wipe over the entire external motor surface with a clean cloth soaked in light oil.

9. Store in an upright position in a dry, well-ventilated room. To prevent accidental starting, leave the spark plug leads disconnected.

10. Remove the battery from the boat and keep it charged while in storage.

PRE-SEASON PREPARATION

1. Remove, clean, inspect, and properly gap spark plugs. Replace defective plugs. (Use new gaskets and torque plugs to manufacturer's recommendations.)

2. Remove oil level plug from gearcase and check for proper oil level.

3. Thoroughly clean and refinish surfaces as required.

4. Check battery for full charge and clean the terminals. Clean and inspect the battery cable connections. Check polarity before installing the battery cables. Cover the cable connections with grease or special protective compound to prevent corrosion.

5. If possible, run the motor in a test tank prior to installing the motor on the boat. Check the water pump and thermostat operation.

SALT WATER CARE

Motors which are used in salt water present special problems and require meticulous care. Aluminum alloys used in outboard motors are highly resistant to corrosion by oxidation (breakdown of metal, caused by its combination with oxygen) but very susceptible to galvanic action (electrical process of depositing atoms of one metal, in solution, on the surface of a different metal). Although oxidation cannot occur under water, it is very prevalent in warm, humid climates. Aluminum parts are protected from galvanization by anodizing (the process of coating metal with a hard shell of aluminum oxide). However, this covering is only protective if it remains unbroken. Following are suggestions for care of all motors used in salt water.

1. After each use, tilt the motor out of the water and flush the entire motor with cool, fresh water.

2. If possible, periodically flush the motor, following manufacturer's recommendations in the appropriate chapter.

3. Be sure the motor is adequately protected with an *approved* paint.

NOTE: *Do not use anti-fouling paint, since these contain copper or mercury and can hasten galvanic corrosion.*

4. Check frequently to be sure that no aluminum parts are left unprotected. Bare metal should be protected quickly.

5. A small self-sacrificing block of susceptible metal, placed near the part to be protected, will sometimes spare a valuable part.

NOTE: *Consult a dealer before attempting to install such a device.*

Submerged Motor Service

Occasionally, through accident or negligence, an outboard motor may be subjected to complete submersion. Mechanical damage could result from the inability of water to compress; however, a more obvious damage is corrosion, especially in the presence of salt water. Corrosive action can start immediately, although it is far more extensive in the presence of heat and oxygen, after the motor is recovered.

Submerged motors must be recovered, cleaned and/or disassembled as quickly as possible. The following procedure can be used as a guide for handling a submerged motor. Consult the specific manufacturer's section for disassembly procedures.

1. Recover the motor as quickly as possible.

2. If some time must elapse before the motor is serviced (it should be serviced within 24 hours), it is best to keep the motor submerged in fresh water. If the motor is too large to be entirely submerged, remove the powerhead and submerge it.

3. Wash the entire motor with clean, fresh water to remove all weeds, mud, and other debris.

4. Remove the carburetor, spark plugs, and reed valve (if possible).

5. Remove water from the cylinders by pointing the spark plug ports down and operating the manual starter (turning the flywheel will do).

CAUTION: *If the motor does not turn over freely, do not force it. This condition indicates mechanical damage, such as a bent connecting rod.*

6. Pour alcohol into the cylinders (alcohol will mix with water). Operate the manual starter again to remove the remaining water and alcohol.

NOTE: *Most manufacturers recommend special engine cleaners in place of alcohol. Engine cleaners frequently contain some type of lubricant also.*

7. Lubricate internal parts by pouring oil through the spark plug ports. Operate the manual starter.

8. Disassemble the entire motor and wash in hot, soapy water and air dry.

9. Immerse all parts (excluding gaskets, which are renewed, and sensitive electrical components) in oil or spray with an oil mist until completely covered.

NOTE: *Alcohol will best protect electrical components.*

10. Ball and roller bearings which cannot be disassembled, should be replaced with new ones. Even minute traces of silt and sand will quickly ruin bearings and necessitate replacement.

11. Check the crankshaft journals (especially the lower one) for traces of moisture or sand scoring.

12. Assemble the motor using new parts as necessary, along with new gaskets and rubber parts.

13. If in doubt concerning the serviceability of any part, consult a dealer.

Boat Performance and Propeller Selection

Many variables will influence, if not dictate, the performance characteristics of any boat. Some, of course, will have a greater influence than others. Assuming that the motor itself is in good condition and properly tuned, the following factors must be considered (not necessarily in order) when attempting to influence or evaluate boat performance.

HULL DESIGN

Basically, hull designs are of two types: displacement hulls or planing hulls. In practice, however, pleasure craft are a variation of one of the two basic types. The displacement hull, common to larger yachts, is characterized by a round bottom which forces its way through the water. The center of gravity is very low, providing a smooth, stable ride in heavy seas. Since the amount of water displaced by this type of hull remains practically the same, regardless of speed, this has the effect of reducing the maximum speed capability. Simply as a matter of interest, the maximum speed of a displacement type hull is fixed by the length of the waterline. No matter how much horsepower is applied to drive the hull, its speed (mph) will not exceed 1½ times the square root of its waterline. The following formula will calculate the maximum speed of a large displacement hull.

$$\text{Speed (mph)} = \frac{3\sqrt{\text{waterline length}}}{2}$$

Planing hulls are designed to gain speed by lifting out of the water. Because the lifting effect supports only part of the weight of the boat, displacement and fric-

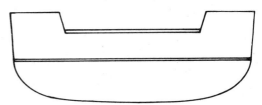

Schematic representation of the aft portion of a planing hull

Aft portion of a slightly modified planing hull

tional resistance are decreased, resulting in an increased speed. In theory, planing hulls are perfectly flat. In practice, however, perfect planing hulls do not exist because of poor maneuverability at slow speeds when the hull is not planing. Practical design combinations of displacement and planing hulls supply the answer to speed and maneuverability problems for pleasure craft.

V-type hulls employ planing characteristics and are much faster than true displacement hulls. V-type hulls tend to stabilize themselves at high speeds, but act as inefficient displacement hulls at lower speeds.

Modified V-hulls are combinations of displacement and V-type hulls. The bow section is characteristic of a displacement hull, while the aft tapers off to a flat "V" shape. These hulls are much better for use in rough water, since the displacement type bow tends to cut through the water, rather than rise above swells and then slap

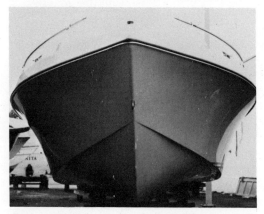

Bow section of a V type hull slightly altered by overextended chines. On most smaller pleasure craft using this type bow, a planing type aft section is employed.

down. At higher speeds, the planing type aft section provides lift and stability.

Deep V-hulls have a much sharper rise from the keel to the chine (where the bottom meets the side) than a traditional V-bottom design. The "V" shape is present along the entire length of the boat and provides good stability in heavy seas. The modified V-type is much faster in calm water because of its planing type aft section.

Aft view of a deep V type hull

Catamarans were the forerunner of the modern tri-hull or trihedral design. A trihedral will not reach planing speed as fast as V-bottom craft; however, this disadvantage is offset by their inherent lateral stability and vast amount of useful space, particularly in the bow.

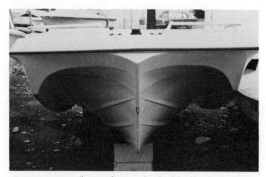

Bow section of a modern trihedral hull

CENTER OF GRAVITY

For maximum speed, move the weight aft until the boat just begins to "porpoise." This will reduce wetted surface to a minimum, only the aft portion being actually in the water.

TRANSOM HEIGHT

Pleasure craft manufactured specifically for use with outboard motors have transoms ranging from approximately 15 to 20 in. high. Too short a motor leg or too high a transom will cause the motor to cavitate, particularly in sharp turns. This is due to the motor running wild in an air pocket, rather than in water. The effect of transom height is small at low speeds, but quite important at high speeds. It is important that the proper motor (short or long leg) is used for a given transom height. See the "Transom and Motor Well Dimensions" chart for general recommendations. As a general rule, for average use, the motor cavitation plate should be ½–1 in. below the bottom of the keel at the transom or (if there is no keel) the bottom of the boat. In the event that the motor and transom cannot be satisfactorily matched to cure cavitation, cutting a notch in the transom to lower the motor will sometimes prove satisfactory.

TILT PIN ADJUSTMENT

The tilt pin, located on the outboard side of the mounting bracket at the bottom, controls the angle of the motor with relation to the transom. In general, the tilt pin should be adjusted so that the motor cavitation plate is about parallel to the water. The speed of boats with weight located forward will sometimes be improved by tilting the engine out one pin hole. This will tend to raise the bow of the boat and reduce wetted surface. If the motor is

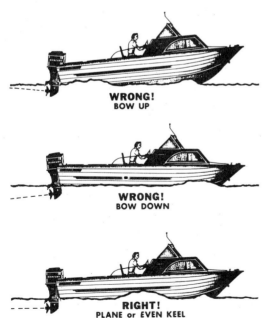

WRONG!
BOW UP

WRONG!
BOW DOWN

RIGHT!
PLANE or EVEN KEEL

Effects of tilt pin adjustment on planing angle (© Kiekhaefer Mercury)

tilted in, the boat will ride with the bow down, wetting more of the bottom and reducing speed. This will generally improve operation in rough water. It should be noted that experimentation is necessary to determine the optimum tilt pin setting. Variations in design, power, weight distribution, and transom angle will dictate the correct tilt pin setting.

NOTE: *If it is found that the tilt pin cannot be satisfactorily adjusted, check for water in the bottom of the boat, since this will cause a constantly shifting mass of weight with a constantly changing weight distribution.*

BOTTOM CONDITION

Surface Roughness

Moss, barnacles, and other surface irregularities that increase friction will cause a considerable loss of speed. It was found in one specific test that a boat, anchored in salt water for forty days, suffered almost a 50 per cent reduction in speed, due to marine growth on the hull.

PROPELLER SELECTION

NOTE: *The following information on propeller selection is taken from the Boating Industry Association's Marine Service Manual of Recommended Practices and reproduced with the permission of the Boating Industry Association.*

The only way to be absolutely sure that the engine will achieve its full horsepower, and will operate efficiently and safely, is to use a reliable tachometer to test the engine rpm at full throttle. Knowing that the engine will turn up to the manufacturer's recommended test wheel range, select a propeller from one of the many charts supplied by your engine or propeller supplier. Make a few test runs at full throttle, with the same load as the rig will normally carry, and note the average rpm reading indicated on the tachometer. If the reading is above or below the manufacturer's indicated operating range, it is imperative that you change propellers.

Since the diameter of the propeller is generally limited by the engine lower unit design, the pitch and blade area will be of the greatest concern. Pitch is the theoretical distance that the propeller will travel in a solid substance if it made one com-

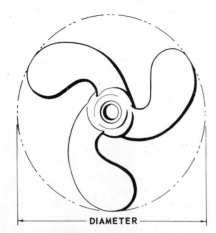

Propeller diameter

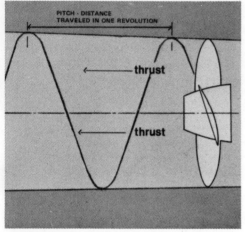

Propeller pitch

plete revolution, without slippage. Increasing the pitch reduces rpm at full throttle, while reducing the pitch will increase rpm at full throttle.

If the full throttle tachometer reading is below the manufacturer's recommended operating range, you must try propellers of less pitch until a propeller is obtained that will allow the engine to continually operate within the recommended rull throttle operating range. If the full throttle tachometer reading is above the manufacturer's recommended operating range, you must try propellers of greater pitch, until a propeller is found that will allow the engine to continually operate within the recommended full throttle operating range.

The number of blades for outboard propellers generally varies from two to four. When selecting a propeller for a light boat, two- or three-blade props will give the best results. As the weight increases,

the blade area should increase. On large, heavy boats, the blade area should be increased by using three or four blades, to obtain optimum performance.

In a situation where both a two- and three-blade prop or three- and four-blade prop will allow the engine to operate within the full throttle operating range, choose the one that will give the greatest forward speed.

IMPORTANCE OF LOAD CHANGES

To properly complete the job of propping, the rig should be checked with both the minimum and maximum expected loads—including skiers. It will often be necessary to have available several propellers (or one variable pitch propeller) and information on when to use them and how to change them as loads vary.

Many times, however, a propeller operating at the high end of the recommended range with light loads will still operate within the range with a maximum load.

PROPELLER CARE

A bent or nicked propeller will set up vibrations in the motor which will have a damaging effect on many of the operating parts. There will be a definite loss of power and efficiency with a damaged propeller. Propellers should be checked frequently to be sure that all blades are in good condition. Be sure to check the propeller for nicks and pitch on all service jobs. Consult your engine or propeller supplier for information on propeller repairs or familiarize yourself with the nearest repair service.

Boat Performance Troubleshooting

NOTE: *The following chart is taken from the Boating Industry Association's Marine Service Manual of Recommended Practices and reproduced with the permission of the Boating Industry Association.*

NOTE:

These are the most common problem areas affecting performance.
1. Improper motor tilt angle or transom height
2. Incorrect propeller selection
3. Improper load distribution
4. Water under cockpit floor

BOAT REACTION	CHECK POINTS
1. Poor speed— light load	A. Incorrect propeller selection B. Load too far forward C. Motor too low in water D. Engine malfunction E. Motor tilt too far in F. Marine growth on hull or lower unit
2. Poor speed— heavy load	A. Under-powered B. Engine malfunction C. Incorrect propeller selection D. Motor tilt too far out E. Marine growth on hull or lower unit
3. Slow to plane —heavy load	A. Motor tilt too far out B. Incorrect propeller selection C. Too much load in stern D. Water under cockpit floor E. Hull has a hook
4. Speed loss	A. Water under cockpit floor B. Marine growth on hull or lower unit C. Weeds on propeller D. Damaged propeller
5. Hard ride in rough water	A. Too much load in stern B. Motor tilt too far out C. Poor speed management
6. Runs wet in rough water	A. Load too far forward B. Motor tilt too far in C. Overloaded
7. Lists on straight when heavily loaded	A. Load not evenly distributed B. Motor tilt too far in C. Water under cockpit floor D. Hull has a hook
8. Lists or rolls on straight when lightly loaded	A. Loose steering B. Water under cockpit floor C. Motor tilt too far in D. Incorrect transom height E. Load too far forward F. Hull has a hook
9. Nose heavy— catches on waves and in turns	A. Motor tilt too far in B. Load too far forward C. Hull has a hook
10. Porpoises on straight run	A. Motor tilt too far out B. Motor too low in water C. Too much load in stern D. Hull has a rocker
11. Porpoises on turns only	A. Motor tilt too far out B. Motor too low in water C. Overloaded
12. Banks too much in turns	A. Overloaded B. Load too far forward C. Motor tilt too far in D. Overpowered E. Hull has a hook
13. Excessive Cavitation	A. Incorrect propeller selection B. Motor too high on transom

BOAT REACTION	CHECK POINTS
	C. Motor tilt too far out D. Overpowered E. Load too far forward F. Water under cockpit floor G. Keel extends too far aft; thru-hull fittings disturb water flow H. Weeds on propeller

Tune-Up and Troubleshooting

Neither tune-up nor troubleshooting can be considered independently, since each has a direct relationship with the other.

An engine tune-up is a service to restore the maximum capability of power, performance, and economy in an engine, and, at the same time, assure the owner of a complete check and more lasting results in efficiency and trouble free performance. Each year tune-up has become more important, with increased power and performance capabilities. It is advisable to follow a definite and thorough procedure of analysis and correction of all items affecting power, performance, and economy. The extent of an engine tune-up is usually determined by the length of time since the last service; however, specific maintenance should be performed at regular intervals (see manufacturer's section for "Periodic Maintenance") depending on operating conditions.

Troubleshooting is a logical sequence of procedures which will most likely lead the owner or serviceman to the particular cause of trouble. The troubleshooting charts in this manual are general in nature, intended to apply to all outboards, two- and four-stroke, respectively. In some cases, more specific troubleshooting procedures for component parts may be found in the manufacturer's section. Service usually comprises two areas: diagnosis and repair. While the apparent cause of trouble in many cases is worn or damaged parts, performance problems are less obvious and the first job is to isolate the problem and cause. Once the cause has been determined through troubleshooting, refer to the manufacturer's section for removal and/or repair procedures. An orderly diagnostic procedure cannot be stressed too frequently, since this could prove invaluable in repairing a stalled or disabled motor in an emergency (on the open water) where no other help is available.

TUNE-UP

Lubrication and Fuel

Since two-cycle engines are lubricated by oil mixed with the fuel, it is important that the correct oil/fuel ratio be maintained at all times. Follow the instructions in the manufacturer's section for recommended oil/fuel ratio. When filling the fuel tank, add about a gallon of fuel, then the oil. Fill the rest of the tank with fuel and shake thoroughly. Never add oil after the tank has been filled.

Of equal importance is the fuel used in outboard motors. Avoid the use of stale fuel, because of the harmful deposits (varnish) which build up in the engine and fuel system, and clog the small drillings and calibrated orifices in the carburetor. See the manufacturer's section for recommended grades of fuel. If no recommendations are available, use a good grade of marine gasoline.

NOTE: *Leaded hi-test fuel is recommended for many four-stroke outboards. If in doubt, consult a dealer.*

Compression

A compression check should be the first step of any tune-up, because an engine showing low or uneven compression will not respond to a tune-up. It is essential that the cause of poor compression be found and corrected before further tune-up procedures are attempted.

Remove the spark plugs, one at a time, and disconnect the coil to prevent the engine from starting. Install a compression gauge in each spark plug hole in turn and crank the engine through at least 4 compression strokes to obtain the maximum reading. Record the compression of each cylinder and compare it to the manufacturer's specifications. If no specifications are available, compression is usually satisfactory if it is even or if there is less than 10 psi variation between cylinders. Poor compression is usually indicative of damage to the cylinders, pistons, rings, or head gasket(s). If poor compression is found between two adjacent cylinders, check for a

Compression gauge installed

blown cylinder head gasket between those two cylinders.

If the powerhead shows any indication of overheating (scorched or discolored paint), inspect the cylinders through the transfer ports for scoring or wear. It is possible for a cylinder to be slightly scored and still exhibit adequate compression.

While working with the powerhead, some manufacturers advocate soaking the cylinders (with the engine horizontal) with a recommended engine cleaner to remove accumulated carbon deposits. When using an engine cleaner, use the manufacturer's recommended brand and follow instructions on the container.

Spark Plugs

The recommended spark plug and gap for a particular motor is given in the "Tune-Up Specifications" chart in each manufacturer's chapter. The particular designation of a spark plug gives, among other information, the heat range. The hot or cold rating (heat range) refers to the ability of the spark plug to conduct heat away from firing tip. The heat range has no bearing on the intensity of the spark. In general, cold plugs are required when the engine is subjected to large loads (pulling skiers, for example) and hot plugs are required for lower intensity operation (trolling).

CAUTION: *Too hot a spark plug will not allow the electrode to cool sufficiently between power strokes and cause*

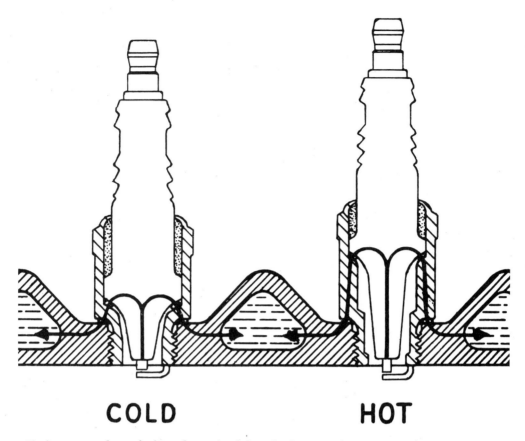

COLD   HOT

The heat range of a spark plug refers to the ability of a plug to conduct heat away from the firing tip.

A piston damaged by pre-ignition (© Kiekhaefer Mercury)

the electrode to glow red-hot. This in turn, causes excessively high temperatures, bringing about detonation and pre-ignition.

It is best to consult a dealer before installing plugs which differ from the manufacturer's recommendations.

CONVENTIONAL SPARK PLUGS

Each spark plug should be removed and inspected individually and compared to the spark plug diagnosis chart to determine the cause of malfunction and possible corrective measures. Replace spark plugs as necessary. In normal service, spark plugs are replaced in sets, corresponding to the number of cylinders. Inspect each spark plug for make, type, and heat range. All plugs must be of the same make and heat range. Adjust each spark plug gap (new or old) to the manufacturer's specification, using a round feeler gauge, as illustrated. Before adjusting the gap, file the center electrode flat with a point file.

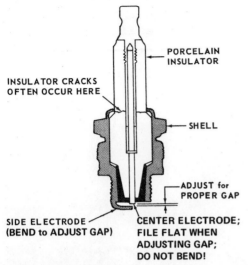

PORCELAIN
INSULATOR

INSULATOR CRACKS
OFTEN OCCUR HERE

SHELL

ADJUST for
PROPER GAP

SIDE ELECTRODE
(BEND to ADJUST GAP)

CENTER ELECTRODE;
FILE FLAT WHEN
ADJUSTING GAP;
DO NOT BEND!

Cross-sectional view of a conventional spark plug
(© Kiekhaefer Mercury)

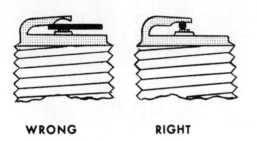

WRONG   **RIGHT**

Gapping conventional spark plugs

CAUTION: *Never bend the center electrode to adjust the gap; always adjust
the gap by bending the side electrode.*

SURFACE GAP SPARK PLUGS

Remove the spark plugs and inspect the
center electrode as illustrated. If worn or
burned back more than $\frac{1}{32}$ in. (0.8 mm)
below the insulator, it will not function
properly. Do not replace surface gap plugs
for any other reason than this. Be sure that
the plugs being replaced are definitely
misfiring; the accumulation of deposits can
be deceiving.

CAUTION: *Due to the high voltage requirements with surface gap spark plugs,
do not use this type of plug, unless specifically recommended by the manufacturer.*

Surface gap spark plug, illustrating proper gap
(© Kiekhaefer Mercury)

SPARK PLUG INSTALLATION

Inspect the spark plug hole threads and
clean before installing the spark plugs.
Crank the engine several times to blow out
any material which might have been dis-
lodged during the cleaning operation. Install the spark plugs in the powerhead
with new gaskets and torque to manufacturer's specification. Since improper installation is one of the largest single causes of
unsatisfactory spark plug performance, improper installation is the result of one or
more of the following practices.

Cause	Result
Insufficient torque (to fully seat gasket)	Compression loss— early plug failure
Excessive torque	Reduced operation life— complete destruction from inability to dissipate heat
Dirty gasket seal	High temperatures— early plug failure
Corroded hole threads	Excessively high tempera- tures—early failure (over- heating)

Always use a new gasket seal and wipe the
seats in the head clean. The gasket must
be fully compressed on clean seats to ensure complete heat transfer and provide a
gas-tight seal in the cylinder. For this reason, as well as the necessity of maintaining
the proper plug gap, the correct torque
when installing the spark plugs is extremely important.

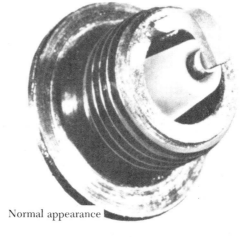

Spark Plug Diagnosis

Plugs with even-colored tan or light gray deposits and moderate electrode wear.

Normal appearance

Can be identified in a negative ground system by lack of wear at the center electrode and a semicircular wear pattern at the side electrode. The primary coil leads are reversed from proper position.

Reversed coil polarity

Usually occurring in a relatively new set splash deposits may form after a long delayed tune-up when accumulated cylinder deposits are thrown against the plugs at high rpm. Clean and install plugs.

Splash fouled

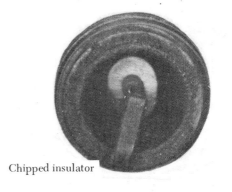

If one or more plugs in a set have chipped insulators, severe detonation is the probable cause. Bending the center electrode to adjust the gap can also crack the insulator. Replace with new plugs of the correct gap and heat range. Check for overadvanced timing.

Chipped insulator

Results from fused deposits which appear as tiny beads or glasslike bubbles; caused by improper oil/fuel ratio and high speed operation following sustained slow speeds.

Gap bridged

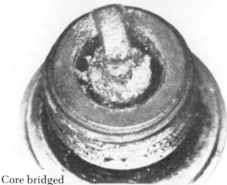

See "Gap Bridging."

Core bridged

Oil or wet, black carbon covering the entire end of the plug, caused by excessive oil in the fuel, too rich fuel mixture, sustained slow speed operation, or incorrect heat range plugs.

Oil fouled

Usually caused by severe pre-ignition or detonation. Likely causes are improper heat range plugs, low octane gasoline, neglected engine maintenance (even with high octane fuel), overadvanced ignition timing or inadequate engine cooling.

Mechanical damage

If set of plugs has dead white insulators and badly worn electrodes, check for over-advanced ignition timing. Install the next colder heat range plugs.

Overheating

Usually caused by an extremely rich air/fuel mixture and characterized by a dry, black appearance of the plug.

Cold fou.

Fuel System

CARBURETOR

The most common causes of problems in the carburetor are improper fuel and the formation of gum or varnish in the calibrated drillings and jets. Over a period of time, hard varnish and other deposits will build up and block the calibrated drillings. The carburetor should be removed, disassembled, and thoroughly cleaned. (Refer to the manufacturer's section exploded views, removal and repair procedures.) Before disassembling the carburetor, thoroughly clean the external surface to remove all traces of dirt and grease. Disassemble the carburetor and soak all components (except cork washers, gaskets, and seals) in a good carburetor solvent. Blow all parts dry with compressed air or allow to air dry. Never attempt to clean the calibrated drillings or jets with wire, since this will only lead to damage and unnecessary replacement of parts.

Inspection

Even though wear damage is minimal on outboard carburetors, the following inspections should be made after the carburetor is disassembled and cleaned.

1. Be sure that the throttle shaft moves freely and is not worn. If the throttle shaft sticks, check further for gum or varnish on the pivot points.

2. Check the mixture adjustment needle for a groove around the tapered point.

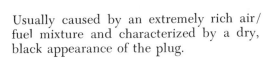

WORN   GOOD

Check the mixture adjustment needle for wear in the form of a groove around the tip of the needle. (© Outboard Marine Corp.)

This is usually the result of overtightening the needle in its seat. If it is found that the motor will not hold an adjustment, investigate this as a possible cause. If the needle is grooved or bent, replace it with a new one.

3. Check the needle valve seat for wear, as this may also prohibit a satisfactory adjustment.

4. Inspect the float for free movement. It should not bind or stick.

5. Check to see that the carburetor linkage moves freely and does not bind.

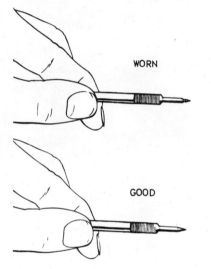

Replace bent or broken needles. (© Outboard Marine Corp.)

6. Be sure that the carburetor body is not cracked, as this will cause carburetor flooding.

Assemble the carburetor, following the instructions in the manufacturer's section. Rather than risk unsatisfactory performance, it is standard practice to replace the jets at every disassembly. These are inexpensive and available from your local dealer. The use of carburetor overhaul kits is also suggested because these contain all new gaskets and seals which should be replaced at every overhaul. Be sure to adjust the float to the manufacturer's specification.

NOTE: *When installing new jets, do not overtighten in the seats. This will damage the jets and necessitate replacement.*

Adjustments

Refer to the manufacturer's section for all adjustments. Also included in the manufacturer's section are data on available jets for use in different altitudes.

FUEL PUMP

Most outboard motors are equipped with one or more diaphragm-type fuel pumps, operated either mechanically, electrically, or by vacuum from the crankcase.

Remove the fuel pump, disassemble it (see manufacturer's section) and wash all parts thoroughly (except diaphragm). Blow dry with compressed air or air dry. Carefully inspect each part for wear or damage. Especially inspect the fuel pump diaphragm, as problems in this area are often mistakenly diagnosed as ignition trouble. A tiny pin-hole in the diaphragm will permit gas to enter the crankcase and wet-foul a particular cylinder at idle speed. At higher speeds this is not as noticeable since the fuel is metered and the plug will fire normally. Replace the diaphragm if conditions warrant.

Assemble the fuel pump and tighten the elbows and check valve connections firmly. After assembly, check the valves by blowing through the outlet hole. Air should be drawn through the valve but should close immediately when you are attempting to blow through it. Check the intake valve in a reverse manner. When installing the fuel valves and fittings, use a suitable sealant, but do not use an excessive amount or the lines will be plugged. Always use new gaskets when assembling. If, after overhaul, poor high speed performance is still noticeable, check the fuel pump delivery pressure, as described in the manufacturer's section.

FUEL LINES AND FILTERS

Inspect the fuel lines for kinks, leaks, or restrictions. If necessary, remove the fuel lines and blow out with compressed air. When installing the fuel lines, be sure that they are not twisted.

Remove the fuel filters (see manufacturer's section) and wash the parts in solvent, allowing them to air dry.

CAUTION: *Do not operate an outboard motor with the filters removed. This will only lead to frequent carburetor clogging.*

If frequent fuel starvation is encountered, check all of the above in addition to the fuel tank.

REED VALVES

If all other possibilities have been exhausted and the motor still performs poorly at slow speed (but satisfactorily otherwise), an inspection of the reed valve unit is warranted. Remove the reed valve unit as described in the manufacturer's section and check for broken or bent reeds. Be sure that all other possibilities have been thoroughly checked, since the removal of the reed valves on some motors involves removal of the powerhead.

Ignition System

BREAKER POINTS

On most outboards, the breaker points are located under the flywheel and the flywheel must be removed to service the breaker points. Refer to the manufacturer's section for removal procedures. Inspect the breaker points for burning or pitting. The contacts should appear clean and light gray in color. A simple test light can be constructed (see illustration) to be used as a continuity tester. Disconnect the coil lead from the points and connect one end of the tester to the points (insulated terminal) and the other to a good ground.

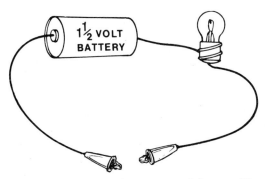

A simple test light can be constructed from readily available materials.

CAUTION: *Before servicing the ignition system (particularly CD type) disconnect the battery.*

With the points closed, the light should burn; it should go out when the points open. If this does not happen, replace the breaker points, making sure that the light oil or wax is cleaned from the points. Adjust the point gap to the manufacturer's specification. It is standard practice to replace the condenser when the points are replaced.

MAKER POINTS

High primary voltage in systems using maker points, will quickly roughen these points. This is not cause for concern as points in this condition will continue to function satisfactorily. Do not replace maker points unless an obvious malfunction is present or the contacts are loose or burned away. See the manufacturer's section for maker point service.

CONDENSER

The condenser can be checked using the continuity tester described above. Check the condenser case for cracks and remove the condenser. Connect a lead of the continuity tester to the condenser wire and the other lead to the condenser case. A short in the condenser is indicated if the light comes on. If the breaker points are observed to pit very rapidly, check the condenser as this is usually at fault.

IGNITION TIMING

Consult the manufacturer's section for specific timing specifications and procedures.

MAGNETO AIR GAP

On motors where the armature and coil are mounted outside the flywheel, turn the engine to locate the flywheel magnets under the armature core legs. Measure the clearance between the armature core legs and the flywheel magneto. If the measured clearance does not meet manufacturer's specifications, loosen the armature mounting screws and adjust to specifications.

If the armature is located under the flywheel, a slot or opening is usually provided to adjust the air gap.

MAGNETO EDGE GAP

This is a service specification and is usually non-adjustable. However, magneto edge gap can change due to a loose flywheel or drive key, excessive breaker cam wear, or improperly adjusted breaker points. Correction of the problem will usually bring the magneto edge gap within specifications.

BATTERY

Normally, batteries in marine use are kept in special plastic boxes. No maintenance is normally necessary, other than keeping the charge up and keeping the terminals clean and lightly coated with petroleum jelly. Check the charge of the battery frequently with a hydrometer. Consult the chart to determine the charged condition from the specific gravity reading.

If the motor is to be unused for a long period of time, it is wise to remove the battery and store it in a cool, dry place. Be sure to keep battery fully charged.

SPECIFIC GRAVITY READING	CHARGED CONDITION
1.260-1.280	Fully Charged
1.230-1.250	Three Quarter Charged
1.200-1.220	One Half Charged
1.170-1.190	One Quarter Charged
1.140-1.160	Just About Flat
1.110-1.130	All The Way Down

Specific gravity vs. charged condition

Cooling System

If overheating is encountered, check the water intakes for blockage. If these appear clear, refer to the manufacturer's section for water pump and impeller service procedures.

Lower Unit

GEARCASE

Check the level and condition of gearcase lubricant at specified manufacturer's intervals. These can be found in the manufacturer's section, along with the specified lubricant.

PROPELLER

Check the propeller for nicks, gouges, or other damage which will affect performance. If the motor is equipped with shear pins, check these for wear or damage. Small nicks on the propellor may be filed smooth or hammered out with a light hammer. Be sure to place the propeller on a block of wood before attempting to correct any nicks with this method.

Troubleshooting 2-Stroke Outboard Motors

NOTE: *The following troubleshooting chart is taken from the Boating Industry Association's Marine Service Manual of Recommended Practices and reproduced with the permission of the Boating Industry Association.*

Start all major diagnoses with a compression test and check wheel rpm. Do not run the motor out of water.

MOTOR REACTION	CHECK POINTS
1. Manual starter rope pulls out, but pawls do not engage	A. Friction spring bent or burred B. Excess grease on pawls or spring C. Pawls bent or burred
2. Starter rope does not return	A. Recoil spring broken or binding B. Starter housing bent C. Loose or missing parts
3. Clattering manual starter	A. Friction spring bent or burred B. Starter housing bent C. Excess grease on pawls or spring D. Dry starter spindle
4. Electric starter inoperative	A. Loose or corroded connections or ground B. Starting circuit safety switch open or out of adjustment C. Under capacity or weak battery, or corroded battery terminals D. Faulty starter solenoid E. Moisture in electric starter motor F. Broken or worn brushes in starter motor G. Faulty fields H. Faulty armature I. Broken wire in harness or connector J. Faulty starter key, push button, or safety switch K. Worn or frayed insulation
5. Electric starter does not engage but solenoid clicks	A. Loose or corroded connections or ground B. Weak battery C. Faulty starter solenoid D. Broken wire in electric harness E. Loose or stripped post on starter motor F. See steps in number 4
6. Hard to start or won't start	A. Empty gas tank B. Gas tank air vent not open C. Fuel lines kinked or severely pinched

MOTOR REACTION	CHECK POINTS
	D. Water or dirt in fuel system
	E. Clogged fuel filter or screens
	F. Motor not being choked to start
	G. Engine not primed—pump primer system
	H. Carburetor adjustments too lean (not allowing enough fuel to start engine)
	I. Timing and synchronizing out of adjustment
	J. Manual choke linkage bent—auto choke out of adjustment
	K. Spark plugs improperly gapped, dirty, or broken
	L. Fuel tank primer inoperative (pressurized system)
	M. Ignition points improperly gapped, burned or dirty, or triggering (CD) system inoperative
	N. Loose, broken wire or frayed insulation in electrical system
	O. Reed valves not seating or stuck shut
	P. Weak coil or condenser
	Q. Faulty gaskets
	R. Cracked distributor cap or rotor, or shorted rotor
	S. Loose fuel connector
	T. Amplifier (CD) inoperative
	U. Poor engine or ignition ground
	V. Faulty ignition or safety switch
7. Low-speed miss or motor won't idle smoothly and slowly enough	A. Too much oil—too little oil
	B. Timing and synchronizing out of adjustment
	C. Carburetor idle adjustment (mixture lean or rich)
	D. Ignition points improper (gap, worn, or fouled) or triggering (CD) system inoperative
	E. Weak coil or condenser
	F. Loose or broken ignition wires
	G. Loose or worn magneto plate
	H. Spark plugs (improper gap or dirty)
	I. Head gasket, reed plate gasket (blown or leaking)
	J. Reed valve standing open or stuck shut
	K. Plugged crankcase bleeder, check valves, or lines
	L. Leaking crankcase halves
	M. Leaking crankcase seals (top or bottom)
	N. Exhaust gases returning through intake manifold
	O. Poor distributor ground
	P. Cracked or shorted distributor cap or rotor
	Q. Fuel pump diaphragm punctured
	R. Accessory tachometer shorted

MOTOR REACTION	CHECK POINTS
	or not compatible with ignition system
	S. Faulty ignition or safety switch
8. High-speed miss or intermittent spark	A. Spark plugs improperly gapped or dirty
	B. Loose, leaking, or broken ignition wires
	C. Breaker points (improper gap or dirty; worn cam or cam follower) or triggering (CD) system faulty
	D. Weak coil or condenser
	E. Water in fuel
	F. Leaking head gasket or exhaust cover gasket
	G. Spark plug heat range incorrect
	H. Engine improperly timed
	I. Carbon or fouled combustion chambers
	J. Magneto, distributor, or CD triggering system poorly grounded
	K. Distributor oiler wick bad
	L. Accessory tachometer shorted or not compatible with ignition system
	M. Faulty ignition or safety switch
9. Coughs, spits, slows	A. Idle or high-speed needles set too lean
	B. Carburetor not synchronized
	C. Leaking gaskets in induction system
	D. Obstructed fuel passages
	E. Float level set too low
	F. Improperly seated or broken reeds
	G. Fuel pump pressure line ruptured
	H. Fuel pump (punctured diaphragm), check valves stuck open or closed, fuel lines leak
	I. Poor fuel tank pressure (pressurized system)
	J. Worn or leaking fuel connector
10. Vibrates excessively or runs roughly and smokes	A. Idle or high-speed needles set too rich
	B. Too much oil mixed with gas
	C. Carburetor not synchronized with ignition properly
	D. Choke not opening properly
	E. Float level too high
	F. Air passage to carburetor obstructed
	G. Bleeder valves or passages plugged
	H. Transom bracket clamps loose on transom
	I. Prop out of balance

MOTOR REACTION	CHECK POINTS	MOTOR REACTION	CHECK POINTS
	J. Broken motor mount K. Exhaust gases getting inside motor cover L. Poor ignition—see steps in number 8	14. No acceleration, idles well but when put to full power dies down	A. High-speed or low-speed needle set too lean B. Dirt or packing behind needles and seats C. High-speed nozzle obstructed D. Float level too low E. Choke partly closed F. Improper timing and synchronization G. Fuel lines or passages obstructed H. Fuel filter obstructed. Fuel pump not supplying enough fuel I. Not enough oil in gas J. Breaker points improperly gapped or dirty K. Bent gearcase or exhaust tube L. Marginal CD amplifier M. Faulty spark plugs
11. Runs well, idles well for a short period, then slows down and stops	A. Weeds or other debris on lower unit or propeller B. Insufficient cooling water C. Carburetor, fuel pump, filter, or screens dirty D. Bleeder valves or passages plugged E. Lower unit bind (lack of lubrication or bent) F. Gas tank air vent not open G. Not enough oil in gas H. Combustion chambers and spark plugs fouled, causing pre-ignition I. Spark plug heat range too high or too low J. Wrong propeller (pre-ignition) K. Low-speed adjustment too rich or too lean		
		15. Engine runs at high speed only by using hand primer	A. Carburetor adjustments B. Dirt or packing behind needles and seat C. Fuel lines or passages obstructed D. Fuel line leaks E. Fuel pump not supplying enough fuel F. Float level too low G. Fuel filter obstructed H. Fuel tank or connector at fault
12. Won't start, kicks back, backfires into lower unit	A. Spark plug wires reversed B. Flywheel key sheared C. Distributor belt timing off (magneto or battery ignition) D. Timing and synchronizing out of adjustment E. Reed valves not seating or broken F. Poor engine or distributor ground		
		16. No power under heavy load	A. Wrong propeller B. Weeds or other debris on lower unit or propeller C. Breaker points improperly gapped or dirty D. Stator plate loose E. Ignition timing over-advanced or late F. Faulty carburetion and/or faulty ignition G. Prop hub slips H. Scored cylinders or rings stuck I. Carbon buildup on piston head at deflector

13. No acceleration, low top rpm	A. Improper carburetor adjustments
	B. Improper timing and synchronization
	C. Spark plugs (improper gap or dirty)
	D. Ignition points (improper gap or faulty), or triggering (CD) system
	E. Faulty coil or condenser
	F. Loose, leaking, or broken ignition wires
	G. Reed valves not properly seated or broken
	H. Blown head or exhaust cover gasket
	I. Weeds on lower unit or propeller
	J. Incorrect propeller
	K. Insufficient oil in gas
	L. Insufficient oil in lower unit
	M. Fuel restrictions
	N. Scored cylinder—stuck rings
	O. Marine growth, hooks, rockers, or change in load of boat
	P. Sticky magneto plate or distributor
	Q. Carbon buildup on piston head at deflector
	R. Marginal CD amplifier
		17. Cranks over extremely easy on one or more cylinders	A. Low compression
			  1. Worn or broken rings
			  2. Scored cylinder or pistons
			  3. Blown head gasket
			  4. Loose spark plugs
			  5. Loose head bolts
			  6. Crankcase halves improperly sealed
			  7. Burned piston

		18. Engine won't crank over	A. Manual start lock improperly adjusted B. Pistons rusted to cylinder wall C. Lower unit gears, prop shaft rusted or broken D. Broken connecting rod, crankshaft, or driveshaft E. Coil heels binding on flywheel F. Engine improperly assembled

MOTOR REACTION	CHECK POINTS
19. Motor overheats	A. Motor not deep enough in water
	B. Not enough oil in gas or improperly mixed
	C. Bad thermostat
	D. Seals or gaskets (burned, cracked, or broken)
	E. Impeller key not in place or broken
	F. Plugged water inlet, outlet, or cavity
	G. Obstruction in water passages
	H. Broken, pinched, or leaking water lines
	I. Improper ignition timing
	J. Motor not assembled properly
	K. Shorted heat light wiring
	L. Bad water pump impeller, plate, housing, or seal
20. Motor stops suddenly, freezes up	A. No oil in gas, or no gas
	B. Insufficient cooling water
	C. No lubricant in gearcase
	D. Rusted cylinder or crankshaft
	E. Bent or broken rod, crankshaft, driveshaft, prop shaft, or stuck piston
	F. Bad water pump or plugged water passages
21. Motor knocks excessively	A. Too much or not enough oil in gas
	B. Worn or loose bearings. pistons, rods, or wrist pins
	C. Overadvanced ignition timing
	D. Carbon in combustion chambers and exhaust ports
	E. Manual starter not centered
	F. Flywheel nut loose
	G. Flywheel hitting coil heels
	H. Bent shift rod (vibrating against exhaust tube)
	I. Loose assemblies, bolts or screws
22. Generator will not charge	A. Battery condition
	B. Connections loose or dirty
	C. Drive belt loose or broken
	D. Faulty regulator or cutout relay
	E. Field fuse or fusible wire in regulator blown
	F. Generator not polarized (DC generators)

MOTOR REACTION	CHECK POINTS
	G. Open generator windings
	H. Worn or sticking brushes and/or slip rings
	I. Faulty rectifier diodes (AC generators)
	J. Faulty ammeter
	K. CD voltage regulator faulty
	L. Rectifier not grounded
	M. CD safety circuit grounded
23. Low generator output and a low battery	A. High resistance at battery terminals
	B. High resistance in charging circuit
	C. Faulty ammeter
	D. Low regulator setting
	E. Faulty rectifier diodes (AC generators)
	F. Faulty generator
24. Excessive battery charging	A. Regulator set too high
	B. Regulator contacts stuck
	C. Regulator voltage winding open
	D. Regulator improperly grounded
	E. High resistance in field coil
	F. Regulator improperly mounted
25. Excessive fuel consumption	A. Hole in fuel pump diaphragm
	B. Deteriorated carburetor gaskets
	C. Altered or wrong fixed jets
	D. Jets improperly adjusted
	E. Carburetor casting porous
	F. Float level too high
	G. Loose distributor pulley
26. Shifter dog jumps	A. Worn shifter dog or worn gear dogs
	B. Worn linkage
	C. Remote control adjustment
	D. Gearcase loose or sprung
	E. Exhaust housing bent
	F. Linkage out of adjustment
27. Electric shift inoperative or slips	A. Improper remote control installation
	B. Faulty coils
	C. Faulty springs
	D. Faulty clutch and gear
	E. Faulty bearings
	F. Wrong lubricant
	G. Loose or sprung gearcase
	H. Shorted wiring

2·Chrysler Outboard Corporation

NOTE: *Specifications for Chrysler racing models are not included since these are limited-production motors. In general, however, service procedures for regular production motors will also apply to racing models. If in doubt, consult an authorized Chrysler dealer or contact the factory directly.*

Chrysler service procedures, contained herein, also apply to the following manufacturers and models:

a. **Chrysler of Canada**

    35 hp—1966–72
    45 hp—1966–72
    50 hp—1966
    55 hp—1967–72
    70 hp—1969–72
    75 hp—1966–68
    85 hp—1969–72
    105 hp—1966–72
    105 hp (Racing)—1968–71
    120 hp—1970–72
    120 hp (Racing)—1970–71
    130 hp—1972
    135 hp (Racing)—1969–71
    150 hp (Racing)—1972

b. **Montgomery Ward (Sea King)**

    35 hp—1966–71
    45 hp—1966–68
    50 hp—1966
    55 hp—1967–71
    80 hp—1967

c. **Eaton's of Canada (Viking)**

    35 hp—1966–70
    55 hp—1966–70

Introduction

Chrysler Outboard Corporation has expanded its line in 1972 to include the limited-production, 150 horsepower racing model, the highest outboard horsepower ever certified by the OBC. Other models range from the 35 horsepower to the 130 horsepower, high-performance model.

All Chrysler outboards in 1972 incorporate a new fuel recycling system which eliminates the overboard discharge of unburned fuel. The new system assures that excess fuel accumulations are recirculated and burned in the combustion chamber.

Faster and more efficient starts are made possible by the Magnapower CD ignition system. Do-it-yourselfers are aided by easily removable, one-piece hoods and easily accessible carburetors, spark plugs, fuel pumps, and electrical components.

Chrysler lower units are protected by a spline-drive propeller and a rubber cushioned hub which acts as a shock absorber if an underwater object is struck. A seal guard protects the lower unit from damage if weeds or fish line become entangled.

Other notable Chrysler features include: dripless carburetors, electrical waterproofing, self-cleaning water pumps, underwater exhaust outlets, and corrosion-resistant finishes.

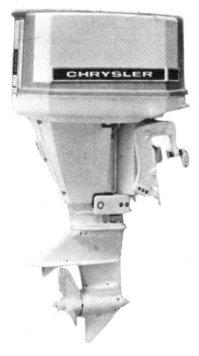

Two-cylinder 35 hp (© Chrysler Outboard Corp.)

Two-cylinder 45 hp (© Chrysler Outboard Corp.)

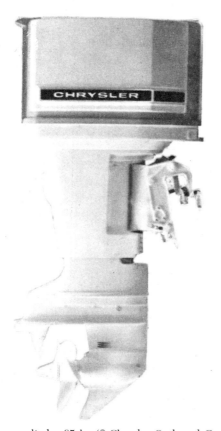

Three-cylinder 85 hp (© Chrysler Outboard Corp.)

Four-cylinder 105 hp (© Chrysler Outboard Corp.)

Model Identification

Year	Model(s)	No. of Cyls	HP (OBC)	Cu In. Displace	Year	Model(s)	No. of Cyls	HP (OBC)	Cu In. Displace
1966	35601, 35631 (M)	2	35	35.9	1969	3525, 3527, 3543 (M) 3545, 3553, 3554 3583, 3585 (M)	2	35	35.7
	45621, 45631 (M)	2	45	42.18		4503, 4505, 4525 (M) 4527, 4535, 4543 4545, 4553, 4555 4565, 4575	2	45	42.18
	50621, 50631 (M)	2	50	44.7					
	50661, 50671 (A)	2	50	44.7		5543, 5545, 5553, 5555 (M) 5563, 5565, 5573, 5575 (A)	2	55	44.7
	75661, 75671 (A)	3	75	72.39					
	105661, 105671 (A)	4	105	96.55		7061, 7071 (CD)	3	70	72.39
1967	35701, 35731 (M)	2	35	35.9		8561, 8571 (CD)	3	85	72.39
	35741, 35751	2	35	35.9		10565, 10575 (CD)	4	105	96.55
	45701, 45711 (M) 45721, 45731 45781	2	45	42.18		10583 (CD)	4	105 Racing	96.55
	55721, 55731 (M) 55761, 55771 (A)	2	55	44.7		1358 HA (CD)	4	135 Racing	96.55
	75761, 75763 (A)	3	75	72.39	1970	35249 HA, 35349 (M) 350 HA, 352 HA, 352 HB 353 HA, 353 HB, 354 HA 354 HB, 355 HA, 355 HB	2	35	35.9
	75771, 75773	3	75	72.39					
	105761, 105763(A)	4	105	96.55					
	105771, 105773	4	105	96.55		45249, 45349, 450 HA (M) 450 HB, 452 HA, 452 HB 453 HA, 453 HB, 454 HA 455 HA, 455 HB	2	45	42.18
1968	35018, 35218 (M)	2	35	35.9					
	35318, 35418 35518	2	35	35.9					
	45018, 45038 (M) 45218, 45238 45318, 45338 45418, 45438 45518, 45538	2	45	42.18		554 HA, 544 HB, 555 HA, 555 HB (M)	2	55	44.7
	55418, 55518 (M) 55618, 55718 (A)	2	55	44.7		556 HA, 556 HB, 557 HA, 557 HB (A) 558 HA, 558 HB, 559 HA, 559 HB (CD)	2	55	44.7
	75618, 75638 (CD) 75718, 75738 (CD)	3	75	72.39					
	105638, 105738 (CD)	4	105	96.55		706 HA, 706 HB, 707 HA, 707 HB (CD)	3	70	72.39
	105748 (CD)	4	105 Racing	96.55					

Model Identification (cont.)

Year	Model(s)	No. of Cyls	HP (OBC)	Cu In. Displace
1970	856 HA, 857 HA (CD)	3	85	72.39
	1056 HA, 1057 HA (CD)	4	105	96.55
	1058 HA (CD)	4	105 Racing	96.55
	1206 HA, 1207 HA (CD)	4	120	96.55
	1208 HA (CD)	4	120 Racing	96.55
	1358 HA (CD)	4	135 Racing	96.55
1971	350 HC, 354 HC, 355 HC 356 HA, 357 HA	2	35	35.9
	452 HC, 453 HC, 450 HC, 454 HC 455 HC, 456 HC, 457 HC, 458 HA 459 HA	2	45	42.18
	551 HA	2	55 Logger	44.7
	554 HC, 555 HC, 556 HC, 557 HC 558 HC, 559 HC	2	55	44.7
	706 HC, 706 HD, 707 HC, 707 HD	3	70	72.37
	856 HB, 856 HC, 857 HB, 857 HC	3	85	72.39
	1056 HB, 1056 HC, 1057 HB, 1057 HC	4	105	96.55

Year	Model(s)	No. of Cyls	Horsepower	Cubic Inch Displacement
1971	1058 HB, 1058 HC	4	105 Racing	96.55
	1206 HB, 1206 HC, 1207 HB, 1207 HC	4	120	96.55
	1208 HB, 1208 HC	4	120 Racing	96.55
	1358 HB, 1358 HC	4	135 Racing	96.55
1972	350 HD, 354 HD, 355 HD, 356 HD 357 HB	2	35	35.9
	452 HD, 453 HD, 450 HD, 454 HD 455 HD, 456 HD, 457 HD, 458 HD 459 HB	2	45	42.18
	554 HD, 555 HD, 556 HD, 557 HD 558 HD, 559 HD	2	55	44.7
	706 HE, 707 HE	3	70	72.39
	856 HD, 857 HD	3	85	72.39
	1056 HD, 1057 HD	4	105	96.55
	1206 HD, 1207 HD	4	120	96.55
	1306 HA, 1307 HA	4	130	96.55
	1508 HA	4	150 Racing	96.55

(M)—Magneto Ignition
(A)—Alternator
(CD)—Capacitive Discharge

General Engine Specifications

Year	Model	Cu In. Displacement	Horsepower (OBC) @ rpm	Full Throttle rpm Range	Bore (in.)	Stroke (in.)	Fuel/Oil Ratio
1966	35	35.9	35 @ 4750	4400–5100	3.000	2.540	50/1①
	45	42.18	45 @ 4750	4400–5100	3.250	2.750	50/1①

General Engine Specifications (cont.)

Year	Model	Cu In. Displacement	Horsepower (OBC) @ rpm	Full Throttle rpm Range	Bore (in.)	Stroke (in.)	Fuel/Oil Ratio
1966	50	44.7	50 @ 4750	4400–5100	3.188	2.800	50/1①
	75	72.39	75 @ 4750	4400–5100	3.312	2.800	50/1①
	105	96.55	105 @ 5000	4500–5500	3.312	2.800	50/1①
1967	35	35.9	35 @ 4750	4400–5100	3.000	2.540	50/1①
	45	42.18	45 @ 4750	4400–5100	3.125	2.750	50/1①
	55	44.7	55 @ 5250	4500–5500	3.188	2.800	50/1①
	75	72.39	75 @ 4750	4400–5100	3.312	2.800	50/1①
	105	96.55	105 @ 5000	4500–5500	3.312	2.800	50/1①
1968	35	35.9	35 @ 4750	4400–5100	3.000	2.540	50/1①
	45	42.18	45 @ 4750	4400–5100	3.125	2.750	50/1①
	55	44.7	55 @ 5250	4500–5500	3.188	2.800	50/1①
	75	72.39	75 @ 4750	4400–5100	3.312	2.800	50/1②
	105	96.55	105 @ 5000	4500–5500	3.312	2.800	50/1②
1969	35	35.9	35 @ 4750	4400–5100	3.000	2.540	50/1③
	45	42.18	45 @ 4750	4400–5100	3.125	2.750	50/1③
	55	44.7	55 @ 5250	4500–5500	3.188	2.800	50/1③
	70	72.39	70 @ 4750	4400–5100	3.312	2.800	50/1③
	85	72.39	85 @ 5000	4500–5500	3.312	2.800	50/1③
	105	96.55	105 @ 5000	4500–5500	3.312	2.800	50/1③
1970	35	35.9	35 @ 4750	4400–5100	3.000	2.540	50/1③
	45	42.18	45 @ 4750	4400–5100	3.125	2.750	50/1③
	55	44.7	55 @ 5250	5000–5500	3.188	2.800	50/1③
	70	72.39	70 @ 4750	4400–5100	3.312	2.800	50/1③
	85	72.39	85 @ 5000	4500–5500	3.312	2.800	50/1③
	105	96.55	105 @ 5000	4500–5500	3.312	2.800	50/1③

General Engine Specifications (cont.)

Year	Model	Cu In. Displacement	Horsepower (OBC) @ rpm	Full Throttle rpm Range	Bore (in.)	Stroke (in.)	Fuel/Oil Ratio
1971	35	35.9	35 @ 4750	4400–5100	3.000	2.540	50/1③
	45	42.18	45 @ 4750	4400–5100	3.125	2.750	50/1③
	55	44.7	55 @ 5250	5000–5500	3.188	2.800	50/1③
	55 Logger	44.7	55 @ 5250	4200–4800	3.188	2.800	50/1③
	70	72.39	70 @ 4750	4400–5100	3.312	2.800	50/1③
	85	72.39	85 @ 5000	4500–5500	3.312	2.800	50/1③
	105	96.55	105 @ 5000	4500–5500	3.312	2.800	50/1③
	120	96.55	120 @ 5250	5000–5500	3.312	2.800	50/1③
1972	35	35.9	35 @ 4750	4400–5100	3.000	2.540	50/1③
	45	42.18	45 @ 4750	4400–5100	3.125	2.750	50/1③
	55	44.7	55 @ 5250	5000–5500	3.188	2.800	50/1③
	70	72.39	70 @ 4750	4400–5100	3.312	2.800	50/1③
	85	72.39	85 @ 5000	4500–5500	3.312	2.800	50/1③
	105	96.55	105 @ 5000	4500–5500	3.312	2.800	50/1③
	120	96.55	120 @ 5250	5000–5500	3.312	2.800	50/1③
	130	96.55	130 @ 5250	5000–5500	3.312	2.800	50/1③

① 24/1 for first 10 hours of operation and continuously for racing or commercial applications.
② 24/1 for first 60 gallons of fuel and continuously for racing or commercial applications.
③ 24/1 for first 4 hours of operation. If motor is used commercially or for racing, you may use 50/1 Chrysler Outboard Oil or 24/1 of any other heavy duty outboard oil.

NOTE: *Consult your dealer as to the use of "break-in" additives during the "break-in" period.*

Tune-Up Specifications

Year	Model	Firing Order	Spark Plugs ° Type	Gap (in.)	Breaker Point Gap (in.)	Compression Pressure (psi)
1966	35	Alternate	Ch–J4J	0.030	0.020	95–105
	45	Alternate	AC–M42K	0.030	0.020	130–140
	50	Alternate	AC–M42K	0.030	0.020	130–140

Tune-Up Specifications (cont.)

| Year | Model | Firing Order | Spark Plugs ° | | Breaker Point Gap (in.) | Compression Pressure (psi) |
			Type	Gap (in.)		
1966	75	1–2–3	Ch–J4J	0.030	0.013–0.015	③
	105	1–3–2–4	Ch–J4J	0.030	0.009–0.011	③
196᷍	35	Alternate	Ch–J4J	0.030	0.020	95–105
	45	Alternate	Ch–J4J	0.030	0.020	130–140
	55	Alternate	Ch–L4J	0.030	0.020	130–140
	75	1–2–3	Ch–L4J	0.030	0.013–0.015	③
	105	1–3–2–4	Ch–J4J	0.030	0.009–0.011	③
1968	35	Alternate	Ch–L4J	0.030	0.020	95–105
	45	Alternate	Ch–L4J	0.030	0.020	130–140
	55	Alternate	Ch–L4J	0.030	0.020	130–140
	75	1–2–3	Ch–L4J	0.030	0.013–0.015	③
	105	1–3–2–4	Ch–L19V	——	0.009–0.011	③
1969	35	Alternate	① Ch–L4J	0.030	0.020	95–105
	45	Alternate	Ch–L4J	0.030	0.020	130–140
	55	Alternate	Ch–L4J	0.030	0.020	130–140
	70	1–2–3	Ch–L19V	——	0.013–0.015	③
	85	1–2–3	Ch–L19V	——	0.013–0.015	③
	105	1–3–2–4	Ch–L19V	——	0.009–0.011	③
1970	35	Alternate	Ch–L4J	0.030	0.020	95–105
	45	Alternate	Ch–L4J	0.030	0.020	130–140
	55	Alternate	② Ch–L4J	0.030	0.020	130–140
	70	1–2–3	Ch–L20V	——	0.013–0.015	③
	85	1–2–3	Ch–L20V	——	0.013–0.015	③
	105	1–3–2–4	Ch–L20V	——	0.009–0.011	③

Tune-Up Specifications (cont.)

Year	Model	Firing Order	Spark Plugs * Type	Gap (in.)	Breaker Point Gap (in.)	Compression Pressure (psi)
1970	105	1–3–2–4	Ch–L20V	——	0.009–0.011	③
	120	1–3–2–4	Ch–L20V	——	0.009–0.011	③
1971	35	Alternate	Ch–L4J	0.030	0.020	95–105
	45	Alternate	Ch–L4J	0.030	0.020	130–140
	55	Alternate	Ch–L4J	0.030	0.020	130–140
	55 Logger	Alternate	Ch–L4J	0.030	0.020	130–140
	70	1–2–3	Ch–L20V	——	0.013–0.015	③
	85	1–2–3	Ch–L20V	——	0.013–0.015	③
	105	1–3–2–4	Ch–L20V	——	0.009–0.011	③
	120	1–3–2–4	Ch–L20V	——	0.009–0.011	③
1972	35	Alternate	Ch–L4J	0.030	0.020	95–105
	45	Alternate	Ch–L4J	0.030	0.020	130–140
	55	Alternate	Ch–L4J	0.030	0.020	130–140
	70	1–2–3	Ch–L20V	——	0.013–0.015	③
	85	1–2–3	Ch–L20V	——	0.013–0.015	③
	105	1–3–2–4	Ch–L20V	——	0.009–0.011	③
	120	1–3–2–4	Ch–L20V	——	0.009–0.011	③
	130	1–3–2–4	Ch–L20V	——	0.009–0.011	③

① Magnapower models use Ch–L19V
② Magnapower models use Ch–L20V
③ All cylinders within 15 psi of each other
 * Surface gap spark plugs are used on all Magnapower capacitor discharge ignition systems.
—— Surface gap spark plugs. All surface gap plugs used on Chrysler outboards have a fixed gap of 0.050 in. This should not be altered.

Torque Specifications

Year	Model (hp)	Flywheel (ft lbs)	Cylinder Head (in. lbs)	Main Bearings (in. lbs)	Kingpin (ft lbs)	Connecting Rod (in. lbs)
1966–72	35, 45, 50, 55	75	270	270	90	150

NOTE: *Due to the extensive use of aluminum and white metal to resist corrosion, torque specifications must be adhered to strictly.*

Standard Screw Torque Specifications

Year	Model (hp)	Screw Size (in.)	Torque (in. lbs)
1966–72	35, 45, 50, 55	6–32	9
		10–24	30
		10–32	35
		12–24	45
		$\frac{1}{4}$–20	70
		$\frac{5}{16}$–18	160
		$\frac{3}{8}$–16	270

NOTE: *Due to the use of aluminum and white metal to resist corrosion, torque specifications must be adhered to strictly.*

Torque Sequences

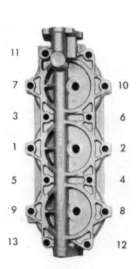

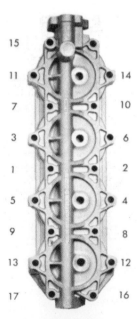

Three-cylinder head bolt tightening sequence (© Chrysler Outboard Corp.)

Four-cylinder head bolt tightening sequence (© Chrysler Outboard Corp.)

Wiring Diagrams

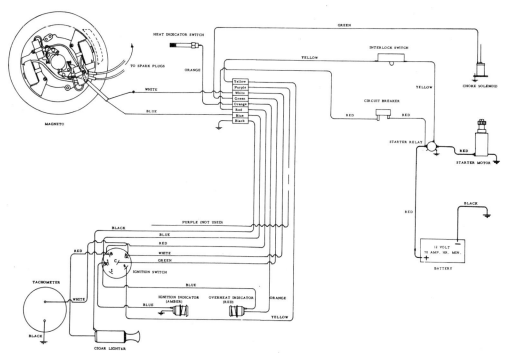

1966–70 35–55 hp with magneto (© Chrysler Outboard Corp.)

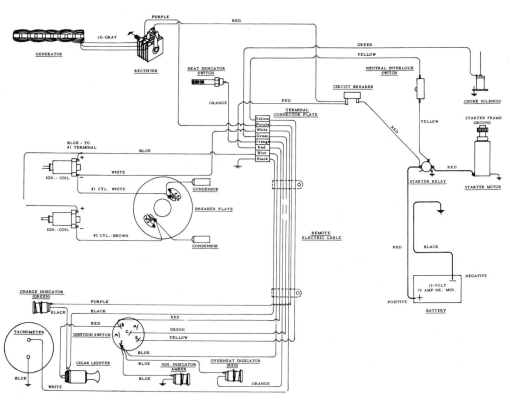

1966–70 35–55 hp with battery ignition and generator (© Chrysler Outboard Corp.)

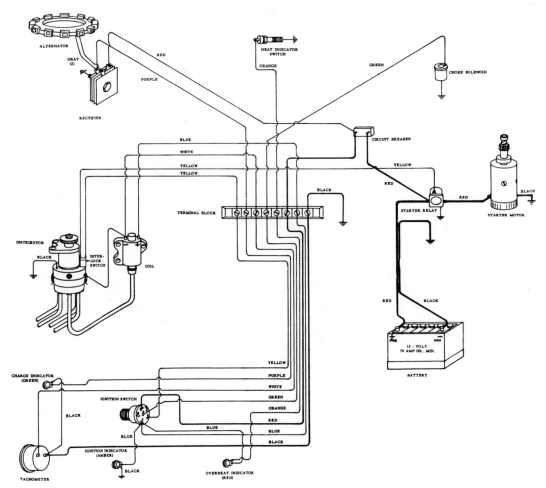

1966–70 70–120 hp with battery ignition and generator (© Chrysler Outboard Corp.)

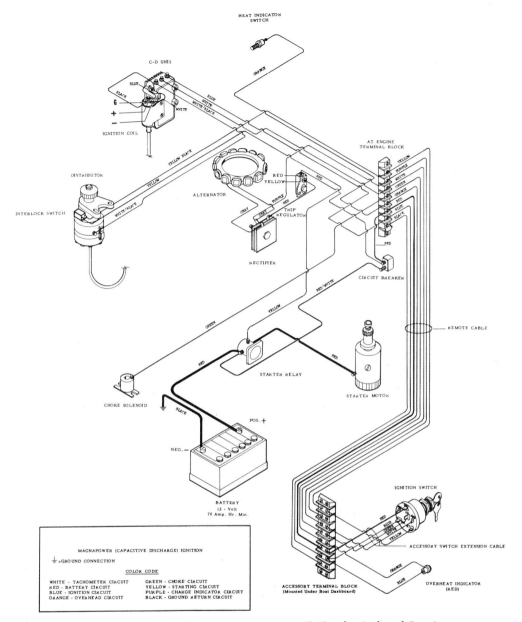

HEAT INDICATOR SWITCH

C-D UNIT

IGNITION COIL

DISTRIBUTOR

INTERLOCK SWITCH

ALTERNATOR

TRIP REGULATOR

RECTIFIER

AT ENGINE TERMINAL BLOCK

CIRCUIT BREAKER

REMOTE CABLE

CHOKE SOLENOID

STARTER RELAY

STARTER MOTOR

BATTERY
12 - Volt
70 Amp. Hr. Min.

POS. +

NEG. -

IGNITION SWITCH

ACCESSORY SWITCH EXTENSION CABLE

ACCESSORY TERMINAL BLOCK
(Mounted Under Boat Dashboard)

OVERHEAT INDICATOR
(RED)

MAGNAPOWER (CAPACITIVE DISCHARGE) IGNITION

= GROUND CONNECTION

COLOR CODE

WHITE - TACHOMETER CIRCUIT   GREEN - CHOKE CIRCUIT
RED - BATTERY CIRCUIT   YELLOW - STARTING CIRCUIT
BLUE - IGNITION CIRCUIT   PURPLE - CHARGE INDICATOR CIRCUIT
ORANGE - OVERHEAD CIRCUIT   BLACK - GROUND RETURN CIRCUIT

1966–70 70–120 hp with Magnapower ignition (© Chrysler Outboard Corp.)

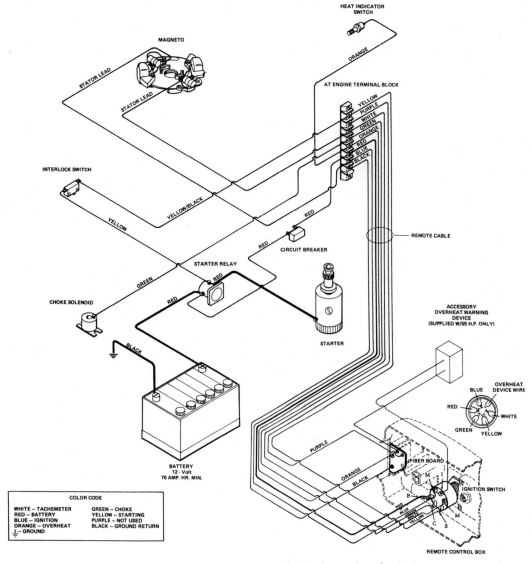

1971–72 35–55 hp with magneto (© Chrysler Outboard Corp.)

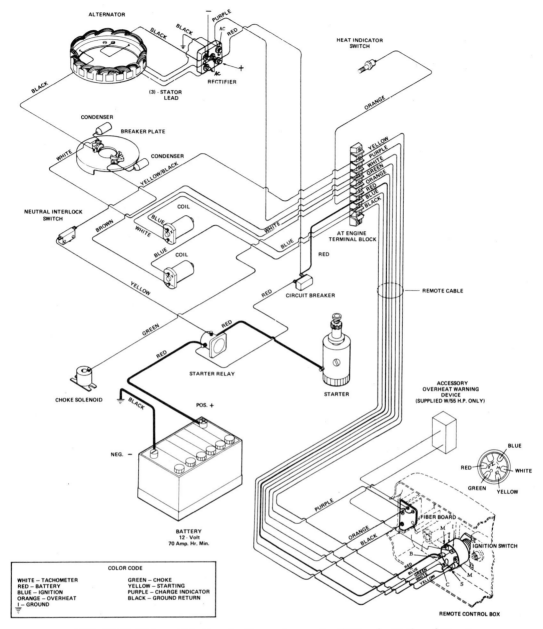

1971–72 35–55 hp with battery ignition and generator (© Chrysler Outboard Corp.)

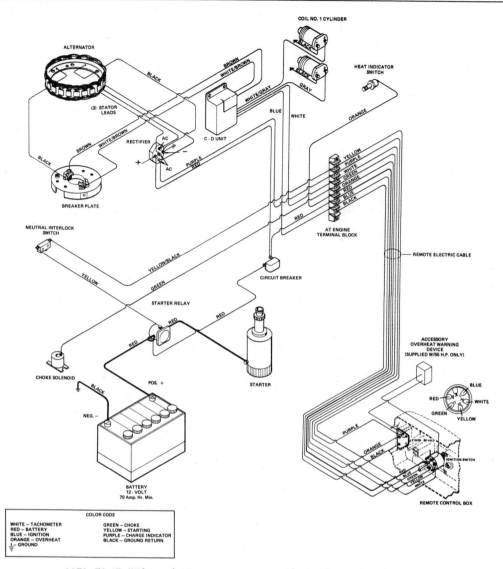

1971–72 45–55 hp with Magnapower ignition (© Chrysler Outboard Corp.)

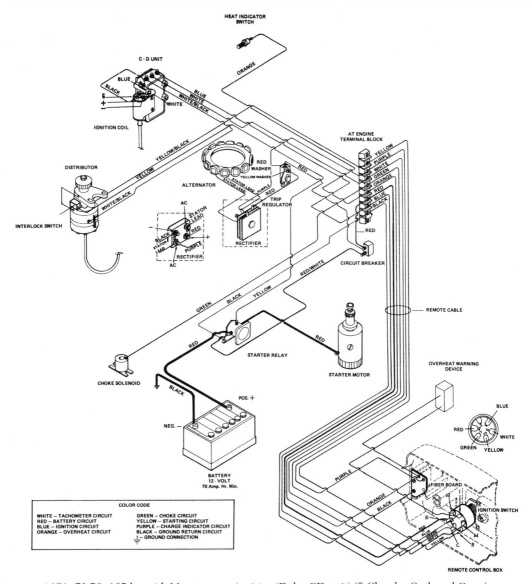

1971–72 70–135 hp with Magnapower ignition (Delta CD unit) (© Chrysler Outboard Corp.)

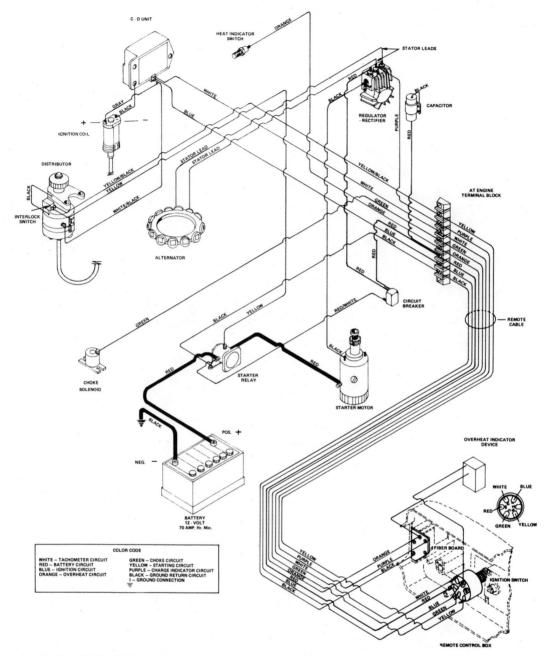

1971–72 70–135 hp with Magnapower ignition (Motorola CD unit) (© Chrysler Outboard Corp.)

Model Identification

SERIAL AND MODEL NUMBER IDENTIFICATION

The serial number and model number are stamped on a plate which is located under the engine hood on the forward floor of the motor support plate. The engine hood must be removed to reveal this plate.

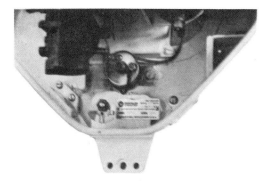

Location of engine identification plate (© Chrysler Outboard Corp.)

MODEL NUMBER INTERPRETATION

The model numbers for all motors, over thirty horsepower are given in the "Model Identification" chart in the specifications section.

1966–67

The first two (or three for motors over 100 horsepower) digits denote the horsepower of the motor. The next digit represents the last number of the model year. The following digit is the variation code (see following chart). The last digit gives the country for which the motor is intended.

1968

The first two (or three) digits give the engine horsepower. The next digit denotes the variation code (see following chart). The next digit gives the country for which the motor was intended. The last digit is the last number of the model year.

1969–72

The first two (or three) digits give the horsepower of the engine. The last numeral is the motor variation code. The let-ters following the number denote the country for which the motor was intended.

Variation Code—1966–69

Code	Interpretation
0	Standard shaft, manual starter
1	Long shaft, manual starter
2	Standard shaft, manual starter, w/tiller
3	Long shaft, manual starter, w/tiller
4	Standard shaft, electric starter
5	Long shaft, electric starter
6	Standard shaft, electric starter, w/alternator
7	Long shaft, electric starter, w/alternator
8	Standard shaft, electric starter, w/alternator, and Magnapower ignition
9	Long shaft, electric starter, w/alternator, and Magnapower ignition

Production Code

Before 1970

1, 3, 5—U.S. Models
2, 4, 6—Canadian Models

1970–72

HA—U.S. Models
HB—Canadian Models

Variation Code—1970–72

Code	Interpretation
6	Standard shaft
7	Long shaft
8	Racing, standard shaft

General Care and Maintenance

SALT WATER

Chrysler Outboard Corporation has taken care to chemically treat all parts that contact salt water. However, the owner must also take some special precautions after running the engine in salt water.

1. Always tilt the engine out of the water when not in use.

2. Periodically run the engine in fresh

water to flush out salt deposits that form in the cooling system and passageways. A flushing adaptor is available from Chrysler to allow the owner to flush the motor with an ordinary garden hose.

3. Wash the engine down with fresh water at regular intervals. Apply an automotive-type wax to protect the finish.

4. Periodically, remove the propeller and lubricate the propeller shaft. While you are about it, check the condition of the propeller and of the lower unit. Be sure that the blades of the propeller are not nicked and that the protective coating of paint on the entire lower unit and leg is unbroken. Paint which is chipped allows the breakdown of the metal at an even faster rate. Be sure you touch up those places where the paint coat is broken.

5. Whenever the engine will not be used for a day or longer, disconnect the negative battery cable to prevent battery rundown and electrolysis.

PREVENTIVE MAINTENANCE AND PERIODIC SERVICE

The following precautions and services, if heeded, should assure a long and satisfactory life for your outboard.

1. Use the type of fuel, oil, and grease specified by the manufacturer.

2. Be sure that the correct fuel/oil ratio is maintained at all times.

3. Never run the outboard motor out of water.

4. Do not overspeed clutch-type models in Neutral. The speed control should not be advanced beyond the Start position.

5. Follow the break-in period as detailed later in this chapter.

6. Every thirty hours of use, check the gear housing and add gear lube if necessary. Completely drain and replace the grease at least once every six months.

7. Prepare the motor for off-season storage (winterizing) as directed in this chapter.

8. The propeller shaft seals should be checked at least after every year's use or immediately after contact with monofilament fishing line, nylon rope, or similar foreign material.

9. Never use the electric starter continuously for more than fifteen seconds without allowing at least three minutes for the armature and field coils to cool.

10. Shift the gears rapidly at the proper engine speed. Do not ease the gears, as this will cause excessive wear to the gears and clutch.

11. Be sure to have the authorized Chrysler dealer perform the initial inspection as required.

12. Check items which are subject to normal wear (water pump impeller, breaker points, spark plugs, starter ropes, starter pawls, shear pins, and items of a similar nature) at least once every season. Twice a season is preferable.

13. Do not tip the motor upside down or store in an inverted position. This practice will lead to corrosion from water seeping into the crankcase from the lower leg.

14. Perform an outboard motor tune-up at the beginning of each season or at the time of winterizing. Check the motor frequently to be sure that it is not in need of a tune-up. Peroidically, clean, inspect, and adjust the carburetor to ensure optimum performance.

15. Always operate the outboard motor within the recommended rpm range. See "General Engine Specifications" or the motor identification plate.

16. Be sure that your boat and motor are rated to accept each other. Power greater than that specified on the hull plate can be considered misuse and could void the warranty.

17. Be sure that the motor is adequately protected against excessive spray and backwash. Any spray or backwash that "drowns" the motor or causes premature corrosion on electrical or carburetor parts may void the warranty.

MOTOR INSTALLATION

It is recommended that the dealer make the first installation of the outboard. However, the owner can do this in accordance with the following suggestions and safety precautions. (See also the introductory chapter.)

1. Mount the engine at the center of the transom and tighten the stern bracket clamp screws alternately. Do not tighten with a wrench.

2. If the engine is not centered on the transom, the torque of the propeller will cause the boat to run erratically and off course.

CAUTION: *Due to the immense amount of thrust delivered by the propeller, it is essential that larger (above 35 hp) en-*

gines be bolted to the transom, using the holes in the mounting bracket provided for this purpose. Be sure that the stern brackets remain parallel to each other. When installing the mounting bolts, the holes through the transom should be caulked liberally to prevent leakage. Chrysler outboards are designed to be installed on a fifteen-inch transom (standard shaft model) or a twenty-inch transom (long shaft model). Most outboards do not adapt well to curved or reverse-angle transoms. If the motor is to be mounted on this type of transom, contact your Chrysler dealer for special mounting instructions.

PROPELLER AVAILABILITY

Chrysler Outboard Corporation offers the propellers listed on the following chart as replacements for the standard equipment propeller. This will allow the owner to match the proper propeller to his boat for particular applications and, at the same time, operate the motor within the recommended operating range.

Propeller Chart

Part No.	Diameter x Pitch (in.)	No. of Blades	Material	Horsepower	Model Year	Application
P367	10⅜ x 7	4	Al.	35–55	66–72	Work
P366	10⅜ x 8½	4	Al.	35–55	66–72	Work
P328	10 x 10	4	Al.	35–55	66–72	Work
P377	10⅜ x 11½	4	Al.	35–55	66–72	Work
P296	10½ x 7	3	Al.	35–55	66–72	Heavy Load
P278	10⅜ x 10	3	Al.	35–55	66–72	Heavy Load
P287	10⅜ x 11½	3	Al.	35 45, 55	66–72 66–72	Medium Load Heavy Load
P293	10⅜ x 12½	3	Al.	45, 55 35	66–72 66–72	Medium Load Light Load
P273	10⅜ x 13½	3	Al.	35–55	66–72	Light Load
P297	10½ x 15	2	Br.	35–55	66–72	Light Load
P428	12 x 8½	3	Br.	55 Logger	71–72	Work
P39	13 x 12	3	Al.	75 75 105 70, 85	66–67 68 66–67 69–70	Medium Load Heavy Load Heavy Load Heavy Load
P47	13 x 14	3	Al.	105 75 70, 85 75 105 105	66–67 68 69–70 66–67 68 69–70	Medium Load Medium Load Medium Load Light Load Heavy Load Heavy Load

Propeller Chart (cont.)

Part No.	Diameter x Pitch (in.)	No. of Blades	Material	Horsepower	Model Year	Application
P322	13 x 16	3	Al.	105 105 75 70, 85	68–70 66–67 68 69–70	Medium Load Light Load Light Load Light Load
P381	13 x 11	3	Al.	70–130	71–72	Barge & Houseboat
P391	13 x 13	3	Al.	70, 85 105–130	71–72 70–72	Heavy Load Barge & Houseboat
P389	13 x 15	3	Al.	70, 85 105–130 120	71–72 71–72 70–72	Medium Load Heavy Load Heavy Load
P372	13 x 17	3	Al.	120 105–130 70, 85	70 71–72 71–72	Medium Load Medium Load Light Load
P383	13 x 19	3	Al.	120 70–130	70 71–72	Light Load Light Load
P404	13 x 21	3	Al.	70–130	71–72	Light Load
P373 °	10 x 15	2RH	Br.	RLU70–135	66–70	Racing—Solid Hub
P374 °	10 x 16	2RH	Br.	RLU70–135	66–70	Racing—Solid Hub
P320 °	10 x 17	2RH	Br.	RLU70–135	66–70	Racing—Solid Hub
P375 °	10 x 18	2RH	Br.	RLU70–135	66–70	Racing—Solid Hub
P411	10 x 16	2RH	Br.	RLU70–150	71–72	Racing—Solid Hub
P412	10 x 16	2LH	Br.	RLU70–150	71–72	Racing—Solid Hub

° Pin drive—All others spline drive

WINTERIZING

Before storing your motor for an extended period of time, it is necessary to protect it against rust, freezing, and corrosion. In lieu of having the motor winterized by a Chrysler dealer, the following procedure is recommended.

NOTE: *The following procedure must be performed on the boat or in a test tank.*

1. Run the engine until it is thoroughly warmed up.

2. Place the gear shift in Neutral and allow the engine to run at fast idle. Remove the fuel line from the fuel tank.

3. Rapidly inject a rust-preventive oil into the carburetor air intakes (for about 10–20 seconds) until the engine stops. On three-cylinder models, it is necessary to remove the carburetor cover to facilitate the injection of oil.

4. Remove the motor from the boat or from the test tank. Drain all fuel from the fuel lines and carburetor(s).

5. Disconnect the battery and remove the spark plugs. Pour an ounce or two of

Chrysler outboard oil into each cylinder. Manually, rotate the crankshaft to distribute the oil over the pistons, cylinders, and rings.

6. Drain and refill the lower unit.

7. Lubricate all parts as described under "Lubrication."

8. Clean the exterior of the engine and apply an automotive-type wax to protect the finish.

9. Remove the propeller and apply a coating of marine lubricant on the propeller shaft. If necessary, replace the shear pin.

10. Store the engine in an upright position in a dry, well-ventilated area.

11. This is an excellent time to have the propeller cleaned up and to perform any maintenance.

Preparation for Use After Storage

1. Remove the spark plugs and replace as necessary.

2. Check the lubricant level in the lower unit.

3. Lubricate all moving parts described under "Lubrication."

4. Clean the exterior of the engine and apply an automotive wax to protect the finish (especially in salt water areas).

5. Check the condition of the battery.

6. Start the motor in a test tank (or on the boat) and be sure that it is operating correctly. Replace any parts as necessary.

STEERING FRICTION ADJUSTMENT

Steering friction is controlled by a friction screw in the top starboard side of the swivel bracket. Adjust to the desired tension by turning the screw in or out.

THRUST PIN (SHEAR PIN) REPLACEMENT

1. To prevent accidental starting, put the engine in Neutral or disconnect the spark plug wires.

2. Remove the cotter pin from the propeller shaft nut and remove the nut and seal.

3. The thrust pin (shear pin) is located behind the propeller in the hub. Remove the damaged or broken thrust pin by driving it out with a new pin if necessary.

4. To remove the propeller, pull it straight back and off the propeller shaft. The propeller is splined to the shaft.

5. If necessary, the propeller may be re-

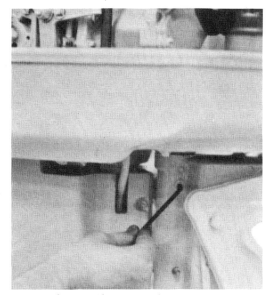

Steering friction adjustment (allen screw) (© Chrysler Outboard Corp.)

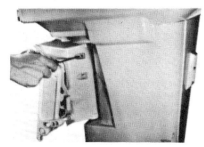

Steering friction adjustment (slotted screw) (© Chrysler Outboard Corp.)

moved by tapping it off with a soft block of wood.

6. If removed, reinstall the propeller.

7. Install a new thrust pin, propeller nut seal, propeller nut, and cotter pin.

8. It is wise to always carry a spare cotter pin, propeller nut, propeller nut seal, and thrust pin, for use in emergencies.

COOLING SYSTEM

Thermostat

Chrysler outboard engines are equipped with a thermostat which controls the temperature of the cooling water. Temperature control provides good idling characteristics and more complete combustion of the fuel charge.

IMPORTANT: *Never operate a Chrysler outboard without the thermostat installed.*

Checking Water Pump Operation

35–55 HP MODELS

Normal operation of the water pump is indicated by a spray of water flowing from the port located on the back of the motor leg. Water should be clearly visible at all operating speeds. If water is not visible, stop the motor immediately. Check the water intake passages on the side of the motor-leg gear housing to make sure that they are not obstructed by weeds and foreign material. If trouble persists, check the water pump impeller.

Operation of the water pump is necessary to avoid internal damage due to overheating.

70–130 HP MODELS

The preceding paragraphs apply. In addition, a heat indicator light is supplied with your motor or a temperature gauge is supplied. This must be installed to warn the operator to shut off the engine due to overheating. Overheating is indicated by the light being on or by the needle on the gauge reaching into the red band.

> NOTE: *Warranty on the engine will be voided if motor installation on the boat does not include the heat indicator lamp or temperature gauge.*

TILT PIN ADJUSTMENT

Location

The tilt pin is located on the bottom of the mounting bracket. It consists of a long pin which can be moved into different holes to change the angle of the motor relative to the transom.

Adjustment

See the introductory chapter of this book for the method of adjusting the tilt pin setting.

Lubrication

GENERAL

The lubrication system of Chrysler outboards is the standard type used on most all two-stroke engine designs. Oil is mixed with the fuel in the recommended propor-

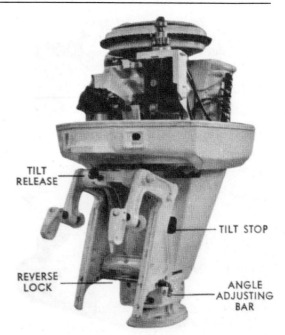

Location of tilt-angle adjusting bar (© Chrysler Outboard Corp.)

tion and, as the fuel is distributed, the oil in the fuel lubricates the pistons, cylinder walls, bearings, rings, and other moving parts, except the lower unit. The lower unit is lubricated by a self-contained supply of special lubricant.

It is worthy to note that in many cases, Chrysler recommends a greater amount of oil if you are not using Chrysler Outboard Oil.

BREAKING IN A NEW MOTOR

The following recommendations should be used when breaking in a new motor or when breaking in a motor which has been overhauled. Consult the following chart for oil ratio recommendations.

Chrysler Outboard Oil should be used in a Chrysler outboard motor but several other oils are acceptable for use when Chrysler Outboard Oil is not available. Oil which is certified TC-W by the Boating Industry Association may be used as well as high quality SAE 30 or 40 Heavy Duty Outboard Oil, as a limited substitute for Chrysler Outboard Oil.

FUEL RECOMMENDATIONS

1966–68

Marine white or regular grade automotive gasoline (approximately 85 octane) is recommended. Avoid the use of premium fuel (approximately 95 octane) with anti-knock additives. Gasolines and oils containing TCP, phosphorus additives, friction-reducing compounds, and break-in oils are unnecessary and not recommended for use in Chrysler outboards.

1969–70

Non-leaded (or low lead) high octane gasolines such as marine white, automotive, or light aircraft are highly recommended for Chrysler outboards.

Regular grade automotive gasolines of 90 octane minimum can be used and are considered acceptable.

The use of premium fuels which contain phosphorus compounds and other additives should be avoided.

1971–72

Unleaded marine white gas, unleaded automotive gas, and light aircraft gas are preferred fuels. These low-lead fuels should be of at least 87 octane.

Regular grade automotive gas, premium grade automotive gas (containing no phosphorus), and automotive gasoline of at least 85 octane are considered acceptable.

Do not use low octane white fuel (lamp gas), motor fuel containing phosphorus or excessive lead, or any fuel not intended for use in modern automotive engines.

Fuel Mixing Procedure

The following procedure will ensure that the oil and fuel are completely mixed and that a minimum of contaminants are allowed to enter the fuel system. Obviously, it is not wise to smoke while filling the gas tank or to fill the tank in an unventilated area where a chance spark could ignite the fumes.

1. Always maintain a clean fuel tank.
2. If possible, strain all fuel through a clean mesh filter.
3. Pour one gallon of fresh gasoline into an empty tank.
4. Add the proper amount of Chrysler Outboard Oil, SAE 30 or SAE 40 Heavy Duty Outboard Oil to the tank.
5. Add the balance of the gasoline and mix the oil and fuel thoroughly.
6. It cannot be stressed too thoroughly to add the recommended amount of oil to the fuel. This is the method of lubricating your outboard and nothing will cause it to wear out faster than using too little oil. Nothing will foul the engine faster than using too much oil.

Fuel Ratio Conversion Table

Fuel/Oil Ratio	Gasoline Quantity	Oil Quantity	
16/1 6 percent oil	1 gallon	½ pt	8 oz
	6 gallon	3 pt	48 oz
	12 gallon	6 pt	96 oz
24/1 4 percent oil	1 gallon	⅓ pt	5.3 oz
	6 gallon	2 pt	32 oz
	12 gallon	4 pt	64 oz
50/1 2 percent oil	1 gallon	⅛ pt	2.6 oz
	6 gallon	1 pt	16 oz
	12 gallon	2 pt	32 oz

Fuel Oil Mixture Requirements

| | | Break-In Period | | | | | Oil Ratio After Break-in | | | |
| | | Oil Ratio | | | | | Pleasure | | HD or Racing | |
Year	Model	Chrysler Outboard Oil	Other Oils	Minimum Hours Req'd	Special Run-in Period (hrs)	Minimum Hrs Prior to Continuous WOT Operation	Chrysler Outboard Oil	Other Oils	Chrysler Outboard Oil	Other Oils
1966	35–50	24/1	24/1	10	——	10	50/1	50/1	24/1	24/1
	75–105	24/1	24/1	10	1	10	50/1	50/1	24/1	24/1
1967	35–55	24/1	24/1	10	1	10	50/1	50/1	24/1	24/1
	75–105	24/1	24/1	10	1	10	50/1	50/1	24/1	24/1
1968	25–55	24/1	24/1	10	1	10	50/1	50/1	24/1	24/1

Fuel Oil Mixture Requirements (cont.)

| | | Break-In Period | | | | | Oil Ratio After Break-in | | | |
| | | Oil Ratio | | | Special Run-in Period (hrs) | Minimum Hrs Prior to Continuous WOT Operation | Pleasure | | HD or Racing | |
Year	Model	Chrysler Outboard Oil	Other Oils	Minimum Hours Req'd			Chrysler Outboard Oil	Other Oils	Chrysler Outboard Oil	Other Oils
1968	75–105	24/1	24/1	2	3	——	50/1	50/1	24/1	24/1
1969	35–55	24/1	24/1④	3	1⑤	3	50/1	50/1	50/1	24/1
1970	35–55	24/1	24/1④	3	1⑤	3	50/1	50/1	50/1	24/1
	70–120	24/1	24/1④	3	1⑤	3	50/1	50/1	50/1	50/1
1971	35–120	25/1	25/1④	3	1⑤	3	50/1	50/1	50/1	25/1
1972	35–130	25/1	25/1④	3	1⑤	3	50/1	50/1	50/1	35/1

1. During the first hour of operation, run the engine in gear between 900–3000 rpms. Do not exceed this limit for one hour of operation.
2. First 60 gallons of fuel.
3. After first fifteen minutes running time, move throttle to WOT for short bursts, gradually increasing the duration.
4. For the first tank of fuel, use a good commercial additive to aid break-in. Consult a dealer for a good brand of additive.
5. Momentary bursts of WOT.

PERIODIC LUBRICATION

In order to keep your Chrysler outboard in as close to its original condition as possible, it is advisable to follow the lubrication schedule listed below.

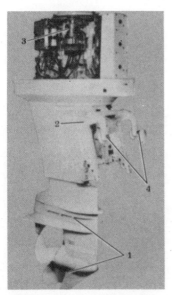

Starboard side lubrication points (© Chrysler Outboard Corp.)

1. Gear housing   3. Distributor (if equipped)
2. Swivel bracket   4. Clamp screws

Lubrication Chart

Lubrication Points	Lubricant	Frequency
Gear housing	1	Every 30 hours of use—drain and replace every 6 months
Swivel bracket	2	Every 60 days
Distributor	2	Every 60 days
Stern bracket	3	Every 60 days
Control linkage	3	Every 60 days
Starter pinion gear	3	Every 30 days
Propeller shaft	3	Every 60 days

Recommended Lubricants (See Chart Above)

Code	Lubricant
1	Chrysler Outboard Gear Lube (if not available, use non-corrosive, leaded, EP 90 outboard gear lube)
2	All-purpose automotive chassis lubricant
3	Rykon No. 2 EP or SAE 40 Motor Oil

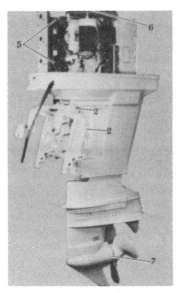

Port-side lubrication points (© Chrysler Outboard Corp.)

2. Swivel bracket 6. Starter
5. Linkage 7. Propeller shaft

LOWER UNIT LUBRICATION

The lubricant in the lower unit (gear housing) should be checked every 30 hours of operation and should be replaced every 100 hours (6 months) or at least once each season (prior to storage). The recommended gear lube is Chrysler Outboard Gear Lube. If this is not available, use a non-corrosive, leaded EP 90 outboard gear lube. Do not use corrosive, hypoid gear lubricants.

Inspection

1. Loosen, but do not remove, the gear-housing drain screw and allow a small amount of lubricant to drain. If water is present, it will drain out, prior to the actual lubricant.

2. Should water be present in the lower unit lubricant, the cause of the entry of water must be found and corrected. The propeller seal is an excellent place to begin.

Lubricant Replacement

1. With the engine in an upright position, remove the upper and lower plug screws and allow the lubricant to drain.

2. Insert the tube into the lower drain hole and fill the gear housing with gear lube until it appears at the top vent hole.

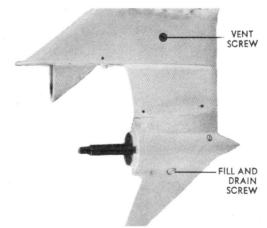

Lower unit lubrication (© Chrysler Outboard Corp.)

3. Install the top plug and washer.

4. Remove the tube of lubricant and install the lower plug screw and washer. Tighten securely.

5. Allow the engine to stand in an upright position for at least one-half hour with the upper screw removed. This will allow the gear lube to completely fill all of the cavities in the gear housing.

6. Recheck the gear lube level. Add lubricant as necessary, using the procedure above.

Fuel System

CARBURETOR

All Models (1966–72)

Removal

1. When disconnecting the throttle link, use caution not to bend the link. It is recommended that it be replaced with a new one, since it is extremely important that the correct geometry be maintained for this setting.

2. Remove the fuel line from the carburetor.

3. Disconnect the choke wire from the choke shaft.

4. Remove the two nuts which hold the carburetor on the adaptor flange.

5. Pull the carburetor forward and remove the studs.

Checking Inlet Needle and Seat

The inlet needle and seat are located in the top half of the carburetor.

1. Separate the body halves.

2. Remove the float lever pin from the top half of the carburetor and lift out the float.

3. Remove the inlet needle and check for excessive wear on the point. If the needle is notched or pitted, replace both the needle and seat with new parts.

4. Reassemble the carburetor and check the float level.

Checking Float Level

1. Separate the body halves and tip the top half upside down. Note the position of the float.

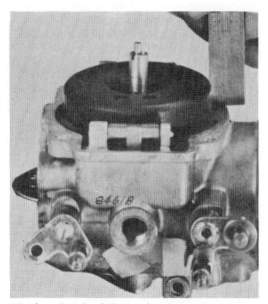

Checking float level (© Chrysler Outboard Corp.)

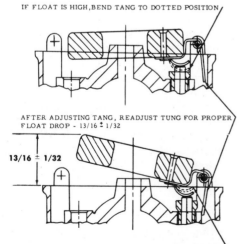

IF FLOAT IS HIGH, BEND TANG TO DOTTED POSITION

AFTER ADJUSTING TANG, READJUST TUNG FOR PROPER FLOAT DROP – 13/16 ± 1/32

13/16 ± 1/32

IF FLOAT IS LOW, BEND TANG TO DOTTED POSITION

Checking float drop (© Chrysler Outboard Corp.)

2. The float should be perfectly level and the edge should extend $13/32$ in. + $1/64$ in. above the edge of the body casting.

3. Adjust the float level by bending the short, curved actuating arm on the float in the direction desired. Do not press down on the float when the float is assembled to the carburetor since the needle valve may be damaged.

Cleaning the Idle Tube

The idle tube is located in the upper half of the carburetor and is replaceable.

1. Remove the idle adjustment needle from the top half of the carburetor.

2. Remove the plug screw, center top half of the carburetor. This will allow access to the idle tube screw.

3. Using a small screwdriver, remove the idle tube from the bore (the same bore as the plug screw).

4. Soak the idle tube in fresh gasoline or carburetor solvent and air-dry.

5. Reassemble in the reverse order of disassembly.

Main nozzle gasket in place (© Chrysler Outboard Corp.)

NOTE: *Be sure that the main nozzle boss gasket is in place. If this is left out, the engine will show all indications of an excessively rich fuel mixture.*

DISASSEMBLY

1. Remove the following parts (in order) from the bowl casting: bowl retaining screws, drain-valve channel plug screw, drain valve spring, drain valve, and main fuel adjustment.

2. From the body casting, remove the following parts (in order): main nozzle gasket, body gasket, float fulcrum pin, float, inlet seat, inlet needle, idle adjustment screw and spring, and idle channel plug screw.

3. Remove the throttle plate and shaft assembly.

4. Remove the choke plate and shaft assembly.

5. Remove the welch plugs covering the idle discharge ports.

6. After all parts have been removed and thoroughly washed in clean gasoline, blow out the following channels with compressed air.

   a. Main nozzle and main air-bleed tube.

   b. Idle supply tube, idle mixture passage, and idle discharge holes.

   c. Fuel supply channel.

   d. Main fuel adjusting orifice and channel.

   e. Drain valve channels.

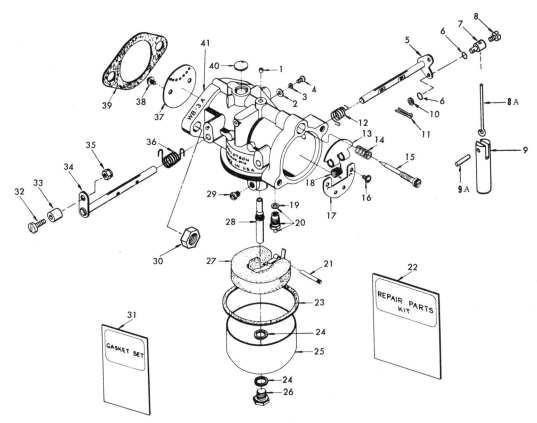

Exploded view of typical carburetor used on Chrysler outboards (© Chrysler Outboard Corp.)

1. Body channel cup plug	13. Choke relief valve	28. Main nozzle
2. Throttle shaft position retaining screw washer	14. Idle mixture screw spring	29. Main fuel jet (0.0785) (Standard)
3. Throttle shaft position retaining screw lockwasher	15. Idle mixture screw	30. Hex nut
4. Throttle shaft position retaining screw	16. Choke shutter retaining screw and lockwasher	31. Gasket set
5. Choke shaft and lever	17. Choke shutter	32. Throttle roller shaft
6. Seal, choke arm swivel	18. Choke relief valve spring	33. Roller
7. Swivel, choke rod	19. Inlet seat gasket	34. Throttle shaft and lever
8. Screw	20. Inlet needle, seat and gasket	35. Stop nut
8A. Choke solenoid rod	21. Float lever pin	36. Throttle shaft return spring
9. Choke solenoid plunger	22. Repair parts kit	37. Throttle shutter
9A. Gear pin	23. Fuel bowl gasket	38. Throttle shutter retaining screw and lockwasher
10. Plain washer	24. Fuel bowl retaining screw gasket	39. Flange gasket
11. Cotter pin	25. Fuel bowl	40. Body channel welch plug
12. Choke shaft return spring	26. Fuel bowl retaining screw	41. Carburetor complete (WB-3C)
	27. Float	

ASSEMBLY

1. Carburetor overhaul kits are available from Chrysler dealers. These are recommended any time a carburetor is being overhauled. They contain all necessary gaskets and seals which should be replaced. However, it may be necessary to purchase some replacement parts separately.

2. It is recommended that a new carburetor flange and bowl gasket be installed at any time the carburetor is removed from the engine and disassembled.

3. Use care when installing the bowl gasket. If it is not properly installed, it can interfere with the carburetor float, which, in turn, will cause the engine to run richly.

4. Assemble the carburetor in reverse order of disassembly.

CARBURETOR ADJUSTMENTS

Low-Speed Jet

ALL MODELS—EXCEPT 1971–72 3 AND 4 CYLINDER MODELS

1. Turn the idle adjustment needle in (clockwise) until it seats lightly. Do not overtighten, as this will damage the needle and seat.

Low-speed carburetor adjustment (© Chrysler Outboard Corp.)

2. Back the idle adjustment out one full turn. On 75 hp models it is necessary to remove the three rubber plugs before any adjustment can be made.

3. Start the engine and run until fully warm.

4. Place the shift lever in the Neutral position.

5. Turn the idle adjustment needle counterclockwise (open) until the engine loses power and begins to run roughly from an overly rich mixture.

6. Slowly turn the needle in until the cylinders fire evenly and the motor runs smoothly.

7. Continue turning the needle in until the engine begins to stall from a mixture which is too lean.

8. Set the adjustment screw halfway between the two points (above). Do not adjust leaner than necessary to obtain a smooth idle. It is better to have a mixture which is too rich than too lean.

1971–72 3 CYLINDER MODELS

1. Remove the three rubber plugs on the carburetor cover.

2. Turn the idle adjustment needles in (clockwise) until they seat lightly. Do not overtighten.

3. Back the needles out ⅞ of a turn. The engine will run at this point but must be adjusted further.

4. Set the control lever in Neutral.

5. Turn the idle adjustment needle on the top carburetor counterclockwise until the engine loses power and begins to miss. Here the mixture is too rich.

6. Turn the needle clockwise until the engine begins to stall due to a lean mixture.

7. Set the adjustment halfway between these two points (steps 5 and 6).

8. Repeat the procedure to adjust the center carburetor.

9. Compute the average number of turns required to adjust the top and center carburetors. Reset all three carburetors at this average adjustment position.

10. It may be necessary to repeat steps 5, 6, and 7 for a finer adjustment.

11. Install the rubber plugs in the carburetor cover.

NOTE: *Do not adjust leaner than is necessary to obtain smooth idling. It is better to have the mixture too rich than too lean.*

1971–72 4 CYLINDER MODELS

1. Perform the adjustment procedure for "All Models—Except 1971–72 3 and 4 cylinder models."

2. The only difference is that four-cylinder models use two carburetors and the adjustment procedure must be repeated on the other carburetor.

3. Be sure that you do not adjust the carburetors any leaner than is necessary to obtain a smooth idle. It is better to have a mixture which is too rich than a mixture which is too lean.

High-Speed Jet—All Models (1966–72)

The high-speed jet is a fixed size (non-adjustable) but can be replaced in accordance with fuel demands when operating the motor at altitudes where barometric pressure affects the fuel/air ratio.

The jet size should only be changed in accordance with the advice of a dealer. The use of a jet size smaller than that recommended for a given altitude can result in cylinder head seizure and piston

where it is inoperative and will allow the throttle lever to retard the magneto sufficiently to shut off the engine. Second, the throttle stop screw can be adjusted to maintain a set idle speed with the throttle fully retarded. If this method of adjustment is used, it will be necessary to choke the engine to stop it.

55 HP (MAGNAPOWER IGNITION)

1. Set the remote control lever in Neutral.

Throttle stop adjustment on 35 hp Magnapower models (© Chrysler Outboard Corp.)

burning. It is best to consult a dealer when you wish to change main jets, as the sizes and part numbers are constantly changing.

When replacing high-speed jets, or whenever the high-speed jet is removed, be sure that the gaskets are in place. In some instances, when not using the gasket, erratic engine operation will result.

Throttle Stop

35–55 HP (1966–72)— EXCEPT MAGNAPOWER

1. The throttle stop is used to adjust the engine to the correct idle speed. It is located on the tower shaft.
2. The throttle stop should be adjusted for an idle of approximately 700–800 rpm in Forward and Reverse, and for approximately 800–900 rpm in Neutral.
3. To increase the idle speed, loosen the locknut and turn the throttle stop screw in (clockwise).
4. To decrease the idle speed, turn the throttle stop screw out (counterclockwise).
5. Be sure to tighten the locknut after completing adjustments.

NOTE: *If using a motor equipped with Duo-drive remote controls, which are not equipped with an ignition shorting switch, two methods of adjusting the throttle stop are possible. First, the throttle stop can be adjusted to a point*

2. Loosen the locknut on the throttle stop screw.
3. Turn the throttle stop screw in or out until the engine idles at 850–900 rpm.
4. Tighten the locknut on the throttle stop screw.

70–130 HP (1966–72)

1. The throttle stop screw located on the tower shaft can be adjusted to obtain the correct idling speed.
2. Idling speed is 600–800 rpm in Reverse or Forward, and 700–900 rpm in Neutral.
3. To increase the idle speed, loosen the locknut and turn the throttle stop screw clockwise. To decrease the idle, turn the throttle stop screw counterclockwise.
4. Be sure to tighten the locknut after adjusting.

Point of Throttle Opening

35–55 HP (1966–72) STANDARD IGNITION

The amount of throttle opening is synchronized with the degree of spark advance, through the throttle cam and related linkage. This adjustment varies and should be checked when servicing a motor.

1. Unsnap the ball joint connector from the throttle tower shaft.
2. With the throttle plate in the closed

position, adjust the eccentric screw holding the throttle roller to the throttle shaft, so that the pick-up line on the lower end of the throttle cam is exactly centered on the throttle roller.

3. Advance the throttle tower shaft and throttle cam to the full-advance position (throttle plate horizontal).

4. Adjust the ball joint connectors until the spacing is identical to the spacing between the connector stud on the throttle cam and the throttle tower shaft.

5. Snap the ball joint connectors in place on the throttle tower shaft.

NOTE: *The point of throttle opening will have to be readjusted if the correct high-speed warm-up rpm (in Neutral) of 1800–2500 rpm cannot be reached.*

55 HP (MAGNAPOWER IGNITION)

1. Set the tower shaft at idle position. This is indicated by the throttle plate in the closed position.

5. Adjust the throttle roller shaft by turning it until the throttle roller just contacts the throttle cam at the index line. Tighten the locknut securely.

6. Connect the throttle link to the tower shaft. Move the tower shaft to the wide-open-throttle stop.

7. Adjust the throttle link between the tower shaft and the throttle cam until the throttle plates are in the horizontal position.

Wide-Open-Throttle Adjustment

55 HP (MAGNAPOWER IGNITION)

1. This adjustment should follow the "Point of Throttle Opening" adjustment for this model.

2. Set the tower shaft at the full throttle position.

3. Adjust the length of the throttle control rod until the throttle plate is in the horizontal position. Tighten the locknut on

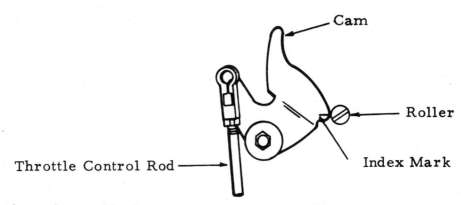

Adjusting the point of throttle opening on 55 hp Magnapower models. (© Chrysler Outboard Corp.)

2. Disconnect the throttle rod from the ball joint on the tower shaft.

3. Hold the throttle cam lightly against the roller on the carburetor throttle shaft. Turn the screw in until the roller is centered on the index mark of the throttle cam.

70–120 HP (1966–72)

1. Loosen the throttle tie-bar screws and set the throttle plates in the closed position.

2. Open the throttle plates by hand until the plates are perfectly parallel with each other.

3. Tighten the tie-bar screws securely.

4. Disconnect the throttle link from the tower shaft.

the throttle control rod. (The throttle control rod is attached to the throttle cam.)

FUEL PUMP

All Models—1962–72

The fuel pump is a two-stage, vacuum-operated, diaphragm-type pump, mounted on the rear starboard side of the powerhead.

The first stage, consisting of a fuel sediment bowl, screen, gasket, diaphragm, and two valves, draws fuel from the tank, pumping it to the second stage. The second stage consists of a diaphragm and single outlet valve. At the outlet of the second stage is an elbow, which distributes fuel to the carburetor(s).

Removal

1. Remove the fuel lines from the intake, outlet, and air pressure fittings on the pump.

2. Remove the screws holding the fuel pump and bracket to the cylinder, and remove the pump.

Disassembly

Under normal conditions, it is not necessary to remove the fuel pump from the engine to disassemble it. To service the pump, proceed as follows:

1. Disconnect the air pressure hoses from the top of the pump cover.

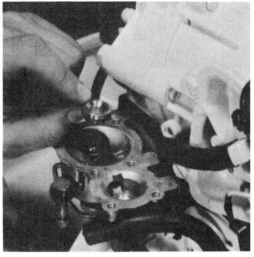

Inspecting the first-stage intake valve (© Chrysler Outboard Corp.)

Separating fuel pump body halves (© Chrysler Outboard Corp.)

2. Remove the screws and separate the body halves.

3. Carefully remove the fuel pump diaphragm and inspect for punctures or tears. The diaphragm should be replaced if it is punctured or excessively distorted.

4. Remove the center fuel-pump valve retaining screws and lift out the valve. Inspect and replace the valve if it shows signs of wear, or if the disc is cracked or distorted. The fuel pump valve is to be replaced with the latest type, which can be identified by the brass body.

5. Remove the fuel sediment bowl. Clean the bowl and filters with clean gasoline.

6. Inspect the first-stage intake valve, but do not try to remove it, unless replacement is necessary. If it must be replaced, use a ½ in. diameter punch to drive it from the bottom of the pump. Obtain a new gasket and valve, and tap the new valve into place, using great care.

7. Inspect the outlet valve of the second stage. This valve cannot be removed without completely destroying the valve. If it must be replaced, follow these steps:

a. Remove the fuel pump from the motor.

b. Remove the outlet fuel elbow from the bottom of the second stage.

c. Drive the second-stage valve out of the bottom of the pump, using a punch.

d. With a new gasket and valve, tap the new valve into place with an $^{11}/_{16}$ in. punch. Use extreme care to avoid damaging the valve.

e. Reinstall the elbow to the bottom of the second stage.

Inspection

Because of the relatively small volume of fuel displaced by the movement of the diaphragm, there must be no leaks in the fuel system and there must be no restriction to the flow of fuel.

1. The diaphragm must be free from holes and must completely cover the crankcase gasket surface.

2. When assembling the diaphragm to the crankcase, be sure that it is not wrinkled and that it extends beyond the gaskets all the way around. The screw holes in the diaphragm, reed plate, gaskets, and cover are irregularly spaced; they must be indexed to fit the boss on the crankcase. Tighten all screws before squeezing the bulb. Do not use gasket cement.

3. Examine all gaskets, connections, and fuel lines for leaks.

4. Check the tension of the fuel pump reeds. The reeds should be flat and cover the holes in the reed plate. The reeds must not exceed 0.0015 in. warpage at the center. When the reeds are assembled to the reed plate, they must seat flush with no initial tension to a maximum of 0.003 in. open. The reeds should not stand open, be bent, or broken.

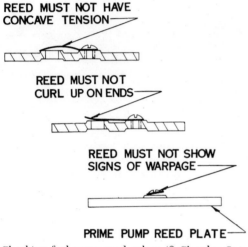

Checking fuel pump reed valves (© Chrysler Outboard Corp.)

ASSEMBLY

1. Reinstall the sediment bowl, using a new gasket and tighten the thumb-screw finger-tight.

2. Using a new gasket, assemble the first stage outlet valve to the pump body.

3. Install the fuel pump gasket, diaphragm, and pump cover on the pump body—in that order.

4. Install the retaining screws and tighten securely.

INSTALLATION

1. Install the pump to the engine.

2. Install the outlet fuel line and pressure hoses. The pressure hose from the first stage is connected to the elbow on the top of the transfer port cover, and the pressure hose from the second stage is connected to the elbow on the lower transfer port cover.

REED VALVES—ALL MODELS

The reed valves in a two-stroke engine permit fuel to enter the crankcase on the upstroke of the piston and close (sealing the crankcase to prevent fuel from escaping) on the downstroke of the piston.

If a reed cracks or breaks off, it can always be detected by the presence of blow-back through the carburetor and by an engine that misses and runs on all but one cylinder. Blow-back will occur when the piston for the cylinder that has the broken reed is on the downstroke.

Inspection

To visually inspect or replace the reed valves, proceed as follows:

1. On hand-start models, remove the starter rope handle and tie a knot in the rope.

2. On electric-start models, remove the electric-start mounting brackets from the crankcase and adaptor flange. Remove the lead wire from the starter terminal on the lower-front of the starter motor.

3. Remove the carburetor and linkage.

4. Remove the carburetor adaptor-flange attaching screws.

5. Inspect the reeds. Replace any that are cracked, broken, or warped. A reed must seat lightly against the reed plate along its entire surface. It must completely cover the holes in the reed plate.

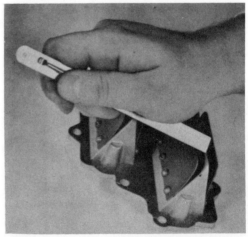

Inspecting the reed stop spacing (© Chrysler Outboard Corp.)

6. Inspect the reed stop spacing. The reed stop is to be set at a maximum of $9/32$ in. opening. The assembled reeds must not stand open more than 0.010 in. The reed stop must be pushed ahead and the reed must be pushed back as far as the reed will allow. This will give the reed stops maximum overlap.

7. When replacing the reeds, the reed stops should also be checked. Especially check the reed stop spacing if broken reeds have been found, as this is one of the contributing causes of reed failure.

RECOVERING BROKEN REEDS

Should reed breakage occur, the pieces can be removed without disassembling the powerhead. It is extremely important to recover broken reeds before they have a chance to enter the engine and cause considerable damage.

1. Remove the reed plate and examine the crankcase.

2. Remove the transfer port cover(s) and look for the broken reed.

3. Remove the cylinder head and examine the combustion chamber. Rotate the flywheel very slowly during this inspection.

4. Replace the cylinder head and transfer port cover(s). Always use new gaskets.

5. It is not necessary to disassemble the powerhead any further than outlined above, even though the broken portion of the reed is not found. Experience at the factory shows that large pieces of the broken reed will be found in the crankcase or transfer port passage. Small pieces will probably pass through the combustion chamber and be discharged with the exhaust gases.

NOTE: *Any time the carburetor is removed, new gaskets should be used at installation.*

FUEL LINE

If the engine will not prime properly, make the following checks:

1. Check the fuel supply in the tank. Fuel must cover the lower end of the filter on the pick-up end, which is approximately 1/2 in. from the bottom.

2. Be sure that the fuel tank vent screw on the tank or gauge is open.

3. Check the fuel line, primer bulb, and connections for leaks.

4. Check the entire fuel line for kinks or restrictions.

5. Check the fuel line coupler to be sure that it is functioning properly.

6. The rubber seals in the fuel line couplers become distorted, cracked, and swelled after prolonged use. These seals are available as replacement parts from dealers.

7. Check the fuel tank adaptor. On models that do not have the check valve in the primer bulb, the check valve is located in the fuel tank adaptor. In some cases, small deposits of sealant accumulate in the check valve and cause it to stick open or closed. A sticking check valve will cause hard priming, hard starting, and electric-start motor failure, due to prolonged cranking. If faulty adaptors are found, replace the entire assembly.

8. The fuel line components are available individually as replacement parts.

FUEL FILTERS

Fuel Tank Filter

REMOVAL

1. Remove the fuel line from the fuel tank.

2. Remove the fuel tank adaptor to gain access to the fuel filter on the bottom of the pick-up tube.

3. Wash the filter in clean gasoline. Replace if rusty or corroded.

4. Be sure to observe fire prevention rules when working on the fuel system.

INSTALLATION

1. Installation is the reverse of removal.

Fuel Pump Filter Bowl Screen

REMOVAL

1. Unscrew the retainer nut below the sediment bowl on the fuel pump.

2. Remove the sediment bowl and filter screen. Wash in clean gasoline.

Exploded view of fuel pump filter bowl (© Chrysler Outboard Corp.)

INSTALLATION

1. Installation is the reverse of removal.

PUDDLE DRAIN SYSTEM

The puddle drain system is located just forward of the transfer port covers on the starboard side of the engine.

The puddle drain system on Chrysler outboards performs the function of keeping the crankcase free of raw fuel which accumulates in the lower portions. These puddles of raw fuel are formed by condensation of fuel on the cylinder walls while the fuel charge is present in the crankcase. The greatest puddle accumulation occurs when the engine is operated for extended periods of time in the low rpm ranges. This is due to the fact that the fuel charge is delayed in the crankcase for a longer period of time.

Puddle drain (© Chrysler Outboard Corp.)

If these puddles of raw fuel were allowed to remain, they would tend to enrich the fuel mixture and force the engine to display characteristics of an overly rich mixture. An engine which has a faulty puddle drain system will stutter and falter during acceleration and generally run roughly.

Reed Adjustment

The puddle drain reeds must not stand open and the reed stop must be set so that they are open 0.017–0.023 in. at the top. Be sure that the screens for the puddle drain reed plate are in place.

Electrical System

All Chrysler outboards use a color-coded wiring system. An understanding of the color coding will greatly facilitate the repair and maintenance of the motor.

Check the color of the insulation on the wire itself. If it has a distinctive color (other than black), such as red, orange, yellow, or blue, then this is the color code of the wire. If the wires are black or gray, check the color of the protective sleeve over the terminal end of the wire. The color of the sleeve indicates the color of the wire code.

The following colors are assigned to each of the electrical circuits in the motor.

Black—Whenever a black wire appears, it indicates that the wire is attached to the negative terminal of the battery and is, therefore, ground.

Red—All wires coded red are connected to the battery positive post and are "hot."

Blue—All blue color-coded wires are part of the ignition primary circuit and are "hot" when the ignition is on.

Yellow—All yellow coded wires are part of the electric start circuit and are "hot" when the ignition switch is in the Start position.

White—Any wire color-coded white is part of the tachometer control circuit.

Orange—All wires color-coded orange are part of the temperature indicator circuit. This circuit is only operative after the heat indicator switch is installed on the engine and the indicator light or gauge is installed.

Green—All wires coded green are part of the choke circuit and "hot" only when the choke is activated.

Purple—All purple color-coded wires are part of the charge indicator circuit and are "hot" when the engine is running.

35–55 HP (1966–72)

Electric Starter

The electric starter used on these models is a lightweight, high-output type. A certain amount of care and attention is necessary however. Dirt, salt, and water accumulation should be removed from the starter as soon as possible.

NOTE: *Never operate the starter motor for a continuous period of more than fifteen seconds without allowing the starter to cool for not less than three minutes in between.*

INSTALLATION

1. Mount the electric starter in the upper and lower brackets with the termi-

nals facing forward and slightly to the port side of the engine.

2. Mount the starter to the bracket with two long $1/4$ x 20 thru-bolts. Do not tighten the thru-bolts at this time.

NOTE: *When removing the starter, use care not to let the starter come apart when the thru-bolts are removed.*

3. Install the starter and bracket assembly on the engine.

4. After all mounting bolts have been installed, torque the lower mounting bracket to crankcase cover screws to 70 in. lbs.

5. Torque the screws securing the upper, starter mounting bracket to the large flange on the crankcase cover to 160 in. lbs.

6. Tighten the long, starter thru-bolts, turning the armature shaft while tightening the bolts. This will ensure that tightening the bolts does not cause armature shaft binding.

7. After completing starter installation, check the backlash between the starter pinion gear and the flywheel teeth. This clearance should be 0.015–0.040 in.

Starter Rope Replacement

1. Remove the starter-rope handle plug.

2. Allow the rope to rewind on the starter spool.

3. Remove the starter pinion nut which retains the starter pinion pin.

4. Drive out the starter pinion pin.

CAUTION: *It is necessary to secure the starter rewind spring as it will unwind when the starter pinion pin is removed.*

5. It is not necessary to remove the starter to replace the starter rope. Simply allow the rewind spring to unwind and remove the old starter rope. Replace it with a new rope.

6. Rewind a new starter rope onto the spool and lubricate the starter rewind spring. Insert the entire spring assembly into the spool with the retainer end down. Make sure that the retainer extension is inserted in the lower end of the spool before installing the rewind spring.

7. Pull the starter rope through the motor control panel and attach the starter handle and plain washer. Tie a knot in the end of the starter rope. Pull the knot securely into the end of the handle and install the plug.

8. Hold the spool firmly with the rope fully wound, and turn the rewind spring assembly eight turns counterclockwise to obtain the proper tension on the rewind spring.

9. Align the hole in the starter rewind-spring drive with the hole in the spool and insert the starter pin through the slot in the starter pinion gear so that the pin engages all parts.

10. Install the screw used to retain the starter pinion pin.

Magneto Ignition

MAGNETO REMOVAL

1. Remove the flywheel from the power-head.

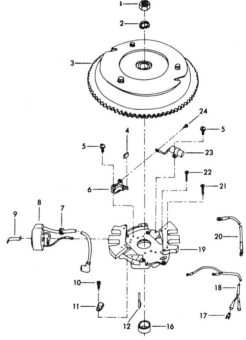

Exploded view of magneto on 35–55 hp (© Chrysler Outboard Corp.)

1. Hex nut
2. Lockwasher
3. Flywheel and starter gear
4. Cam wiper felt
5. Breaker point and condenser screw
6. Breaker point set
7. Grommet
8. Coil
9. Coil retaining clip
10. Cable clip screw
11. Cable clip
12. Key
13. Starter rope w/handle
14. Connector, shift cable
15. Connector, throttle cable
16. Cam
17. Terminal male slide
18. Primary terminal wire
19. Stator plate w/coil, condenser, points, lead, wires and screw
20. Wire, stator ground
21. Lamination screw
22. Lamination screw
23. Condenser w/mount
24. Breaker arm terminal screw

2. Remove the screw retaining the spark control bearing to the throttle tower shaft.

3. Disconnect the magneto from the stator ring.

4. Remove the spark plug lead wires and magneto ground wire from the center forward screw in the transfer port cover.

5. Disengage the wiring harness from the terminal connector plate.

6. Lift the magneto off the engine. If powerhead repairs are to be made, remove the magneto cam and key.

Magneto Installation

1. Lubricate all moving parts, linkages, magneto pilot bore, stator plate, and cam wiper felts with Rykon 2 EP lubricant.

2. Install the magneto breaker cam and key, if removed. The breaker cam must be installed with the arrow or part number up.

3. Further installation is the reverse of removal.

Coil Replacement

1. The coils are held in place by coil wedge springs which pass between the coil and the core.

2. To remove the coil, disconnect the primary and secondary lead wires and pry away one end of the coil wedge.

3. It may be necessary to bend one of the coil core laminations to remove the coil.

4. After removing the spring and bending the lamination, pry the coil from the core with two screwdrivers.

5. When replacing the coil, bend the core lamination down to be sure that the coil does not move out and damage the flywheel.

Condenser Replacement

1. Normally, a condenser does not need replacement, except in the event of leakage. The condenser can be checked using the instruction in the introductory chapter of this book.

2. Disconnect the lead wire attached to the breaker plate and remove the screw securing it to the stator plate.

3. Installation is the reverse of removal.

Alternator Equipped Models

The alternator used on these models is a constant-current, three-phase alternator with a self-regulating output of nine amps.

It does not use a voltage regulator since the stator and flywheel are so designed as to be self-regulating. The rectifier accepts and converts alternating current to what is essentially direct current.

Alternator Removal

1. Remove the flywheel.

2. Disconnect the breaker point lead wire and the lead wire from the breaker point to the ignition coil. The latter must be disconnected from the dual male terminal on the stator plate.

Removing breaker point lead wires (© Chrysler Outboard Corp.)

3. The yellow coil lead wire will have to be pulled through the holes in the bottom of the stator plate. Note the correct routing of this wire for later assembly.

4. Remove the three breaker plate shoes from the stator.

Removing breaker plate shoes (© Chrysler Outboard Corp.)

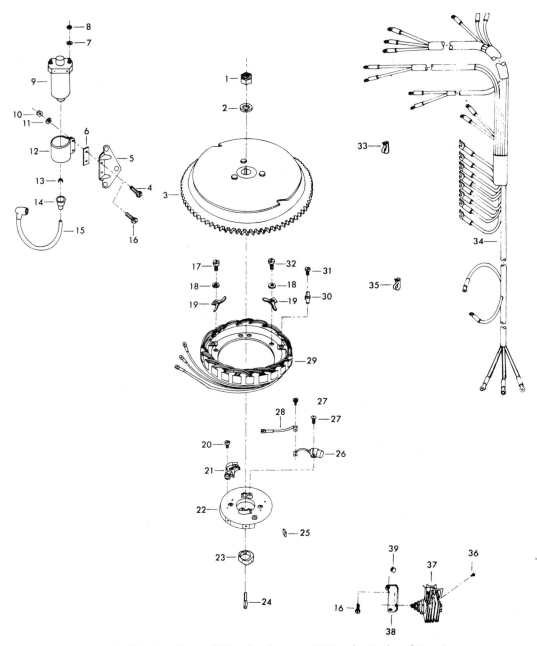

Exploded view of typical Chrysler alternator (© Chrysler Outboard Corp.)

1. Hex nut
2. Spring lockwasher
3. Flywheel
4. Screw
5. Coil bracket
6. Vibration pad
7. Lockwasher
8. Hex nut
9. Coil w/boot, clip, washer, and nut
10. Stop nut
11. Lockwasher
12. Coil clamp
13. Terminal clip

14. Boot
15. Lead wire, long
    Lead wire, short
16. Hex slot head screw
17. Screw
18. Spring lockwasher
19. Breaker plate shoe
20. Breaker contact screw
21. Breaker point set
22. Breaker plate w/condenser points and screws
23. Cam
24. Key
25. Cam wiper felt

26. Condenser
27. Condenser clamp screw
28. Primary interlead group
29. Stator
30. Terminal bracket
31. Screw
32. Screw
33. Clamp
34. Wiring harness
35. Clamp
36. Screw
37. Rectifier
38. Rectifier mounting bracket
39. Grommet

5. Remove the three gray stator lead wires attached to the rectifier and lift the stator group up off the engine.

Rectifier Removal

1. Remove the black and purple lead wires from the terminals on the rectifier.

2. Remove the two screws attaching the rectifier to the mounting bracket on the cylinder bracket.

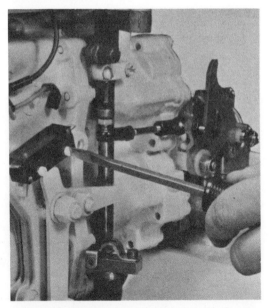

Removing the neutral interlock switch (© Chrysler Outboard Corp.)

Removing the rectifier mounting bracket (© Chrysler Outboard Corp.)

IMPORTANT: *Always remove the rectifier from the engine in the manner described above. Do not use a wrench on the coated mounting bolt head. Any indications of wrench marks on the mounting bolt head will automatically void the rectifier warranty.*

Neutral Interlock Switch Removal

1. Remove the yellow lead wires from the neutral interlock switch and remove the switch.

2. Remove the cable clamps that retain the lead wires to the cylinder block. Allow the cable clamp to remain attached to the wires.

Ignition Coil Removal

1. Remove all wires attached to the ignition coil.

2. Remove the spark plug wires.

3. Remove the three cylinder-head bolts that retain the port coil and mounting bracket to the cylinder block.

Removing the ignition coil (© Chrysler Outboard Corp.)

4. Apply step 3 to the starboard coil and mounting bracket.

Starter Removal

1. Remove the heavy lead wire from the post on the lower front side of the starter motor.

2. Remove the screws from the lower mounting bracket to the carburetor adaptor flange.

3. Remove the upper mounting bracket from the crankcase cover.

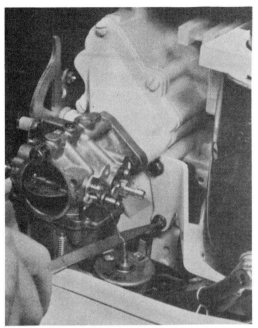

Starter attaching screws on carburetor adaptor flange (© Chrysler Outboard Corp.)

felts) with Rykon 2 EP lubricant prior to installation.

2. The order of installation is the reverse of removal.

3. Mount the alternator stator group on the crankshaft bearing cage so that the mounting holes align with the threaded holes in the matching bosses on the bearing cage. Properly mounted, the lead wires will be on the port side of the engine. The three breaker-plate friction screws are held in place by the stator mounting screws.

4. Install the red, spark-control swivel bearing and link to the underside of the breaker plate and install the breaker plate with the spark control link protruding through the starboard slot in the crankshaft bearing cage.

5. Adjust the tension of the breaker shoes so that all six "feet" are touching and so that the maximum force required to move the breaker plate in the advance direction is two pounds.

Adjustments

BREAKER POINTS

1. Remove the flywheel nut and the flywheel.

2. Inspect the breaker points. If they are burned or pitted, they should be replaced; do not file breaker points.

3. If the breaker points have been used for some time, they must be cleaned before the gap can be set. A small strip of 320 grit emery cloth, folded and inserted between the points, will do this. Hold the points closed on the emery cloth and rotate the cloth using the points as a pivot.

4. Clean the oxide dust from the points by performing the same operation with a piece of hard-surface cardboard. If the breaker points are excessively pitted, check the condition of the condenser, as a defective or leaking condenser will cause pitting and burning of the points.

5. Set the engine controls at the full or wide-open throttle position. This will establish a common, stationary location for setting breaker points.

6. Rotate the crankshaft to open the breaker point being adjusted. Always rotate the engine in the direction of engine rotation. For alternator models, stop at a point about 10° past the top of the ramp on the cam. The top of the ramp is the

4. Remove the ground strap from the lower screw of the throttle conduit bracket on the starboard side of the powerhead or from the lower screw in the lower transfer port cover.

5. Remove the cable clamps which retain the engine wiring harness. Make a note of the correct routing of the wiring to aid in assembly.

STARTER RELAY REMOVAL

1. Remove all lead wires from the terminals on the starter relay.

2. Remove the screws holding the relay to the support plate and remove the relay.

CHOKE SOLENOID REMOVAL

1. Remove the green lead wire from the terminal on top of the solenoid.

2. Remove the choke plunger wire from the choke arm on the carburetor.

3. Remove the screws holding the solenoid to the support plate and remove the solenoid.

INSTALLATION—ALTERNATOR, RECTIFIER, NEUTRAL INTERLOCK SWITCH, IGNITION COIL, STARTER, STARTER RELAY, AND CHOKE SOLENOID

1. Lubricate all moving parts (linkages, pilot bores, breaker plate, and cam wiper

point where no further breaker point opening occurs.

For magneto ignition models, stop at the mark on the cam. This also is the point where no further opening of the points occurs.

7. Set the breaker points to the specification listed in the specifications section of this chapter. Correct gap is obtained when a feeler gauge of the correct thickness will have a slight drag when slipped between the points.

8. Adjust the other set of points in the same manner.

ENGINE TIMING

NOTE: *The timing tool described in this procedure is a Chrysler special tool, designated by its number in the text. The tool can be ordered from your Chrysler dealer for a modest price and is almost necessary to have when timing the engine. Other methods will time the engine but not as easily or as accurately.*

Timing tool (T-2937) showing timing marks (arrows) on the rod (© Chrysler Outboard Corp.)

1. Adjust the breaker points as detailed previously.

2. Check to be sure that the throttle tower shaft is advanced to its maximum position.

3. The wide-open-stop arm on the tower shaft cover must be against the crankcase cover.

4. Remove the spark plug from the top cylinder and install the barrel of the timing tool (part no. T–2937) into the spark plug hole.

5. Install the rod of the timing tool into the barrel with the two 40 hp marks on the outside.

6. Hold the rod tight against the piston and rotate the crankshaft in the direction of engine rotation and locate Top Dead Center.

7. Screw the barrel of the timing tool in or out until the inside line of the two 40 hp marks aligns with the edge of the barrel.

8. Connect a test light between the coil lead wire and ground on magneto ignition models or between the positive terminal of no. 1 ignition coil and ground for alternator models.

9. Turn the crankshaft clockwise until the outer mark on the rod aligns with the edge of the barrel. The piston in the top cylinder is now positioned exactly at 32° BTDC.

10. Turn the crankshaft slowly until the test light goes out.

Adjusting the spark control link on 35–55 hp models (© Chrysler Outboard Corp.)

11. Loosen the locknut on the spark control link and adjust the spark control link in the direction required to make the light go on and off as the mark on the rod passes the edge of the barrel of the timing tool.

12. Install the flywheel.

Adjustments—55 hp Magnapower Models

WARNING: *The Magnapower ignition system operates at very high voltage. When possible, disconnect the battery before performing any service to the system. Use well-insulated tongs to handle high tension leads when the battery is connected.*

BREAKER POINT ADJUSTMENT

1. Remove the flywheel nut and flywheel.

2. Remove the spark plugs.

3. Set the throttle at the wide-open position.

4. Rotate the crankshaft in the direction of engine rotation; for breaker point ad-

justment, always rotate the engine this way.

5. Inspect the breaker point contact surfaces. If they are pitted or burned severely, they must be replaced. It is not advisable to file points.

6. Dirty points can be cleaned with 320 grit emery cloth by using the procedure listed under the breaker point adjustment for standard ignition models.

7. Rotate the crankshaft to open the breaker points being adjusted. Turn the crankshaft so that the rubbing block rests against the highest point of the cam. Mark the high point of the cam to use as a reference point in adjusting the other set of points.

the rubbing block on the other set of points. Adjust the second set of points in the same manner.

ENGINE TIMING

NOTE: *The timing tool described in this procedure is a Chrysler special tool, designated in the text by its part number. The tool can be ordered from your Chrysler dealer at a modest price and is almost essential in timing the engine. Other methods will do the job, but not as easily or as accurately.*

1. Set the throttle at WOT (wide open throttle).

2. Remove the spark plugs from the engine.

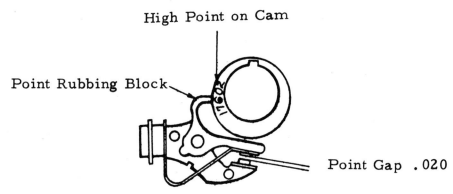

Measuring point gap on 55 hp Magnapower models (© Chrysler Outboard Corp.)

8. Set the point gap to specification (see specifications section) with a feeler gauge. Adjust the points until a slight drag is felt on the feeler gauge when slipped between the points.

9. Rotate the crankshaft one full turn. Align the part number on the cam with

3. Install the barrel portion of timing tool (part no. TA2937–1) in the spark plug hole of the top cylinder.

4. Install the rod portion of the timing tool in the barrel with the two marks on the rod (25–55 hp) facing outside the barrel.

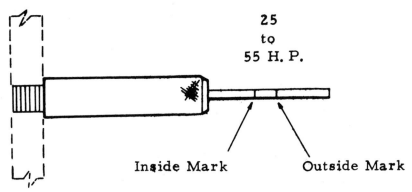

Timing tool (TA-2937) installed (© Chrysler Outboard Corp.)

5. Hold the rod tight against the top of the piston and rotate the crankshaft in the direction of engine rotation. Locate Top Dead Center.

6. Screw the barrel in or out until the inside mark on the rod aligns with the edge of the barrel. Do not disturb the position of the barrel.

7. Connect a test light between the terminal of no. 1 cylinder on the breaker plate (white/brown wire terminal) and ground.

8. Rotate the crankshaft in the direction of engine rotation (one full revolution) until the outer mark on the rod is even with the edge of the timing barrel. Always align the mark when the rod is coming out of the barrel.

9. Loosen the locknut on the spark control link. Turn the spark control link until the test light goes out, indicating the points are open.

10. Turn the spark control link back until the light comes on and glows dimly, indicating the points are beginning to close.

11. Hold the spark control link firmly and tighten the locknut.

12. Rotate the crankshaft one full revolution and align the outer mark on the rod with the edge of the timing tool barrel. The test light should be glowing dimly.

13. For ultra-fine tuning, it is recommended that the procedure be repeated on no. 2 cylinder. Install the timing tool in no. 2 cylinder and connect the test light to the no. 2 set of points and to ground. Repeat the entire procedure above.

14. Remove the test light from the engine.

15. Install the flywheel and torque the flywheel nut to 80 ft lbs.

16. Install the spark plugs and connect the cables to the battery.

NOTE: *If the spark plugs on these engines appear to have pitted or eroded*

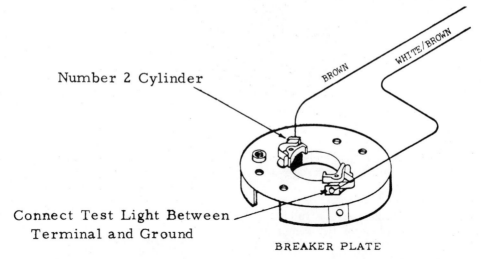

Test light connections (© Chrysler Outboard Corp.)

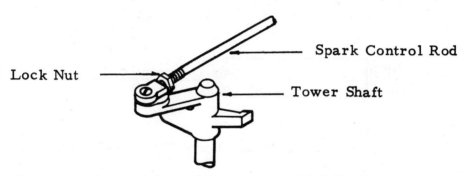

Adjusting the spark control link on 55 hp Magnapower models (© Chrysler Outboard Corp.)

side electrodes, install new Champion L-20V plugs. These are surface gap plugs with non-adjustable gaps and are used as replacement plugs for the Champion L-19V which were installed as original equipment on 55 hp Magnapower models.

70–130 HP (1966–72)

Electrical Component Removal

1. Remove the flywheel nut from the crankshaft. Remove the flywheel.
2. Disconnect the electrical leads from the rectifier and remove the rectifier and mounting bracket from the powerhead.
3. Disconnect the wiring from the starter solenoid and remove the starter solenoid from the support plate.
4. Remove the bolts securing the lower starter mounting bracket and remove the starter from the bracket on the powerhead.
5. Remove the distributor pulley belt from the distributor and remove the distributor from the engine. Remove the distributor cap.
6. Remove the electrical leads from the starter interlock switch.
7. Remove the bolts securing the distributor bracket to the powerhead and remove the distributor.
8. Disconnect the electrical leads from the ignition coil and remove the coil from the engine.
9. Disconnect and remove the circuit breaker.
10. Remove the leads from the solenoid and terminal block.
11. Remove the clamps from the engine wiring harness and remove the wiring harness.

DISTRIBUTOR DISASSEMBLY

1. Remove the nuts, terminal insulation, and terminal screw from the housing.
2. Remove the condenser.
3. Remove the breaker point set and the wick bracket.
4. Remove the screws, washers, and interlock switch.
5. Remove the stop-nut, distributor pulley, spacer, thrust washers, distributor shaft, and spacer.
6. Remove the lead wire and starter interlock cam.
7. Remove the retaining ring and pull the distributor bracket off the housing.

8. Remove the screws, cap cover, cap seal, and cap gasket from the cap base.
9. Remove the felt cam wick from the bracket and discard the wick.

DISTRIBUTOR INSPECTION

1. Inspect the rotor for cracks and wear.
2. Inspect the brushes for wear.
3. Inspect the cap base for chips, cracking, and evidence of arcing.

DISTRIBUTOR ASSEMBLY

1. Install the barrel of the housing in the distributor bracket. Secure with the retaining ring.
2. Measure the clearance between the top face of the distributor bracket and the retaining ring. The clearance must be 0.001–0.005 in. If it is not, install shims under the retaining ring to correct the clearance.
3. Install the key in the distributor shaft.
4. Install the thrust washers and spacer on the shaft.
5. Install the distributor pulley and secure with the stop nut.
6. Install the breaker points and wick bracket, and tighten the screws securely.
7. Install the condenser.
8. Attach the lead wire to the breaker point terminal.
9. Install the condenser lead wire on the terminal screw.
10. Slip one end of the terminal insulators over the terminal screw and push the terminal screw through the hole in the distributor.
11. Install the remaining terminal insulator, terminal, and nut.
12. Install the lockwasher and tighten the nut finger-tight.
13. Install the starter interlock cam and tighten the screws securely. Do not overtighten.
14. Install the interlock switch with screws and washers.
15. Set the points to the gap specified in the specifications section of this manual.

Electrical Component Installation

1. Remove the nuts from the thru-bolts in the starter, being careful not to let the starter come apart.
2. Install the starter in the upper starter mounting bracket. Install the nuts on the thru-bolts.

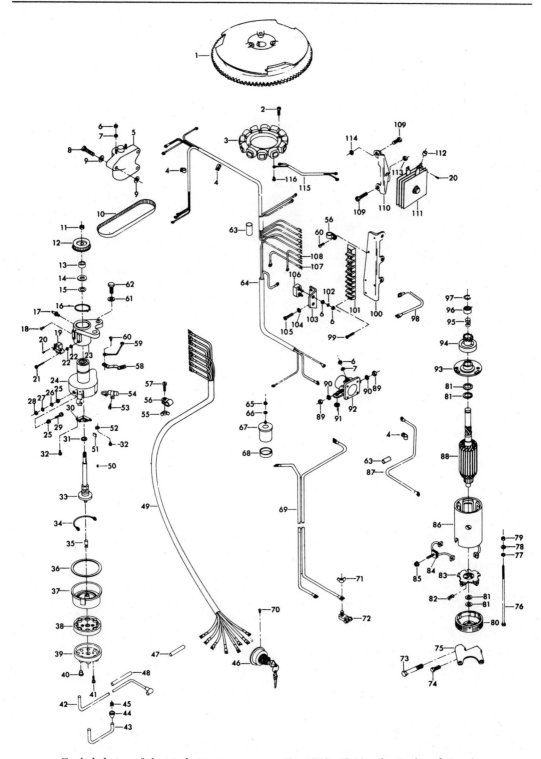

Exploded view of electrical system components 70–130 hp (© Chrysler Outboard Corp.)

1. Flywheel
2. Screw
3. Stator
4. Clamp
5. Coil w/boot
6. Hex nut
7. Spring lockwasher
8. Hex bolt
9. Plain washer
10. Distributor belt
11. Stop nut
12. Distributor pulley

13. Spacer
14. Thrust washer
15. Thrust washer
16. Retaining ring
17. Grease fitting
18. Screw
19. Interlock switch
20. Screw
21. Screw
22. Plain washer
23. Distributor bracket
24. Housing w/bearings
25. Terminal insulator
26. Plain washer
27. Lockwasher
28. Hex nut
29. Terminal screw
30. Breaker point set
31. Spacer
32. Breaker point set screw
33. Distributor shaft
34. Lead wire
35. Brush
36. Cap gasket
37. Cap base
38. Cap seal
39. Cap cover
40. Rubber plug
41. Cap screw
42. Lead wire
43. Coil wire
44. Boot
45. Terminal clip
46. Ignition switch w/keys
47. Sleeve
48. Sleeve

49. Remote electric cable
50. Woodruff key
51. Cam felt wick
52. Wick bracket
53. Condenser screw
54. Condenser
55. Wing nut
56. Clamp
57. Screw
58. Starter interlock cam
59. Lead wire
60. Screw
61. Plain washer
62. Hex bolt
63. Sleeve
64. Engine wiring harness
65. Hex nut
66. Lockwasher
67. Choke, solenoid
68. Retaining band
69. Battery cable
70. Screw
71. Wing nut
72. Battery cable clamp
73. Hex bolt
74. Screw
75. Lower starter bracket
76. Thru-bolt package
77. Lockwasher
78. Plain washer
79. Hex nut
80. Head ass'y commutator end
81. Thrust washer package
82. Spring set
83. Brush plate and holder
84. Brush terminal set

85. Hex locknut
86. Frame and field ass'y
87. Starter lead
88. Armature
89. Hex nut
90. Spring lockwasher
91. Plain washer
92. Starter relay
93. Head ass'y drive end
94. Bendix drive
95. Spring
96. Retainer
97. Retaining ring
98. Ground wire
99. Screw
100. Terminal block bracket
101. Terminal block
102. Lockwasher
103. Circuit breaker bracket
104. Plain washer
105. Screw
106. Circuit breaker
107. Wire, terminal block ground
108. Wire, circuit breaker
     terminal block
109. Screw
110. Rectifier bracket
111. Rectifier
112. Grommet
113. Hex nut
114. Plain washer
115. Wiring harness, generator
     stator
116. Screw

3. The electrical terminal on the starter must face forward to the powerhead. Install the starter relay on the port side of the support plate.

4. Install the heavy red lead between the electrical terminal on the starter and the rear terminal on the starter relay.

5. Install the circuit breaker and the terminal block mounting bracket.

6. Install the terminal block mounting bracket on the port side of the powerhead.

7. Install the rectifier on the port side of the powerhead.

8. Install the choke solenoid on the front of the powerhead.

9. Install the distributor and coil on the starboard side of the powerhead.

10. Install the distributor and coil on the starboard side of the powerhead.

11. Install the alternator stator on top of the powerhead.

12. Install the wiring harness on the engine and make the electrical connections.

13. Install the flywheel on the crankshaft and torque the flywheel nut to 70 ft lbs.

Adjustments

TIMING POINTER ALIGNMENT

NOTE: *To perform this adjustment, it is almost essential to have the Chrysler special timing tool, identified in the text by its part number. Other methods will allow the engine to be timed, but not as easily or as accurately.*

1. Remove the spark plug from the top cylinder and install the barrel of the timing tool (part no. T–2937A) into the spark plug hole.

2. Insert the rod portion of the timing tool into the barrel portion.

3. Hold the rod tight against the piston, rotate the crankshaft and locate Top Dead Center.

4. The "O" mark on the flywheel and the index mark (I) on the timing pointer should be in alignment. If not, shift the timing pointer and align these two marks.

BREAKER POINT ADJUSTMENT

1. Remove the distributor cap and the two bolts which secure the distributor housing to the powerhead.

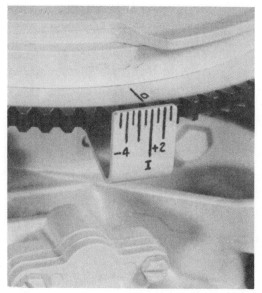

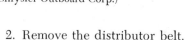

Timing pointer alignment on 70–130 hp models (©Chrysler Outboard Corp.)

Alignment of the tower shaft arm with the distributor swivel screw

2. Remove the distributor belt.

3. Inspect the breaker points and replace if necessary.

4. Using a feeler gauge, set the breaker point gap to the specification in the specifications section of this chapter.

5. Install the distributor loosely to the powerhead.

6. Turn the flywheel to align the 0° mark on the flywheel with the pointer index line (I). Turn the distributor pulley to align the index mark on it with the outside diameter of the flywheel.

7. Install the distributor belt over the distributor pulley. Adjust the distributor to obtain a slight deflection (¼ in. with 1 lb exerted).

8. Be sure that the belt is not too tight as the tower shaft linkage is apt to bind.

9. Set the throttle at maximum spark advance.

10. Turn the flywheel to align the 36° mark on the flywheel with the index line (I) on the timing pointer.

11. Turn the tower shaft to align the tower shaft arm (in a straight line with the distributor swivel screw).

12. Connect a test light between the distributor primary (white) wire and the ground.

13. Adjust the distributor control rod by turning counterclockwise until the breaker point closes—this is indicated by the light coming on. Turn the control rod clockwise

until the breaker point just opens, as indicated by the light going out. Lock the control rod in this position.

NOTE: *The breaker points must be gapped before performing this step.*

14. Advance the controls to the wide-open throttle position.

15. Turn the flywheel to align the 36° mark on the flywheel with the (−4) line on the timing pointer.

16. Adjust the wide-open throttle-stop adjusting screw until the breaker light just

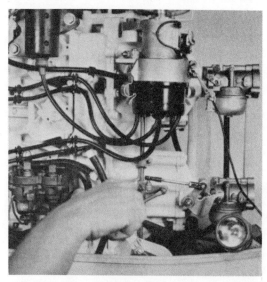

Adjusting the wide-open throttle stop screw (© Chrysler Outboard Corp.)

begins to open as indicated by the light dimming.

17. Remove the test equipment, replace the spark plugs, and test the engine.

NEUTRAL INTERLOCK SWITCH ADJUSTMENT

1. Place the engine gearshift in Neutral.
2. Connect a test light to the terminals of the interlock switch.
3. Advance the tower shaft to the Neutral stop.
4. Adjust the neutral interlock cam until the light just comes on.
5. Tighten the cam screws.

MAGNAPOWER IGNITION MODELS

Magnapower ignition models are timed and adjusted in the same manner as conventional ignition system models of the same horsepower range.

Powerhead

35–55 HP (1966–72)

Removal

1. On manual-start models, remove the starter handle and tie a knot in the starter rope to prevent it from rewinding. Perform the removal steps for electrical equipment detailed in the electrical section.
2. Remove the E-ring from the stabilizer link on the port side of the cylinder block just to the rear of the crankcase parting line.
3. Remove the magneto or alternator as described previously. When removing electrical equipment, allow as much wiring as possible to remain intact. This will greatly facilitate assembly of components.
4. Remove the fuel line from the carburetor intake and remove the puddle drain hoses from the fittings on the carburetor adaptor flange.
5. Remove the carburetor, fuel pump, and reed plate as outlined previously.
6. Remove the thermostat water tube and the cylinder head.
7. Remove the two screws which attach the upper engine shock mount bracket to the shock mount, located directly above the kingpin nut.
8. If the cylinder block is to be replaced, remove as many components as

possible from the powerhead before removing the powerhead from the motor leg. This will allow greater leverage on heavily torqued screws.

9. Remove the nine powerhead-to-lower leg attaching screws. One of these screws is located under the motor leg exhaust cover. On models equipped with motor leg covers, the covers must be removed to gain access to these screws.
10. Lift the powerhead up and off, separating the powerhead from the spacer plate at the upper, cylinder exhaust gasket.

Disassembly

1. Remove the crankshaft bearing-cage attaching screws and remove the bearing cage.
2. Remove the main bearing bolts and dowel pins.
3. Remove the throttle tower shaft from the starboard side of the powerhead.
4. Remove the crankcase cover-to-cylinder block attaching screws.
5. Separate the crankcase cover from the cylinder block by inserting a screwdriver into the slotted openings near the dowel pin holes, and pry the halves apart.
6. Loosen the connecting rod cap screws and remove the cap and screws from the rod. Match mark the bearing cap and connecting rod.
7. Remove the connecting rod needle bearings and cages. Keep the cages and rollers in sets and keep these together with the matching connecting rod. To prevent loss of the needle bearings, wrap these in a clean, lint-free cloth.
8. Remove the crankshaft.
9. Pull the connecting rod and pistons out of the cylinder and mark the pistons with the proper cylinder number. Cylinders are numbered from the top, beginning with no. 1.
10. Using a piston ring expander, remove the rings from the pistons.
11. It is not advisable to separate the connecting rods from the pistons. If it is necessary to replace a piston, the connecting rod and piston should be replaced as an assembly.

COMPONENT INSPECTION

1. Inspect the cylinder bores for rust, scoring, or pitting. The cylinder block should be replaced if the bores are scored excessively or exhibit an out-of-round con-

dition. Small score marks can be removed by honing.

2. Inspect all water passages for obstructions.

3. Check all bearings for rust, corrosion, or pitting. Under normal conditions, all bearings will last the life of the engine.

4. Clean all carbon and salt deposits from the exhaust chamber and water jackets.

5. Cylinder walls, after running, develop a hard, tough glaze, which causes new piston rings to require an abnormally long time to break in. This glaze can be removed with a cylinder hone or deglazer. If a cylinder hone is used, exercise extreme care; only a very minute amount of the cylinder wall can be removed.

Assembly

CONNECTING ROD AND PISTON

1. Install the piston rings to the pistons, using a piston ring expander. If a ring expander is not available, this can be done by hand if great care is used. Align the open end of the rings with the anchor pin in the piston, with the inside beveled edge to the top.

2. The connecting rod and piston must be installed in the powerhead so that the sloping side of the piston dome faces the exhaust chest of the cylinder. The matchmarks and oil hole in the connecting rod must be facing up (toward the flywheel).

3. Coat the pistons, rings, and cylinder walls with a light coating of oil and install

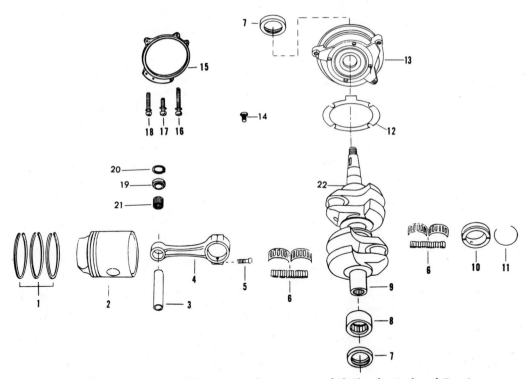

Exploded view of crankshaft, piston, and connecting rod (© Chrysler Outboard Corp.)

1. Piston ring set
2. Piston
3. Piston pin
4. Connecting rod w/cap and screws
5. Connecting rod screws
6. Bearing cage w/rollers
7. Crankshaft seal
8. Crankshaft lower main bearing
9. Crankshaft w/bearing
10. Crankshaft center main bearing race w/snap-ring

11. Snap-ring
12. Bearing cage gasket
13. Crankshaft bearing cage w/seal and gasket for magneto ignition models
   Crankshaft bearing cage w/seal and gasket for alternator models
14. Screw
15. Magneto stator ring
16. Screw w/lockwasher
17. Screw w/lockwasher

18. Screw w/lockwasher
19. Spacer
20. Retainer, piston pin
21. Bearing, all models
22. Crankshaft thrust bearing upper, not sold separately, contact factory for authorization to return crankshaft to factory for bearing replacement

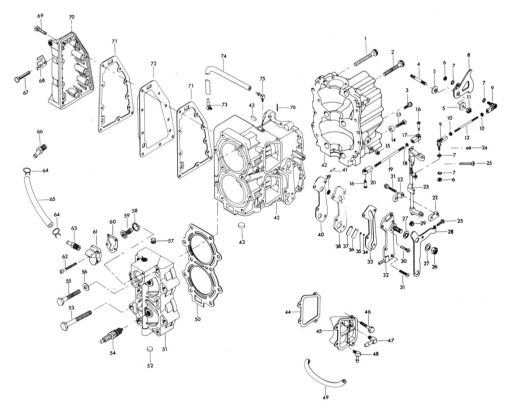

Exploded view of two-cylinder powerhead (© Chrysler Outboard Corp.)

1. Cap screw
2. Cap screw
3. Screw
4. Stud, throttle cam
5. Throttle cam bearing
6. Hex nut
7. Internal tooth lockwasher
8. Throttle cam
9. Ball joint w/bearing
10. Hex nut
11. Elastic stop nut
12. Throttle link
13. Fill head screw
14. Bumper
15. Stop nut
16. Spark control swivel
17. Spark control bearing
18. Hex nut
19. Spark control link
20. Spark control bearing
21. Fill head screw
22. Bearing, towershaft
23. Towershaft
24. Plastic rivet
25. Fill head screw
26. Stop nut
27. Shift arm bearing
28. Shift arm

29. Nyliner
30. Hex slot head screw
31. Screw
32. Cylinder drain cover
33. Cylinder drain cover gasket
34. Pan head screw
35. Plain washer
36. Cylinder drain reed stop
37. Reed, cylinder drain
38. Cylinder drain reed plate
     w/reeds, reed stops, screws,
     and screen
39. Screen, cylinder drain reed
     plate
40. Cylinder drain reed plate
     gasket
41. Dowel pin
42. Cylinder w/crankcase cover,
     deflector plate, and screws
43. Welch plug
44. Transfer port cover gasket
45. Transfer port cover
46. Hex slot head screw
47. Elbow, fuel line
48. Elbow
49. Hose
50. Cylinder head gasket
51. Cylinder head w/pipe plug

52. Welch plug
53. Cap screw
54. Spark plug
55. Cap screw
56. Plain washer
57. Pipe plug
58. Grommet, thermostat
59. Thermostat
60. Thermostat cover gasket
61. Thermostat cover
62. Fill head screw
63. Fitting, thermostat
64. Clamp
65. Water tube, thermostat
66. Fitting, thermostat
67. Hex head screw
68. Lead wire clip
69. Hex slot head screw
70. Exhaust port cover
71. Exhaust port plate gasket
72. Exhaust port plate
73. Fitting
74. Hose w/check valve
75. Elbow w/metering cup
76. Spring pin

the pistons in the cylinder with a piston ring compressor. This also can be done by hand if care is used.

Crankshaft

1. The crankshafts on these models use an upper-main thrust bearing which is pressed onto the crankshaft and cannot be replaced, except at the factory. If this bearing must be replaced, write Chrysler Outboard Corporation, Field Service Department, Hartford, Wisconsin 53027 to arrange to have the crankshaft returned for service.

2. Inspect the crankshaft journals, keyway, splines, and seal. The crankshaft must be replaced if excessively scored or discolored from heat.

3. If the center main bearing was removed, or is to be replaced, assemble the crankshaft as follows.

4. Install the bearing brace halves so that the snap-ring groove is toward the bottom of the crankshaft. The center main bearing is removed by fracturing and must be replaced in matched pairs only.

5. Coat both bearing halves with light grease. One edge of each cage has a small cutout. Install the cages so that the notches are aligned together. They must also point to the flywheel end of the crankshaft.

Installing center main bearing (© Chrysler Outboard Corp.)

6. Install sixteen roller bearings in the cages.

7. Install one-half of the bearing cage to the underside of the crankshaft center main journal.

8. Place the remaining half on the top of the crankshaft, making sure that the snap-ring grooves and bearing notches are aligned as described above.

9. Install the snap-ring in the groove.

Crankshaft and Connecting Rod Needle Bearings

1. Place the crankshaft in position on the cylinder block. Lift the connecting rods toward the crankshaft, adjusting positions of both if necessary. Position the connecting rod bearing surfaces about 1/8 in. below the crankshaft journal surface.

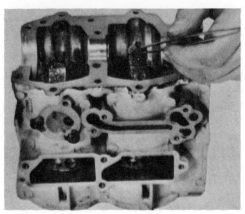

Installing connecting rod needle bearings (© Chrysler Outboard Corp.)

2. Remove the crankshaft from the cylinder block.

3. Coat the bearing surfaces of the connecting rod with a light coating of grease.

4. These models use caged needle bearings—sixteen on each connecting rod. Place half of the bearing cage on the bearing surface of the lower connecting rod journal, with the notches facing up, toward the flywheel. Install eight needle bearings in the bearing cage.

5. These bearing cages are machined together for accuracy and must be installed in pairs.

6. Repeat steps 3 and 4 for the upper portion of the connecting rod.

7. Carefully install the crankshaft on the cylinder block. Use care so that the needle bearings are not disturbed. Rotate the center main bearing race until the holes in the bearing align with the locating pins in the cylinder block.

8. Apply a light film of grease to the top half of the crankshaft journal.

9. Lay the remaining bearing cage over the top half of the crankshaft journal, making sure that the notches on the bearing cage halves match.

10. Place the remaining eight roller bearings in the bearing cage.

11. Carefully install the connecting rod

caps so that the loose roller bearings are not disturbed. The caps must be installed to the connecting rod from which they were removed. They must also be installed with the matchmarks on the side of the cap together and facing the flywheel end of the crankshaft.

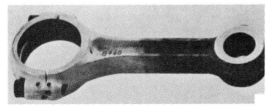

Two-cylinder connecting rod matchmarks (© Chrysler Outboard Corp.)

12. Install the connecting rod screws. Tighten the screws gradually and gently move the cap back and forth until it is properly aligned with the connecting rod. Inspect the joint between the connecting rod cap and the lower portion of the connecting rod. If a joint is visible, improper alignment is indicated. Loosen the screws and realign the caps and connecting rods. Make sure that the roller bearings are not disturbed.

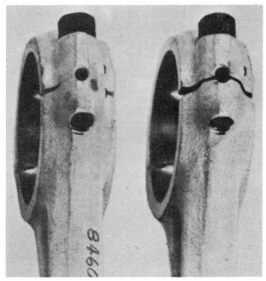

Connecting rod joints—proper on the left and improper on the right (© Chrysler Outboard Corp.)

13. Torque the connecting rod screws to 150 in. lbs.

SEALING THE CRANKCASE

1. Soak a clean lint-free rag in cleaning solution or pure grain alcohol and wipe the cylinder block crankcase joint until it is free of all foreign matter. The crankcase bearing cage mounting surface and O-ring seat must also be wiped clean or the sealer will not set properly.

2. Apply sealant to the cylinder block crankcase joint line, crankcase bearing cage mounting surface, and O-ring recess. Wipe all excess sealant from the bearing cage mounting surface and O-ring recess. Be sure to keep sealant away from bearing surfaces.

3. Apply Permatex No. 1 to all screws with holes through the crankcase.

4. Apply Loctite D to the upper and lower main bearing bores in the cylinder block and crankcase cover. Using the long, rubber-type seal, lay the new seal in the cylinder block groove and cut off flush with the bearing OD.

5. Apply 3M EC70 sealant from the OD of the upper main bearing bore to the outside edge of the $3/8$ in. tapped hole. Avoid the crankcase-to-cylinder block joint line by $1/8$ in. on both sides. Apply the same sealant to the lower edge of the center main bearing bore and lower main bearing bore on the entire web avoiding the crankcase-to-cylinder block joint line by $1/8$ in.

6. Apply Permatex No. 1 to all cylinder head screws, motor leg-to-powerhead screws (on the exhaust side which break into the exhaust cavity), screws with holes through the crankcase, and the two $3/8$ in. screws at the center main bearing.

7. The welch plug in the top of the cylinder head is replaceable. When installing, make sure that the counterbore in the head is free of burrs and foreign matter. Coat the outside edge of the plug with Loctite D before inserting the plug. The plug must be installed with the convex side up. Drive the plug in against the seat until it is flat and stake it in three places around the diameter.

8. Install and torque all main bearing bolts holding the crankcase cover to the cylinder block. At this time, turn the crankshaft several times to be sure that all parts are free and not binding. If any binding or knocking exists, the powerhead must be disassembled and the cause must be found and corrected before proceeding.

CRANKSHAFT BEARING CAGE

1. Inspect the bearing and seals on the crankshaft bearing cage. If pitted, rusted,

or scored, they must be replaced. The complete bearing cage must be replaced, as special equipment is necessary to install the bearing.

2. There are two seals on the bearing cage. One is pressed into the top of the cage and the other is an O-ring installed in the lower diameter of the cage. If the seals are cracked or worn, they must be replaced. Pry out the old seal, being careful not to gouge the seal bore. Apply Loctite H Non-Drying Sealer to the OD of the seal and grease the lip of the seal liberally with Aero Shell 14 Cam Grease or its equivalent prior to installation.

3. Assemble the seal with the spring down (toward the cylinder) and drive the seal into the seal bore so that the lower edge extends to within 0.150 in. of the recess on the bottom of the bearing cage. NOTE: *35–55 horsepower models with A203144 or A213144 bearing cage do not have a pressed-in bearing. The bearing is pressed onto the crankshaft. The crankshaft bearing cage can be serviced without removing the powerhead. Remove the flywheel, stator, magneto key and cam, and the top two screws attaching the crankcase cover to the cylinder block. The bearing cage is accessible and can be removed.*

4. Apply 3M EC750 sealer, as described in "Closing and Sealing the Crankcase," to the crankshaft bearing cage mounting surface on the cylinder block.

5. Apply Rykon 2 EP lubricant to the recess on the ID of the stator ring and hold the ring to the underside of the crankshaft bearing cage.

6. Install the bearing cage and stator ring assembly to the cylinder block. Be sure that the rubber O-ring is in place on the lower side.

Lower Crankshaft Seal

1. Apply Aero Shell 14 Cam Grease or its equivalent to the inside sealing lip of the lower crankshaft seal.

2. Install the seal to the lower end of the crankshaft with the spring down (toward the motor leg).

3. Securely tighten the two main bearing bolts directly below the crankshaft bearing cage and the screws in the lower end of the cylinder block. Tighten all the remaining crankcase-cover attaching screws. Torque the main bearing bolts to 270 in. lbs.

Installation

1. Lightly lubricate the lower spline in the end of the crankshaft and the spline on the driveshaft, down to the rubber O-ring seal. Use Aero Shell 14 Cam Grease or its equivalent and be sure that the O-ring seal is in place on the driveshaft.

Installing the upper driveshaft O-ring seal (© Chrysler Outboard Corp.)

2. Install a new cylinder-block exhaust gasket on the motor leg and place the powerhead in position. Tighten all screws securely. It is a good practice to apply 3M EC750 or Permatex No. 1 sealant to both sides of the cylinder-block exhaust gasket.

3. Clean all carbon buildup from the dome cavities in the cylinder head and check the flatness of the cylinder head with a straightedge and a feeler gauge.

4. Using a new cylinder head gasket, install the cylinder head. NOTE: *Some cylinder head gaskets are marked for easy installation, while others must be laid up against the cylinder block to match the configurations. Incorrect installation can cut off the cooling water supply to the powerhead. Apply Loctite H to the cylinder head bolts.*

5. Torque the cylinder head bolts to 270 in. lbs, starting at the center and working out in either direction. The cylinder head bolts must be retorqued after break-in and after the engine has cooled. When retorquing the bolts, hold the torque for fifteen seconds to allow the torque to set.

6. Install the thermostat, grommet, thermostat gasket, and cover to the cylinder head. The thermostat must be installed

with the V-slot up. If the thermostat fitting was removed from the exhaust port, be sure that it is installed.

7. Check the condition of the spark plugs. If satisfactory, install and torque to 10–15 ft lbs.

8. Install the exhaust water-jacket cover and gasket to the exhaust chamber on the port-side of the cylinder block.

9. Install the exhaust-port plate gasket, exhaust port plate, exhaust-port cover gasket, and exhaust-port cover on the cylinder block. Apply sealant to both sides of the exhaust-port plate gasket (between the cylinder and the exhaust-port plate) on the following areas: around the lower, rear, intake hole, from the top, forward, mounting hole across the top to the thin section of the gasket, and the entire forward, lower, corner to just above the first mounting hole.

10. Using new gaskets, install the transfer port covers to the starboard side of the motor.

11. Route the fuel line down from the pump outlet in front of the powerhead ground strap, behind the gearshift arm, under the cylinder drain cover, and up to the carburetor intake.

12. Assemble the two, split, flanged bearings to the throttle tower shaft with the shoulder up (on the top bearing) and down (on the lower bearing). Lubricate the ID of the bearing.

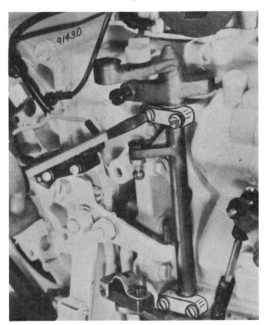

Installing the tower shaft bearing cups (© Chrysler Outboard Corp.)

13. Lubricate the tower shaft bearing surfaces on the crankcase cover and the ID of the tower shaft bearing caps.

14. Install the tower shaft on the crankcase cover and the tower shaft bearing caps. Tighten the bearing caps so that the tower shaft will move freely without excessive binding.

15. Install the throttle link assembly from the throttle cam to the ball connector on the tower shaft.

16. Assemble the puddle drain lines to the carburetor adaptor flange.

17. Install the two screws which attach the upper engine bracket shock mount to the upper shock mount. Use the lower set of holes in the bumper bracket.

18. Install the stabilizer link over the stabilizer screw and install the E-ring on the screw to lock the assembly in place.

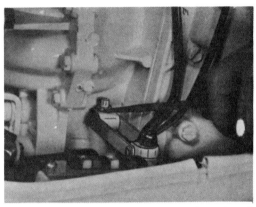

Installing the stabilizer link (© Chrysler Outboard Corp.)

19. Assemble one shift arm bearing over the stud in the cylinder drain cover.

20. Insert the cotter pin through the hole in the gearshift rod. Place one plain washer over the shift rod against the cotter pin.

21. Install the shift arm over the stud in the cylinder drain cover and shift rod, with the hooked arm forward.

22. Assemble one shift arm bearing over the stud in the cylinder drain cover and one plain washer over the end of the gearshift rod.

23. Lubricate the bearings and washers on the shift-rod cylinder drain-cover stud.

24. Install the long, elastic, stopnut to the stud on the cylinder drain cover. Install the short, elastic, stop nut to the gearshift rod. Tighten the locknuts securely, then back off just enough to allow free movement of the shift arm mechanism.

25. Install the neutral interlock switch to the top two holes in the cylinder drain cover. The button should face down. Do not tighten the mounting screws too tight or the switch may crack. No adjustment of the switch is required as the switch is self-aligning.

26. Install the electrical system components. See "Electrical System."

27. Install the white, spark control bearing and locknut to the spark control link on the magneto or alternator. Assemble the spark-control-link bearing assembly to the top arm on the throttle tower shaft.

28. Adjust all linkages, point of throttle opening, and engine timing as detailed in the appropriate section.

NOTE: *If new parts have been installed in the powerhead, it is good practice to break in the engine (see "Lubrication") before attempting sustained, full-throttle operation.*

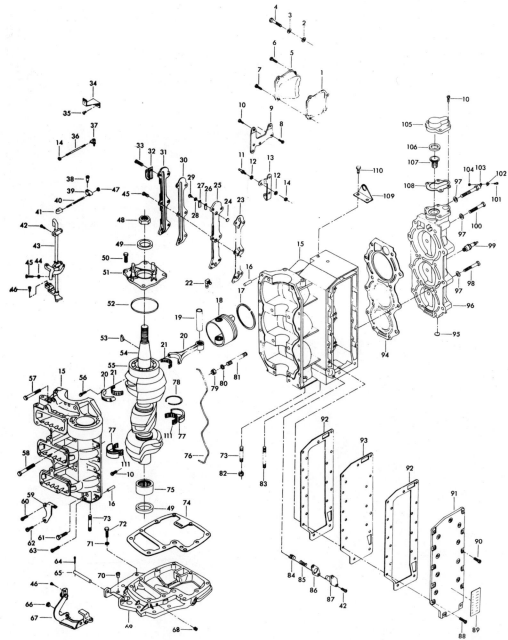

Exploded view of three-cylinder powerhead (© Chrysler Outboard Corp.) (Key is on facing page)

1. Gasket, transfer port cover
2. Plain washer
3. Plain washer
4. Hex bolt
5. Transfer port cover
6. Screw
7. Screw
8. Screw
9. Fuel pump bracket
10. Screw
11. Rod end connector stud
12. Internal tooth lockwasher
13. Bracket
14. Hex nut
15. Cylinder w/seal and screws
16. Dowel pin
17. Piston ring set
18. Piston w/bearing
19. Piston pin
20. Connecting rod w/cap and screw
21. Bearing cage w/roller
22. Elbow
23. Gasket, cylinder drain reed plate
24. Screen
25. Cylinder drain reed plate w/reeds, stops and screws
26. Reed, cylinder drain
27. Reed stop
28. Plain washer
29. Screw
30. Gasket, cylinder drain cover
31. Cylinder drain cover
32. Clamp
33. Screw
34. Timing pointer
35. Screw
36. Throttle link
37. Ball joint w/stud
38. Swivel
39. Distributor control rod end

40. Distributor control rod
41. Towershaft control rod
42. Screw
43. Towershaft w/bearings, swivels and screws
44. Hex nut
45. Hex slot head screw w/lock-washer
46. Screw w/lockwasher
47. Hex nut
48. Flywheel nut
49. Seal
50. Hex bolt
51. Crankshaft bearing cage w/seal
52. Seal, crankshaft bearing cage
53. Flywheel key
54. Crankshaft w/bearing
55. Crankshaft thrust bearing upper, not sold separately, contact factory for authori- zation to return crankshaft to factory for bearing re- placement
56. Connecting rod screw
57. Hex bolt
58. Hex bolt
59. Bracket, remote electric cable
60. Screw
61. Hex bolt
62. Screw
63. Screw
64. Cotter pin
65. Gearshift arm pin
66. Bearing
67. Gearshift arm w/interlock, swivel & rivets
68. Hex countersunk headless pipe plug
69. Spacer plate w/welch plug
70. Bearing
71. Spring lockwasher

72. Hex bolt
73. Stud
74. Cylinder exhaust gasket, upper
75. Lower main bearing
76. Parting line seal
77. Crankshaft main bearing w/snap-ring
78. Snap-ring
79. Hex nut
80. Spring lockwasher
81. Stud
82. Stop-nut
83. Stud
84. By-pass valve
85. Spring, by-pass valve
86. Gasket, by-pass valve
87. By-pass valve cover
88. Screw
89. Decal, wiring
90. Screw
91. Exhaust port cover
92. Gasket, exhaust port plate
93. Exhaust port plate
94. Head gasket
95. Welch plug
96. Cylinder head w/welch plug
97. Plain washer
98. Bolt
99. Spark plug
100. Cap screw
101. Screw
102. Internal tooth lockwasher
103. Thermoswitch
104. Nut
105. Thermostat cover
106. Grommet
107. Thermostat
108. Gasket, thermostat cover
109. Lifting bracket
110. Screw w/lockwasher
111. Bearing cage w/roller

70–135 HP (1966–72)

Removal

1. Remove the flywheel nut from the crankshaft. Remove the flywheel with the aid of a puller. An automotive flywheel holder may be used to remove the nut from the flywheel.

2. Remove the electrical leads from the rectifier. Remove the rectifier and mounting bracket.

3. Remove the electrical leads from the starter solenoid. Remove the starter solenoid from the support plate.

4. Remove the bolts securing the starter mounting bracket to the powerhead. Remove the starter from the engine.

5. Remove the distributor pulley, belt, and distributor cap from the powerhead.

6. Disconnect the electrical leads from the starter interlock switch.

7. Unbolt the distributor bracket and remove the distributor.

8. Disconnect the coil leads and remove the coil.

9. Remove the circuit breaker after disconnecting the leads.

10. Remove the electrical leads from the terminal block and choke solenoid.

11. Remove the clamps from the engine wiring harness and remove the harness from the engine.

12. Remove the clamp and intake drain hose from the elbow.

13. Remove the intake baffle from the carburetors.

14. Remove the throttle and choke linkages from the carburetors.

15. Unclamp and remove the fuel line from the elbows.

16. Remove the carburetors and gaskets.

17. Remove the intake manifold, gasket, and reed plate adaptor.

18. Remove the reed plates.

19. Remove the screws from the support plate.

20. Remove the nut from the upper shift rod and remove the shift rod from the shift lever.

21. Unbolt and remove the rear leg cover.

22. Unbolt the spacer plate.

23. Remove the nuts from the studs on the powerhead and carefully lift the powerhead from the motor leg.

24. Remove the bolts from the exhaust tube and remove the exhaust tube from the spacer plate.

25. Remove the spacer plate and gasket from the powerhead.

Disassembly

1. Remove the thermo-switch, washers, cylinder head, and head gasket. Discard all gaskets removed from the powerhead during disassembly.

2. Remove the thermostat cover, packing, thermostat, and gasket.

3. Remove the exhaust port cover, gasket, and exhaust port plate.

4. Remove the by-pass valve cover, gasket, spring, and by-pass valve.

5. Remove the electric, remote cable bracket.

6. Remove the cylinder drain cover, gasket, and cylinder drain reed plate.

7. Remove the fuel pump bracket, the transfer port covers, and the gaskets.

8. Unbolt and remove the tower shaft.

9. Remove the screws securing the outer edge of the crankcase cover to the cylinder block.

10. Remove the crankshaft bearing cage and seal.

11. Unscrew and remove the crankcase cover. The crankcase cover can be easily removed by twisting a large bladed screwdriver in the slots located at the upper right-hand and left-hand corners of the joint line between the crankcase cover and the cylinder block.

12. The pistons, wrist pins, connecting rods, connecting rod caps, connecting rod bearings, and screws are matched assemblies. These items must be identified as to

their original location as they are removed so that they can be returned to their proper location.

13. Remove the connecting rod screws, rod caps, and connecting rod bearings.

14. Carefully lift the crankshaft from the cylinder block.

15. Remove the seal and lower main bearing from the crankshaft.

16. Mark the pistons as to front and cylinder number, and push them out of the bores.

17. Using a ring expander, remove the piston rings from the pistons.

18. The piston and connecting rod can be replaced independently, but it is best to replace the entire connecting rod, piston, and bearing assembly, if necessary.

19. The crankshaft main bearing races and bearing cages are matched assemblies. These must be marked as to their original locations.

20. Remove the snap-rings, crankshaft main bearing races, and crankshaft bearing cages from the crankshaft.

21. Remove all grease and carbon from all powerhead components with degreaser or other suitable solvent.

CAUTION: *Use flammable solvents only in well-ventilated areas and keep away from sparks, flames, and electrical appliances.*

Inspection

1. After degreasing, air-dry all components.

2. Remove the glaze from the cylinder bores with a cylinder hone. Be extremely careful since only a minute amount of the cylinder wall can be removed.

3. Inspect the cylinder bore for cracks or scoring. Replace if cracked or excessively scored.

4. Install the crankcase cover and torque the mounting screws to 270 in. lbs.

5. With an inside micrometer, measure the diameter of the cylinder bore at the cylinder head end. The diameter must be 3.3130–3.3148 in.

6. Measure the diameter of the upper main bearing bore. It must be 2.8338–2.8345 in.

7. Using a micrometer, measure the diameter of the piston. At the top it must be 3.286–3.288 in. At the bottom it should be 3.3065–3.3075 in.

8. If any of the dimensions in steps 5,

6, or 7 are not as specified, the appropriate part should be replaced.

9. Inspect the connecting-rod bearing bore diameter. If the silver plating is worn off the connecting rod in the area of the bearing bore, the rod must be replated or replaced.

10. Inspect the bearing rollers for scoring or discoloration from overheating.

Assembly

1. Install the lower main bearing and seal on the crankshaft. The lipped edge of the seal must face the bottom, splined end of the crankshaft. Bearing cage halves are matched assemblies and should be installed in their original locations.

2. Install the bearing cage halves on the center main bearing journals of the crankshaft. The matchmarks on the bearing cage halves must point toward the flywheel (threaded) end of the crankshaft.

3. Install the center main bearing race halves with the grooved end of the race toward the flywheel end of the crankshaft. Lock the bearing in place with the snap-ring.

4. Remove all oil, grease, and fingerprints from the crankshaft upper main bearing bore of the cylinder block with alcohol or a similar solvent.

5. Apply a thin coat of Loctite H to the upper main bearing bore of the cylinder block.

6. Install the crankshaft in the cylinder block. Turn the center and lower main bearings until the bearing locating holes slip over the bearing locating pins.

7. Install the crankshaft bearing cage and bolt it to the cylinder block.

8. Lock the lower end of the crankshaft with a block of wood (as shown).

9. Install the rings on the pistons, using a ring expander. If a ring expander is not available, this can be done by hand, if care is used. The bevel on the inside edge of the ring must face the top of the piston.

10. Turn the rings until the ring alignment pin is approximately centered in the ring gap.

11. Apply a light coat of engine oil to the cylinder bores.

12. Push the pistons into the cylinders with a ring compressor. The rings can be compressed by hand if care is used. The high crown side of the piston must face the intake port side of the cylinder block.

Locking the lower end of the crankshaft with a block of wood (© Chrysler Outboard Corp.)

Centering the ring alignment pin in the ring gap (© Chrysler Outboard Corp.)

13. Install the lower bearing race half in the connecting rod. The matchmarks on the bearing cage halves must face the flywheel end of the crankshaft.

Location of bearing cage matchmarks (© Chrysler Outboard Corp.)

Installing the bearing rollers (© Chrysler Outboard Corp.)

14. Install the bearing rollers into the bearing cage.

15. Pull the connecting rod up until the bearing contacts the journal of the crankshaft.

16. Install the upper bearing cage half, rollers, and connecting rod cap.

17. Torque the bolts securing the connecting rod cap to the connecting rod to 180 in. lbs.

18. Insert the seals in the groove of the joint line between the crankcase cover and the cylinder block.

19. Remove the block of wood holding the crankshaft in place (step 8).

20. Remove the crankshaft bearing cage from the cylinder block.

21. Clean the upper main bearing bore of the crankcase cover with alcohol or a similar solvent.

22. Apply a coat of Loctite H to the upper main bearing bore in the crankcase cover.

NOTE: *Be sure that the locating holes in the main bearings are in place over the bearing locating pins in the cylinder block.*

23. Apply Loctite H to the threaded portion of the ⅜ in. bolts securing the crankcase cover.

24. Install the crankcase cover and bolts, torquing the bolts to 270 in. lbs.

25. Install the remaining ¼ in. screws securing the crankcase cover. Torque these screws to 70 in. lbs.

26. Apply Loctite H to the threaded portion of the stud and install the lock-washer and nut. Torque the nut to 270 in. lbs.

27. Install the seal on the crankshaft bearing cage and install the crankshaft bearing cage on the cylinder block, torquing the mounting bolts to 270 in. lbs.

28. Install the reeds and reed stops on the cylinder drain reed plate.

29. Install, in order, the gasket, reed plate, gasket, and cylinder drain cover. Torque the screws to 70 in. lbs.

30. Install the exhaust port cover, exhaust port plate and gaskets, and torque the screws to 70 in. lbs.

31. Attach the rod end connector studs to the bracket and torque the attaching nuts to 35 in. lbs.

32. Install the gaskets and transfer port covers on the cylinder intake ports and torque the mounting screws to 70 in. lbs.

33. Attach the fuel pump bracket to the fuel pump, torquing the mounting screws to 70 in. lbs.

NOTE: *If the powerhead is to be painted, install the fuel pump after painting.*

34. Install the timing pointer on the crankcase cover and torque the mounting screws to 30 in. lbs.

35. Install the lifting bracket with screws torqued to 270 in. lbs.

36. Install the by-pass valve, spring, gasket, and by-pass valve cover, and torque the screws to 30 in. lbs.

37. Install the cylinder head gasket and cylinder head, and torque the bolts to 270 in. lbs, in increments of 25 in. lbs. The cylinder head bolts should be torqued according to the illustration in the specifications. Install the thermo-switch and tighten the mounting securely.

38. Install the gasket, thermostat, grommet, and thermostat cover, torquing the screws to 70 in. lbs.

39. Install the electric, remote-control bracket and torque the screws to 70 in. lbs.

40. Install the elbows on the cylinder block.

41. Install the tower shaft and tighten the screws to 70 in. lbs.

42. Install the studs and tighten securely.

NOTE: *If the powerhead is to be painted, remove all grease and oil from the powerhead with alcohol or a similar solvent. Mask the bottom (water) side of the powerhead, crankshaft and upper main bearing, intake ports on the crankcase cover, and the spark plug holes. Suspend the powerhead from a rope securely fastened to the lifting ring. Paint the powerhead with frost-white (Chrysler part no. K 734), spray bomb.*

Installation

1. Install the gasket and spacer plate on the powerhead. Nuts are installed on the four short studs located at the front of the powerhead.

2. Install the exhaust tube on the support plate and secure with screws.

3. Place the gasket on the motor leg.

4. Carefully set the powerhead on the motor leg and tighten the mounting nuts securely.

5. Secure the front edge of the support plate to the motor leg.

6. Thread the nut onto the shift rod and slip the rod through the attaching hole on the shift lever. Install the nut on the shift rod.

7. Install the exhaust idle boot, spring, and clamp on the exhaust idle outlet of the motor leg.

8. Install the rear leg cover on the motor leg and align the exhaust idle boot with the rear leg cover.

9. Secure the support plate to the rear leg cover.

10. Install the reed assemblies in the intake manifold of the powerhead.

11. Install the intake manifold, gasket, and adaptor plate on the powerhead.

12. Install the gaskets and carburetors on the intake manifold.

13. Install the choke throttle linkages on the carburetors. Adjust the throttle linkage so that all throttle plates are horizontal when at WOT (wide-open throttle). Throttle plates must be parallel to each other at WOT.

14. Install the fuel supply lines to the carburetors.

15. Install the fuel pump on the powerhead.

16. Connect the air hose between the elbow on the large diameter end of the fuel pump and the bottom elbow on the side of the powerhead.

17. Connect the air hose between the elbow on the bottom of the fuel pump and the elbow on the bottom carburetor.

18. Connect the drain line between the elbow located on the bottom of the intake baffle and the fitting on the bottom of the intake manifold.

19. Install the intake baffle on the carburetors.

20. Remove the nuts from the thru-bolts on the starter. Do not let the starter come apart as the nuts are removed.

21. Install the starter in the upper, starter, mounting bracket. Install the nuts on the thru-bolts. The electrical terminal on the starter must face the powerhead.

22. Install the starter relay on the port side of the support plate.

23. Install the large red lead between the starter terminal and the starter relay.

24. Install the circuit breaker and terminal block mounting bracket (on the port side of the powerhead).

25. Install the rectifier on the port side of the powerhead.

26. Install the choke solenoid on the front of the powerhead.

27. Install the distributor and coil on the starboard side of the powerhead.

28. Install the alternator and stator on top of the powerhead.

29. Install the electrical harness on the engine and be sure that all connections are made and are tight.

30. Install the flywheel on the crankshaft and torque the flywheel nut to 70 ft lbs.

Motor Leg and Water Pump

35–55 HP (1966–72)

Gear Housing

REMOVAL

1. Drain the lubricant from the gear housing as detailed in the lubrication section of this chapter.

2. Disconnect the coupler between the intermediate and upper shift rods. On models with acoustical motor leg covers, it is necessary to remove the covers to gain access to the coupler.

3. Remove the four screws which attach the gear housing to the motor leg and remove the gear housing.

WATER PUMP REMOVAL

The water pump on these models acts as a positive-displacement type at low speeds

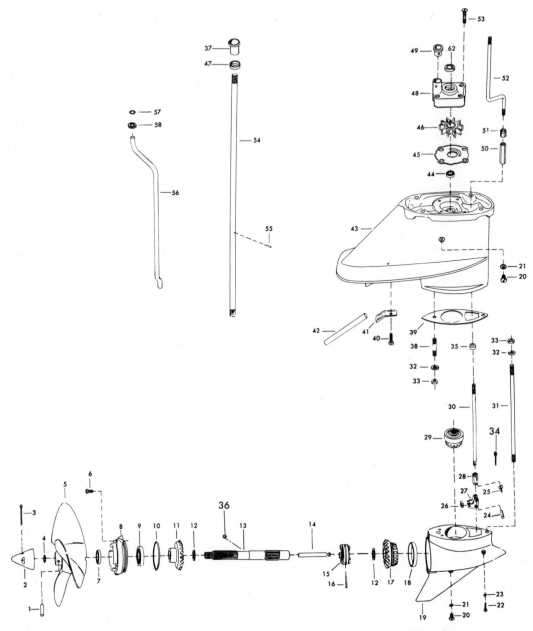

Exploded view of gear housing, lower unit, and water pump (© Chrysler Outboard Corp.)

1. Propeller pin
2. Propeller nut w/seal and cotter pin
3. Cotter pin
4. Seal propeller nut
5. Propeller (Accessory Item)
6. Cap screw
7. Seal, propeller shaft
8. Propeller shaft bearing cage w/seal
9. Ball bearing, propeller shaft
10. Seal propeller shaft bearing cage
11. Bevel gear rear w/bushing
12. Thrust washer, bevel gear

13. Propeller shaft
14. Gearshift pin w/yoke
15. Clutch
16. Spring pin
17. Bevel gear front w/bearing
18. Propeller shaft thrust bearing cup
19. Gear housing lower w/plug, washer, and thrust bearing cup
20. Plug, gear housing
21. Washer, gear housing plug
22. Gearshift arm pin
23. Nyltite washer
24. Spring pin

25. Pin
26. Gearshift arm yoke w/pin
27. Gearshift arm w/bushing
28. Coupling, shift arm
29. Bevel pinion w/bearing
30. Gearshift rod lower
31. Stud, long
32. Lockwasher
33. Nut
34. Cotter pin
35. Seal, shift rod, lower
36. Ball, prop shaft
37. Boot
38. Stud, short
39. Gasket, gear housing

Disconnecting the gearshift rod coupler (© Chrysler Outboard Corp.)

3. Remove the water pump impeller drive pin and back plate.

WATER PUMP INSTALLATION

1. Install the water pump back plate to the gear housing.

2. Install the water pump drive pin and install the impeller over the driveshaft.

3. Place the water pump top plate in the pump body. Place a small amount of grease on the back of the top plate to hold it to the pump body.

4. Slide the pump bolt down over the driveshaft. Rotate the driveshaft and push the pump body over the impeller.

5. Install the three, pump body retaining screws.

Gearshift Linkage Adjustment

1. Shift the gear housing into Forward gear.

2. Scribe a mark on the gearshift rod where it emerges from the motor leg.

and as a centrifugal pump at high speeds. It is located at the top of the gear housing and consists of a water pump body, impeller, and top and back plates of stainless steel. The impeller is driven by the driveshaft which passes through the center of the water pump body.

A thermostat is used to control the temperature of the cooling water in the powerhead. When the engine is cold and the thermostat closed, water flows through the by-pass line between the cylinder head and the exhaust port cover. After the engine has reached operating temperature, approximately 165° F, the thermostat is fully open and the by-pass line is restricted. If the thermostat is removed for operation, water will continue to flow through the by-pass line and overheating will result.

1. Remove the three screws securing the water pump body to the gear housing.

2. Slide the water pump body and impeller off the driveshaft.

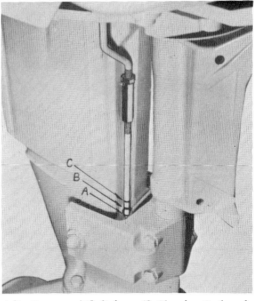

Adjusting gearshift linkage (© Chrysler Outboard Corp.)

40. Screw	50. Coupling, gearshift rod, lower	56. Intake water line for standard shaft models
41. Inlet water plate	51. Coupler	Intake water line for long shaft models
42. Inlet water tube	52. Gearshift rod intermediate for short shaft models	57. Seal
43. Gear housing upper w/seal, washer, plug, and inlet water tube	Gearshift rod intermediate for long shaft models	58. Plain washer
44. Seal, driveshaft	53. Screw	62. Driveshaft seal
45. Water pump back plate	54. Driveshaft for standard shaft models	
46. Water pump impeller	Driveshaft for long shaft models	
47. Retainer		
48. Water pump body with seals	55. Water pump inpeller drive-pin	
49. Seal, inlet water line lower		

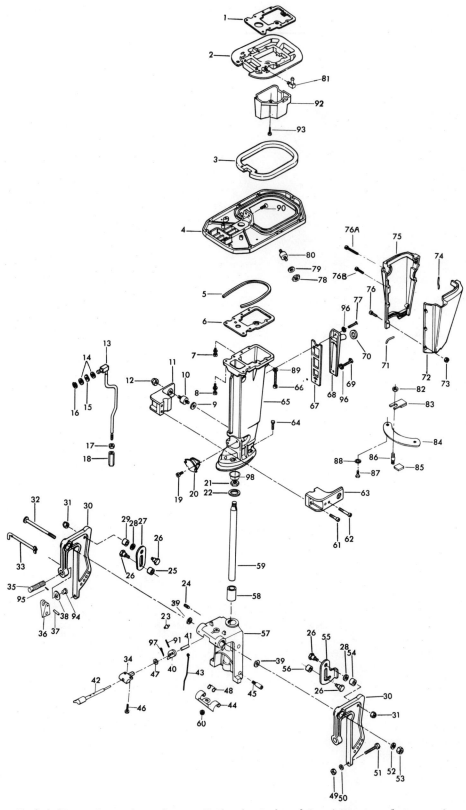

Exploded view of motor leg and covers (© Chrysler Outboard Corp.) (Key is on facing page)

1. Cylinder exhaust gasket upper
2. Spacer plate
3. Seal, kingpin plate
4. Kingpin plate
5. Dampening pad
6. Cylinder exhaust gasket lower
7. Screw w/lockwasher
8. Screw w/lockwasher
9. Shock mount spacer for models with serial no.'s 5000 and under
10. Shock mount side lower w/spacer
11. Shock mount lower cover, starboard for models with serial no.'s 5000 and under
    Shock mount lower cover, starboard for models with serial no.'s 5001 and over
12. Stop-nut
13. Gearshift rod upper
14. Plain washer
15. Bowed spring washer
16. Retaining ring
17. Hex nut
18. Gearshift rod coupling
19. Screw
20. Shock mount lower
21. Kingpin nut
22. Swivel bracket washer
23. Grease fitting
24. Set screw, oval point
25. Spacer, tilt-stop
26. Tilt-stop pivot
27. Tilt-stop, starboard
28. Bowed spring washer
29. Spacer, tilt-stop
30. Stern bracket
31. Stop nut
32. Stern bracket pivot bolt
33. Stern bracket lock bar w/end
34. Bearing
35. Clamp screw w/foot
36. Clamp screw handle
37. Spring pin
38. Clamp screw foot
39. Stern bracket friction washer
40. Arm
41. Bearing
42. Handle and shaft
43. Link
44. Lock
45. Pin
46. Screw
47. Plain washer
48. Reverse lock spring
49. Hex nut
50. Plain washer
51. Screw
52. Plain washer
53. Elastic stop nut
54. Spacer, tilt-stop
55. Tilt-stop, port
56. Spacer, tilt-stop
57. Swivel bracket w/bearings and grease fitting
58. Swivel bracket bearing
59. King pin w/welch plug
60. Stop-nut
61. Cap screw
62. Screw
63. Shock mount lower cover, port for models with serial no.'s 5000 and under
    Shock mount lower cover, port for models with serial no.'s 5001 and over
64. Screw
65. Motor leg for models with serial no.'s 5000 and under
    Motor leg for models with serial no.'s 5001 and over
66. Screw
67. Motor leg exhaust cover gasket
68. Motor leg exhaust cover
69. Screw
70. Grommet, motor leg exhaust cover
71. Packing, leg cover lower
72. Motor leg cover, port
73. Nut
74. Packing, leg cover upper
75. Motor leg cover, starboard
76. Screw
76A. Screw
76B. Screw
77. Screw
78. Hex nut
79. Plain washer
80. Shock mount, side upper
81. Drain fitting
82. Lock nut
83. Friction shoe adjusting arm w/shoe
84. Friction shoe plate
85. Friction shoe
86. Stud
87. Screw
88. Spring lockwasher
89. Spring lockwasher
90. Screw
91. Spring pin
92. Leg exhaust tube
93. Screw w/lockwasher
94. Stud
95. Spring pin
96. Spring lockwasher
97. Cotter pin
98. Plug

3. Shift the engine into Neutral. Again scribe a mark on the gearshift rod.

4. Shift the engine into Reverse gear. Scribe another mark on the gearshift rod. The distance between the marks should be equal.

5. Adjust the gearshift rod coupling until the distance between the marks is equal.

Friction Adjustments

1. See "Steering Friction Adjustment" in the maintenance section of this chapter.

Motor Leg Covers

1. The following procedure has been developed to facilitate installation of motor leg covers.

2. Coat the grooves in the leg covers with a silicone, rubber-adhesive sealant and install rubber packing. Tape the packing in place.

3. Be sure that the motor leg covers are aligned and installed properly. If not, they will rub together, creating vibrations and noises.

4. Install both cover halves around the motor leg.

5. Install one standard size mounting screw in the center hole in the forward set of mounting holes.

6. Install one long (2 in.) screw in the center hole in the rear set of mounting holes.

7. Install the balance of the standard screws and tighten securely.

8. Remove the long screw installed in step 6 and install a standard screw.

70–135 HP (1966–72)

Gear Housing

REMOVAL

1. Remove the pin connecting the upper and lower gearshift rods.

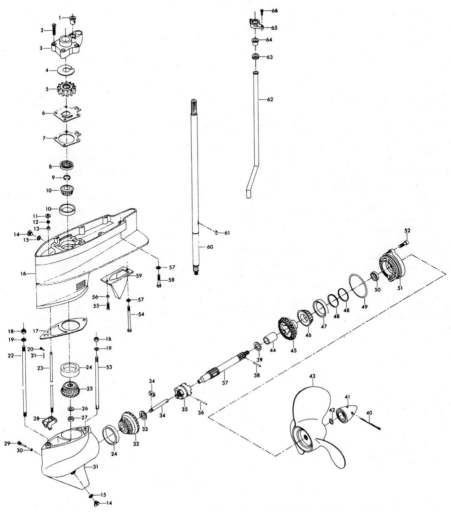

Exploded view of gear housing and lower unit (© Chrysler Outboard Corp.)

1. Seal, Intake water line lower
2. Screw
3. Water pump body w/seal
4. Water pump top plate
5. Water pump impeller
6. Water pump back plate
7. Gasket, water pump
8. Seal, driveshaft
9. Retaining ring
10. Bearing, driveshaft w/cup
11. Retainer, gearshift rod seal
12. Spacer, gearshift rod
13. Seal, gearshift rod
14. Plug, gear housing
15. Washer, gear housing plug
16. Gear housing upper w/plug and washer
17. Gasket, gear housing
18. Stop-nut
19. Plain washer
20. Pin, gearshift rod lower
21. Cotter pin
22. Stud, gear housing front
23. Gearshift rod lower
24. Bearing cup

25. Bevel pinion gear w/bearing
26. Washer, bevel pinion retaining
27. Nut, bevel pinion retaining
28. Coupling, gearshift arm w/bushing
29. Pin gearshift arm
30. Washer
31. Gear housing lower
32. Bevel gear front w/bearing
33. Spacer, bevel gear front
34. Pin, gearshift w/yoke
35. Clutch
36. Spring pin
37. Propeller shaft
38. Propeller pin pack
39. Thrust washer, bevel gear, rear
40. Cotter pin
41. Propeller nut w/cotter pin and seal
42. Seal, propeller nut
43. Propeller
44. Bearing, bevel gear, rear
45. Bevel gear, rear
46. Bearing w/cup
47. Bearing cup

48. Shim propeller shaft bearing cage
49. Seal, propeller shaft bearing cage
50. Seal, propeller shaft
51. Propeller shaft bearing cage w/seal
52. Cap screw
53. Stud, gear housing, rear
54. Bolt
55. Screw
56. Countersunk external tooth lockwasher
57. Spring lockwasher
58. Bolt
59. Exhaust outlet
60. Driveshaft w/nut
61. Drive key, water pump
62. Intake water line
63. Grommet, water line
64. Seal, Intake water line, upper
65. Bracket water line
66. Screw

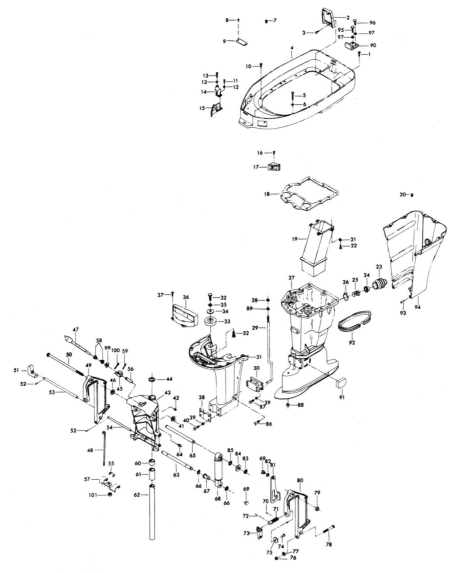

Exploded view of motor leg and support plate (© Chrysler Outboard Corp.)

1. Screw	17. Battery cable grommet	35. Spring lockwasher
2. Latch bracket	18. Gasket, exhaust lower	36. Baffle air intake
3. Screw w/lockwasher	19. Exhaust tube	37. Screw
4. Support plate	20. Plug	38. King pin cap
5. Screw	21. Spring lockwasher	39. Spring lockwasher
6. Lockwasher	22. Screw	40. Bolt
7. Plug	23. Boot, idle exhaust	41. Friction washer
8. Screw	24. Insert	42. Set screw
9. Identification plate w/screws	25. Spring	43. Swivel bracket w/bearing
for U.S.A. models	26. Clamp	and grease fitting
Identification plate w/screws	27. Motor leg	44. Washer
for Canada models	28. Stop-nut	45. Reverse lock arm
10. Screw	29. Gearshift rod upper	46. Friction washer
11. Screw w/lockwasher	w/coupler	47. Handle and shaft
12. Plain washer	30. Shock mount lower	48. Link
13. Screw w/lockwasher	31. Leg cover, front w/pin	49. Stern bracket, starboard
14. Cap, cable bushing	32. Screw	50. Stern bracket pivot bolt
15. Bushing, cable entry	33. Shock mount upper	51. Lock bar handle
16. Screw w/lockwasher	34. Washer	52. Spring pin

53. Stern bracket lock bar
    w/handle
54. Reverse lockpin
55. Reverse lockspring
56. Bearing
57. Reverse lock
58. Bearing
59. Spring pin
60. Bearing extension
61. Bearing
62. King pin w/plugs
63. Shaft, shock mount lower
64. Grease fitting
65. Shaft shock mount upper
66. Retaining ring
67. Bearing
68. Shock absorber w/bushing

69. Tilt-stop pivot
70. Spring pin
71. Clamp screw
72. Spring pin
73. Clamp screw handle
74. Stud
75. Clamp screw foot
76. Nut
77. Plain washer
78. Screw
79. Stop-nut
80. Stern bracket, port
81. Tilt-lock
82. Spring bowed washer
83. Retaining ring
84. Plain washer
85. Spring bowed washer

86 Screw
87. Bolt
88. Seal, gearshift rod
89. Locknut
90. Deflection stop
91. Shock mount side
92. Seal motor leg
93. Spring pin
94. Motor leg cover, rear
95. Screw
96. Screw
97. Lockwasher

99. Washer
100. Cotter pin
101. Locknut

For Long Shaft Models
27. Motor leg
92. Seal, motor leg
94. Motor leg cover, rear

For Short Shaft Models
27. Motor Leg
92. Seal, motor leg
94. Motor leg cover, rear

2. Remove the bolts securing the gear housing to the motor leg.

3. Pull the gear housing from the motor leg.

Water Pump Removal

1. Remove the plug from the gear housing and drain the lubricant as described under "Lubrication."

2. Remove the cotter pin, propeller nut, seal, propeller pin, and propeller from the propeller shaft.

3. Remove the screws, water pump body, water pump top plate, impeller, water pump back plate, and water pump gasket.

4. Remove the water pump drive key from the driveshaft.

Water Pump Installation

1. Install the water pump drive key in the driveshaft keyway.

2. Install the gasket, back plate, impeller, top plate, body, and screws. Tighten the screws securely.

3. Install the water line intake seal in the water pump body.

4. Remove the vent plug from the upper gear housing and fill the gear housing as detailed under "Lubrication."

Installation

1. Install the gear housing on the motor leg, making sure to align the water pick-up tube with the outlet on the water pump.

2. Install the bolts on the side of the gear housing and tighten securely.

3. Attach the lower shift rod to the upper shift rod with the shift pin and cotter pin.

4. Adjust the gear shift linkage as described under "Gear Shift Linkage Adjustment" for 1966–72 35–55 hp motors.

5. Position the shift lever so that the Neutral interlock stop on the lever is aligned with the neutral interlock stop on the tower shaft. Tighten the nuts.

3 · Kiekhaefer Mercury

Introduction

Kiekhaefer Mercury has long been recognized as the performance leader among outboard manufacturers. The first Mercury outboard was produced in 1939, and, during its 32 years of production, has been continually improved through many marine engineering achievements. Mercury was the first manufacturer to produce a four-cylinder inline outboard. In 1957 Mercury was again first, with the revolutionary six-cylinder, inline outboard; and in 1962 Mercury built the first production 100 horsepower, six-cylinder outboard. This engine has set more performance and endurance records than any other outboard.

Mercury outboards are easily recognizable by their slim, high profile. This small bore, short stroke, inline engine design features smaller and lighter pistons and connecting rods. As a result, piston speeds are decreased, providing longer service life and smoother operation. Other notable Mercury features include a patented "Direct Charge" fuel induction system, a "Jet-Prop" exhaust which discharges exhaust gases into a vacuum in the slipstream, the use of anti-corrosion alloys, "Thunderbolt" ignition system for hotter spark, and shear-proof drive with the propeller splined to the hub. A live, rubber safety clutch protects the drive train against impact damage.

Engine Serial Number

The engine serial number is stamped on a plate which is located on the swivel bracket and also on the powerhead. This number is the manufacturer's key to many engineering details and should be included in any correspondence with a dealer or the manufacturer.

Model Identification

Year	Model	No. of Cyls	Horsepower	Cubic Inch Displacement
1966	350	2	35.0	32.5
	500	4	50.0	44.0
	(Jet Prop)			
	650	4	65.0	60.0
	950, 950SS	6	95.0	90.0
	1100, 1100SS	6	110.0	93.5
1967	350	2	35.0	32.5
	500M, 500S,			
	500SS	4	50.0	44.0
	650S, 650SS	4	65.0	62.5
	950SS	6	95.0	90.0
	1100SS	6	110.0	93.5

1971 Mercury 1350 6-cylinder

1971 Mercury 400 2-cylinder

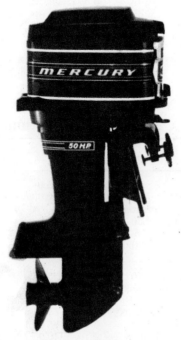

1971 Mercury 500 4-cylinder

Model Identification (cont.)

Year	Model	No. of Cyls	Horsepower	Cubic Inch Displacement
1968	350	2	35.0	32.5
	500SS	4	50.0	44.0
	650SS	4	65.0	62.4
	1000SS, 1000BP	6	100.0	90.0
	1250SS, 1250BP	6	125.0	99.81
1969	350	2	35.0	32.5
	500SS	4	50.0	44.0
	650SS	4	65.0	62.4
	800	4	80.0	66.6
	1000SS	6	100.0	99.81
	1000 Super BP	6	100.0	99.81
	1250SS	6	125.0	99.81
	1250 Super BP	6	125.0	99.81
1970– 1971	400	2	40.0	33.3
	500	4	50.0	43.8
	650	4	65.0	62.42
	800	4	80.0	66.6
	1150	6	115.0	99.81
	1350	6	135.0	99.81

General Engine Specifications

Year	Model	Cubic Inch Displacement	Horsepower (OBC)	Full Throttle Range (rpm)	Bore (in.)	Stroke (in.)
1966	350	32.5	35.0	4800–5200	3.000	2.300
	500 Jet Prop	44.0	50.0	5200–5600	2.562	2.125
	650	60.0	65.0	4800–5200	2.875	2.300
	950, 950SS	90.0	95.0	4800–5200	2.875	2.300
	1100, 1100SS	93.5	110.0	4800–5200	2.938	2.300
1967	350	32.5	35.0	4800–5300	3.000	2.300
	500M, 500S, 500SS	44.0	50.0	5200–5600	2.562	2.125
	650S, 650SS	62.4	65.0	4800–5200	2.938	2.300
	950SS	90.0	95.0	4800–5200	2.875	2.300
	1100SS	93.5	110.0	4800–5200	2.938	2.300
1968	350	32.5	35.0	4800–5300	3.000	2.300
	500SS	44.0	50.0	5200–5500	2.562	2.125
	650SS	62.4	65.0	4800–5300	2.938	2.300
	1000SS	90.0	100.0	4800–5300	2.875	2.300
	1000BP	90.0	100.0	6200–6500	2.875	2.300
	1250SS	99.81	125.0	4800–5300	2.875	2.562
	1250BP	99.81	125.0	5000–5600	2.875	2.562
1969	350	32.5	35.0	4800–5300	3.000	2.300
	500SS	44.0	50.0	5200–5500	2.562	2.125
	650SS	62.4	65.0	4800–5300	2.938	2.300
	800	66.6	80.0	4800–5300	2.875	2.562
	1000SS	90.0	100.0	4800–5300	2.875	2.300
	1000 Super BP	99.81	100.0	6200–6500	2.875	2.300
	1250SS	99.81	125.0	4800–5300	2.875	2.562
	1250 Super BP	99.81	125.0	5000–5600	2.875	2.562
1970– 1971	400	33.3	40.0	4800–5300	2.875	2.562
	500	43.8	50.0	4800–5500	2.562	2.125
	650	62.42	65.0	4800–5300	2.938	2.300
	800	66.6	80.0	4800–5300	2.875	2.562
	1150	99.81	115.0	4800–5300	2.875	2.562
	1350	99.81	135.0	4800–5300	2.875	2.562

Tune-Up Specifications

NOTE: *When analyzing compression test results, look for uniformity among cylinders, rather than specific pressure. Variation between cylinders should not exceed 15 psi.*

Year	Model	Spark Plugs Type	Gap (in.)	Firing Order	Ignition Timing (in.)	Ignition Timing (deg)	Breaker Point Gap (in.)	Dwell Angle (deg)	Idle Speed (rpm)
1966	350	J4J①	0.025	Alternate	0.300B	——	0.020	——	500
	500	J4J	0.025	90° con.	0.200B	32½B	0.010	48	550
	650	J4J	0.025	1–3–2–4	0.222B	32½B	0.010	48	550
	950, 1100	L4J	0.030	60° con.	0.235B	34½B	——	90	550
	950SS, 1100SS	L19V	②	60° con.	0.275B	36½B	——	45	550
1967	350	L4J③	0.030	Alternate	0.300B	——	0.020	——	500
	500M, 500S	L4J	0.030	1–3–2–4	——	35B	0.010	48	550–600
	500SS	L19V	②	1–3–2–4	0.232B	35B	——	——	550

Tune-Up Specifications (cont.)

NOTE: *When analyzing compression test results, look for uniformity among cylinders, rather than specific pressure. Variation between cylinders should not exceed 15 psi.*

Year	Model	Spark Plugs Type	Gap (in.)	Firing Order	Ignition Timing (in.)	(deg)	Breaker Point Gap (in.)	Dwell Angle (deg)	Idle Speed (rpm)
1967	650S	L4J	0.030	1–3–2–4	——	38B	0.010	48	550–600
	650SS	L19V	②	1–3–2–4	0.300B	38B	⑩	⑩	550
	950SS,								
	1100SS	L19V	②	60° con.	0.275B	36½B	⑩	⑩	550
1968	350	L4J③	0.030	Alternate	0.300B	——	0.020	——	500
	500SS	L19V④	②	1–3–2–4	0.232B	35B	⑩	⑩	550
	650SS	L19V④	②	1–3–2–4	0.300B	38B	⑩	⑩	550
	1000SS	L19V④	②	60° con.	——	36½B	⑩	⑩	550–600
	1250SS	L19V④	②	60° con.	——	34B	⑩	⑩	550–600
	1000BP	L19V④	②	60° con.	——	N.A.	⑩	⑩	N.A.
	1250BP	L19V④	②	60° con.	——	N.A.	⑩	⑩	N.A.
1969	350	L4J③	0.030	Alternate	0.300B	——	0.020	——	500
	500SS	L19V④	②	1–3–2–4	0.232B	35B	⑩	⑩	550
	650SS	L19V④	②	1–3–2–4	0.300B	38B	⑩	⑩	550
	800	L19V④	②	90° con.	——	23B	⑩	⑩	550–600
	1000SS	L19V④	②	60° con.	——	36½B	⑩	⑩	550–600
	1250SS	L19V④	②	60° con.	——	34B	⑩	⑩	550–600
	1000 Super BP	L19V④	②	60° con.	——	N.A.	⑩	⑩	N.A.
	1250 Super BP	L19V④	②	60° con.	——	N.A.	⑩	⑩	N.A.
1970–1971	400	V40FFM	②	Alternate	⑤	⑤	⑥	⑩	550–650
	500	V40FFM	②	1–3–2–4	0.237B	——	⑩	⑩	550
	650	V40FFM	②	90° con.	——	38B⑦	⑩	⑩	550–600
	800	V40FFM	②	90° con.	——	23B⑧	⑩	⑩	550–600
	1150, 1350	V40FFM	②	60° con.	——	23B⑨	⑩	⑩	550–600

① Alternate plug—L4J or M42FF
② Spark plug gap not adjustable
③ Alternate plug—M42FF
④ Alternate plug—V40FF
⑤ Primary throttle pick-up—5–7° BTDC
  Secondary throttle pick-up—27° BTDC
⑥ Thunderbolt ignition trigger gap—0.050–
  0.060 in.
⑦ Primary throttle pick-up—7–9° BTDC

⑧ Primary throttle pick-up—5–7° BTDC
⑨ Primary throttle pick-up—
  to serial no. 2928768—5–7° BTDC
  from serial no. 2928768—TDC–2° BTDC
⑩ Equipped with Thunderbolt breakerless ignition
  —— Not applicable
B—BTDC (Before top dead center)
con.—Consecutive

Carburetor Specifications

NOTE: *Because Mercury has used many carburetors over the years, it is necessary to positively identify the carburetor before attempting to use the specifications charts. The carburetor manufacturing number is the only positive identification, and is stamped on the front of the carburetor.*

1350, 1250SS, and 1250BP

Merc Model	1350	1350	1250SS–1	1250SS	1250SS	1250 BP	1250 BP
Carburetor mfg. no.	KD7A	KD7B	KD2A	KD1A	KD1B	KD1BR1	KD3A1
High speed system Nozzle ID	25	25	23	28	28	28	28

Carburetor Specifications (cont.)

Merc Model	1350	1350	1250SS–1	1250SS	1250SS	1250 BP	1250 BP
Carburetor mfg. no.	KD7A	KD7B	KD2A	KD1A	KD1B	KD1BR1	KD3A1
Nozzle cross holes	60(6)	60(6)	60(6)	60(4)	60(4)	60(4)	60(6)
Nozzle air bleed	0.065	0.065	0.065	0.065	0.065	0.065	0.0465
Fixed jet	0.0785	0.0785	0.076	0.082	0.082	0.080	0.074
Idle system—pick-up tube Bottom—ID or restriction	59	59	59				0.053
Top—ID or restriction				65	65	65	
Air bleed—body or tube	60	60	58	60	60	60	60
Idle adjustment Restriction—orifice	50	50	47	50	50	50	50
By-Pass holes 1st under welch plug	52	52	58(2)	58(2)	58(2)	58(2)	54
2nd under welch plug	58	62	53	54	54	54	58
3rd under welch plug							
Throttle bore—top					68		
Miscellaneous Inlet seat	3⁄32	0.094	3⁄32	3⁄32	3⁄32	3⁄32	3⁄32
Shutter valve—hole (cutoff) side			By-Pass	By-Pass	By-Pass	By-Pass	

1150, 1100, 1100SS, 1000, 1000SS, 1000BP, and 1000

Merc Model	1150	1150	1100 1100SS 1100SS–1 1000–2	1000SS–1	1000SS	1000BP	1000 1000–1
Carburetor mfg no.	KD6A	KD6B	KC7A	KC14A	KA10A	KC7B1	KC1A
High speed system Nozzle ID	25	25	22	22	22	22	28
Nozzle cross holes	60(6)	60(6)	55	55(4)	55(4)	55(4)	56
Nozzle air bleed	0.038	0.038	55	0.055	0.055	55	58
Fixed jet	0.066	0.066	0.065	0.059	0.059	0.059	0.069

Carburetor Specifications (cont.)

Merc Model	*1150*	*1150*	*1100* *1100SS* *1100SS–1* *1000–2*	*1000SS–1*	*1000SS*	*1000BP*	*1000* *1000–1*
Carburetor mfg no.	KD6A	KD6B	KC7A	KC14A	KA10A	KC7B1	KC1A
Idle system—pick-up tube Bottom—ID or restriction	63	63	0.065	0.053–0.056	0.053–0.056	0.065	52
Top—ID or restriction			50		60(2)	50	50
Air bleed—body or tube	60	60	70	62	62	70(2)	70
Idle adjustment Restriction—orifice	50	50	48	48	48	48	48
By-Pass holes 1st under welch plug	54	54	50	60(2)	53(2)	54(2)	55
2nd under welch plug	58	65	56	53	55	55	56
3rd under welch plug			55	55		56(2)	50
Throttle bore—top			68			68	68
Miscellaneous Inlet seat	3/32	0.094	42	3/32	3/32	3/32	42
Shutter valve—hole (cutoff) side				By-Pass	By-Pass	By-Pass	

950, 950SS, 800, 650, and 650SS

Merc Model	*950* *950SS* *950SS–1*	*800* *(4 Cyl)*	*650* *650–1*	*650–2* *650–3*	*650–4* *650SS*
Carburetor mfg no.	KC6A	KD4A	KC2A	KC5A	KC5B
High speed system Nozzle ID	22	25	26	22	22
Nozzle cross holes	55	60(6)	55	55	55(4)
Nozzle air bleed	0.053	0.065	58	0.057	0.057
Fixed jet	0.051	0.074	0.069	0.071	0.061
Idle system—pick-up tube Bottom—ID or restriction	0.065	63	52	0.065	0.065
Top—ID or restriction	50		50	50	50

Carburetor Specifications (cont.)

Merc Model	950 950SS 950SS–1	800 (4 Cyl)	650 650–1	650–2 650–3	650 4 650SS
Carburetor mfg no.	KC6A	KD4A	KC2A	KC5A	KC5B
Air bleed—body or tube	68	60	70	70	70(2)
Idle adjustment Restriction—orifice	48	50	48	48	48
By-Pass holes 1st under welch plug	47	58(2)	44	44	44
2nd under welch plug	56	52	$\frac{1}{16}$	$\frac{1}{16}$	$\frac{1}{16}$(2)
3rd under welch plug	55				
Throttle bore—top	68		68	68	
Miscellaneous Inlet seat	42	$\frac{3}{32}$	42	42	$\frac{3}{32}$
Shutter valve—hole (cutoff) side		By-Pass			Float

650 and 500

Merc Model	650–7	650–8	650	500–2 500–3	500–4	500–5	500–6 500SS
Carburetor mfg no.	KC5C	KA11A	KC15A	KA19A	KA21A	KA21B	KA21C
High speed system Nozzle ID	22	22	22	28	27	27	27
Nozzle cross holes	55(4)	55(4)	55(4)	60 54	60 54	56	56(2)
Nozzle air bleed	0.055	0.055	0.055	65	65	55	55
Fixed jet	0.061	0.061	0.061	0.059	0.057	0.061	0.065
Idle system—pick-up tube Bottom—ID or restriction	0.065	0.065	0.065	53	60	60	0.060
Top—ID or restriction	60(2)			50	50	50	
Air bleed—body or tube	60	60	60	65	70	70	60
Idle Adjustment Restriction—orifice	48	48	48(2)	50	50	50	50
Discharge holes—in tube			60				

Carburetor Specifications (cont.)

Merc Model	650-7	650-8	650	500-2 500-3	500-4	500-5	500-6 500SS
Carburetor mfg no.	KC5C	KA11A	KC15A	KA19A	KA21A	KA21B	KA21C
By-Pass holes 1st under welch plug	53(2)	60(2)	55	56	53	53	50(2)
2nd under welch plug	55	53(2)	53	56	56	1.15mm	1.15mm(2)
3rd under welch plug		55		50	46	46	51
Throttle bore—top				60	60		
Miscellaneous Inlet seat	3/32	3/32	3/32	42	42	42	3/32
Shutter valve—hole (cutoff) side	By-Pass	By-Pass					By-Pass

500, 400, and 350

Merc Model	500-7	500-9 500-8	400	350 350-1 (2 Cyl)	350-2	350-3	350-3	350-4 350-5	350-6
Carburetor mfg no.	KA21D	KA24A	KD5A	KC4A	KC8A	KC9A	KC9B	KC9C	KC13A
High speed system Nozzle ID	27	27	25	24	22	22	22	22	22
Nozzle cross holes	56(2)	56(2)	60(6)	55	55	55(4)	55(4)	55(4)	55(4)
Nozzle air bleed	0.052	0.052	0.065	58	58	58	58	54	54
Fixed jet	0.063	0.063	0.065	0.069	0.069	0.067	0.069	0.063	0.061
Idle system—pick-up tube Bottom—ID or restriction	60	0.060	0.0785	52	50	0.065	0.065	0.065	0.065
Top—ID or restriction			59	50	50	50	50	50	50
Air bleed—body or tube	58	58	60	70	70	70(2)	68(2)	68(2)	68(2)
Idle adjustment Restriction—orifice	50	50	50	48	48	48	48	48	48
By-Pass holes 1st under welch plug	50(2)	50(2)	52	50	50	47	47	52	52
2nd under welch plug	1.15mm	1.15mm(2)	58	1/16	1/16	1/16(2)	1/16(2)	54	54
3rd under welch plug	51	51			60	60	60		

Carburetor Specifications (cont.)

Merc Model	500–7	500–9 500–8	400	350 350–1 (2 Cyl)	350–2	350–3	350–3	350–4 350–5	350–6
Carburetor mfg no.	KA21D	KA24A	KD5A	KC4A	KC8A	KC9A	KC9B	KC9C	KC13A
Throttle bore—top				65	65	65	65		
Miscellaneous Inlet seat	³⁄₃₂	³⁄₃₂	³⁄₃₂	42	42	³⁄₃₂	³⁄₃₂	³⁄₃₂	³⁄₃₂
Shutter valve—hole (cutoff) side	By-Pass	By-Pass					Float		Bottom	Bottom

Jet Changes for Elevation

	Jet Sizes for Elevations		
Engine Model	Up to 4000 ft	4000– 7000 ft	7000– 10000 ft
Merc 1350	0.078 in.	0.076 in.	0.074 in.
Merc 1250SS	0.082 in.	0.080 in.	0.0785 in.
Merc 1150	0.066 in.	0.064 in.	0.062 in.
Merc 1100SS–1100	0.065 in.	0.063 in.	0.061 in.
Merc 1000SS (1968)	0.059 in.	0.057 in.	0.055 in.
Merc 950	0.051 in.	0.049 in.	0.047 in.
Merc 950SS–900	0.049 in.	0.047 in.	0.045 in.
Merc 800 (4 Cyl)	0.074 in.	0.072 in.	0.070 in.
Merc 650	0.061 in.	0.059 in.	0.057 in.
Merc 500 (1966–68)①	0.063 in.	0.061 in.	0.059 in.
Merc 500 (1967)	0.065 in.	0.063 in.	0.061 in.
Merc 500 (1966)②	0.057 in.	0.055 in.	0.053 in.
Merc 400 (2 Cyl)	0.078 in.	0.076 in.	0.074 in.
Merc 350–200 (1967–68)	0.063 in.	0.061 in.	0.059 in.
Merc 350 (2 Cyl)	0.069 in.	0.067 in.	0.065 in.

NOTE: *Jet sizes are intended as a guide. Try a size smaller or larger if in doubt.*
No change in spark advance is recommended for elevation. Propellers of lower pitch should be used at high elevation to allow proper engine rpm.
① Serial no. 2010163 and up
② Serial no. 2010162 and down

Reed Stop Openings

Model	Reed Stop Opening (in.)
350	0.191
350 (1967–68)	0.156
400	0.162
500	0.156
650	0.191
800 (4 cyl)	0.162
950, 950SS	0.156
1000SS (1968), 1100, 1100SS	0.191
1150	0.075
1250SS, 1350	0.162

Cylinder Block Finish Hone Diameter

Model	Cylinder Block Finish Hone Diameter (in.)
1350, 1250, 1250BP, 1150	2.875
1000 Super BP (1969)	2.875
1000 (1968–69), 1000BP (1968)	2.875
1100, 650 (1967)	2.938
1000, 950	2.875
950 (1967)	2.875
800 (1969–71)	2.875
650 (1968–71)	2.938
650	2.875
500 (1968–71)	2.565
400	2.875
350 (1966–69)	3.000

Torque Specifications (2 and 4 Cyl Models)

Model	650	500–450–400 350–300	400 (1970–71)
Part			
Connecting rod nuts	180 in. lbs	180 in. lbs	180 in. lbs
Flywheel-to-crankshaft	65 ft lbs	65 ft lbs	65 ft lbs
Water pump (plastic)	①	①	①
Spark plugs	20 ft lbs	20 ft lbs	20 ft lbs
Centermain bearing lockscrew *	150 in. lbs	②	——
Centermain bearing reed stop-screw	35–40 in. lbs	35–40 in. lbs	20–25 in. lbs
Exhaust outer cover	150 in. lbs	150 in. lbs	250 in. lbs
Cylinder block cover	70 in. lbs	70 in. lbs	70 in. lbs
Crankcase-to-cylinder block	150 in. lbs	150 in. lbs	200–220 in. lbs
Gear housing-to-driveshaft housing	200 in. lbs	200 in. lbs	——
Starter motor-to-crankcase	125 in. lbs	85 in. lbs	——
Powerhead-to-driveshaft housing	30 ft lbs	18 ft lbs	18 ft lbs
Bottom bearing retriever	——	——	100 in. lbs
Upper and lower end cap nuts	150 in. lbs	150 in. lbs	150 in. lbs
Distributor shaft nut	65–75 in. lbs	——	65–75 in. lbs

—— Does not apply

* Merc 650 (1970 and newer)

① ¼–28 (nut thread)—24–30 in. lbs
  ⁵⁄₁₆–24 (nut thread)—35–40 in. lbs
  ¼–20 (bolt thread)—15–20 in. lbs

② ⅜–16 thread—120 in. lbs
  ⅜–24 thread—150 in. lbs

NOTE: *Due to the extensive use of aluminum and white metal, to resist corrosion, torque specifications must be adhered to strictly.*

Torque Specifications (6 Cyl Models)

Model	1350–1150	1250–800 1000 (1968–69)	1250BP Super BP	1100–1000	1000BP	950 (90 cu in.)	800
Part							
Connecting rod nuts	180 in. lbs	180 in. lbs	180 in. lbs	180 in. lbs	180 in. lbs	180 in. lbs	180 in. lbs
Flywheel-to-crankshaft	100 ft lbs	100 ft lbs	100 ft lbs	85 ft lbs	85 ft lbs	85 ft lbs	85 ft lbs
Water pump (plastic)	①	①	——	①	——	——	——
Spark plugs	20 ft lbs	20 ft lbs	20 ft lbs	20 ft lbs	20 ft lbs	20 ft lbs	20 ft lbs
Centermain bearing lockscrew	——	150 in. lbs	150 in. lbs	150 in. lbs	150 in. lbs	②	②
Centermain bearing reed stop-screw	20–25 in. lbs	35–40 in. lbs	——	35–40 in. lbs	——	35–40 in. lbs	35–40 in. lbs
Exhaust outer cover	250 in. lbs	150 in. lbs	150 in. lbs	150 in. lbs	150 in. lbs	150 in. lbs	250 in. lbs
Cylinder block cover	70 in. lbs	70 in. lbs	70 in. lbs	70 in. lbs	70 in. lbs	70 in. lbs	70 in. lbs
Crankcase-to-cylinder block	220 in. lbs	150 in. lbs	150 in. lbs	150 in. lbs	150 in. lbs	150 in. lbs	150 in. lbs
Gear housing-to-drive-shaft housing	200 in. lbs	200 in. lbs	200 in. lbs	200 in. lbs	200 in. lbs	200 in. lbs	200 in. lbs
Starter motor-to-crankcase	125 in. lbs	125 in. lbs	125 in. lbs	125 in. lbs	125 in. lbs	125 in. lbs	85 in. lbs
Powerhead-to-driveshaft housing	30 ft lbs	30 ft lbs	30 ft lbs	30 ft lbs	30 ft lbs	30 ft lbs	30 ft lbs
Upper and lower end cap nuts	150 in. lbs	150 in. lbs	150 in. lbs	150 in. lbs	150 in. lbs	150 in. lbs	150 in. lbs
Distributor shaft nut	65–75 in. lbs	65–75 in. lbs	65–75 in. lbs	——	——	——	65–75 in. lbs
Inner exhaust water jacket cover	150 in. lbs	150 in. lbs	150 in. lbs	150 in. lbs	150 in. lbs	150 in. lbs	150 in. lbs

① ¼–28 (nut thread)—25–30 in. lbs ② ⅜–16 thread—120 in. lbs
5⁄16–24 (nut thread)—35–40 in. lbs ⅜–24 thread—150 in. lbs
¼–20 (bolt thread)—15–20 in. lbs
NOTE: *Due to the extensive use of aluminum and white metal, to resist corrosion, torque specifications must be adhered to strictly.*

Tightening Sequences

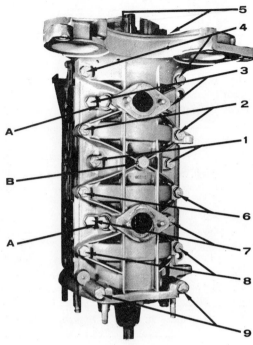

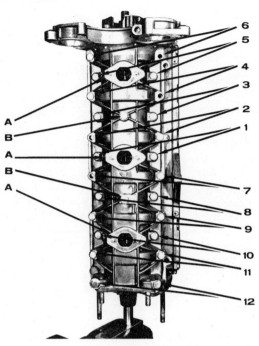

4-cylinder crankcase—torque lettered bolts first, then numbered bolts (© Kiekhaefer Mercury)

6-cylinder crankcase—torque lettered bolts first, then numbered bolts (© Kiekhaefer Mercury)

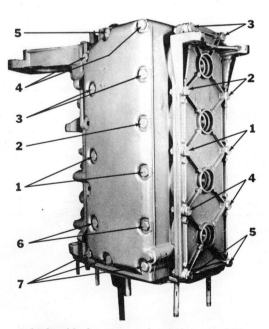

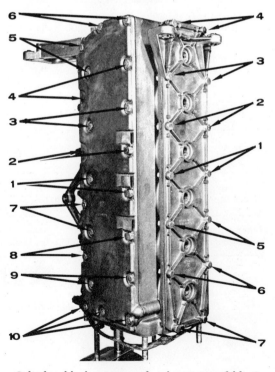

Cylinder block cover and exhaust manifold—4-cylinder models (© Kiekhaefer Mercury)

Cylinder block cover and exhaust manifold—6-cylinder models (© Kiekhaefer Mercury)

NOTE: *For two-cylinder engine torque sequence, start with the center bolts and work to the top; then, from the center to the bottom. This will prevent distortion and leakage.*

Wiring Diagrams

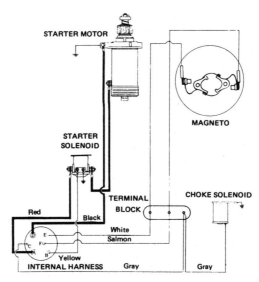

Mercury 350 (2-cylinder) (© Kiekhaefer Mercury)

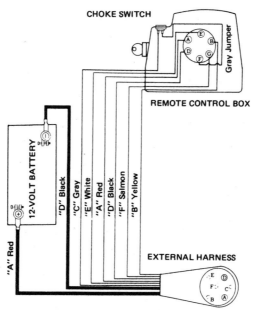

Mercury 350 (2-cylinder) harness (© Kiekhaefer Mercury)

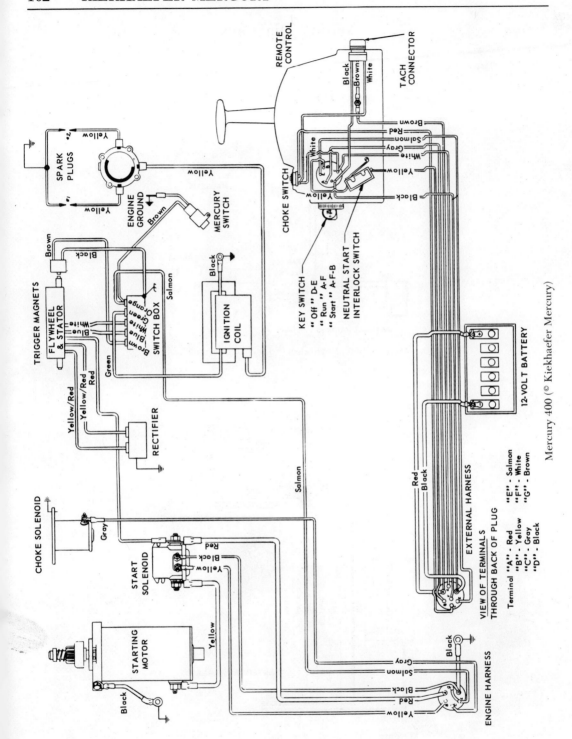

Mercury 400 (© Kiekhaefer Mercury)

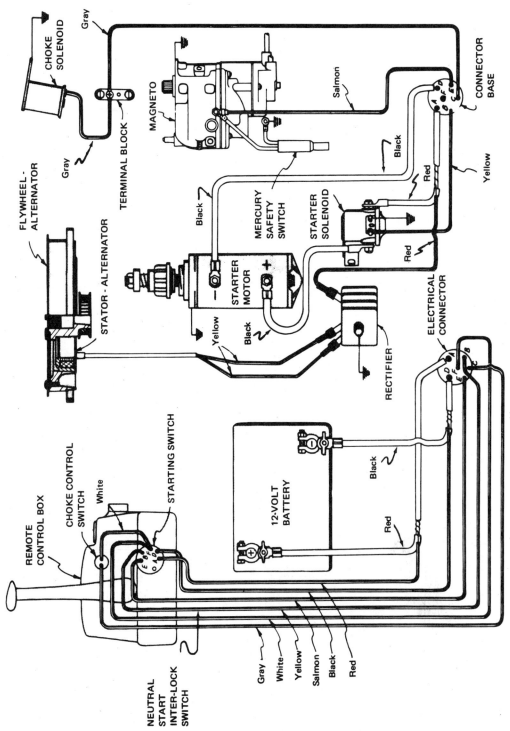

Mercury 4-cylinder with Kiekhaefer Mercury magneto (© Kiekhaefer Mercury)

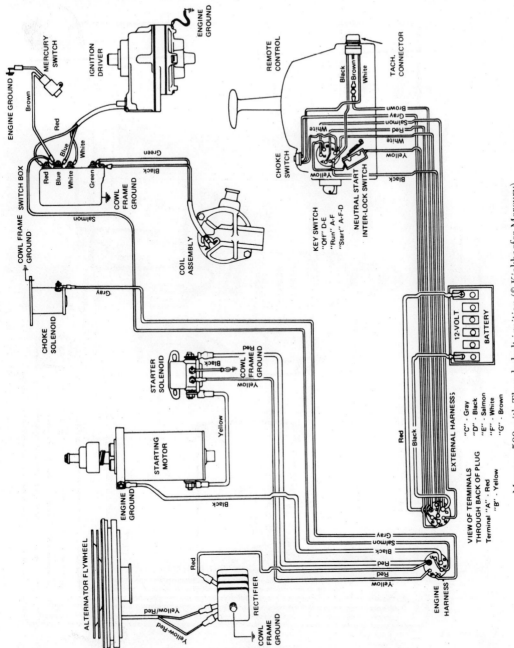

Mercury 500 with Thunderbolt ignition (© Kiekhaefer Mercury)

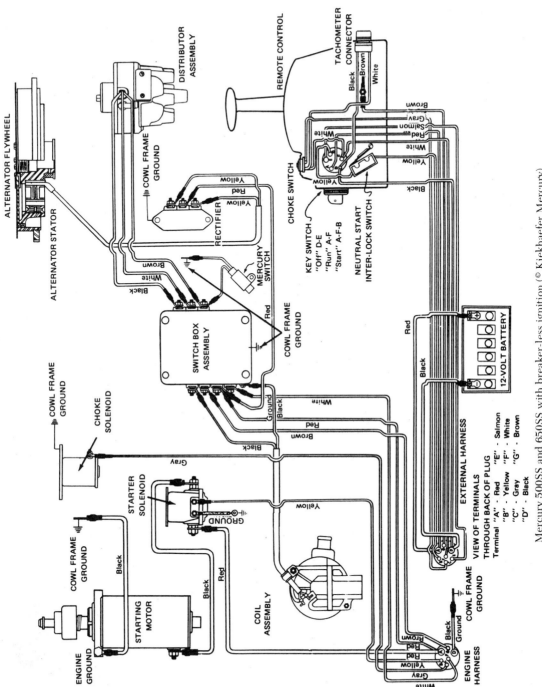

Mercury 500SS and 650SS with breaker-less ignition (© Kiekhaefer Mercury)

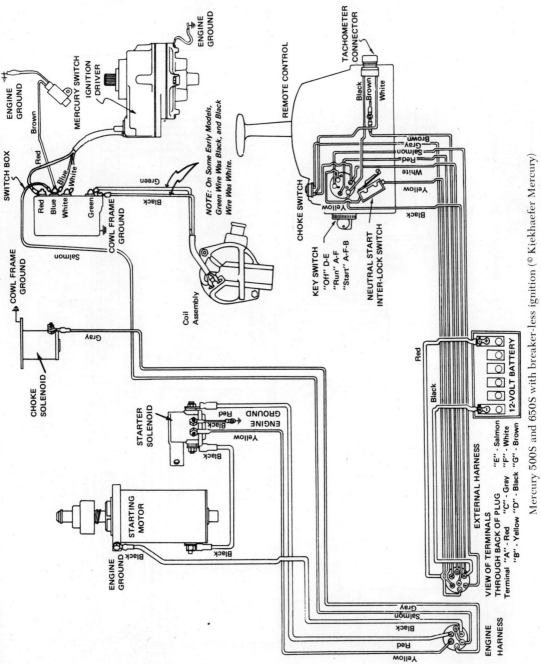

NOTE: On Some Early Models, Green Wire Was Black, and Black Wire Was White.

VIEW OF TERMINALS
THROUGH BACK OF PLUG
Terminal "A" - Red   "C" - Gray   "E" - Salmon
"B" - Yellow   "D" - Black   "F" - White
"G" - Brown

Mercury 500S and 650S with breaker-less ignition (© Kiekhaefer Mercury)

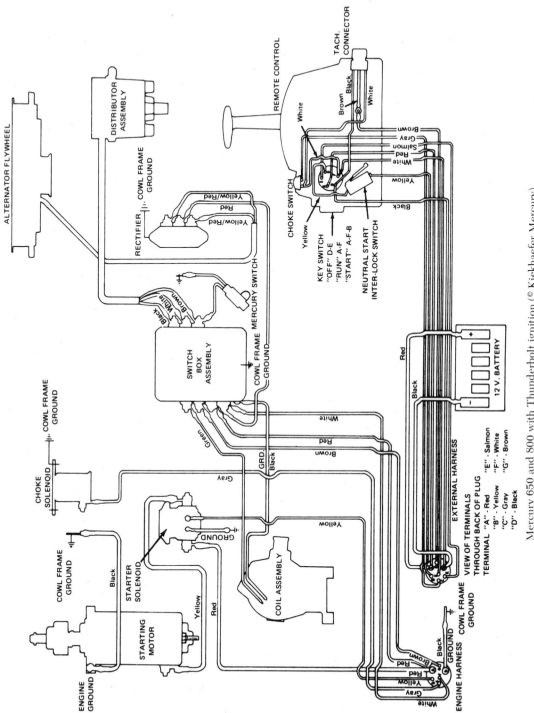

Mercury 650 and 800 with Thunderbolt ignition (© Kiekhaefer Mercury)

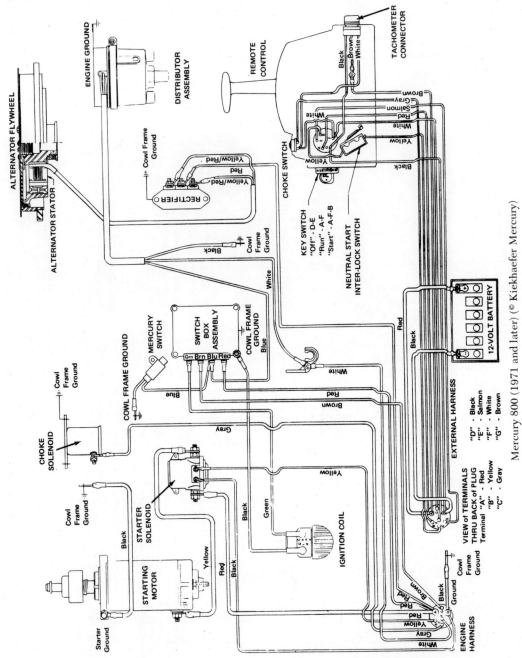

Mercury 800 (1971 and later) (© Kiekhaefer Mercury)

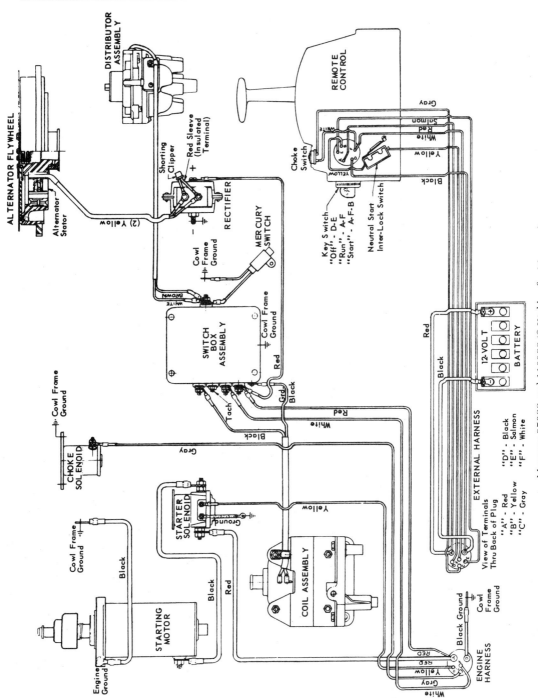

ALTERNATOR FLYWHEEL

DISTRIBUTOR ASSEMBLY

REMOTE CONTROL

Alternator Stator

Shorting Clipper

Red Sleeve (Insulated Terminal)

(2) Yellow

RECTIFIER

Cowl Frame Ground

MERCURY SWITCH

Choke Switch

Key Switch
"Off" - D-E
"Run" - A-F
"Start" - A-F-B

Neutral Start Inter-Lock Switch

Gray

White
Red
Salmon

Yellow

Black

SWITCH BOX ASSEMBLY

Cowl Frame Ground

Red

Grd.

Black

Red

Black

White

Red

Black

12 VOLT
BATTERY

Cowl Frame Ground

CHOKE SOLENOID

Gray

Tach

EXTERNAL HARNESS

"A" - Red
"B" - Yellow
"C" - Gray

"D" - Black
"E" - Salmon
"F" - White

View of Terminals
Thru Back of Plug

STARTER SOLENOID

Ground

Yellow

Cowl Frame Ground

Black

Red

COIL ASSEMBLY

STARTING MOTOR

Black

Engine Ground

Black Ground

Cowl Frame Ground

RED
Yellow
Gray
White

ENGINE HARNESS

Mercury 950SS and 1100SS (© Kiekhaefer Mercury)

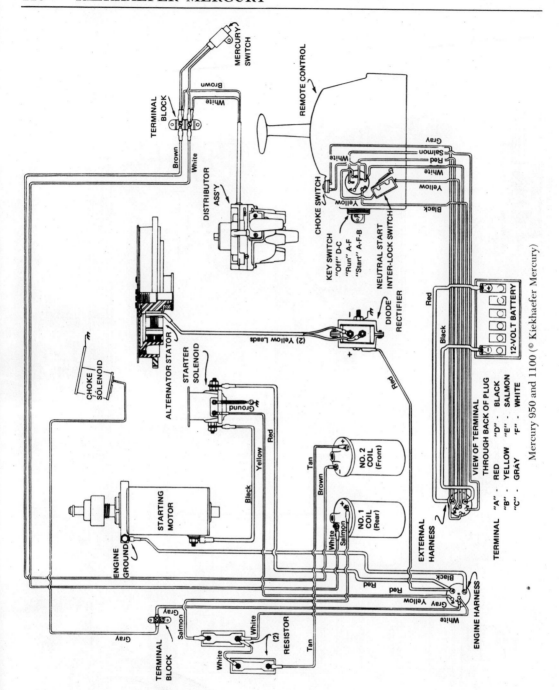

MERCURY SWITCH

REMOTE CONTROL

TERMINAL BLOCK

Brown

White

Brown

White

DISTRIBUTOR ASS'Y

CHOKE SWITCH

KEY SWITCH
"Off" D-C
"Run" A-F
"Start" A-F-B

NEUTRAL START
INTER-LOCK SWITCH

Gray
Salmon
Red
White
Yellow
Black

CHOKE SOLENOID

ALTERNATOR STATOR

STARTER SOLENOID

Ground

(2) Yellow Leads

DIODE RECTIFIER

Red

Red

12-VOLT BATTERY

STARTING MOTOR

Black

Yellow

Red

Tan

Brown

NO. 2 COIL (Front)

NO. 1 COIL (Rear)

White
Salmon

ENGINE GROUND

Gray

Yellow

White

Red

Red

Black

EXTERNAL HARNESS

ENGINE HARNESS

VIEW OF TERMINAL
THROUGH BACK OF PLUG

Red

Black

TERMINAL BLOCK

Gray

Salmon

White

White

RESISTOR (2)

Tan

TERMINAL "A" - RED   "D" - BLACK
"B" - YELLOW   "E" - SALMON
"C" - GRAY   "F" - WHITE

Mercury 950 and 1100 (© Kiekhaefer Mercury)

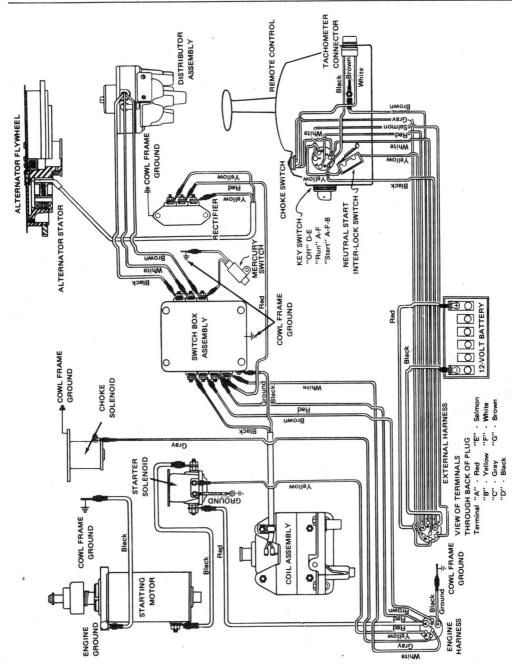

Mercury 950, 1000, 1100 and 1250 with breaker-less ignition (© Kiekhaefer Mercury)

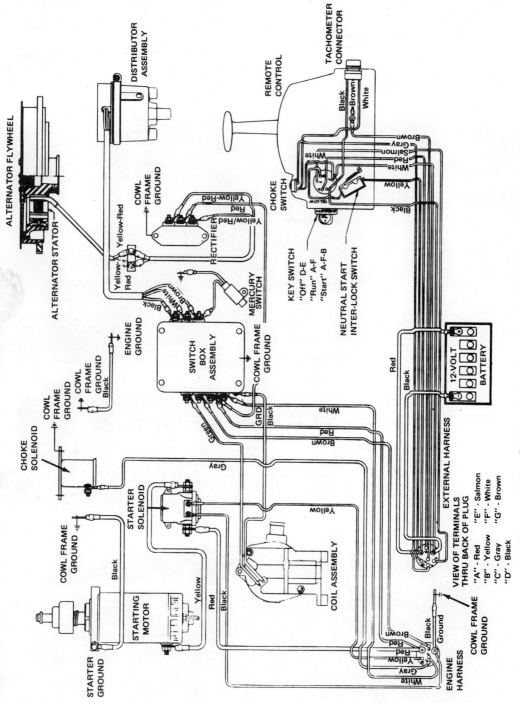

Mercury 1150 and 1350 with Thunderbolt ignition (© Kiekhaefer Mercury)

General Care and Maintenance

FLUSHING THE MOTOR

Motors which are operated primarily in salt water should be flushed periodically to remove deposits of salt which build up in the passages and inhibit cooling. Ideally, motors should be flushed after every use; however this is nearly impossible with today's larger motors. Flushing the motor thoroughly at least two or three times a season should be adequate for motors in normal use. One of the following flushing kits should be used.

Engine Model	Mercury Kit Part No.
200 from ser no. 2432536 All 1969 and newer 4 and 6 cylinder models	C–48755A–1
All 2, 4, and 6 cylinder except those listed above and prior to 1966	C–24789A–1

1. Remove the plug marked FLUSH and the washer from the flushing intake.

2. Connect the flushing attachment and couple a garden hose to the attachment.

3. Turn on the water but *do not operate* the motor. Water pressure from the tap is sufficient to flush the motor, and does not need to be at maximum pressure.

CAUTION: *If the motor must be operated while flushing, to prevent damage to the impeller, it is imperative that a "Flush-Test" device is used which attaches directly over the intake holes in the gear housing strut. Do not operate the motor above idle speed while flushing or engine rpm will be uncontrollable. When flushing, it is advisable to remove the propeller as a precautionary measure.*

4. During and after flushing, keep the motor in an upright position, resting on the skeg, until all water has drained from the driveshaft housing.

PREVENTIVE MAINTENANCE AND PERIODIC SERVICE

25 Hour Service

The following service should be completed approximately every 25 hours.

1. Remove the engine cover and clean all accessible parts thoroughly.

2. Lubricate the lower unit as detailed in the following section.

Ride-Guide lube fitting (© Kiekhaefer Mercury)

3. Lubricate the "Ride-Guide" steering tube.

Throttle shaft and upper shift shaft lubrication (© Kiekhaefer Mercury)

4. Lubricate the throttle linkage and the upper shift shaft.

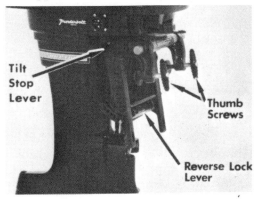

Reverse lock lever and swivel bracket lubrication (© Kiekhaefer Mercury)

5. Lubricate the reverse lock lever and the swivel bracket.

6. Lubricate the distributor adaptor fittings and control handle (if equipped).

Lubrication of distributor adaptor fittings (© Kiekhaefer Mercury)

Lower drive unit lubrication (© Kiekhaefer Mercury)

7. Remove and inspect the propeller. Trim nicks with a file but do not remove more metal than is necessary. Lubricate the propeller shaft with graphite grease or Quicksilver Anti-Corrosion Grease. Install the propeller.

8. Service the spark plugs. See the tune-up section in the front of this book.

9. Inspect the spark plug leads for deterioration, particularly where insulation contacts metal.

10. Inspect the fuel lines (including tank) for deterioration.

11. Inspect the entire surface for corroded areas. Corroded areas may be cleaned thoroughly and repainted with matching paint.

12. Check the entire motor for loose parts, tightening where necessary.

13. Service the fuel filter on the remote tank after every 100 hours (or at least once a season) or whenever performance conditions warrant.

14. Check to be sure that all control fittings are securely attached and properly adjusted.

15. Other than models with Thunderbolt ignition, the breaker points should not be disturbed as long as the engine is operating satisfactorily. If the points are cleaned and adjusted at the mid-season check, they should not normally require service for at least another 100 hours.

16. Check the condition of the starter cable and replace it if cracked or broken.

17. Replace the engine hood.

Lower Unit Lubrication

NOTE: *Use only Quicksilver Super-Duty Gear Lubricant in the lower unit; regular automotive grease is not acceptable. In an absolute emergency, extreme-pressure marine gear lubricant may be used.*

1. Remove the lubricant filler plug which is located on the right side of the gear housing, just above the skeg.

2. Remove the air vent screw which is located just above the cavitation plate.

CAUTION: *Never apply lubricant to the lower unit without first removing the air vent screw. The injected lubricant will displace air which must escape so that the lower unit will be entirely filled.*

3. Inject lubricant through the filler plug hole until the lubricant begins to flow from the air vent hole. This indicates that the housing is filled.

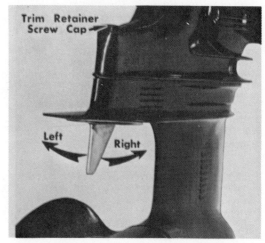

Trim tab adjustment (© Kiekhaefer Mercury)

4. Replace the air vent screw first, then the grease plug, making sure that the washer is located under each, to prevent the entry of water into the gear housing.

Gear Housing Capacities

Model	Capacity (fl oz)
1350, 1250, 1150, 1100, 1000, 950, 800, 650	17
500, 400, 350	9

Trim Tab

The trim tab is an anodic tab and is self-sacrificing to help combat galvanic corrosion on Mercury 200, and larger, models. Periodically inspect the trim tab for corrosion. If the trim tab is being eaten away, it should be replaced.

NOTE: *Do not paint or coat the trim tab or its inhibiting value will be lost.*

REMOVAL AND REPLACEMENT

1. Before removing the trim tab, mark the location of the trailing edge on the cavitation plate.
2. Remove the plug which is located directly above the trim tab.
3. Through the hole in the drive housing, loosen the screw which holds the trim tab.
4. Remove the trim tab and clean the recessed area to assure good metal contact between the drive housing and the trim tab.
5. Install the trim tab by reversing the removal procedure.
6. Test the boat and motor, and adjust the trim tab if necessary.

ADJUSTMENT

1. Operate the boat at the best throttle setting.
2. Adjust the tilt pin setting or trim the boat with "Power-Trim."
3. Turn the steering wheel to the left and right, noting which direction is the easier. With the boat at rest, remove the plug in the driveshaft housing and loosen the trim tab retaining screw.
4. If the steering wheel turns more easily to the right, position the trailing edge of the trim tab to the right, and vice versa.

Tighten the retaining screw and replace the plug.
5. Operate the boat to check the setting. Readjust the trim tab if necessary.

NOTE: *Steering torque may increase even though the trim tab has been adjusted properly. The trim tab will be most effective at the boat speed and trim setting for which it was adjusted.*

WINTERIZING

Because outboard motors are so susceptible to corrosion, care must be taken to properly store the motor when not in use. The motor should always be stored upright in a clean, cool, dry place. The following procedure is recommended by the manufacturer for winterizing.

1. Operate the motor on the boat or in a test tank. Disconnect the fuel line and allow the engine to run at idle.
2. Inject approximately 4 oz of Quicksilver Storage Seal into each carburetor and allow the engine to stall out. This indicates that the carburetors have run dry.
3. Drain the fuel tank and fuel lines.
4. Remove the engine hood.

Fuel Tank Filter

1. Remove the fuel line from the fuel tank and remove the fuel pick-up tube by removing the screws in the top connector housing.
2. The fine mesh, wire filter can be cleaned by rinsing in clean benzine.

Motor Fuel Filter

1. Remove the front bracket by removing the screws which hold it to the front of the bottom cowling.
2. Remove the srew from the top of the filter covers on the carburetors.
3. Remove the fuel filter covers.
4. Inspect the fuel filters, lines, and fittings for signs of wear or leakage.
5. Drain and clean the filters.
6. Replace the filter covers and tighten the screws.
7. Replace the front bracket and cowlings.

Powerhead

1. Lubricate the lower unit (see "25 Hour Service").
2. Lubricate the control linkage (see "25 Hour Service").

3. Lubricate the distributor adaptor (see "25 Hour Service").

4. Thoroughly clean the motor and spray with "Corrosion and Rust Preventive."

5. Install the cowling and apply a thin film of clean, fresh engine oil to all painted surfaces.

6. Remove the propeller and apply Anti-Corrosion Grease or waterproof-type grease to the propeller shaft and install the propeller.

7. Lubricate the swivel bracket (see "25 Hour Service").

Battery Storage

1. Remove the battery from its installation as soon as possible. Remove all grease and sulphate from the top surface. A diluted ammonia or soda solution will neutralize any acid present, and may be flushed away with clean water. Care must be taken to keep the vent plugs tight so that neutralizing solution does not enter the cells.

2. Cover the plates with distilled water, but not over $3/16$ in. above the perforated baffles.

3. Lubricate the terminals with a light cup of cup grease or petroleum jelly.

4. With the battery at full charge (specific gravity 1.260–1.275), store in a dry place where the temperature will not fall below freezing.

5. Remove the battery from storage every 45 days. Check the water level and

charge the battery for 5–6 hours at 6 amps. Do not fast-charge.

6. When ready to return the battery to service, remove excess grease from the terminals (leaving a film on), charge as necessary, and reinstall.

Motor Storage

When storing outboard motors for the winter, be sure that all water drain holes in the gear housing are free and open and that the flushing plug is removed so that all water will drain out. Trapped water may freeze and expand and may crack the gear housing or water pump housing. Be sure that the lower unit is full of grease to protect against water leakage into the gear housing, caused by a loose air vent plug or loose filler plug. Be sure to replace gaskets under the screws and flush plug, renewing any damaged gaskets.

Propeller Selection

The following charts contain almost all propellers available from Mercury for the models contained in this book. Before attempting to use these charts to select a different propeller, it is absolutely imperative that the information in the first chapter under "Boat Performance and Propeller Selection" be read and followed.

Right-Hand Rotation (Facing Bow)

Motor Model	Clockwise RH Rotation	Dia (in.)	Pitch (in.)	No. Bl	Material	① Approx Gross Load (lbs)	Approx Boat Length (ft)	Std Length (in.)	Long Shaft (in.)	Speed Range (mph)
	A-48-32180A1	11	13	2	Bronze	Up to 800	12–14			30–37
Merc 350	A-48-32182A1	11	13	2	Alum.	Up to 800	12–14			30–37
	C-48-38090A1	10¾	13	3	Alum.	Up to 800	12–14	All	All	30–37
2 Cylinder	A-48-32184A1	11	12	2	Bronze	700–1200	13–15			24–31
	A-48-32186A1	11	12	2	Alum.	700–1200	13–15			24–31
	C-48-38094A1	10¾	12	3	Alum.	700–1200	13–15			24–31
	A-48-32188A1	11	11	2	Bronze	1000–1600	15–17			19–25
	A-48-32190A1	11	11	2	Alum.	1000–1600	15–17			19–25
	C-48-38098A1	10¾	11	3	Alum.	1000–1600	15–17			19–25
	A-48-33772A1	10¾	10	3	Bronze	1000–1800	17–19			16–23
	C-48-33774A1	10¾	10	3	Alum.	1000–1800	17–19			16–23
Full Throttle	A-48-32192A1	10¾	9	3	Bronze	1600–2000	18–22	16½	21½	11–19
rpm Range:	C-48-32194A1	10¾	9	3	Alum.	1600–2000	18–22			11–19
4800–5300	C-48-37314A1	11	8	3	Alum.	Aux. Power or Work Boat				1–12
Merc 400	A-48-56250A1	10¾	17	2	Bronze	Up to 750	11–13			36–44
2 Cylinder	A-48-56230A1	10¾	17	2	Alum.	Up to 750	11–13			36–44
	A-48-56252A1	10¾	15	2	Bronze	Up to 800	12–14			32–40

Right-Hand Rotation (Facing Bow) (cont.)

Motor Model	Clockwise RH Rotation	Dia (in.)	Pitch (in.)	No. Bl	Material	① Approx Gross Load (lbs)	Approx Boat Length (ft)	Std Length (in.)	Long Shaft (in.)	Speed Range (mph)
Merc 400	A–48–56232A1	10¾	15	3	Alum.	Up to 800	12–14	All	All	32–40
2 Cylinder	A–48–56254A1	11	13	2	Bronze	700–1200	13–15			29–36
	A–48–56234A1	11	13	2	Alum.	700–1200	13–15			29–36
	A–48–56236A1	10¾	13	3	Alum.	700–1200	13–15			29–36
	A–48–56256A1	11	12	2	Bronze	1000–1600	15–17			26–32
	A–48–56238A1	11	12	2	Alum.	1000–1600	15–17			26–32
	A–48–56240A1	10¾	12	3	Alum.	1000–1600	15–17			26–32
	A–48–56258A1	11	11	2	Bronze	1000–1800	15–19			22–28
	A–48–56242A1	11	11	2	Alum.	1000–1800	15–19			22–28
	A–48–56244A1	10¾	11	3	Alum.	1000–1800	15–19			22–28
Full Throttle	A–48–56260A1	10¾	10	3	Bronze	1600–2000	18–22	16½	20	15–22
rpm Range:	A–48–56246A1	10¾	10	3	Alum.	1600–2000	18–22			15–22
4800–5300	A–48–56262A1	10¾	9	3	Bronze	Aux. Power or Work Boat				To 16
	A–48–56248A1	10¾	9	3	Alum.	Aux. Power or Work Boat				To 16
Merc 500	A–48–56228A1	10¾	19	3	Alum.	Up to 850	12–14			38–45
(1970–71)	A–48–56250A1	10¾	17	2	Bronze	Up to 950	12–15			33–40
	A–48–56230A1	10¾	17	3	Alum.	Up to 950	12–15			33–40
	A–48–56252A1	10¾	15	2	Bronze	700–1200	14–16			28–35
	A–48–56232A1	10¾	15	3	Alum.	700–1200	14–16			28–35
	A–48–56254A1	11	13	2	Bronze	800–1300	13–15			26–30
	A–48–56234A1	11	13	2	Alum.	800–1300	13–15			26–30
	A–48–56236A1	10¾	13	3	Alum.	800–1300	13–15	All	All	26–30
	A–48–56256A1	11	12	2	Bronze	1000–1700	13–17			23–28
	A–48–56238A1	11	12	2	Alum.	1000–1700	13–17			23–28
	A–48–56240A1	10¾	12	3	Alum.	1000–1700	13–17			23–28
	A–48–56258A1	11	11	2	Bronze	1100–2000	14–18	15½	20	20–25
	A–48–56242A1	11	11	2	Alum.	1100–2000	14–18			20–25
	A–48–56244A1	10¾	11	3	Alum.	1100–2000	14–18			20–25
	A–48–56260A1	10¾	10	3	Bronze	1600–2200	16–20			18–23
Full Throttle	A–48–56246A1	10¾	10	3	Alum.	1600–2200	16–20			18–23
rpm Range:	A–48–56262A1	10¾	9	3	Bronze	Aux. Power or Work Boat				0–18
4800–5500	A–48–56248A1	10¾	9	3	Alum.	Aux. Power or Work Boat				0–18
Merc 500SS	A–48–32176A1	10¾	17	2	Bronze	Up to 850	12–14			45–52
500S	C–48–38086A1	10¾	15	3	Alum.	Up to 950	12–15			40–44
500	A–48–32178A1	10¾	15	2	Bronze	Up to 950	12–15			40–44
(Jet Prop)	C–48–38090A1	10¾	13	3	Alum.	700–1300	14–16	All	All	34–38
	A–48–32180A1	11	13	2	Bronze	700–1300	14–16			34–38
	A–48–32182A1	11	13	2	Alum.	700–1300	14–16			34–38
Full Throttle	C–48–38094A1	10¾	12	3	Alum.	950–1500	15–17			30–35
rpm Range:	A–48–32184A1	11	12	2	Bronze	950–1500	15–17			30–35
5200–5600	A–48–32186A1	11	12	2	Alum.	950–1500	15–17			30–35
	C–48–38098A1	10¾	11	3	Alum.	1000–1800	16½–19			26–30
Full Throttle	A–48–32188A1	11	11	2	Bronze	1000–1800	16½–19			26–30
rpm Range:	A–48–32190A1	11	11	2	Alum.	1000–1800	16½–19			26–30
500SS	A–48–33772A1	10¾	10	3	Bronze	1600–2200	18–22			18–28
(1968–69)	C–48–33774A1	10¾	10	3	Alum.	1600–2200	18–22	16½	21½	18–28
5200–5500	A–48–32192A1	10¾	9	3	Bronze	2000 Plus	22 Plus			8–20
	C–48–32194A1	10¾	9	3	Alum.	2000 Plus	22 Plus			8–20
	C–48–37314A1	11	8	3	Alum.	Aux. Power or Work Boat				1–10
Merc 650SS	C–48–31450A3	13¾	23	2	Bronze	Up to 1000	Up to 16			48–56
650	A–48–29654A2	12¼	21	2	Bronze	Up to 1000	Up to 16			43–51
Full Throttle	A–48–29656A2	12½	19	2	Bronze	900–1300	Up to 17			38–46
rpm Range:	A–48–29658A2	13	17	2	Bronze	1000–1800	15–17	All	All	33–40
4800–5300	A–48–31072A2	13	17	2	Alum.	1000–1800	15–17			33–40
	A–48–37902A2	12	17	3	Alum.	1000–1800	15–17			33–40
Full Throttle	A–48–29660A2	13	15	2	Bronze	1200–2000	15–18			27–34
rpm Range:	A–48–31074A2	13	15	2	Alum.	1200–2000	15–18			27–34
650, 650S	A–48–37900A2	12½	15	3	Alum.	1200–2000	15–18			27–34
(1966–67)	A–48–29662A2	13½	13	2	Bronze	1800–2600	18–22			23–29
4800–5200	A–48–31076A2	13½	13	2	Alum.	1800–2600	18–22			23–29
	A–48–37898A2	13	13	3	Alum.	1800–2600	18–22			23–29
	C–48–30396A3	14	11	3	Bronze	2200–3500	21–24			19–26

Right-Hand Rotation (Facing Bow) (cont.)

Motor Model	Clockwise RH Rotation	Dia (in.)	Pitch (in.)	No. Bl	Material	① Approx Gross Load (lbs)	Approx Boat Length (ft)	Std Length (in.)	Long Shaft (in.)	Speed Range (mph)
Merc 650SS	C–48–35936A3	14	11	3	Alum.	2200–3500	21–24	15½	20	19–26
650 (cont.)	C–48–30398A3	14	9½	3	Bronze	3300 Plus	Houseboat			9–20
	C–48–33242A3	14	9½	3	Alum.	3300 Plus	Houseboat			9–20
	C–48–30400A3	14	8½	3	Bronze	7000 Plus	Work Boat			1–10
Merc 650	A–48–49614A4②	13	24	2	Bronze	Up to 1000	Up to 15			43–50
(1970–71)	C–48–31450A3	13¾	23	2	Bronze	Up to 1000	Up to 16			39–45
	C–48–32386A3	13¾	23	2	Alum.	Up to 1000	Up to 16			39–45
	A–48–49612A4②	13	22	2	Bronze	Up to 1000	Up to 17			40–46
	C–48–49630A3	13¾	21	2	Bronze	900–1300	15–17			35–41
	C–48–49632A3	13¾	21	2	Alum.	900–1300	15–17			35–41
	C–48–32744A3	13	21	3	Bronze	900–1300	15–17			35–41
	C–48–32746A3	13	21	3	Alum.	900–1300	15–17			35–41
	A–48–49610A4②	13	20	2	Bronze	900–1300	15–17	All	All	36–42
	C–48–32748A3	13	19	3	Bronze	1000–1800	16–19			31–37
	C–48–32750A3	13	19	3	Alum.	1000–1800	16–19			31–37
	C–48–31458A3	13	17	3	Bronze	1200–2000	18–21	15½	20	26–33
	C–48–32264A4	13	17	3	Alum.	1200–2000	18–21			26–33
	C–48–31460A3	14	15	3	Bronze	1800–2600	19–22			21–28
	C–48–32390A3	14	15	3	Alum.	1800–2600	19–22			21–28
	C–48–30394A3	13½	13	3	Bronze	2000–3000	20–23			16–23
	C–48–32392A3	13½	13	3	Alum.	2000–3000	20–23			16–23
	C–48–30396A3	14	11	3	Bronze	2200–3500	21–24			11–18
Full Throttle	C–48–35936A3	14	11	3	Alum.	2200–3500	21–24			11–18
rpm Range:	C–48–30398A3	14	9½	3	Bronze	3300 Plus	Houseboat			2–13
4800–5300	C–48–33242A3	14	9½	3	Alum.	3300 Plus	Houseboat			2–13
Merc 800	A–48–52010A3	13	25	3	Bronze	950	Up to 15			42–49
(1970)	A–48–52012A3	13	25	3	Alum.	950	Up to 15			42–49
	C–48–31448A3	13½	25	2	Bronze	950	Up to 15			42–49
	A–48–52006A3	13	23	3	Bronze	1000	Up to 16			36–44
	A–48–52008A3	13	23	3	Alum.	1000	Up to 16			36–44
	C–48–31450A3	13¾	23	2	Bronze	1000	Up to 16			36–44
	C–48–32386A3	13¾	23	2	Alum.	1000	Up to 16			36–44
	C–48–31452A3	13¾	21	2	Bronze	800–1400	15–17			33–38
Gear Shift	C–48–31454A3	13¾	21	2	Alum.	800–1400	15–17			33–38
	A–48–53894A3	13¾	21	3	Bronze	800–1400	15–17			33–38
	A–48–53892A3	13¾	21	3	Alum.	800–1400	15–17	All	All	33–38
	C–48–31456A3	13¾	19	2	Bronze	1000–1800	16–18			30–35
	C–48–32388A3	13¾	19	2	Alum.	1000–1800	16–18			30–35
	A–48–53898A3	13¾	19	3	Bronze	1000–1800	16–18			30–35
	A–48–53896A3	13¾	19	3	Alum.	1000–1800	16–18	15½	20	30–35
	A–48–53902A3	14	17	3	Bronze	1500–2400	17–19			27–32
	A–48–53900A3	14	17	3	Alum.	1500–2400	17–19			27–32
	C–48–31460A3	14	15	3	Bronze	1800–2800	19–21			22–29
	C–48–32390A3	14	15	3	Alum.	1800–2800	19–21	All	All	22–29
	C–48–30394A3	13½	13	3	Bronze	2000–3600	21–23			18–24
	C–48–32392A3	13½	13	3	Alum.	2000–3600	21–23			18–24
Full Throttle	C–48–30396A3	14	11	3	Bronze	2400–6000	Houseboat			13–20
rpm Range:	C–48–35936A3	14	11	3	Alum.	2400–6000	Houseboat			13–20
4800–5300	C–48–30398A3	14	9½	2	Bronze	6000 Plus	Work Boat	15½	20	1–15
	C–48–33242A3	14	9½	3	Alum.	6000 Plus	Work Boat			1–15
Merc 800	C–48–59138A4	14	26	2	Bronze	Up to 1000	Up to 16			48–55
(1971)	A–48–49616A4	13	26	2	Bronze	Up to 1000	Up to 16			48–55
	A–48–52010A3	13	25	3	Bronze	Up to 950	Up to 15			42–49
	A–48–52012A3	13	25	3	Alum.	Up to 950	Up to 15			42–49
	A–48–55458A4	14	24	2	Bronze	Up to 1200	Up to 17			44–51
	A–48–49614A4	13	24	2	Bronze	Up to 950	Up to 15			44–51
	C–48–31450A3	13¾	23	2	Bronze	Up to 1000	Up to 16			36–44
	C–48–32386A3	13¾	23	2	Alum.	Up to 1000	Up to 16			36–44
	A–48–52006A3	13	23	3	Bronze	Up to 1000	Up to 16			36–44
	A–48–52008A3	13	23	3	Alum.	Up to 1000	Up to 16			36–44
Gear Shift	A–48–55456A4	14	22	2	Bronze	Up to 1400	Up to 18			38–46

Right-Hand Rotation (Facing Bow) (cont.)

Motor Model	Clockwise RH Rotation	Dia (in.)	Pitch (in.)	No. Bl	Material	① Approx Gross Load (lbs)	Approx Boat Length (ft)	Std Length (in.)	Long Shaft (in.)	Speed Range (mph)
Merc 800	A–48–49612A4	13	22	2	Bronze	Up to 1000	Up to 16	All	All	38–46
(1971)	C–48–49630A3	13¾	21	2	Bronze	1000–1800	15–17			34–42
	C–48–49632A3	13¾	21	2	Alum.	1000–1800	15–17			34–42
	C–48–32744A3	13	21	3	Bronze	1000–1800	15–17			34–42
	C–48–32746A3	13	21	3	Alum.	1000–1800	15–17			34–42
	C–48–59136A4	14	20	2	Bronze	1200–2000	16–19			47–54
	A–48–49610A4	13	20	2	Bronze	1000–1800	15–17			35–40
	C–48–31456A3	13¾	19	2	Bronze	1600–2200	16–18			32–36
	C–48–32388A3	13¾	19	2	Alum.	1600–2200	16–18	15½	20	32–36
	C–48–32750A3	13	19	3	Alum.	1600–2200	16–18			32–36
	C–48–31458A3	13	17	3	Bronze	1900–2600	17–19			28–34
	C–48–32264A3	13	17	3	Alum.	1900–2600	17–19			28–34
	C–48–31460A3	14	15	3	Bronze	2000–2800	19–21			24–29
	C–48–32390A3	14	15	3	Alum.	2000–2800	19–21			24–29
	C–48–30394A3	13½	13	3	Bronze	2000–3600	21–23			18–24
	C–48–58826A3	14	13	3	Bronze	2000–3600	21–23			18–24
Full Throttle	C–48–30396A3	14	11	3	Bronze	2400–6000	Houseboat			13–20
rpm Range:	C–48–35936A3	14	11	3	Alum.	2400–6000	Houseboat			13–20
4800–5300	C–48–30398A3	14	9½	3	Bronze	6000 Plus	Work Boat			1–15
	C–48–33242A3	14	9½	3	Alum.	6000 Plus	Work Boat			1–15
Merc 950SS–950	C–48–31450A3	13¾	23	2	Bronze	1000	Up to 16			45–56
	C–48–32386A3	13¾	23	2	Alum.	1000	Up to 16			45–56
	C–48–32744A3	13	21	3	Bronze	900–1500	Up to 17			40–47
	A–48–31452A3	13¾	21	2	Bronze	900–1500	Up to 17			40–47
	C–48–32746A3	13	21	3	Alum.	900–1500	Up to 17			40–47
	A–48–31454A3	13¾	21	2	Alum.	900–1500	Up to 17	All	All	40–47
	C–48–32748A3	13	19	3	Bronze	1100–1800	16–18			35–42
	A–48–31456A3	13¾	19	2	Bronze	1100–1800	16–18			35–42
	C–48–32750A3	13	19	3	Alum.	1100–1800	16–18			35–42
	A–48–32388A3	13¾	19	2	Alum.	1100–1800	16–18			35–42
Gear Shift	C–48–31458A3	13	17	3	Bronze	1400–2200	17–20			30–37
	C–48–32264A3	13	17	3	Alum.	1400–2200	17–20			30–37
	C–48–31460A3	14	15	3	Bronze	1800–2600	19–22			25–32
	C–48–32390A3	14	15	3	Alum.	1800–2600	19–22			25–32
	C–48–30394A3	13½	13	3	Bronze	2200–3500	21–24			17–27
	C–48–32392A3	13½	13	3	Alum.	2200–3500	21–24	15½	20	17–27
	C–48–30396A3	14	11	3	Bronze	3500 Plus	Houseboat			12–18
	C–48–35936A3	14	11	3	Alum.	3500 Plus	Houseboat			12–18
Full Throttle	C–48–30398A3②	14	9½	3	Bronze	6000 Plus	Work Boat			1–13
rpm Range:	C–48–33242A3②	14	9½	3	Alum.	6000 Plus	Work Boat			1–13
4800–5200	C–48–30400A3	14	8½	3	Bronze	12000 Plus	Work Boat			1–8
Merc 1000SS	A–48–49614A4	13	24	2	Bronze	1000	Up to 16			49–62
(1968–69)	C–48–31450A3	13¾	23	2	Bronze	1000	Up to 16			43–50
	C–48–32386A3	13¾	23	2	Alum.	1000	Up to 16			43–50
	A–48–49612A4	13	21	2	Bronze	1000	Up to 16			45–52
	C–48–32744A3	13	21	3	Bronze	900–1500	Up to 17	All	All	40–47
	A–48–31452A3	13¾	21	2	Bronze	900–1500	Up to 17			40–47
	C–48–32746A3	13	21	3	Alum.	900–1500	Up to 17			40–47
	A–48–31454A3	13¾	21	2	Alum.	900–1500	Up to 17			40–47
	C–48–49630A3	13¾	21	2	Bronze	900–1500	Up to 17			40–47
	A–48–49632A3	13¾	21	2	Alum.	900–1500	Up to 17			40–47
	A–48–49610A4	13	20	2	Bronze	900–1500	Up to 17			42–49
	C–49–32748A3	13	19	3	Bronze	1100–1800	16–18			35–42
	A–48–31456A3	13¾	19	2	Bronze	1100–1800	16–18			35–42
	C–48–32750A3	13	19	3	Alum.	1100–1800	16–18			35–42
	C–48–32388A3	13¾	19	2	Alum.	1100–1800	16–18			35–42
Gear Shift	C–48–31458A3	13	17	3	Bronze	1400–2200	17–20			30–37
	C–48–32264A3	13	17	3	Alum.	1400–2200	17–20	15½	20	30–37
	C–48–31460A3	14	15	3	Bronze	1800–2600	19–22			25–32
	C–48–32390A3	14	15	3	Alum.	1800–2600	19–22			25–32
	C–48–30394A3	13½	13	3	Bronze	2200–3500	21–24			17–27
	C–48–32392A3	13½	13	3	Alum.	2200–3500	21–24			17–27
	C–48–30396A3	14	11	3	Bronze	3500 Plus	Houseboat	All	All	12–18

Right-Hand Rotation (Facing Bow) (cont.)

		Propeller				①		Transom Height		
Motor Model	Clockwise RH Rotation	Dia (in.)	Pitch (in.)	No. Bl	Material	Approx Gross Load (lbs)	Approx Boat Length (ft)	Std Length (in.)	Long Shaft (in.)	Speed Range (mph)
Full Throttle	C–48–35936A3	14	11	3	Alum.	3500 Plus	Houseboat			12–18
rpm Range:	C–48–30398A3②	14	9½	3	Bronze	6000 Plus	Work Boat			4–13
4800–5300	C–48–33242A3②	14	9½	3	Alum.	6000 Plus	Work Boat	15½	20	4–13
Merc 1100SS–	C–48–31448A3	13½	25	2	Bronze	1000	Up to 16			47–60
1100	C–48–31450A3	13¾	23	2	Bronze	1200	Up to 17			43–50
(93.5 Cu.In.)	C–48–32386A3	13¾	23	2	Alum.	1200	Up to 17			43–50
(1532cc)	A–48–31452A3	13¾	21	2	Bronze	1100–1800	16–18			38–45
	A–48–31454A3	13¾	21	2	Alum.	1100–1800	16–18			38–45
Merc 1000	C–48–32744A3	13	21	3	Bronze	1100–1800	16–18	All	All	38–45
(90 Cu In.)	C–48–32746A3	13	21	3	Alum.	1100–1800	16–18			38–45
(1475cc)	A–48–31456A3	13¾	19	2	Bronze	1400–2300	17–20			33–40
	A–48–32388A3	13¾	19	2	Alum.	1400–2300	17–20			33–40
	C–48–32748A3	13	19	3	Bronze	1400–2300	17–20			33–40
	C–48–32750A3	13	19	3	Alum.	1400–2300	17–20			33–40
	C–48–31458A3	13	17	3	Bronze	1800–2600	19–22	15½	20	28–35
	C–48–32264A3	13	17	3	Alum.	1800–2600	19–22			28–35
Gear Shift	C–48–31460A3	14	15	3	Bronze	2200–3000	21–24			23–30
	C–48–32390A3	14	15	3	Alum.	2200–3000	21–24			23–30
	C–48–30394A3	13½	13	3	Bronze	2800–4200	23–27			16–25
	C–48–32392A3	13½	13	3	Alum.	2800–4200	23–27			16–25
	C–48–30394A3	14	11	3	Bronze	4000 Plus	Houseboat			11–17
	C–48–35936A3	14	11	3	Alum.	4000 Plus	Houseboat			11–17
Full Throttle	C–48–30398A3③	14	9½	3	Bronze	12000 Plus	Work Boat			1–12
rpm Range:	C–48–33242A3③	14	9½	3	Alum.	12000 Plus	Work Boat			1–12
4800–5200	C–48–30400A3	14	8½	3	Bronze	12000 Plus	Work Boat			1–8
Merc 1150	□C–48–59138A4	14	26	2	Bronze	1000	Up to 16			60–68
(1970–71)	□C–48–49616A4	13	26	2	Bronze	1000	Up to 16			60–68
	□C–48–52010A3	13	25	3	Bronze	1200	Up to 17			53–63
	□C–48–55458A4	14	24	2	Bronze	1200	Up to 17	All	All	55–63
	A–48–49614A4②	13	24	2	Bronze	Up to 1100	Up to 16			51–63
	C–48–31450A3	13¾	23	2	Bronze	Up to 1100	Up to 17			49–57
* 1970 Only	C–48–32386A3	13¾	23	2	Alum.	Up to 1100	Up to 17			49–57
□ 1971 Only	□C–48–52006A3	13	23	3	Bronze	1400	Up to 18			50–58
	□C–48–55456A4	14	22	2	Bronze	1400	Up to 18			52–60
	A–48–49612A4②	13	22	2	Bronze	Up to 1100	Up to 17			52–60
	C–48–49630A3	13¾	21	2	Bronze	1100–1700	Up to 18			44–51
	C–48–49632A3	13¾	21	2	Alum.	1100–1700	Up to 18			44–51
	C–48–32744A3	13	21	3	Bronze	1100–1700	Up to 18			44–51
Gear Shift	C–48–32746A3	13	21	3	Alum.	1100–1700	Up to 18			44–51
	A–48–49610A4②	13	20	2	Bronze	1100–1700	Up to 18			47–54
	□C–48–59136A4	14	20	2	Bronze	1200–2000	17–19			47–54
	C–48–31456A3	13¾	19	2	Bronze	1400–2100	17–19			39–46
	C–48–32388A3	13¾	19	2	Alum.	1400–2100	16–19			39–46
	C–48–32748A3	13	19	3	Bronze	1400–2100	17–19	15½	20	39–46
	C–48–32750A3	13	19	3	Alum.	1400–2100	17–19			39–46
	C–48–31458A3	13	17	3	Bronze	1700–2500	18–21			33–41
	C–48–32264A3	13	17	3	Alum.	1700–2500	18–21			33–41
	C–48–31460A3	14	15	3	Bronze	2100–2900	20–23			27–35
	C–48–32390A3	14	15	3	Alum.	2100–2900	20–23			27–35
	C–48–30394A3	13	13	3	Bronze	2500–4000	22–25	All	All	20–29
	□C–48–58826A3	14	13	3	Alum.	3000–4500	32–28			20–29
	*C–48–32392A3	13½	13	3	Alum.	2500–4000	22–25			20–29
	C–48–30396A3	14	11	3	Bronze	3700 Plus	Houseboat			12–22
Full Throttle	C–48–35936A3	14	11	3	Alum.	3700 Plus	Houseboat	15½	20	12–22
rpm Range:	C–48–30398A3	14	9½	3	Bronze	9000 Plus	Work Boat			1–14
4800–5300	C–48–33242A3	14	9½	3	Alum.	9000 Plus	Work Boat			1–14
Merc 1250SS	A–48–49614A4	13	25	3	Bronze	Up to 1200	Up to 17			49–62
(1968–69)	C–48–52010A3	13	25	3	Bronze	1200	Up to 17			47–60

Right-Hand Rotation (Facing Bow) (cont.)

Motor Model	Clockwise RH Rotation	Dia (in.)	Pitch (in.)	No. Bl	Material	① Approx Gross Load (lbs)	Approx Boat Length (ft)	Std Length (in.)	Long Shaft (in.)	Speed Range (mph)
Merc 1250SS	C–48–52012A3	13	25	3	Alum.	1200	Up to 17			47–60
(1968–69)	C–48–31448A3	13½	25	2	Bronze	1200	Up to 17			47–60
	C–48–52006A3	13	23	3	Bronze	1400	Up to 18			43–50
	C–48–52008A3	13	23	3	Alum.	1400	Up to 18			43–50
	C–48–31450A3	13¾	23	2	Bronze	1400	Up to 18			43–50
	C–48–32386A3	13¾	23	2	Alum.	1400	Up to 18			43–50
	A–48–49612A4	13	22	2	Bronze	Up to 1400	Up to 18			45–52
	A–48–49630A3	13¾	21	2	Bronze	1200–2000	16–19			38–45
	C–48–49632A3	13¾	21	2	Alum.	1200–2000	16–19			38–45
	A–48–53894A3	13¾	21	3	Bronze	1200–2000	16–19			38–45
	A–48–53892A3	13¾	21	3	Alum.	1200–2000	16–19			38–45
	A–48–31452A3	13¾	21	2	Bronze	1200–2000	16–19			38–45
	A–48–31454A3	13¾	21	2	Alum.	1200–2000	16–19	All	All	38–45
	C–48–32744A3	13	21	3	Bronze	1200–2000	16–19			38–45
	C–48–32746A3	13	21	3	Alum.	1200–2000	16–19			38–45
	A–48–49610A4	13	20	2	Bronze	1200–2000	16–19			40–47
Gear Shift	A–48–31456A3	13¾	19	2	Bronze	1600–2400	17–21			33–40
	A–48–32388A3	13¾	19	2	Alum.	1600–2400	17–21	15½	20	33–40
	A–48–53898A3	13¾	19	3	Bronze	1600–2400	17–21			33–40
	A–48–53896A3	13¾	19	3	Alum.	1600–2400	17–21			33–40
	C–48–32748A3	13	19	3	Bronze	1600–2400	17–21			33–40
	C–48–32750A3	13	19	3	Alum.	1600–2400	17–21			33–40
	A–48–53902A3	14	17	3	Bronze	2000–2800	19–21			28–35
	A–48–53900A3	14	17	3	Alum.	2000–2800	19–21			28–35
	C–48–31458A3	13	17	3	Bronze	2000–2800	19–21			28–35
	C–48–32264A3	13	17	3	Alum.	2000–2800	19–21			28–35
	C–48–31460A3	14	15	3	Bronze	2400–3200	21–25			23–30
	C–48–32390A3	14	15	3	Alum.	2400–3200	21–25			23–30
	C–48–30394A3	13½	13	3	Bronze	3000–4500	23–28			16–25
	C–48–32392A3	13½	13	3	Alum.	3000–4500	23–28			16–25
	C–48–30396A3	14	11	3	Bronze	4000 Plus	Houseboat			11–17
Full Throttle	C–48–35936A3	14	11	3	Alum.	4000 Plus	Houseboat			11–17
rpm Range:	C–48–30398A3③	14	9½	3	Bronze	12000 Plus	Work Boat			1–12
4800–5300	C–48–33242A3③	14	9½	3	Alum.	12000 Plus	Work Boat			1–12
	C–48–30400A3③	14	8½	3	Bronze	12000 Plus	Work Boat			1–8
Merc 1350	□C–48–59138A4	14	26	2	Bronze	Up to 1000	Up to 16			60–68
(1970–71)	□A–48–49616A4	13	26	2	Bronze	Up to 1000	Up to 16			60–68
	□A–48–52010A3	13	25	3	Bronze	Up to 1200	Up to 17			53–63
★ 1970 Only	□A–48–55458A4	14	24	2	Bronze	Up to 1200	Up to 17			55–63
□ 1971 Only	A–48–49614A4②	13	24	2	Bronze	Up to 1200	Up to 17			51–63
	C–48–31450A3	13¾	23	2	Bronze	Up to 1200	Up to 18			49–57
	C–48–32386A3	13¾	23	2	Alum.	Up to 1400	Up to 18			49–57
	□A–48–52006A3	13	23	3	Bronze	Up to 1400	Up to 18			50–58
	A–48–49612A4②	13	22	2	Bronze	Up to 1400	Up to 18			52–60
	□A–48–55456A4	14	22	2	Bronze	Up to 1400	Up to 18			52–60
	C–48–49630A3	13¾	21	2	Bronze	1200–2000	16–19			44–51
	C–48–49632A3	13¾	21	2	Alum.	1200–2000	16–19			44–51
	C–48–32744A3	13	21	3	Bronze	1200–2000	16–19	All	All	44–51
	C–48–32746A3	13	21	3	Alum.	1200–2000	16–19			44–51
	A–48–49610A4②	13	20	2	Bronze	1200–2000	16–19			47–54
	□C–48–59136A4	14	20	2	Bronze	1200–2000	16–19			47–54
	C–48–31456A3	13¾	19	2	Bronze	1600–2400	17–21			39–46
	C–48–32388A3	13¾	19	2	Alum.	1600–2400	17–21			39–46
	★C–48–32748A3	13	19	3	Bronze	1600–2400	17–21	15½	20	39–46
Gear Shift	C–48–32750A3	13	19	3	Alum.	1600–2400	17–21			39–46
	C–48–31458A3	13	17	3	Bronze	2000–2800	19–23			33–41
	C–48–32264A3	13	17	3	Alum.	2000–2800	19–23			33–41
	C–48–31460A3	14	15	3	Bronze	2400–3200	21–25			27–35
	C–48–32390A3	14	15	3	Alum.	2400–3200	21–25			27–35
	C–48–30394A3	13½	13	3	Bronze	3000–4500	23–28			20–29
	□C–48–58826A3	14	13	3	Alum.	3000–4500	23–28			20–29
	★C–48–32392A3	13½	13	3	Alum.	3000–4500	23–28			20–29

Right-Hand Rotation (Facing Bow) (cont.)

Motor Model	Clockwise RH Rotation	Dia (in.)	Pitch (in.)	No. Bl	Material	① Approx Gross Load (lbs)	Approx Boat Length (ft)	Std Length (in.)	Long Shaft (in.)	Speed Range (mph)
		Propeller					*Transom Height*			
Merc 1350 (1970–1971)										
	C–48–30396A3	14	11	3	Bronze	4000 Plus	Houseboat			12–22
Full Throttle	C–48–35936A3	14	11	3	Alum.	4000 Plus	Houseboat			12–22
rpm Range:	C–48–30398A3	14	9½	3	Bronze	12000 Plus	Work Boat			1–14
4800–5300	C–48–33242A3	14	9½	3	Alum.	12000 Plus	Work Boat			1–14

① Gross weights are approximate—include weight of boat, fuel, passengers, and gear.
② High performance Quicksilver propellers.
③ Special applications only.
NOTES—(*Applicable to entire preceding propeller chart*):
(a)—The selection procedure for propellers used in dual installation is the same, but use the next higher pitch propellers on the chart.
(b)—For water skiing, use the next lower pitch propeller on the chart.
(c)—CAUTION: *When using a low-pitch propeller on a light boat for water skiing purposes, do not operate at full throttle when not pulling skis. Over-revving of the engine risks possible damage.*
(d)—Use the next lower pitch propeller for each additional 2500 feet of elevation.
(e)—For commercial application, use the lower listed rpm.

LUBRICATION AND FUEL RECOMMENDATIONS

Fuel

The manufacturer recommends that regular, leaded automotive gasolines be used in Mercury outboards equipped with Thunderbolt (CD) ignition systems and surface gap spark plugs. Some marine white gasolines have been known to cause trouble because of their very low octane rating. Detonation, ring sticking, and port plugging are among the common complaints resulting from the use of low octane marine white fuel. Regular gasolines are of a more uniform quality and readily available from most service stations or marinas.

Mercury outboards with conventional ignition systems and conventional spark plugs operate with much higher plug temperatures than those with Thunderbolt ignition. Do not operate Mercury outboards with new lead-free or no-lead fuels, other than those approved by Kiekhaefer Mercury. To be certain as to the quality of a particular fuel, consult an authorized Mercury dealer. Some oil companies have for years manufactured high grade, lead-free fuel which contains no phosphorus (major cause of piston failure) and is designed for use in two-cycle engines, either directly or as a pre-mixed fuel. Such fuels, if known to be of good quality, may continue to be used.

NOTE: *Kiekhaefer Mercury reserves the right to refuse warranty on parts which are damaged when using improper fuels.*

Internal Lubrication

Kiekhaefer Mercury specifically recommends that only FORMULA 50 Quicksilver 2-Cycle Super Outboard Motor Oil or Formula 2 Quicksilver 2-Cycle Outboard Motor Oil be used in their outboard motors. In an absolute emergency, when FORMULA 50 or Formula 2 Quicksilver Oil is not available, a high grade 2-cycle oil intended for use in outboards may be substituted.

WARNING: *Do not, under any circumstances, use multigrade or other detergent automotive oils or oils which contain metallic additives. This type of oil may result in piston scoring, bearing failure, or both.*

When using FORMULA 50 Quicksilver Super 2-Cycle Outboard Motor Oil, thoroughly mix one 12 ounce can with each 5 gallons of gasoline (8 ounces with each three gallons) in your remote fuel tank.

When using Formula 2 Quicksilver 2-Cycle Motor Oil, thoroughly mix one 30 ounce can with each 6 gallons of gasoline (15 ounces with each 3 gallons) in the remote fuel tank.

For operation in Canada, use 15 ounces of FORMULA 50 Quicksilver 2-Cycle Super Outboard Motor Oil to each 5 Imperial gallons of gasoline, or 35 ounces of

Formula 2 Quicksilver 2-Cycle Outboard Motor Oil to 5 Imperial gallons of gasoline in the remote fuel tank.

WARNING TO MERCURY OUT-BOARD OWNERS: *The use of any other oil than Kiekhaefer Quicksilver FORMULA 50 in the 50/1 ratio may cause piston scoring, bearing failure, or both. The motor warranty may be void if failure should occur with the use of any other oils in the 50/1 fuel/oil mixture.*

Examination of outboard motors with scored pistons which have been returned to Mercury Service Department shows that the use of certain so-called "outboard motor oils" has caused piston scoring.

Break-in Fuel / Oil Mixture

FORMULA 50 Quicksilver Super

For the first two tankfulls, thoroughly mix two 12 ounce cans to each six gallon tank of fuel (or one 12 ounce can to each three gallon tank of fuel). After break-in, refer to "Internal Lubrication."

Operate the new motor at ½ throttle (2500–3500 rpm) for the first two hours. After the first two hours, the motor may be run at any speed but sustained operation at full throttle should be avoided for an additional eight hours of running time.

Formula 2 Quicksilver

For the first two tankfulls, thoroughly mix one 30 ounce can to each 6 gallon tank of fuel (or 15 ounces to each three gallon tank of fuel). After break-in, refer to "Internal Lubrication."

Operate the new motor at ½ throttle (2500–3500 rpm) for the first two hours. After the first two hours, the motor may be run at any speed but sustained operation at full throttle should be avoided for an additional 8 hours of running time.

Fuel Mixing Procedure

Observe all fire prevention rules, particularly regarding smoking. Mix fuel in a well-ventilated area and mix directly in the remote tank.

Measure accurately the required amounts of oil and fuel. Pour a small amount of gasoline into the tank and add a small amount of oil (about the same amount as gas). Mix thoroughly by shaking vigorously. Add the balance of oil and gas (oil first). Cleanliness is of prime importance in mixing fuel, as even a small particle of dirt can clog the jets and calibrated passages in the carburetor. Fresh gasoline should always be used, since gasoline contains gum and varnish deposits, which when left in a tank for a length of time may cause carburetor and spark plug fouling.

Carburetor idle adjustment is sensitive to fuel mixture variations. Careless or inaccurate mixing will necessitate frequent adjustment. Be consistent and prepare each batch of fuel exactly the same. Using less than the recommended proportion of oil will result in serious motor damage, and using more than the recommended proportion will cause spark plug fouling, erratic carburetion, excessive smoking, and faster-than-normal carbon accumulation.

External Lubrication and Maintenance

For best operation and performance, the following maintenance and lubrication charts should be followed in great detail. It is also recommended that the stated lubricant be used.

Lubrication Frequency

Model	Location	Lubricant	Every 30 Days	Every 60 Days	Once in Season	Twice in Season
			Frequency			
All	Lower drive unit	Super-duty gear lubricant (C–92–52650)	●			
All	Propeller shaft splines	Anti-corrosion grease	●			
All	Swivel pin	(C–92–45134A1)	★	●		

Lubrication Frequency (cont.)

Model	Location	Lubricant	Frequency			
			Every 30 Days	Every 60 Days	Once in Season	Twice in Season
4 and 6 cylinder	Magneto/distributor adaptor				●	★
If equipped	Ride-guide tube and cable	New multipurpose lubricant (C–92–49588)	★	●		
400	Reverse lock cam			●		
If equipped	Ride-guide pivot/ball joint		★	●		
All	Throttle/shift linkage		★	●		
All	Upper shift shaft		★	●		
All	Thumb screws	Anti-corrosion oil	★	●		
All	Reverse lock lever	(C–92–39928A1)	★	●		
All	Tilt stop lever		★	●		
200–110–75–40	Stator plate clamps				●	★
110–75–40	Tiller handle pivot/gears		★	●		
Electric start	Starter motor pinion gear	SAE no. 10 oil	★	●		
If equipped	Power trim pump oil level	Formula 4 oil (C–92–33157)	●			

★—Units operated in salt water

Lubrication and Maintenance

Locations ▲	Every 30 Days	Every 60 Days	Once in Season	Twice in Season
Check lubricant level in lower drive unit	A			
Lubricate propeller shaft splines		C-Each prop installation		
Lubricate swivel pin	①	C		
Lubricate magneto/distributor adaptor ★			D	①
Lubricate ride-guide steering tube	①	D		
Lubricate ride-guide steering cable	①	D		
Lubricate ride-guide steering pivot/ball joint	①	E		

Lubrication and Maintenance (cont.)

Locations ▲	Every 30 Days	Every 60 Days	Once in Season	Twice in Season
Lubricate throttle/shift linkage	①	E		
Lubricate thumb screws	①	E		
Lubricate upper shift shaft	①	E		
Lubricate reverse lock lever ★	①	E		
Lubricate reverse locking cams	①	C		
Lubricate tilt stop lever	①	E		
Lubricate starter motor pinion gear		①	J	
Lubricate tiller handle knuckle pivot/gears ★	①	E		
Lubricate stator plate clamps			E	①
Check lubricant level in power trim pump		I		
Check condition of battery/terminals	①			●
Inspect spark plug leads/all electrical connections			●	
Clean fuel filter(s)			●	
Clean fuel tank filter			●	
Inspect all fuel lines/connections				●
Check entire unit/loose, damaged or missing parts			●	
Check condition of spark plugs			●	
Inspect breaker points			●	
Inspect propeller for possible damage				●
Inspect and clean entire unit/touch-up paint			L-M	①

▲—Complete list of maintenance is not applicable to all models
①—Units operated in salt water
★—Includes all pivot points and sliding surfaces unless stated elsewhere
A—Super Duty Quicksilver Gear Lubricant (C–92–52650)
C—Anti-Corrosion Grease (C–92–45134A1)
D—New Multipurpose Quicksilver Lubricant (C–92–49588)
E—Anti-Corrosion Oil (C–92–39928A1)
L—Quicksilver Marine Cleaner (C–92–32172)
M—Quicksilver Spray Paint
I—Quicksilver Formula 4 Oil (C–92–55573–24) or SAE 20–20W Specification MS
J—SAE No. 10 oil

Lubricant and Sealer Application

Lubrication Point	Model								
	350	400	500	650	800	1000	1150	1250	1350
Gear Housing	A	A	A	A	A	A	A	A	A
Drive Shaft Splines	C	C	C	C	C	C	C	C	C
Shift Shaft Coupling	B	B	B	B	B	B	B	B	B
Distributor Pilot Grease Fitting	—	—	C	C	C	C	C	C	C
Magneto Bushing	C	—	—	—	—	—	—	—	—
Swivel Pin Grease Fitting	B	B	B	B	B	B	B	B	B
Tilt to Swivel Bracket	D	D	D	D	D	D	D	D	D
Tilt Tube Inside Diameter (ID)	D	D	D	D	D	D	D	D	D
Propeller Shaft Splines	—	—	—	—	—	—	—	—	—
Reverse Lock Cams	C	—	—	—	—	—	—	—	—
Thumb Screws	D	D	D	D	D	D	D	D	D
Tilt Stop Levers	B	B	—	—	—	—	—	—	—
Reverse Lock Latch in Swivel Bracket	—	—	—	—	—	—	—	—	—
Throttle Linkage *	D	D	D	D	D	D	D	D	D
Throttle Cluster	D	D	D	D	D	D	D	D	D
Shift Linkage *	D	D	D	D	D	D	D	D	D
Tiller Handle Knuckle Pivot	—	—	—	—	—	—	—	—	—
Tiller Handle Knuckle Gears	—	—	—	—	—	—	—	—	—
Tiller Handle Universal Joint	—	—	—	—	—	—	—	—	—
Choke Shutter Stud	D	D	D	D	D	D	D	D	D
Choke Shaft in Bottom Cowl	C	D	—	—	—	—	—	—	—
Starter Sheave Pawls	C	C	C	—	—	—	—	—	—
Distributor or Ignition Driver Shaft Splines	—	—	—	—	—	—	—	—	—
Choke Grommets	—	—	F	F	F	F	F	F	F
Choke Solenoid Plunger Hole	—	F	F	F	F	F	F	F	F
Cylinder Bores	—	E	E	E	E	E	E	E	E
Piston Rod and Crank Needles	C	C	C	C	C	C	C	C	C
Centermain Needles	—	C	C	C	C	C	C	C	C
Top Cowl Mounts	—	—	B	B	B	B	B	B	B
Piston Rings	E	E	E	E	E	E	E	E	E
Bearing Carrier Spool—Gear Housing	C	C	C	C	C	C	C	C	C
Water Pump Base and Housing	C	C	C	C	C	C	C	C	C
Shift Shaft Threaded Bushing—Gear Housing	C	C	C	C	C	C	C	C	C
End Caps—Crankshaft	E	E	E	E	E	E	E	E	E
Impeller Pin and Drive Shaft	C	C	C	C	C	C	A	C	A
Screws—Exhaust Cover	D	D	D	D	D	D	D	D	D
Oil Seals (Outside Diameter) to Spool	H	H	H	H	H	H	H	H	H
Oil Seals (OD) to Threaded Shift Shaft Bushing	H	H	H	H	H	H	H	H	H
Oil Seals (OD) to Water Pump Base	—	H	H	H	H	H	H	H	H
Crankcase to Block Split Line	J	J	J	J	—	J	—	—	—
Pinion Nut	—	—	—	H	H	H	H	H	H
Apply to Inner Water Jacket Cover Screws	—	—	—	—	S	—	G	G	G
Distributor Rotor to Crankshaft	—	K	—	—	—	—	—	—	—
Starter Interlock Slide	—	D	D	—	—	—	—	—	—
High Tension Leads @ Distributor Tower	—	L	—	—	—	—	—	—	—
Anti-Reversing Wire	—	F	—	—	—	—	—	—	—

* Includes all pivot points and sliding surfaces, unless stated elsewhere

A—Super-Duty Quicksilver Gear Lubricant (C–92–52645–1)
B—Anti-Corrosion Grease (C–92–45134A1)
C—New Multipurpose Quicksilver Lubricant (C–92–49588–12)
D—Anti-Corrosion Oil (C–92–39928A1)
E—FORMULA 50 Quicksilver 2-Cycle Motor Oil (C–92–39607–1)

F—DC–4 Compound (C–92–24108–1)
G—Exhaust Tube Sealer (C–92–33749–1)
H—Loctite A (C–92–32609–1)
J—Gasket Sealer (C–92–28804–1)
K—Loctite Primer Grade T (C–92–59327–1) and Compound Grade HV (C–92–36088–1)
L—Bendix Sealing Compound No. 47

MOTOR INSTALLATION

Very special attention should be given to mounting the motor on the transom. The clamp bracket must not only support the weight of the motor but must also accept the stress of thrust, impact, inertia, and steering. These forces are transferred directly to the transom through the clamp bracket.

The motor is designed for a recommended transom height. To avoid damage to the motor, it is important that the clamp screws are tightened securely and equally. Clamp screws should be tightened and positioned near a horizontal plane to allow full tilt and turn of the motor. If this is not observed, damage to the steering may result. It is also advisable to consult the general section, "Mounting the Motor on the Boat," for general instructions.

CAUTION: *Before operating four- or six-cylinder motors, they must be secured to the boat with two bolts placed through the transom into slots provided at the bottom of the clamp bracket. Refer to instructions on the red CAUTION tag attached to a new motor. Upper mounting bolts must be installed if the transom has an extremely hard smooth surface. Occasionally check the clamp screws to be sure that they are tight. Failure to bolt the motor to the transom may result in damage to, or loss of, the motor.*

TILT PIN ADJUSTMENT

Holes are provided in the clamp bracket to permit changing the location of the tilt lock pin for proper adjustment of tilt angle. See "Tilt Pin Adjustment" in the general section at the front of this book.

Fuel System

Mercury outboards are equipped with pressure-type carburetors, remote fuel tanks, and either vacuum-type or diaphragm-type fuel pumps. Most models are also equipped with a fuel filter at the tank or at the carburetor.

CARBURETORS

All Mercury pressure-type carburetors are serviced in an identical manner.

Removal

1. Detach the choke and throttle linkage at the carburetor.
2. Remove the fuel line from the carburetor.
3. If necessary, on some models, remove the starter motor.
4. Remove the two nuts attaching the carburetor to the crankcase and remove the carburetor.

DISASSEMBLY

1. Remove the cap screw and gasket from the fuel filter cover.
2. Detach the filter housing, gasket, filter element, and filter element gasket.
3. Unscrew the idle adjustment screw and remove the spring.
4. Unscrew the idle restriction tube which extends inside the main discharge nozzle of the top carburetor. Do not lose the small restriction tube gasket.

Removing idle restriction tube (© Kiekhaefer Mercury)

5. Remove the discharge jet plug screw. Using a screwdriver of exact size, unscrew the high speed discharge nozzle.
6. Remove the brass hex-head plug and gasket from the carburetor body with a ⅜ in. wrench.
7. Remove the fixed jet and gasket with a screwdriver of exact size.
8. Remove the two screws which hold the float bowl cover and gasket to the carburetor body. Lift off the cover and gasket.
9. Remove the lower float lever pin

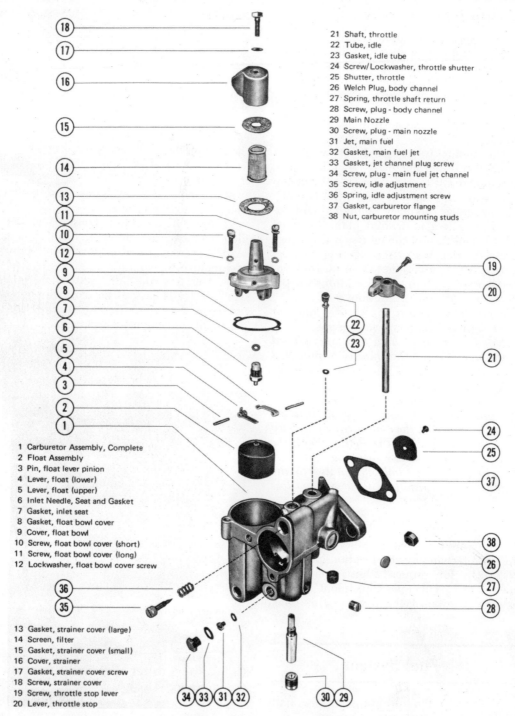

21 Shaft, throttle
22 Tube, idle
23 Gasket, idle tube
24 Screw/Lockwasher, throttle shutter
25 Shutter, throttle
26 Welch Plug, body channel
27 Spring, throttle shaft return
28 Screw, plug - body channel
29 Main Nozzle
30 Screw, plug - main nozzle
31 Jet, main fuel
32 Gasket, main fuel jet
33 Gasket, jet channel plug screw
34 Screw, plug - main fuel jet channel
35 Screw, idle adjustment
36 Spring, idle adjustment screw
37 Gasket, carburetor flange
38 Nut, carburetor mounting studs

1 Carburetor Assembly, Complete
2 Float Assembly
3 Pin, float lever pinion
4 Lever, float (lower)
5 Lever, float (upper)
6 Inlet Needle, Seat and Gasket
7 Gasket, inlet seat
8 Gasket, float bowl cover
9 Cover, float bowl
10 Screw, float bowl cover (short)
11 Screw, float bowl cover (long)
12 Lockwasher, float bowl cover screw

13 Gasket, strainer cover (large)
14 Screen, filter
15 Gasket, strainer cover (small)
16 Cover, strainer
17 Gasket, strainer cover screw
18 Screw, strainer cover
19 Screw, throttle stop lever
20 Lever, throttle stop

Exploded view of typical Mercury pressure type carburetor (© Kiekhaefer Mercury)

and lever, allowing the upper lever to pivot back. This will expose the inlet needle.

10. Remove the inlet needle.

11. Remove the inlet needle seat which has a right-hand thread. A ⅜ in. socket will do this nicely. Do not lose the small gasket behind the inlet needle seat.

12. Remove the float by tipping the carburetor upside down.

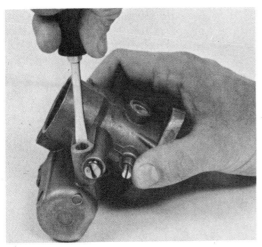

Removing the fixed high speed jet (© Kiekhaefer Mercury)

13. Tap the welch plug, which covers the idle by-pass chamber, with a center punch, and pry it off.

14. Remove the throttle plate from the throttle shaft.

15. Remove the throttle shaft from the top of the carburetor.

16. Remove the throttle plate return spring from the carburetor body.

17. Remove the lead plugs with a sharp punch.

18. Unscrew the two nuts and remove the choke plate and screen.

19. If applicable, remove the choke linkage from the plate.

Cleaning and Inspection

1. Insert the proper size drills in passages. See the carburetor specifications for the proper size drill. Be sure that the passages are clear and free of restrictions.

2. Immerse the carburetor body in carburetor solvent for a short period of time (long enough to remove all dirt and varnish which has accumulated.)

3. Rinse the carburetor thoroughly in clean solvent and blow dry with compressed air. If compressed air is not available, shake the carburetor body to remove most of the solvent and allow to air dry.

4. Check the fuel filter for chips or cracks.

Assembly

1. Check the float for deterioration.

2. Check the float spring adjustment.

3. Check to see that the spring has not been stretched.

4. Place the float in the bowl on the float needle.

5. Place the inlet needle seat gasket in the float bowl cover and thread the inlet needle seat securely into place. Do not overtighten.

6. Set the inlet needle into the neoprene seat.

7. Place the upper float lever in position and insert the float lever pin.

8. Install the lower float lever and pin.

9. Install the float bowl cover. Bend the secondary lever as necessary to obtain a distance of $13/32$ in. $\pm$ $1/64$ in. from the face of the shoulder in the primary lever.

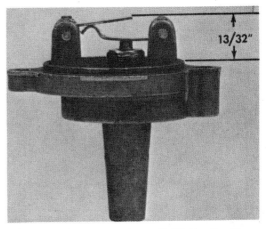

Adjusting the primary lever (© Kiekhaefer Mercury)

10. Be sure that the needle does not stick in the seat. Tip the assembly upright and the needle should move freely on the primary lever.

11. Hold the float bowl cover in an upright position. The distance between the levers as illustrated should be $1/4$ in. Bend the tab on the secondary lever as required to obtain this dimension.

12. Check to see that the float spring measures approximately $3/32$ in. from the top of the float to the end of the exposed spring.

13. Install a new gasket on the end of the float bowl cover and install on the carburetor float bowl. Secure the cover with two screws and lockwashers.

14. Install the fuel filter gasket and fuel filter element with another gasket and the filter bowl cover.

15. Replace the filter bowl cover gasket and install the filter on the carburetor.

16. Assemble the choke plate and screen

Clearance adjustment between levers (© Kiekhaefer Mercury)

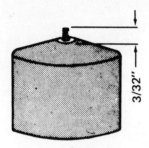

Carburetor float adjustment (© Kiekhaefer Mercury)

on the carburetor throat studs. Install the choke linkage on the choke plate.

17. Install the throttle shaft return spring in the recess at the lower end of the carburetor.

18. Insert the throttle shaft into the top of the carburetor and into the return spring slot. Be sure to have one coil of the spring turned to allow sufficient return of the throttle plate to the closed position from spring tension.

19. Secure the throttle plate to the throttle shaft.

20. Insert the main discharge nozzle into the receptacle at the bottom of the carburetor. Tighten it securely but do not overtighten. Be sure to use a screwdriver of the exact size.

21. Thread the discharge plug into the carburetor.

22. Where applicable, place the gasket on the correct fixed jet and insert the jet (see specifications) into the carburetor.

23. Place the gasket on the ⅜ in. brass hex-head plug and secure the plug.

24. Where applicable, place the gasket on the idle restriction tube and install the idle restriction tube into the carburetor.

25. Insert a new welch plug over the idle by-pass chamber and tap the center of the plug lightly to hold the plug in place.

26. Seal with Liquid Neoprene.

27. Place the spring on the idle adjustment screw and thread the idle adjustment screw into the carburetor.

Installation

1. Installation is the reverse of removal.

Adjustments

HIGH SPEED

The high speed jet is fixed and no adjustment is possible. To alter the high speed jet, it must be replaced with a jet of a different size. Consult the "Jet Changes for Elevation" chart in the specifications for alternate jet sizes or the "Carburetor Specifications" for the standard jet size.

1. Jet size recommendations are intended as a guide. Try a size larger or smaller if in doubt.

2. The manufacturer does not recommend altering the spark advance for operation in higher altitudes. Use a propeller of lower pitch in higher elevations to allow the engine to operate at the recommended rpm.

3. Test the engine in a test tank with a propeller or test wheel.

IDLE SPEED

1. The idle speed is set at the factory for optimum performance. However, due to ambient conditions, it may be necessary to adjust the idle speed periodically.

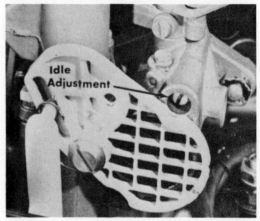

Idle adjustment needle (© Kiekhaefer Mercury)

2. If adjustment is necessary, it can be done with a test wheel or regular propeller in a test tank or on the boat. For optimum low speed performance, adjust the idle mixture and idle speed under actual operating conditions.

3. Warm the engine thoroughly before attempting any adjustment.

4. Start with all idle needles one turn open and adjust for maximum rpm with the distributor retarded to give about 600–700 rpm.

5. With the engine idling in forward gear, turn the low speed mixture adjustment needle counterclockwise until the cylinders fire unevenly. This will indicate an overly rich mixture.

6. Slowly turn the needle clockwise until the cylinders fire evenly and the engine picks up speed.

7. Continue turning the needle clockwise until the motor begins to slow down and fire unevenly. This will indicate a mixture which is too lean.

8. Set the adjustment screw $1/2$ to $3/4$ turn counterclockwise from the too-lean position. This is the approximate true setting. Do not lean the mixture any more than is necessary to obtain a reasonably smooth idle. When in doubt, it is preferable to have a slightly rich mixture rather than a mixture which is too lean.

9. If the motor hesitates during acceleration, after adjusting the idle mixture, the mixture is too lean and should be enriched slightly to produce smooth acceleration.

10. Run the engine at idle and adjust the idle stop screw on the stop bracket until the engine idles at the recommended rpm (see "Tune-Up Specifications") in forward gear.

11. Run the engine at full throttle to clear the cylinders and recheck the idle stop adjustment.

12. It may be necessary to adjust the idle screw up to $1/4$ turn with each change in brand of gasoline to account for differences in volatility and refining process.

Float Level and Float Drop

(See steps no. 9–12 of carburetor assembly procedure.)

Hard Starting

Hard starting is often traced to the improper operation of the choke plate. Adjust the choke linkage and choke return spring for fast, positive action of the choke plate. Be sure that it moves freely and quickly.

Clearance between the choke plate and carburetor body must not be more than 0.015 in. when the choke is closed or the motor will be hard to start.

Fuel Pressure

Fuel pressure at the top carburetor should be checked whenever insufficient fuel supply is suspected or if a fuel tank of other than Kiekhaefer Mercury manufacture is being used. Check fuel tanks (other than Mercury) for the following:

a. Adequate air vent in the fuel cap.

b. Adequate fuel line diameter. The fuel line must be $5/16$–$3/8$ in. in diameter.

c. A clogged or too small filter on the end of the pick-up, or too small pick-up tube. A fuel pick-up assembly (A–32–33909A4) may be used as a comparison.

An insufficient fuel supply will cause the motor to run lean, lose rpm, or cause piston scoring.

1. Connect a pressure gauge into the fuel line that leads to the upper carburetor. The fuel pressure must be at least 2 psi at full throttle.

Throttle Pick-up

Because this adjustment is so closely related to other adjustments made to the electrical system, the adjustment for the throttle pick-up is included among the adjustments in the electrical system.

Throttle Stop

This adjustment is also included in the section dealing with adjustments to the electrical system.

FUEL PUMP

Diaphragm-type fuel pumps are used on most Mercury engines of large horsepower rating. Crankcase pulsating pressure is transferred to the fuel pump diaphragm, which draws fuel from the fuel tank. Before servicing the fuel pump, be sure to obtain replacement parts from a Mercury dealer.

Removal

1. Remove the fuel tank line from the adaptor.

2. Remove the fuel lines from the pump.

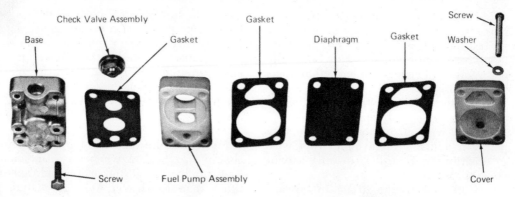

Exploded view of type A-53238A3 fuel pump (© Kiekhaefer Mercury)

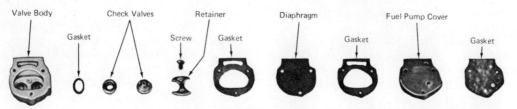

Exploded view of type A-30269A2 and A-23009A1 fuel pump (© Kiekhaefer Mercury)

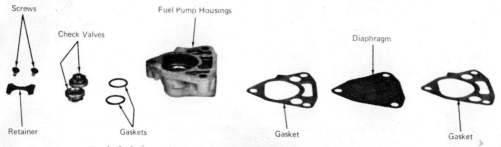

Exploded view of type A-55156A5 fuel pump (© Kiekhaefer Mercury)

3. Remove the screws which secure the fuel pump to the crankcase and remove the fuel pump.

DISASSEMBLY

1. Separate the fuel pump components, referring to the exploded views.

2. Remove the gaskets, diaphragm, and check valve retainer screw.

CLEANING AND INSPECTION

1. Wash all parts thoroughly and allow to air dry.

2. Inspect each part for wear or damage.

3. Replace the pulsator diaphragm and gaskets with new parts.

4. Be sure that the valve seats provide good contact area for the valve disc.

5. Tighten elbows and check valve connections firmly when installing.

6. Do not use Permatex on the valve retainer gasket.

7. Reassemble the fuel pump cover and inspect the check valves. Blow through the outlet hole. Air should be drawn through the valve, but should close immediately when attempting to blow through it.

8. Check the inlet valve by reversing the procedure in Step no. 7. If leakage exists, check for free operation and accurate setting of the valves.

9. A worn or slightly warped valve will cause leakage. Replace worn or slightly warped valves with new ones.

ASSEMBLY

1. Inspect all parts, making sure that they are usable and ready for assembly.

2. Install new check valve gaskets in the seats and set the check valve discs in position. The inlet check valve seat is identified by its tip which protrudes into the casting.

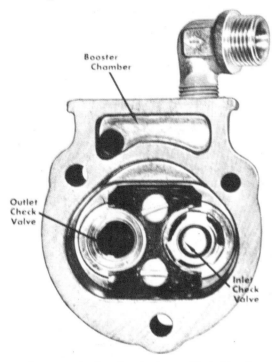

Fuel pump check valve locations (© Kiekhaefer Mercury)

3. The flat side of the check valve fits over this tip. The outlet check valve is installed opposite (flat end up) so that tension is against the valves.

4. Place the retainer on the check valves in the housing and secure with two screws.

5. Place the new gasket on the pump body, followed by the neoprene diaphragm, another gasket, and the fuel pump cover.

VACUUM FUEL TANK AND FUEL LINE

Because the fuel pump on the motor pumps fuel from the tank to the carburetor, only one fuel line is necessary between the tank and motor.

NOTE: *Under law, all gasoline containers must be colored red.*

Priming

1. Prior to starting the motor, the fuel tank must be primed by squeezing the primer bulb on the fuel line.

2. Slowly squeeze the primer bulb by hand. This will draw fuel from the tank to the carburetor bowl.

3. When the bowl on the carburetor is filled, pressure will be felt on the bulb.

Primer Bulb Replacement

1. Remove the damaged or inoperative primer bulb by cutting the fuel line as close to the bulb as possible. Do not damage the check valve assembly.

2. Place a small clamp over the end of the long fuel line (fuel tank to primer bulb) and install the small end of the check valve assembly into the end of the fuel line.

3. Place a large clamp over the end of the primer bulb and fit the primer bulb over the large end of the check valve assembly.

4. Position the clamps on the primer bulb and fuel line as shown (do not pinch the check ball) and pinch the sides of the clamp with a pair of end-cutter pliers. Do not pinch the clamp any more than is necessary to obtain a good seal.

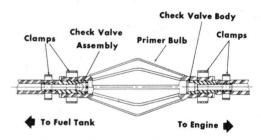

Primer bulb installation (© Kiekhaefer Mercury)

5. Repeat this procedure with the primer bulb-to-engine end of the fuel line, making sure to install the check valve body into the primer bulb.

6. Squeeze the primer bulb several times to be sure that there are no leaks and that the bulb is pumping fuel.

Repairing Fuel Tank Leaks

1. Remove the filler cap and fuel tank cover assembly.

2. If the spot of the leak is known, circle the hole with a pencil, drain the tank completely, and flush with carbon tetrachloride or trichloroethylene.

CAUTION: *Do not use either of these solvents in an unventilated space.*

3. If the spot of the leak is not known, drain and flush the tank, as in step no. 2.

4. Submerge the tank in water and look for bubbles arising from the hole in the tank.

5. Leaks in the tank sheet metal may be repaired by welding according to recommended procedures. It is best to leave this type of work to a shop, where proper facilities are available.

Custom Fuel Tanks

If a tank other than Kiekhaefer Mercury is used, an air vent is the only requirement. Check all "foreign" tanks for the following:

a. Adequate air vent in fuel cap.

b. A large enough diameter fuel line. The fuel line should be $5/16-3/8$ in. inside diameter.

c. Adequate filter on the end of the pick-up, or an adequate pick-up tube.

Electrical System

Motors equipped with electric start are distinguished by the letter E following the model number. The electric start system is a 12 volt type, designed especially for outboard use. There are no adjustments to be made.

STARTER

The starter motor operates under great load and produces a great deal of horsepower for its size. Under no circumstances should the starter be operated for more than 15 seconds at a time. Cranking should not be repeated without a pause of at least 2 minutes to allow the heat to escape.

Inspection

The cranking motor and solenoid are completely enclosed to prevent the entry of moisture and dirt. However, preventive maintenance is required as follows:

1. Inspect the terminals for corrosion and loose connections.

2. Inspect the wiring for worn and frayed insulation.

3. Check the mounting bolts to be sure that they are tight.

Removal

NOTE: *The Delco-Remy starter motor replaces the Bosch unit on later electric start models and is completely interchangeable as a unit.*

1. Be sure that the battery is disconnected before working on the electrical system.

2. Remove the electrical connections from the starter motor.

3. Remove the mounting bolts from the flange and remove the starter motor and drive.

Brush Replacement

2 AND 4 CYLINDER MODELS

Replacement brush sets are available and contain insulated brushes and ground brushes, along with necessary screws, nuts, and washers.

1. Cut off the old brush leads where they attach to the field coils.

2. Clean the ends of the coils by filing or grinding the old brush lead connections. Remove varnish only as far as is necessary to make solder connections.

3. Using resin flux, solder the leads to the field coils—making sure that they are in the correct position to reach the brush holders. It is recommended that the leads be soldered to the back sides of the coils so that excessive solder will not rub the armature. Do not overheat the leads as excessive solder will run onto the leads and it will no longer be flexible.

Solder New Brush Lead Here in Position Shown

Replacing the brush lead to the field coil on 2 and 4 cylinder models (© Kiekhaefer Mercury)

4. Remove the old ground brush holders and attach the new assemblies to the frame with screws, washers, and nuts. Peen the ends of the screws so that they do not vibrate loose.

5. Be sure that none of the soldered

connections are touching the frame and grounding the fields.

6 Cylinder Models

Partial disassembly of the starter motor is necessary to replace the brushes.

1. Loosen and pull out the thru-bolts.
2. Remove the commutator end frame.
3. Remove the armature and drive assembly from the frame and field assembly.

Ground Brushes

1. Remove ground brushes by drilling out the rivets which fasten the holders to the field frame.
2. Care should be taken not to enlarge the hole in the frame.

Insulated Brushes

1. Bend the clip inward to ease brush lead removal.
2. Open the clip which supports insulated brush leads and break the weld which holds the brush lead to the clip.
3. Note which brush has the longer lead and replace with the same length brush lead.
4. Discard all old parts.
5. Install new insulated brushes by placing the proper brush lead into the open clips on the field coils.
6. Tin approximately ¼ in. of field coil assembly and brush lead before placing into the field.
7. Place the brush lead into the clip and crimp the clip to form a good connection.
8. Solder the connection with a heavy-duty soldering iron that will heat quickly so that the field coil and brush lead are not overheated. Use only resin core solder.

RECTIFIER

Three types of rectifiers are used on outboards: plate type, diode type, and the diode type used with Mercury Thunderbolt ignition. The function of the rectifier is to convert alternating current to direct current for recharging of the battery. Failure of the rectifier to discharge a direct current indicates that the rectifier or the alternator is at fault. Rectifiers are rendered useless (discolored appearance) when the battery leads are connected to the wrong terminals. If the rectifier fails, it may be one of the following causes:

    a. Reversed battery wires.
    b. Stopping the engine with the igni-

tion switch when the engine is running above idle speed.
    c. An open circuit such as a broken wire or loose harness connector at the engine.

Removal

1. From the rectifier, remove the two yellow leads which originate at the alternator.
2. From the rectifier, remove the red lead which originates at the electrical harness.
3. Remove the mounting nuts and the rectifier.

Installation

1. Installation is the reverse of removal.

IGNITION SYSTEM

Mercury has used many types of ignition systems since 1966, including magneto, distributor, Thunderbolt triggered by distributor, and the current Thunderbolt breakerless type with removable or built-in trigger. The following chart identifies the model and ignition type. Refer to the specific section for service procedures.

The following precautions should be observed to avoid damaging the Thunderbolt breakerless system.

    A. Do not reverse battery leads.
    B. Do not spark the battery lead wires.
    C. Use only recommended spark plugs. Do not use resistor spark plugs or resistor spark plug wires.
    D. Do not disconnect any wires while the engine is running.
    E. Do not run the engine with a damaged rectifier or with the rectifier removed.
    F. Do not ground any wires to the engine block for checking spark. Ground only to bottom cowl or front cover plate.
    G. Use only approved Mercury tachometers.
    H. Due to the high degree of sophistication on Mercury outboards, only a good quality, transistorized, DC timing light should be used. If the cylinder to which the timing light is connected is shorting out (but fires normally, without the light connected) the probability is that the timing light is of insufficient quality.

CAUTION: *When servicing the ignition*

system, do not touch or disconnect any ignition components while the engine is running, or with the battery connected.

Phelon Magneto

The magneto type ignition has a coil, condenser, and one or two sets of points. This type ignition is self-energizing and requires no external current source (battery). The Phelon-type magneto is used on the 1966–69 Mercury 350.

Removal

1. Remove the flywheel (see "Powerhead").
2. Remove the high tension leads from the spark plugs.
3. On some models, remove the clamp screws which hold the high tension leads to the cylinder block.
4. Rotate the stator plate clockwise and lift off the stator plate.
NOTE: *The magneto unit is an integral part of the flywheel. It is assembled and machined with the flywheel and should never be removed or recharged. Attempts at either of the above will result in magneto replacement.*

Disassembly

1. Remove the primary connection and spark plug wire.
2. Bend down the clip which holds the coil on the core and remove the coil from the core.
3. Remove the condenser mounting screws and the condenser.
4. Remove the breaker points mounting screws and remove the breaker points.

Cleaning and Inspection

1. Wash all parts, except coil and condenser, in cleaning solvent.
2. Check the lead wire to be sure that spark is not leaking through at some point.
3. If points are pitted severely, replace with a new set.
4. Inspect the coil for insulation leakage or for evidence that spark is leaking to a ground.

Assembly

1. Replace the cam breaker (on engines equipped with cam) on the crankshaft with the word "top" up. Install the key into the crankshaft keyway.

2. Replace the thrust washer or flywheel key, whichever is used.
3. Set the magneto on the upper end cap and rotate it to seat it properly.
4. When replacing the coil on the core, be careful not to bend the laminated core. Be sure that the coil is fully seated before bending the core.
5. Check the ground connection for a good contact under the screw.
6. Check the insulation at the breaker point connection to be sure that the lead does not ground against the fixed contact or the spring.
7. If the cam wick becomes dry, it should be replaced. Do not oil the wick. If the breaker arm pivot dries out, lubricate lightly with New Multipurpose Lubricant. Avoid excessive lubrication at this spot.

Kiekhaefer Magneto

The Kiekhaefer magneto is a special type used on all Mercury 4 cylinder models from 1966 through 67. These motors require an ignition spark every 90° of crankshaft rotation. This magneto has a four-lobe breaker cam and produces four sparks per

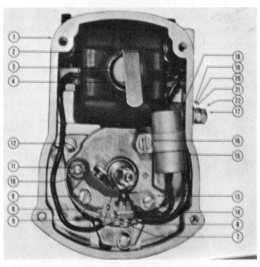

Kiekhaefer 4-cylinder magneto (© Kiekhaefer Mercury)

1. Frame	12. Screw and lockwasher
2. Coil	13. Screw
3. Knob, high tension coil	14. Washer
4. Clip, high tension	15. Condenser
5. Breaker arm assembly	16. Screw and lockwasher
6. Breaker assembly complete	17. Primary ground screw
7. Self-tapping screw	18. Insulator ground switch
8. Washer	19. Washer
9. Screw	20. Washer
10. Washer	21. Lockwasher
11. Hair pin	22. Nut

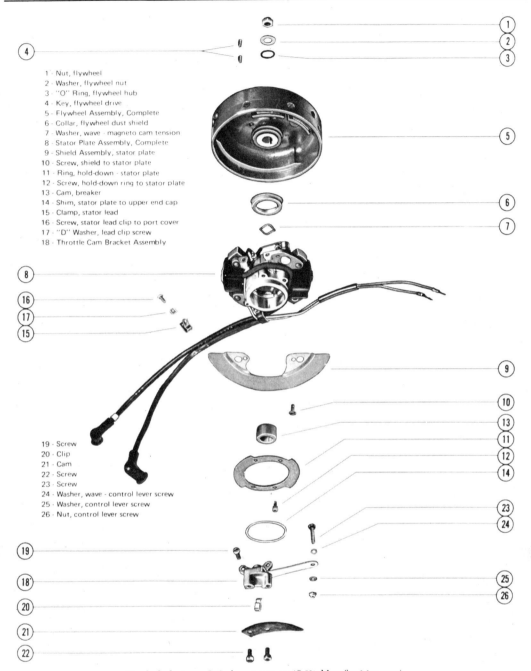

1 - Nut, flywheel
2 - Washer, flywheel nut
3 - "O" Ring, flywheel hub
4 - Key, flywheel drive
5 - Flywheel Assembly, Complete
6 - Collar, flywheel dust shield
7 - Washer, wave - magneto cam tension
8 - Stator Plate Assembly, Complete
9 - Shield Assembly, stator plate
10 - Screw, shield to stator plate
11 - Ring, hold-down - stator plate
12 - Screw, hold-down ring to stator plate
13 - Cam, breaker
14 - Shim, stator plate to upper end cap
15 - Clamp, stator lead
16 - Screw, stator lead clip to port cover
17 - "D" Washer, lead clip screw
18 - Throttle Cam Bracket Assembly

19 - Screw
20 - Clip
21 - Cam
22 - Screw
23 - Screw
24 - Washer, wave - control lever screw
25 - Washer, control lever screw
26 - Nut, control lever screw

Exploded view of Phelon magneto (© Kiekhaefer Mercury)

revolution of the cam which runs at crankshaft speed.

REMOVAL

1. Remove the flywheel (see "Powerhead"), remove the two hold-down clips on the exhaust side of the engine, and detach the high tension leads.

2. Detach the braided ground strap by removing the crankcase screw, leaving the strap attached to the magneto.

3. Remove the lockwasher and nut from the primary ground screw which holds the primary lead to the magneto.

4. Remove the magneto.

DISASSEMBLY

1. Carefully, remove the end cap, rotor, and cover.

2. Remove the breaker assemblies by detaching the breaker terminal screw which holds the primary lead, condenser lead, and coil lead.

3. Remove the condenser and cam wick assembly.

4. Remove the lockring and the breaker assembly.

5. Unscrew and remove the stationary breaker arm.

6. Disconnect the ground wire and lockwire, and remove the coil.

7. Unbolt and remove the bearing support plate from the magneto frame.

Bearing support plate removed from magneto frame (© Kiekhaefer Mercury)

8. Press out the magnetic rotor and shaft. Be careful not to damage either of these parts.

9. To remove the bearing support plate from the magneto, place the support plate in a vise with jaw protectors. Tap on the shaft opposite the drive end while holding the magnetic rotor.

10. If the bearings are worn, replace with new bearings.

11. Do not wipe or wash off sealed bearings. These are pre-packed and require no further lubrication.

Cleaning and Inspection

1. Clean the exterior magneto frame. Compressed air is best for this. Do not submerge the unit in liquid.

2. Check all disassembled parts for wear or damage.

3. Occasionally a vertical crack appears in the magnetic rotor of the four-cylinder magneto. This will not affect the performance of the unit.

Leakage Paths

1. Occasionally, the secondary voltage establishes a path to ground other than across the spark plugs. Once such a path is established, the ignition spark is likely to continue to follow this path.

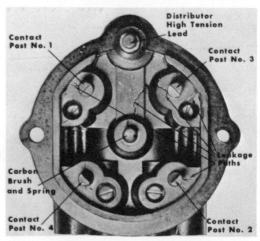

Magneto cap leakage paths (© Kiekhaefer Mercury)

2. Causes of leakage paths are:

a. Broken leads or poor lead connections.

b. Excessive spark plug gap or point gap.

c. Moisture or corrosion in the magneto.

3. A surface leakage path can be located by the burning effect on plastic or other insulating materials.

4. The cause of a leakage path must be determined and corrected. Any part with evidence of heavy (or more than one) leakage paths, should be discarded and replaced.

Oxidation

In most cases, magnetos which have been subjected to corrosion can be cleaned and returned to service. The oxidation or corrosion will be evident from the green deposits which form on the copper and brass parts. A brown deposit is usually found throughout the unit also. There are several common causes of oxidation.

a. A spark gap across a loose connection in the magneto.

b. Carbon paths within the magneto.

c. Broken or sticking brush leads.

d. Plugged vents.

The cause of oxidation should be located and corrected.

Assembly

1. Press the ball bearing drive end into the magneto frame housing.

2. Press the ball bearing opposite end into the bearing support. The bearing support should be tapped with a mallet or

pressed, being careful not to cock the bearing support or the housing.

3. Tighten four screws and lockwashers evenly to support the frame.

4. Rotate the magneto assembly, making sure that the shaft does not bind. A binding condition indicates badly worn or rough bearings. Do not confuse the pull due to magnetic break during rotation with a binding condition.

5. Before installing the movable contacts, apply a very light film of New Multipurpose Lubricant on the post.

6. Install the breaker point assembly with two screws and washers.

7. Install the coil on the magneto housing and tighten the bridge set screws. Install the lockwire into the coil bridge set screws.

8. Install the holder and cam wick assembly along with condenser on the top of the holder.

9. Install the new cam wick which is supplied with each new breaker assembly. The cam wick holder must be set so that the wick has 0.015 in. clearance to the flat of the cam breaker. This is important as too little clearance will cause particles to

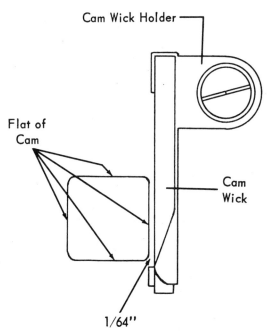

Cam Wick Holder

Flat of Cam

Cam Wick

1/64"

Cam Wick and holder installation (© Kiekhaefer Mercury)

be thrown off and too much clearance will cause insufficient lubrication. A new cam wick should be installed every 100 hours

of operation or each time breaker points are replaced.

10. Install the breaker points.

11. Place a washer on the terminal screw and insert screw into the primary lead of the coil. Place the ground lead on the screw (do not short the leads) and insert the screw in the movable and stationary points and tighten.

12. Start four screws through the new gasket and cover, but do not tighten.

13. Install the gasket and magneto end cap over the cover and tighten the screws.

14. Tighten the four screws on the cover, thus aligning the magneto cap contact post and magneto rotor contact point.

15. Remove two screws from the magneto end cap.

16. Install the rotor, making sure that it aligns with the spline.

17. Reinstall the gasket, end cap, and two screws with ground strap and tighten.

INSTALLATION

1. Attach the other end of the ground strap to the crankcase screw.

2. The magneto rotor shaft and shaft extension are spline-blanked on either shaft for easy installation.

3. Rotate the timing pulley until shaft sets in place.

4. Replace the four screws and secure the magneto to the adaptor.

5. Connect all wires and leads.

6. The magneto must be retimed to the motor. See the specific motor under the timing and adjustments section.

Kiekhaefer Distributor

A Kiekhaefer distributor-type ignition replaces the magneto on 1966–67 Mercury six-cylinder outboard motors.

REMOVAL

1. Remove the four screws which secure the distributor to the distributor adaptor.

2. Remove the ground strap from the distributor ground frame. Remove the spark plug leads from the spark plugs and detach the high tension lead from the screw on the exhaust plate.

3. Pull the air vent tubes from the nylon elbows and pull the secondary leads out of the coils.

4. Disconnect the primary leads.

5. Remove the distributor assembly from the motor.

DISASSEMBLY

1. Remove the two screws securing the side inlet assembly and remove the side inlet. The side inlet cap must be removed before the distributor cap is removed. The side inlet contains the carbon brushes which extend past the inside of the distributor rotor and can be broken off.

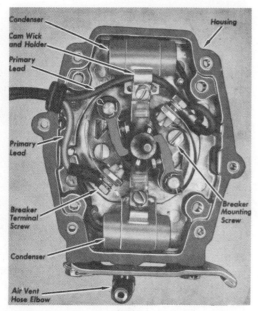

Kiekhaefer distributor with cap removed (© Kiekhaefer Mercury)

2. Remove the secondary lead wires which are threaded into the distributor housing and side inlet. Pull off the neoprene caps and unscrew the leads.

3. Pull the distributor rotor off the distributor shaft. Be careful as the distributor rotor may be secured with Loctite.

4. Remove the distributor adaptor from the distributor frame.

5. Remove the nut which secures the leads to the breaker assemblies.

6. Remove the screw which secures the condenser and cam wick holder to the frame.

7. Remove the cotter pins and fiber washers from the pivot pins.

8. Remove the mounting screws which hold the breaker assemblies to the frame and remove the breaker assemblies.

9. Tap the distributor cam assembly and two sealed ball bearings from the housing with a mallet to remove them.

10. Remove the wave washers.

11. The distributor rotor drive pin is a tight fit in the rotor. To prevent bending

the rotor shaft, be sure to support the cam assembly when driving the pin out for replacement of the ball bearings.

12. If necessary, remove the rotor bearings from the shaft by tapping or pressing.

CLEANING AND INSPECTION

1. See "Cleaning and Inspection" of Kiekhaefer four-cylinder magneto.

2. Be sure that the carbon brush is not worn and that the spring is not corroded.

3. Check the side inlet for cracks or leakage. Replace if found to be defective.

4. Be sure that the carbon brush and spring of the inlet can be depressed easily and returned to the original position.

ASSEMBLY

1. Press the sealed ball bearings onto the shaft, one from each end. Apply pressure from the inner ball race to prevent damaging the ball bearing.

2. Press the distributor cam drive pin into the drive pin hole. Center it evenly in the hole.

3. Insert two wave washers in the recess in the distributor frame. The bearings slip freely into the housing.

4. Install the plastic vent elbow into the frame.

5. Check the breaker points for pitting or misalignment.

6. Lubricate both pivot pins with New Multipurpose Lubricant. Place the breaker point assembly on the pivot pin, making sure that the stationary point is flush with the frame of the housing.

7. Install, but do not tighten, the retaining screw.

8. Set the breaker points to specification with a feeler gauge.

9. Check the spring tension which should be 33–37 ounces.

10. Place the primary and condenser leads on the primary terminals of the breaker assembly and tighten the nut.

11. Install the condensers.

12. Install the cam, cam wick holders, and one primary lead, and tighten the retaining screw. A new cam wick should be installed every 100 hours of engine operation or each time breaker points are installed. The cam wick is specially lubricated and requires no further attention. Any additional lubrication will be detrimental to the life of the points.

13. Set the cam wick holder so that the wick has 1/64 in. to the flat end of the cam-

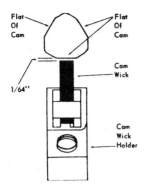

Cam wick and holder installation (© Kiekhaefer Mercury)

shaft (between lobes). A 0.015 in. feeler gauge will set this properly.

14. Tighten the hold-down screw. If the cam wick is set too close to the flat of the cam, the result will be excessive grease from the wick and premature destruction of the points. If the cam wick is set too far from the flat of the cam, rapid cam follower wear will result.

15. Replace the fiberglass adaptor and place a new gasket on the frame.

16. Place a new O-ring and nylon sleeve in the camshaft recess.

17. Apply a few drops of Loctite A in the rotor shaft bore and install the rotor on the shaft.

18. Press on the rotor until it is seated on the drive pin. The rotor is mounted off-center and will only fit one way.

19. Thread the high tension lead for coil No. 1 into the center terminal of the distributor housing. Thread high tension lead of coil No. two into the side inlet assembly.

20. Set a new gasket on the distributor housing and place the housing on the frame and adaptor. For correct alignment, the notch on the housing and frame must match.

21. Fasten the cap with two screws and washers.

22. Set a new gasket on the inlet and place the inlet assembly on the distributor cap. Be sure that the brush is in position on the rotor.

23. Secure the inlet assembly to the distributor housing with two screws.

INSTALLATION

1. Secure the distributor and attach the ground straps from the distributor frames to the crankcase.

2. Replace the vent tubes to the air vent elbow on the distributor frame. Attach the primary wire to the correct location.

3. Place the high tension leads so that two leads will be positioned on each clamp at the rear of the manifold cover. Attach the high tension leads to the respective spark plug terminals.

Thunderbolt Breaker-Less Battery Ignition—4 and 6 Cylinder Distributor Housing with Built-In Trigger

REMOVAL

1. Remove the wraparound and top cowl assemblies.

2. Remove the top cowl support frame and rear support bracket as follows:

   a. Remove three nuts from cowl frame rubber mounts.

   b. Remove two screws and lockwashers from the forward top part of the cowl support frame and four screws from bottom of rear support.

   c. Disconnect the choke solenoid wire.

   d. Remove the top cowl support frame and rear support bracket from the powerhead.

3. Remove the spark plug wires and their retainers. Remove the high tension cable from the coil and remove the air vent tubes.

4. Disconnect the trigger lead wires from the switch box.

5. Remove the screw and driven pulley flange and remove the timing belt from the driven pulley.

6. Disconnect the link rod from the vertical throttle lever and remove the ground strap.

7. Remove the distributor and adaptor assembly.

DISASSEMBLY

1. Bend open the tab washer and unscrew the distributor housing cap from the adaptor.

2. Pull the distributor housing assembly from the economizer collar and distributor adaptor.

3. Remove the clamp from the distributor cap and housing.

4. Remove and inspect the distributor cap and spark plug lead assembly.

5. Remove the upper ball bearing from

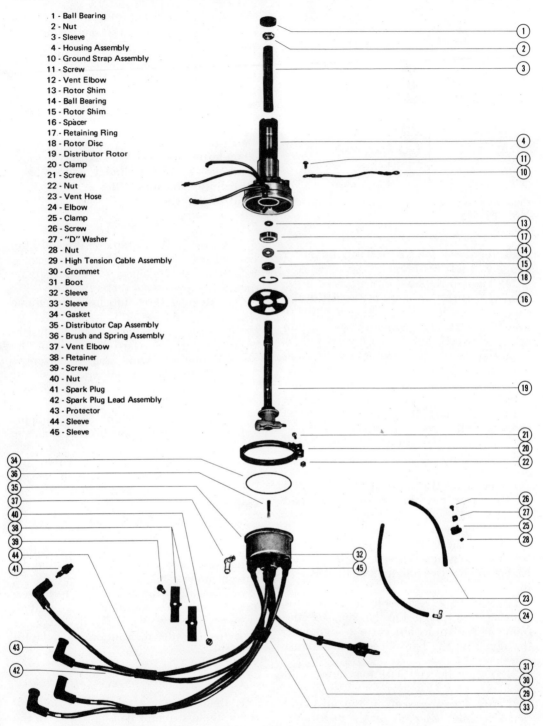

 1 - Ball Bearing
 2 - Nut
 3 - Sleeve
 4 - Housing Assembly
10 - Ground Strap Assembly
11 - Screw
12 - Vent Elbow
13 - Rotor Shim
14 - Ball Bearing
15 - Rotor Shim
16 - Spacer
17 - Retaining Ring
18 - Rotor Disc
19 - Distributor Rotor
20 - Clamp
21 - Screw
22 - Nut
23 - Vent Hose
24 - Elbow
25 - Clamp
26 - Screw
27 - "D" Washer
28 - Nut
29 - High Tension Cable Assembly
30 - Grommet
31 - Boot
32 - Sleeve
33 - Sleeve
34 - Gasket
35 - Distributor Cap Assembly
36 - Brush and Spring Assembly
37 - Vent Elbow
38 - Retainer
39 - Screw
40 - Nut
41 - Spark Plug
42 - Spark Plug Lead Assembly
43 - Protector
44 - Sleeve
45 - Sleeve

Distributor for Thunderbolt breaker-less ignition with built-in trigger (© Kiekhaefer Mercury)

the distributor housing. Press on the outer race of the bearing through the hole on each side of the housing. Do not press against the ball bearing retainer.

6. Remove the nut from the rotor shaft and tap lightly on the rotor shaft to remove from the distributor.

7. Remove the retaining ring from the lower end of the distributor housing and remove the lower ball bearing.

CLEANING AND INSPECTION

1. Inspect the bearings for wear or corrosion.

2. Clean and inspect the parts of the distributor housing, replacing as necessary.

3. Check the distributor cap for leakage paths.

ASSEMBLY

1. Install the lower ball bearing into the distributor housing and retain with the retaining ring.

2. Place the rotor disc into the slot in the distributor housing.

3. Install the rotor and shaft assembly through the disc, making certain that the disc key is inserted into the keyway.

4. Place the rotor shaft sleeve over the rotor shaft and torque the nut on the rotor shaft to 75–80 in. lbs.

5. Press the upper ball bearing into the distributor housing.

6. Place the economizer collar washer in the recess of the distributor housing and install the economizer collar.

7. Place the adaptor washer on the economizer collar and install the adaptor assembly.

8. Install the distributor housing washer, tab washer, wave washer (with wave toward the cap), and distributor housing cap onto the housing. Screw the cap on until tight, back off cap to the first notch and bend up the tab washer.

9. Install the distributor cap clamp and locate the screw as shown.

Locate Clamp Screw & Nut In This Position

Installing the distributor cap clamp. Position the clamp as shown. (© Kiekhaefer Mercury)

INSTALLATION

1. Position the distributor and adaptor assembly into the cylinder block mounting flange. Be sure that the driven pulley spacer and distributor drive key are positioned properly.

2. Secure the distributor adaptor to the cylinder block.

3. Align the arrow on the pulley with the timing mark on the flywheel and install the timing belt.

4. Install the driven pulley flange and torque the screw to 60 in. lbs.

5. Reconnect the ground strap and connect the link rod to the vertical lever.

6. Install the high tension lead to the coil.

7. Reinstall the air vent tube.

8. Cover the switch box terminals with Liquid Neoprene and connect the trigger leads, following the color code on wires and terminals.

9. Install all cowl support brackets.

10. Time and adjust the engine and install all cowls.

Thunderbolt Breaker-Less Battery Ignition—4 and 6 Cylinder with Removable Trigger Assembly

REMOVAL

1. Remove the wraparound and top cowl assemblies as detailed in the previous section.

2. Remove the spark plug wires, the high tension cable from the coil, and the air vent tubes.

3. Disconnect three trigger lead wires from the switch box assembly.

4. Unscrew the adaptor and remove the distributor and adaptor assembly.

5. Remove the distributor housing.

DISASSEMBLY

1. Remove the distributor cap from the adaptor.

2. Separate the trigger housing from the adaptor plate and remove the gasket.

3. Separate the trigger assembly, rotor shaft assembly, and primary housing.

CLEANING AND INSPECTION

1. See "Cleaning and Inspection" in the previous section.

ASSEMBLY

1. Place the wave washer and rotor shaft assembly into the primary housing.

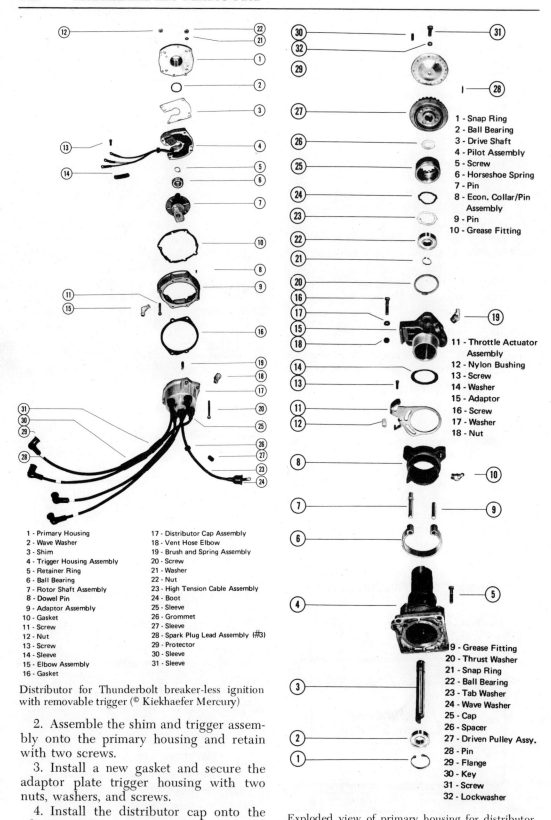

1 - Snap Ring
2 - Ball Bearing
3 - Drive Shaft
4 - Pilot Assembly
5 - Screw
6 - Horseshoe Spring
7 - Pin
8 - Econ. Collar/Pin Assembly
9 - Pin
10 - Grease Fitting

11 - Throttle Actuator Assembly
12 - Nylon Bushing
13 - Screw
14 - Washer
15 - Adaptor
16 - Screw
17 - Washer
18 - Nut

1 - Primary Housing
2 - Wave Washer
3 - Shim
4 - Trigger Housing Assembly
5 - Retainer Ring
6 - Ball Bearing
7 - Rotor Shaft Assembly
8 - Dowel Pin
9 - Adaptor Assembly
10 - Gasket
11 - Screw
12 - Nut
13 - Screw
14 - Sleeve
15 - Elbow Assembly
16 - Gasket

17 - Distributor Cap Assembly
18 - Vent Hose Elbow
19 - Brush and Spring Assembly
20 - Screw
21 - Washer
22 - Nut
23 - High Tension Cable Assembly
24 - Boot
25 - Sleeve
26 - Grommet
27 - Sleeve
28 - Spark Plug Lead Assembly (#3)
29 - Protector
30 - Sleeve
31 - Sleeve

Distributor for Thunderbolt breaker-less ignition with removable trigger (© Kiekhaefer Mercury)

2. Assemble the shim and trigger assembly onto the primary housing and retain with two screws.

3. Install a new gasket and secure the adaptor plate trigger housing with two nuts, washers, and screws.

4. Install the distributor cap onto the adaptor, making sure that the spring and brush assembly is in the distributor cap.

19 - Grease Fitting
20 - Thrust Washer
21 - Snap Ring
22 - Ball Bearing
23 - Tab Washer
24 - Wave Washer
25 - Cap
26 - Spacer
27 - Driven Pulley Assy.
28 - Pin
29 - Flange
30 - Key
31 - Screw
32 - Lockwasher

Exploded view of primary housing for distributor with Thunderbolt ignition with removable trigger (© Kiekhaefer Mercury)

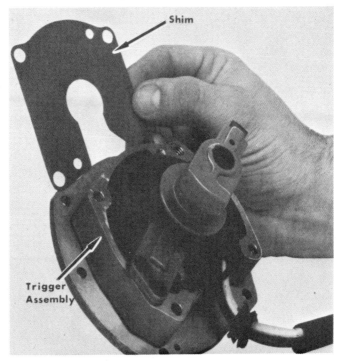

Installing the shim on the removable trigger assembly (© Kiekhaefer Mercury)

INSTALLATION

1. Secure the distributor with four screws and attach the ground straps from crankcase to distributor frame.

2. Replace the vent tubes in the air vent elbows.

3. Attach the trigger lead wires to the switch box assembly.

4. Install the spark plug wires and secure with the retainers on the crankcase.

5. Install the coil high tension lead.

6. Install the top cowl and wrap assembly.

Lightning Energizer Breaker-Less Ignition

REMOVAL

1. Remove the vent hoses from the ignition driver.

2. Remove the ignition driver ground strap.

3. Remove the red, white, and blue leads from the switch box.

4. Detach spark plug wires from the ignition driver.

5. Remove the four screws securing the ignition driver to the adaptor and remove the ignition driver.

DISASSEMBLY

1. Remove the end cap, cover, and rotor.

2. Remove the low- and high-speed coil assemblies by disconnecting the soldered joint (unsolder the connection only if the coils are to be replaced) on the terminal board and loosening the coil bridge set screws. These may be held by Loctite.

3. Remove the bearing cap to ignition drive frame screws and press out the magnetic rotor, shaft, and bearing cap. Do not damage the magnetic rotor or bearing cap.

4. To remove the bearing cap from the rotating magnet, place in a vise with soft jaws, hold the magnetic rotor, and tap on the shaft opposite the driven end.

5. If the bearings are worn or rough, replace with new bearings. Wipe off sealed bearings; do not wash in solvent.

CLEANING AND INSPECTION

1. Check the ignition driver frame housing, for dirt, rust, or corrosion, which can be removed with no. 320 carborundum paper and wiped clean.

2. Check the rotating magnet and shaft, and clean in the same manner (step no. 1).

3. Check the end cap for leakage paths.

1 - Housing
2 - Set Screw
3 - Terminal Board Assembly
4 - Screw
5 - Coil Assembly
6 - Coil Assembly
7 - Harness

8 - Clamp
9 - Screw
10 - Ball Bearing
11 - Shaft Assembly
12 - Ball Bearing
13 - Bearing Cap
14 - Screw
15 - Rotor Assembly
16 - Spring
17 - Gasket
18 - Cover
19 - Screw
20 - Tab Washer
21 - Vent Elbow
22 - Cap Assembly
23 - Brush and Spring Assembly
24 - Gasket
25 - Ground Strap Assembly
26 - Screw
27 - Tab Washer
28 - Lead Assembly
29 - Grommet
30 - Boot
31 - Spark Plug Lead Assembly

32 - Sleeve
33 - Sleeve
34 - Protector Assembly
35 - Sleeve
36 - Clip
37 - Screw
38 - "D" Washer

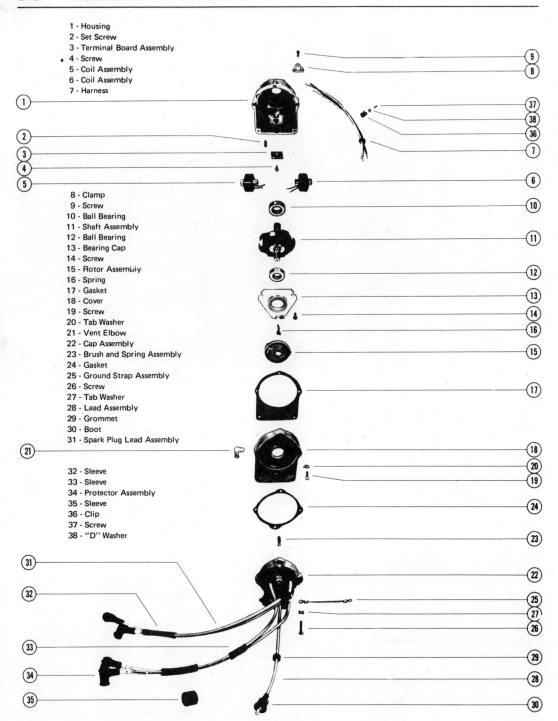

Exploded view ignition driver used with Lightning Energizer ignition system (© Kiekhaefer Mercury)

ASSEMBLY

1. Install the magnetic rotor and bearing assembly into the ignition driver housing. Place a small amount of Loctite on the screws and tighten evenly. Rotate the magnetic rotor by hand, checking to be sure there is no binding.

2. Install the high- and low-speed coils into the ignition driver housing. The low (red) coil goes into the housing on the left

side when viewing it from the driven end.

3. Place a small amount of Loctite on the coil bridge screws, hold the coils against the bottom stops, and tighten the screws.

4. If the coil leads were previously removed from the terminal board, resolder the leads, using 50–50 solder and resin flux. After soldering, coat the terminals with Liquid Neoprene.

5. Install a new cover gasket and install the ignition driver housing.

6. Clean the splines of the rotor and shaft. Apply three drops of Loctite to the bottom of the splined hole in the rotor. Install the rotor. Make sure that the spring is pressed into the bottom of the splined hole before applying Loctite.

7. Install a new distributor cap gasket and install the distributor cap.

INSTALLATION

1. The ignition driver rotor shaft and shaft extension are each provided with a space for easy installation.

2. With the flywheel and pulley aligned, install the ignition driver on the motor.

3. Rotate the timing pulley until the shaft sets in place. A $1/16$ in. groove is located at the end of the shaft coupling in the centerline of the blank tooth to locate for easy installation.

4. Secure the ignition driver to the adaptor with four screws.

Thunderbolt Breaker-Less Ignition—Merc 400 (2 Cylinder)

REMOVAL

1. Remove the wraparound cowl. Unscrew the top cowl from the powerhead and remove the starter rope handle and top cowl.

2. Remove the rewind starter as follows:

a. Remove the cotter pin, washer, and screw from the neutral starter lockout cable. Remove the cable from the rewind starter.

b. Remove the brown and black wires from the switch box.

c. Remove the linkage screw from the spark advance lever.

d. Unscrew and remove the rewind starter.

3. Remove the two centerhub screws and lockwashers.

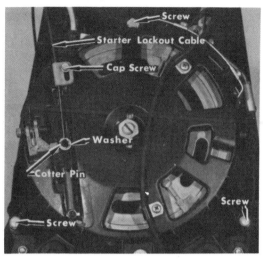

Disassembling the neutral starter lockout cable (© Kiekhaefer Mercury)

4. Remove the flywheel nut and washer, using an automotive flywheel holder to hold the flywheel.

5. Carefully, remove the flywheel with a puller and two bolts.

DISASSEMBLY

1. Remove the stator as follows:

a. Remove the four allen head screws and washers.

b. Remove the screw and D washer from the clamp.

c. If a manual model, remove the blue and white wires from the switch box.

d. If an electric model, remove the blue and white wire from the switch box and the two yellow wires from the rectifier.

e. Remove the stator.

2. Remove the distributor body as follows:

a. Remove the spark plug wires.

b. Remove the high tension leads from the clip.

c. Remove the high tension lead from the coil.

d. Remove the vent hose from the distributor body.

NOTE: *On early Merc 400s, the rotor was not secured by Loctite and will come off when the distributor body is pried up. Later models have the rotor secured by Loctite and must be removed as follows:*

3. Remove the four end cap screws.

4. Using a universal puller (installed

with 10–32x3½ in. bolts) in any two holes of the distributor body, pull the end cap assembly off.

5. Unscrew the high tension lead from the distributor body.

6. Remove the front support, the coil, and the switch box.

CLEANING AND INSPECTION

1. Check the high tension leads for cracking or fraying.

2. Check for carbon tracks or leakage.

ASSEMBLY

1. Install the coil and switch box on the front cowl support and install the front support.

2. Check the O-ring and install the end cap with four screws.

3. To reduce possible wear on the distributor, the rotor must be installed with Loctite Grade AV. If Loctite AV is not available, Loctite Pipe Sealant (available commercially) may be substituted. Do not use Loctite Type A.

4. Apply Loctite as follows:
CAUTION: *LocQuic primer must be sprayed on crankshaft before distributor body is installed as the primer will deteriorate the plastic body.*

a. Spray LocQuic Primer Grade T on crankshaft between the top oil seal and taper.

b. Install new distributor body and stator.

c. Apply Loctite AV to bottom of bore in the distributor rotor. Do not allow Loctite to run into the top oil seal.

d. Press the rotor in place by hand.

5. Place the high tension lead wires into the new distributor housing on the engine. Use longer boots (A–60096) and no. 47 sealant on the posts.

INSTALLATION

1. Install the vent tube restrictor in the upper end of the vent tube. Push the restrictor into the vent tube about 1 in. and install vent tube to elbow.

2. Install the flywheel using a new O-ring.

3. Install the starter rewind housing.

4. Install the linkage on the spark advance lever.

5. Connect the wires to the switch box and to the rectifier (if applicable).

6. Install the neutral starter lock and cable.

7. Pull the rewind rope through the top cowl.

8. Install the top cowl.

9. Install the starter rope handle.

10. Install the wraparound cowl.

BREAKER POINT REPLACEMENT

See the appropriate section concerning ignition system service.

Breaker Point Adjustment

PHELON MAGNETO

1. The flywheel must be removed to adjust the points.

2. Care must be taken when adjusting the points gap. The high point of the cam is not the keyway, but as shown in the illustration.

High point of the cam location—Phelon magneto (© Kiekhaefer Mercury)

3. Adjust the breaker points so that breaker cam follower arm is at the high point of the cam. This is approximately ¼ in. after the points open.

4. A degree plate should be used to set the points, however, if a degree plate is not available, set the breaker arms at the highest point of the cam lobe.

5. Using a feeler gauge, between the open faces of the points, set the gap at 0.020 in, by loosening the screw on the base plate.

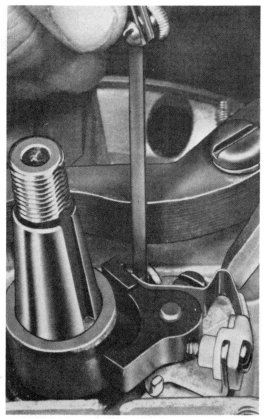

Adjusting the breaker points—Phelon magneto (© Kiekhaefer Mercury)

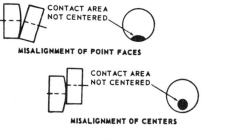

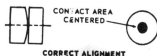

Correct and incorrect alignment for breaker points on all Mercury engines (© Kiekhaefer Mercury)

6. Rotate the crankshaft 180° and set the other set of points in the same manner.

7. Check the breaker cam for looseness due to wear. It should be tight on the crankshaft and installed with the arrow or part number to the top. If this is loose, it will probably cause misfiring at idle.

NOTE: *Some models have the breaker cam cut into the crankshaft as a one-piece assembly.*

8. Reinstall the flywheel.

KIEKHAEFER 4 CYLINDER MAGNETO

1. The points must be closed for 48° of rotation to allow sufficient current to build up in the coil.

2. Prior to synchronization, clean the faces of the points to remove oil and dirt film.

3. Check the point faces for proper alignment. Any misalignment will result in premature wear or pitting.

4. The breaker points should be aligned properly by bending or twisting the fixed contact only.

5. Check the breaker point spring tension, which should be 33–37 ounces. If the spring tension is less than thirty-three ounces, the breaker arm will flutter and cause a miss at high rpm. On the other hand, if the spring tension is greater than thirty-seven ounces, the rubbing block will wear and the points will close in about 4–6 hours of operation.

6. To check spring tension, hook a spring scale in the crook of the fiber cam follower, and pull the spring scale at a right angle to the movable arm until the breaker point just begins to open. If the spring tension is too great, bend the breaker point spring inward to the fiber cam follower. If the tension is too small, bend the spring outward from the cam follower. Do not bend the spring with pliers to create a sharp bend. Bend only by hand.

7. Set the point gap at 0.008 in. when the cam follower fiber arm is on the highest part of the cam lobe.

8. A more exact adjustment is to adjust the dwell to 48°. An automotive dwell meter can be used to do this, if one is available.

NOTE: *Do not use an automotive dwell meter on Thunderbolt ignition.*

KIEKHAEFER 6 CYLINDER DISTRIBUTOR

1. Clean the face of the points to remove dirt and film.

2. Check the spring tension as described in the previous section. Spring tension should be 33–37 ounces.

3. Breaker assemblies are pre-tensioned and pre-aligned; however, the alignment

and spring tension should be checked at installation.

4. It is essential that both distributor gaps are the same or the engine will run erratically. One set of points, firing three cylinders, will be out of time with the second set of points.

5. Place the rubbing block of no. 1 set of points (white lead; brown lead on Thunderbolt ignition) on the highest part of the distributor cam lobe and set the points at 0.007 in.

6. Set the second set of points in the same manner.

NOTE: *An automotive-type dwell meter may be used to set the dwell on standard type ignition. Do not use an automotive-type dwell meter on Thunderbolt ignition. A Mercury dealer is best equipped with the special tools to synchronize the points on Thunderbolt ignition models.*

7. On standard ignition models the dwell should be 90° and should be 45° on Thunderbolt ignition models.

All Breaker-Less Ignitions

1. Thunderbolt and Lightening Energizer breakerless ignitions have no breaker points to be serviced.

Timing and Additional Adjustments

NOTE: *All timing procedures for the pulley and distributor or magnetic pulley assume that the magneto, distributor, or pulley have been removed or disturbed. If these have not been disturbed, it is wise to check the timing anyway.*

MERC 350 (1966–69) FULL
GEARSHIFT

Maximum Spark Advance

1. For this operation, it is best to spend a few dollars and acquire a timing device which threads into the spark plug port. This will take the place of the special tool that is used by dealer to position the piston at the proper BTDC position. These little timing devices are available (with complete instructions) at most good automotive, boat, cycle, or snowmobile outlets.

2. The flywheel must be removed for this operation.

3. Remove the no. 1 (top) spark plug

and thread the timing gauge into the hole. Set no. 1 piston at Top Dead Center (TDC) and zero the timing gauge.

4. Place the no. 1 piston at 0.300 in. (7.62 mm) BTDC by rotating the crankshaft in a clockwise direction from TDC.

5. Advance the magneto slowly against the magneto stop. At this time, the breaker points should open. A continuity tester can be used to determine the moment the points open. If they did not open, or opened before touching the magneto stop, adjust the magneto linkage and tighten the locknut.

6. Recheck the magneto advance to assure the correct setting.

7. Advance the magneto against the magneto stop. Loosen the two screws on the throttle pick-up plate and adjust to obtain full throttle, then tighten the screws. Allow 0.010–0.015 in. play in the carburetor shaft to avoid forcing the linkage. Do not bend the pick-up with the nylon sleeve.

Magneto stop and linkage—1966–69 Merc 350 (© Kiekhaefer Mercury)

Full throttle adjustment—1966–69 Merc 350 (© Kiekhaefer Mercury)

8. It should not be necessary to adjust the linkage on the port side of the engine, as this is pre-set at the factory. Should the setting be disturbed, adjust the linkage so that ½ in. of thread remains exposed.

MERC 400 (1970–71)

Timing and Synchronizing

1. Check that the trigger pick-up in the trigger plate is positioned approximately in the center of the elongated slots.

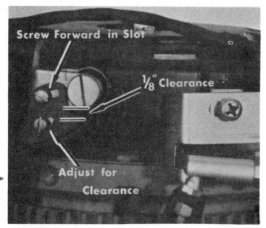

Throttle lockout cam position—Merc 400 (© Kiekhaefer Mercury)

2. If necessary to adjust this position, place the throttle lockout cam as shown in the illustration.

3. Check to see that the gap between the trigger pick-up head and the trigger housing is 0.050–0.060 in. wide. If necessary, adjust this clearance by shimming between the trigger plate and the starter housing.

4. Connect a timing light.

5. With the engine running, align the flywheel timing mark (two white dots) in the timing window. Loosen the two screws on the carburetor pick-up plate, and slide the plate so that the cam just touches the primary pick-up arm on the carburetor cluster. Tighten the two screws.

6. Adjust the engine speed to 5000–5200 rpm. This must be done on the boat or in a test tank.

NOTE: *An ordinary automotive tachometer will not register the impulses of this ignition. Consult a Mercury dealer as to what type of tachometer to use.*

Flywheel timing marks properly aligned—Merc 400 (© Kiekhaefer Mercury)

7. Adjust the spark stop screw to align the flywheel timing mark (white line) in the timing window. Tighten the locknut.

8. With the spark arm against the stop, but not actuating the throttle arm, adjust the throttle pick-up arm to just touch the secondary pick-up on the carburetor cluster. Bend the arm to adjust.

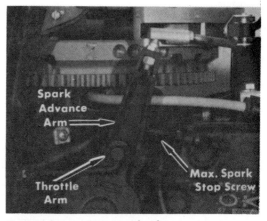

Setting the maximum spark advance stop screw—Merc 400 (© Kiekhaefer Mercury)

9. Rotate the throttle arm to wide open throttle and adjust the throttle stop screw to allow full carburetor plate opening, with 0.010–0.015 in. clearance to prevent binding. Tighten the locknut.

10. Remove the timing light from the engine.

MERC 500 (1966–67)

The following procedure is necessary in the event that the timing has been dis-

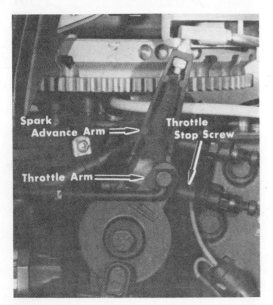

Adjusting the throttle stop screw—Merc 400
(© Kiekhaefer Mercury)

turbed or that the magneto has been removed (which will disturb the timing).

Timing the Flywheel and Magneto Pulley

1. The flywheel has one mark (a straight line), which, when aligned with the arrow on the magneto driven pulley, indicates that no. 1 piston is at TDC (Top Dead Center).

2. Rotate the flywheel until the timing mark on the flywheel is aligned with the center of the crankshaft and distributor pulley center.

Timing magneto pulley and flywheel—Merc 500 1966–67 (© Kiekhaefer Mercury)

3. Position the arrow on the pulley to point at the timing mark on the flywheel.

4. Replace the timing belt, plate, screw, and washers.

Maximum Spark Advance

1. To set the maximum spark advance, it is advisable to acquire a timing tool (explained under Merc 350 "Maximum Spark Advance Adjustment").

2. Remove the no. 1 spark plug (top) and thread the timing tool into the spark plug port.

3. Set the no. 1 piston at TDC (Top Dead Center) and set the timing gauge at zero.

4. Rotate the crankshaft in a clockwise direction and set no. 1 piston at 0.200 in. (5.08 mm) BTDC.

5. Slowly advance the magneto until the points break. This can be seen with a continuity tester which is described in the first section of this book.

6. Hold the magneto in this position and adjust the spark advance screw to just touch the pilot assembly. Tighten the locknut.

Spark advance screw adjustment—Merc 500 1966–67 (© Kiekhaefer Mercury)

7. Recheck the magneto setting by actuating the throttle control lever.

Carburetor Throttle Pick-up Plate

1. Adjust the carburetor throttle pick-up plate position with a 0.015 in. feeler gauge to obtain this clearance between the second pick-up pin and the no. 2 lever or the carburetor cluster when the magneto is against the stop in full advance.

2. Be sure that the throttle moves freely in all positions and that both throttle plates close fully at idle.

Full Throttle Stop

1. Set the full throttle stop screw to allow 1/64 in. free movement of the cluster lever (in a clockwise direction) when the throttle is held against the full stop. Push the cluster lever with the finger.

NOTE: *If the timing stop is readjusted, the adjustment for maximum spark advance must be repeated.*

MERC 500E (SER NO. 2406035 & UP)
MERC 500M (SER NO. 2307056 & UP)
MERC 500S (SER NO. 2306756 & UP)
MERC 650E (SER NO. 2446775–2606853)
MERC 650S (SER NO. 2312311–2446775)

The following timing procedure assumes that the ignition driver has been removed or otherwise disturbed.

Timing the Flywheel and Distributor Pulley

1. Rotate the flywheel until the alignment mark (a straight white line on Merc 500s or three white dots on Merc 650s) is

Timing alignment marks—Merc 650 (© Kiekhaefer Mercury)

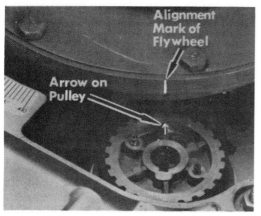

Timing alignment marks—Merc 500 (© Kiekhaefer Mercury)

aligned with the arrow on the distributor pulley.

2. Install the timing belt, plate, cap, washers, and screw, and torque to 60 in. lbs.

3. Connect a timing light (a DC timing light must be used); one lead to no. 1 spark plug, another lead to positive post on the battery, and a third lead to negative battery terminal.

4. On manual start engines, install a jumper wire from the negative battery terminal to a ground on the bottom cowl or front cover plate.

Spark Advance

5. Start the engine and hold the ignition driver at full retard. Adjust the idle stop screw to produce an idle speed of 550–600 rpm in forward.

Idle stop adjustment—Merc 650, 500 (© Kiekhaefer Mercury)

6. Advance the ignition driver so that the timing mark aligns with 7–9° BTDC.

7. Slide the actuator plate forward so that the primary pick-up on the throttle plate just touches the primary pick-up arm on the carburetor cluster. Tighten the locking screws.

8. It is necessary to run the engine at wide open throttle to know the approximate rpm when adjusting for maximum spark advance. Refer to the following chart for maximum spark advance adjustments at differing wide open throttle rpms.

NOTE: *The engine may be timed on the boat, but it must be timed at wide open*

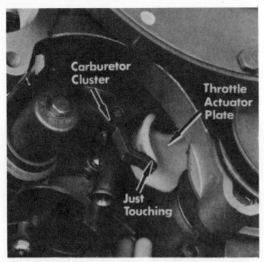

Primary pickup just touching the carburetor cluster —Merc 650, 500 (© Kiekhaefer Mercury)

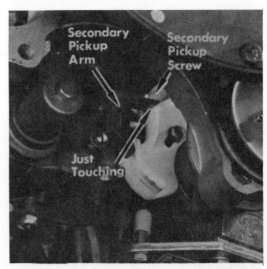

Secondary pickup arm adjustment—Merc 650, 500 (© Kiekhaefer Mercury)

throttle. The rpms will vary according to pitch of the propeller and other factors listed in the opening chapter of the book.

Wide Open Throttle (rpm)	Spark Advance 650S	Spark Advance 500S, 500M
2000–4000	41–42 BTDC	38–39 BTDC
4000–4800	40–41 BTDC	37–38 BTDC
4800–5200	38 BTDC	——
5200–5600	——	35 BTDC

9. With the engine running at wide open throttle, adjust the spark advance screw to align the flywheel timing mark with the appropriate (see chart) degree mark on the timing decal. Tighten the spark-advance screw jam-nut and recheck the timing.

10. With the ignition driver against the spark advance stop, but not actuating the economizer collar, adjust the secondary pick-up with the screw on the throttle actuator plate. Turn the screw until it just touches the secondary pick-up arm on the carburetor cluster. Tighten the nut.

Throttle Stop

1. Rotate the economizer collar to the wide open throttle position.

2. Adjust the throttle stop screw on stop bracket to allow full throttle plate opening, but do not allow the throttle plates to act as a stop. Do not let the carburetor cluster hit the filter bowl on the carburetor.

Throttle stop adjustments—Merc 650, 500 (© Kiekhaefer Mercury)

Idle stop screw adjustment—Merc 650, 500 (© Kiekhaefer Mercury)

3. Idle the engine and adjust the idle stop screw on the stop bracket so that the engine idles at 550–600 rpm in forward gear.

4. Run the engine at full throttle to clear the motor and recheck the idle.

Merc 650 (1966–67)

Timing the Flywheel and Magneto Pulley

1. Rotate the flywheel until the timing mark on the flywheel (straight white line) aligns with the center of the crankshaft and magneto pulley center.

Timing marks on 1966–67 Merc 650 (© Kiekhaefer Mercury)

2. Position the arrow on the magneto pulley (not the plate) to align with the mark on the flywheel.

3. Install the timing belt, plate, cap, washers, and screws and torque to 60 in. lbs.

Maximum Spark Advance

1. Adjust the maximum spark advance by following steps no. 1–7 under "Maximum Spark Advance, Merc 500 (1966–67)." The only difference is that no. 1 piston is set at 0.222 in. (5.6388 mm) BTDC.

Pick-up Plate

1. This operation is best performed with a timing gauge described under Merc 350 "Maximum Spark Advance."

2. Remove the no. 1 spark plug and thread the timing gauge into the spark plug port.

3. Set the no. 1 piston at TDC (Top Dead Center) and set the timing gauge at zero.

4. Rotate the crankshaft in a clockwise direction and set the no. 1 piston at 0.015 in. (0.381 mm) BTDC.

5. Retard the magneto against the idle stop screw.

6. Rotate the magneto slowly (counterclockwise) until the points open. This point can be determined by the use of a simple test light.

7. Loosen the throttle pick-up plate screws.

8. Slide the throttle pick-up plate so that the tab (without the nylon sleeve) just touches the carburetor cluster.

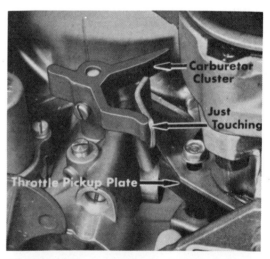

Throttle pickup tab adjustment—1966–67 Merc 650 (© Kiekhaefer Mercury)

Throttle pickup pin adjustment—1966–67 Merc 650 (© Kiekhaefer Mercury)

9. Tighten the throttle pick-up plate screws.

10. Turn the magneto against the 0.222 in. spark advance stop.

11. Bend the second throttle pick-up pin (with nylon sleeve) against the carburetor cluster leaving 0.000–0.015 in. clearance to avoid binding.

12. Lubricate the cam and nylon pin with New Multipurpose Quicksilver Lubricant.

Throttle Stop Adjustment

1. Use the procedure under "Throttle Stop Adjustment" for Merc 500E, 500M, 500S, 650E, and 650S.

MERC 950 AND 1100 (1966) STANDARD IGNITION

Timing the Flywheel and Distributor Pulley

1. Refer to the procedure for timing the flywheel and magneto pulley for the Merc 650 (1966–67).

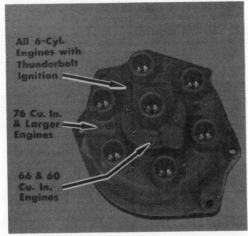

Distributor cap identification (© Kiekhaefer Mercury)

Spark Advance

1. To set the spark advance stop, it is advisable to acquire a timing gauge, described under Merc 350 "Maximum Spark Advance Adjustment."

2. Position the distributor with the air vent elbow facing approximately forward.

3. Remove the no. 3 (from top) spark plug and thread the timing gauge into the spark plug port.

4. Set no. 3 piston at TDC (Top Dead Center) and set the timing gauge at zero.

5. Rotate the crankshaft in a clockwise direction, and set no. 3 piston at 0.235 in. (5.969 mm) BTDC.

6. Retard the distributor against the idle speed stop screw.

7. Slowly, turn the distributor rotor counterclockwise to touch the distributor drive coupling.

8. Holding the rotor, turn the distributor slowly counterclockwise, until the points break. This can be determined by a continuity tester described in the opening chapter of the book.

9. Hold the distributor in this position and adjust the spark advance stop screw to just touch the pilot assembly and tighten the locknut.

10. Recheck steps no. 6, 7, and 8 to be sure that the adjustment is correct.

Pick-up Plate

1. This adjustment is essentially the same as the pick-up plate adjustment for the Merc 650 (1966–67). The 1966 950 and 1100 standard ignition models were equipped with a distributor instead of a magneto. Therefore, the following procedure is valid.

2. Perform steps no. 1–4 of the Merc 650 (1966–67) pick-up plate adjustment.

3. Retard the distributor against the idle screw.

4. Turn the distributor rotor (clockwise) to touch the drive coupling.

5. Hold the rotor in this position and slowly rotate the distributor counterclockwise until the points break, which can be determined by the use of a simple test light.

6. Perform steps no. 8–12 of the Merc 650 (1966–67) pick-up plate adjustment.

Throttle Stop

1. Use the procedure under Merc 500E, 500M, 500S, 650E, and 650S throttle stop adjustment.

MERC 1100SS, 950SS WITH THUNDERBOLT IGNITION

Timing the Flywheel and Distributor Pulley

1. Rotate the flywheel until the timing mark (a straight line on the flywheel edge) is aligned with the arrow on the pully (not the plate).

2. Install the timing belt, cap, plate,

Timing marks on 1966 950SS, 1100SS (© Kiekhaefer Mercury)

washers, and screw, and torque to 60 in. lbs.

Spark Advance Adjustment

There are two ways of adjusting the spark advance on these motors. A timing light may be used, provided it is of good quality. The sophistication of the ignition on these models will interfere with a poor quality timing light. (Refer to the list of precautions under "Ignition System".)

A second method, the mechanical method, requires the use of a simple timing gauge and will accomplish virtually the same purpose.

Timing Light Method

1. Connect the timing light; one lead to ground on the bottom cowl or front cover plate, one lead to the hot post of the starter solenoid, and another lead to no. 1 (top) spark plug.
2. Start the engine and let it run for a few minutes.
3. Aim the timing light at the degree markings on the top cowl support frame and advance the throttle until the timing mark on the flywheel is aligned with the 36½° mark on the timing decal.
4. Adjust the advance stop screw in or out until the correct timing is obtained.
5. Tighten the nut on the stop screw and recheck the timing.
6. Return the throttle lever to neutral position.

Pick-up Plate Adjustment (Timing Light Method)

1. Connect the timing light as above.
2. Advance the throttle until the line on the flywheel aligns with the throttle pick-up line on the timing decal.
3. At this point, the carburetor pick-up should just touch the carburetor cluster.
4. Loosen the screws which hold the throttle pick-up plate and adjust if necessary.

Spark Advance Adjustment (Mechanical Method)

1. The mechanical method of adjusting the spark advance on 1100SS and 950SS motors is identical to the method used on 1100 and 950 motors with standard ignition. The only changes are as follows:
   A. Disconnect the battery leads and the distributor leads (brown and white from terminal A.)
   B. Set no. 1 piston (not no. 3) at 0.275 in. (6.985 mm) BTDC.

Pick-up Plate Adjustment (Mechanical Method)

1. It is advisable to acquire a timing gauge, described under Merc 350 maximum spark advance adjustment.
2. Remove the spark plug from no. 3 cylinder and thread the timing gauge into the spark plug port.
3. Set no. 3 piston at TDC (Top Dead Center) and set the timing gauge at zero.
4. Rotate the crankshaft in a clockwise direction, and set no. 3 piston at 0.015 in. (0.381 mm) BTDC.
5. Retard the distributor against the idle stop screw.
6. Slowly, turn the distributor rotor counterclockwise to contact the drive coupling.
7. Hold the rotor in this position and rotate the distributor counterclockwise until the points open (this can be seen with a simple test light).
8. Loosen the throttle pick-up plate screws.
9. Slide the throttle pick-up plate so that the first throttle tab (without the nylon sleeve) just touches the carburetor cluster.
10. Tighten the throttle pick-up plate screws.
11. Turn the distributor against the 0.275 in. spark advance stop.

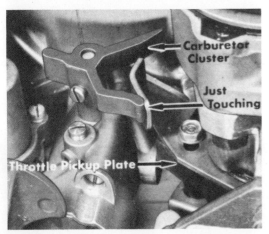

Throttle pickup tab adjustment—1966 Merc 950SS, 1100SS (© Kiekhaefer Mercury)

Timing marks on 1967 1100SS, 950SS, 500SS (© Kiekhaefer Mercury)

12. Bend the second throttle pick-up pin (with nylon sleeve) against the carburetor cluster, leaving 0.000–0.015 in. gap to avoid binding.

13. Lubricate the cam and nylon pin with New Multipurpose Quicksilver Lubricant.

14. Replace the distributor cap.

Throttle Stop Adjustment

1. Refer to the procedure under Merc 500E, 500M, 500S, 650E, and 650S throttle stop adjustment.

MERC 1100SS, 950SS, 650SS,
AND 500SS (1967)

Timing the Flywheel and Distributor Pulley—650SS

1. Rotate the flywheel until the alignment mark (a straight white line on the side surface of the flywheel) is aligned with the arrow on the distributor pulley.

2. Install timing belt, plate, cap, washers, and screw, and torque to 60 in. lbs.

Timing the Flywheel and Distributor Pulley—650SS

1. Rotate the flywheel until the timing mark (three white dots on the side of flywheel) is aligned with the arrow on the distributor pulley.

2. Install timing belt, plate, cap, washers, and screw, and torque to 60 in. lbs.

NOTE: *Some early engines are timed with a different procedure and will run satisfactorily as timed. If these early engines are timed with the above method,*

Timing marks on 1967 650SS (© Kiekhaefer Mercury)

the stops and controls will have to be readjusted.

Spark Advance Adjustment

1. Disconnect the fuel tank from the motor and run the carburetors dry before performing the following.

2. Disconnect the throttle cable at the motor.

3. Connect a good timing light; one lead to no. 1 spark plug, one lead to ground on the bottom cowl or front cover plate and one lead to the hot post of the starter solenoid.

4. Crank the engine and hold the timing light over the degree decal on the top cowl plate.

5. Advance the vertical lever until the timing mark on the flywheel aligns with the timing mark on the decal (36½° BTDC for 1100SS and 950SS; 38° BTDC for 650SS and 35° BTDC for 500SS).

Spark advance adjustment on 1967 SS models (© Kiekhaefer Mercury)

6. Adjust the spark advance stop screw in or out to obtain the correct timing.

7. Tighten the spark advance stop screw locknut and recheck the timing.

*Pick-up Plate Adjustment—
1100SS, 950SS, and 650SS*

1. Use the timing light and advance the throttle until the timing mark (three dots) on the flywheel aligns with the throttle pick-up line on the timing decal.

2. At this point, the carburetor pick-up should be adjusted to touch the carburetor cluster with 0.000–0.005 in. clearance to avoid binding.

Pick-up Plate Adjustment—500SS

1. Use the timing light, advance the throttle until the timing marks (2 dots) on the flywheel align with the no. 1 TDC line on the timing decal.

2. At this point, the carburetor pickup should just touch the carburetor cluster with 0.000–0.005 in. clearance to avoid binding.

3. Loosen the screws to the throttle pick-up plate, and adjust if necessary.

4. Without running the engine, rotate the distributor against the spark advance stop.

5. Bend the second throttle pick-up pin (if necessary) so that it touches the carburetor cluster with 0.000–0.015 in. clearance to avoid binding.

6. Lubricate the nylon pin with New Quicksilver Multipurpose Lubricant.

Throttle Stop Adjustment

1. Refer to the procedure under Merc 500E, 500M, 500S, 650E, and 650S throttle stop adjustment.

Vertical lever and idle stop screw (© Kiekhaefer Mercury)

MERC 1250SS AND 1000SS
(1968–69)

*Timing the Flywheel and
Distributor Pulley*

1. Rotate the flywheel until the alignment mark (a straight white line on the edge of the flywheel) is aligned with the arrow on the distributor pulley.

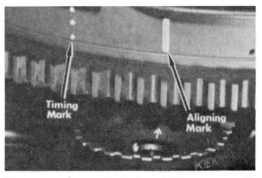

Timing marks on 1968–69 1250SS, 1000SS (© Kiekhaefer Mercury)

2. Install the timing belt, plate, cap, washers, and screw, and torque to 60 in. lbs.

NOTE: *Disconnect the fuel tank and run the carburetors dry before performing the following checks and adjustments.*

Spark Advance Adjustment—
Merc 1250SS

1. Disconnect the throttle cable from the engine.

2. Connect a timing light; one lead to no. 1 spark plug, one lead to ground on the front cover plate or bottom cowl, and another lead to the hot side of the starter solenoid.

3. Back out the throttle stop screw completely.

4. Advance the vertical lever to wide open throttle. Adjust the stop screw until it touches the throttle stop. Turn the throttle stop an additional ¾ turn to prevent jamming the linkage.

5. Advance the vertical lever to the wide open throttle position and crank the engine. Shine the timing light at the degree decal on the top cowl. Adjust the spark advance linkage until the timing mark (dots on the flywheel) aligns with the 34° BTDC mark on the timing decal.

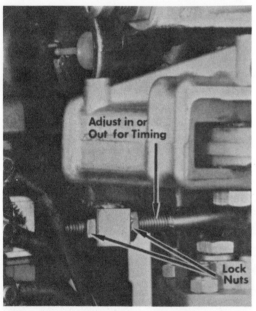

Adjusting spark advance linkage—1968–69 1250SS (© Kiekhaefer Mercury)

6. Tighten the locknuts and recheck the timing.

Primary Pick-up Plate Adjustment—
Merc 1250SS

1. Connect the timing light and advance the throttle until the timing mark on the flywheel aligns with the 7–9° BTDC mark on the timing decal.

2. At this point the carburetor pick-up should just touch the carburetor cluster with 0.000–0.005 in. clearance to avoid binding.

3. If necessary to adjust, loosen the screws on the pick-up plate and adjust to obtain the desired clearance.

Secondary Pick-up Plate Adjustment
Merc 1250SS

1. Advance the vertical lever to the wide open throttle position and adjust the screw on the nylon adaptor (port side of the engine) to allow full throttle plate opening.

2. Allow play in the carburetor shaft, at full throttle, but do not allow the throttle plates to act as stops or allow the carburetor cluster to contact the filter bowl.

Spark Advance Adjustment—
Merc 1000SS

1. Refer to the spark advance adjustment procedure for Merc 1100SS, 950SS, 650SS, and 500SS.

Spark advance adjustment—1968–69 1000SS (© Kiekhaefer Mercury)

Pick-up Plate Adjustment—
Merc 1000SS

1. Connect a timing light as detailed previously, and advance the throttle until the timing mark (three dots) aligns with the 5–7° BTDC mark on the timing decal.

2. At this point, carburetor pick-up should just contact the carburetor cluster with 0.000–0.005 in. clearance to avoid binding.

3. If necessary, adjust the pick-up plate by loosening the screws on the throttle pick-up plate.

*Secondary Pick-up Plate
Adjustment—Merc 1000SS*

1. Without running the engine, rotate the distributor against the spark advance stop.

2. Adjust the secondary pick-up with the screw on the throttle-actuator plate. Turn the screw until it just contacts the secondary pick-up arm on the carburetor cluster. Tighten the locknut.

*Throttle Stop Adjustment—
Merc 1250SS and 1000SS*

1. Refer to throttle stop adjustment, Merc 500E, 500M, 500S, 650E, and 650S.

Timing marks—Merc 800 and 650 (1970–71) (© Kiekhaefer Mercury)

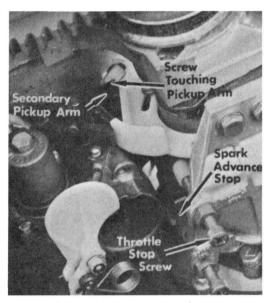

Secondary pickup adjustment—1968–69 1250SS, 1000SS (© Kiekhaefer Mercury)

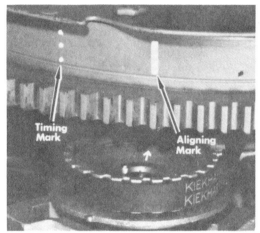

Timing marks—Merc 800 and 650 (1970–71) (© Kiekhaefer Mercury)

MERC 800 (1969–71) AND
MERC 650 (1970–71)

*Timing the Flywheel and
Distributor Pulley*

1. Rotate the flywheel until the alignment mark (a white dot and punch marks) is aligned with the arrow on the distributor pulley.

NOTE: *Merc 800 engines up to serial number 2881081 have a straight white line on the flywheel. On these engines, align the white line with the arrow on the distributor pulley.*

2. Install the timing belt, plate, cap, washers, and screw, and torque to 60 in. lbs.

CAUTION: *Before performing the following adjustments and checks, disconnect the fuel tank and run the carburetors dry.*

Spark Advance Adjustment

1. Disconnect the throttle cable from the engine.

2. Connect a good timing light—one lead to no. 1 spark plug, one lead to ground on the front cover plate or bottom cowl, and another lead to the hot side of the starter solenoid.

3. Turn the ignition key on and crank the engine while holding the timing light in line with the degree markings on the top cowl support frame. Advance the vertical lever until the timing mark on the flywheel aligns with the 27° BTDC mark on the timing decal.

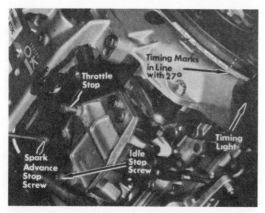

Spark advance adjustment—Merc 800 and 650 (1970–71) (© Kiekhaefer Mercury)

4. Adjust the timing by turning the spark advance screw in or out until correct timing is obtained.

5. Tighten the locknut and recheck the timing.

Pick-up Plate Adjustment

1. Using the timing light, connected above, advance the throttle until the timing mark on the flywheel aligns with the 5–7° BTDC mark (for Merc 800s) or the 7–9° BTDC mark (for Merc 650s).

2. At this point, the carburetor pick-up should just touch the carburetor cluster, with 0.000–0.005 in. clearance to avoid binding.

3. Loosen the screws which hold the pick-up plate and adjust if necessary.

4. Without running the engine, rotate the distributor against the spark advance stop. Adjust the secondary pick-up with the screw on the throttle plate actuator. Turn the screw until the actuator plate just touches the secondary pick-up arm on the carburetor cluster. Tighten the locknut on the adjusting screw.

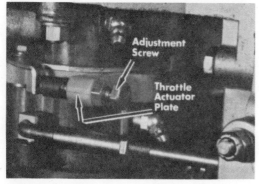

Throttle actuator plate adjustment—Merc 800 and 650 (1970–71) (© Kiekhaefer Mercury)

Throttle Stop Adjustment

1. Rotate the economizer collar to the wide open throttle position.

2. Adjust the throttle stop screw on the throttle stop bracket to allow full throttle-plate opening. Do not allow the throttle plates to act as stops or allow the carburetor cluster to contact the filter bowl.

Timing Decal Location—
1969 Merc 800

If, for any reason, the timing decal on these engines is disturbed, or must be replaced, the no. 1 piston TDC mark on the decal must be aligned with the mark on the top cowl support bracket. If not, the timing cannot be properly adjusted.

MERC 1150 AND 1350

Timing the Flywheel and
Distributor Pulley

1. The procedure is identical to that for the Merc 800 (1969–71) and the 650 (1970–71), except that all timing marks on the flywheel are three dots, located by a white dot.

Timing marks on Merc 1150 and 1350 (© Kiekhaefer Mercury)

Primary Throttle Pick-up
Adjustment

1. Connect a timing light as detailed—one lead to no. 1 spark plug, one lead to ground on the bottom cowl or front cover plate, and the other lead to the hot side of the starter solenoid.

2. Disconnect the throttle cable from the engine.

3. Start the engine and shine the timing light on the degree markings.

4. Advance the throttle until the timing mark aligns with the 5–7° BTDC mark (up to serial number 2928768) or with the TDC-2° BTDC mark (serial number 2928768 and up) on the timing decal.

5. With the timing marks aligned thusly, the primary pick-up should touch the carburetor cluster.

6. To adjust, loosen the screws which hold the throttle pick-up plate. Tighten the screws after adjustment.

Maximum Throttle Pick-up

1. With the engine running, and timing light attached, advance the distributor until the flywheel timing mark aligns with the 23° mark on the timing decal and adjust the maximum spark advance screw to just touch the distributor.

2. Tighten the locknut and remove the timing light.

3. With the distributor against the spark advance screw, but not actuating the econ-

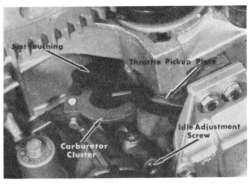

Secondary pickup adjustment—Merc 1150 and 1350 (© Kiekhaefer Mercury)

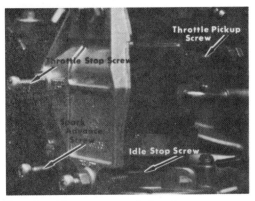

Throttle pickup screw and throttle stop screw—Merc 1150 and 1350 (© Kiekhaefer Mercury)

omizer collar, adjust the throttle pick-up screw on the throttle actuator so that it just touches the secondary pickup on the carburetor cluster. Tighten the locknut.

BATTERY MAINTENANCE

Specific Gravity

See the first chapter of this book for battery procedures relating to specific gravity.

Electrolyte Level

The electrolyte level in the battery should be checked regularly. In hot weather, check more frequently. If the electrolyte level is found to be low, distilled (or colorless, in an emergency) water should be added to bring the level to about 3/16 in. above the level of the plates. The electrolyte level should never be allowed to fall below the level of the plates.

MANUAL STARTING

Automatic Rewind Starters

REMOVAL

1. Remove the cowling from the motor.

2. Unbolt the three screws securing the automatic rewind housing and remove it from the motor.

DISASSEMBLY

1. Pull the handle out of the housing (fully extended) and pry the end cap out of the rubber handle. Tie a knot in the rope to prevent its return into the housing.

2. Remove the cable from the rubber handle and release the cable so that the spring unwinds.

3. Bend down the locktabs on the nut and place a screwdriver in the sheave shaft slot to hold the shaft while removing the nut (left-hand thread).

4. Remove the nut securing the internal parts to the top of the housing.

CAUTION: *When removing the following parts, be sure that the rewind spring does not fly out of the sheave, causing bodily injury. The best practice is to wrap a large heavy cloth around the hand (or wear a heavy glove) and pull the spring out, allowing it to uncoil slowly.*

5. Remove the retainer plate, shaft, starter pawls, wave washers, bushings, spring guide, retainer spring, sheave shaft

1 - Nut	8 - Washer	15 - Sheave	22 - Wave Washer
2 - Tab Washer	9 - Screw	16 - Wave Washer	23 - Retainer Plate
3 - Starter Housing	10 - Screw	17 - Pawl	24 - Sheave Shaft
4 - Rope Guide	11 - Retainer	18 - Nylon Bushing	25 - Cable
5 - Seal	12 - Spring	19 - Spacer	26 - Handle
6 - Pulley	13 - Bushing	20 - Retainer	27 - Retainer
7 - Spacer	14 - Pin	21 - Washer	

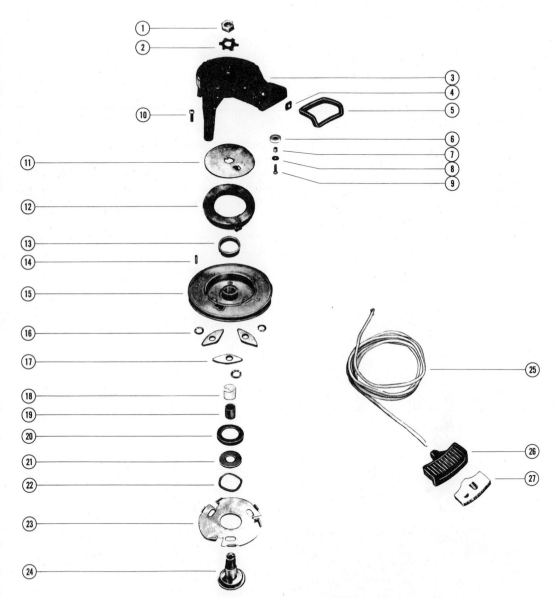

Exploded view of automatic recoil starter (© Kiekhaefer Mercury)

spacer, wave washer, and wave washer retainer.

6. Remove the cable from the sheave by unwinding and twisting the end near the anchor ½ turn.

ASSEMBLY

1. Replace the starter cable in the starter sheave by attaching the anchor end of the cable in the slot. Slide in sideways

and twist ½ turn after the anchor is in the hole.

2. Wind the cable on the sheave (clockwise) working from the bottom of the sheave. Leave enough free end to insert through the starter housing opening.

3. Place the sheave in a vise and engage the outer loop of the spring in the slot of the spring recess in the sheave.

4. Wind counterclockwise until the spring is in place.

5. Install the spring guide bushing on the sheave hub, with the chamfered end towards the sheave.

6. Install the spring retainer on top of the spring and engage the inner loop in the anchor pin of the spring retainer plate.

7. Lubricate the spring and spring guide bushing.

8. Assemble the starter pawl to the sheave with the identification mark side toward the rim of the sheaves.

9. Mount the three, starter-pawl wave washers on the anchor pins and place the starter pawls on top of the pins. Lubricate all parts as they are being installed. Be careful installing the pawls, as they are all installed the same way. The radii of the pawls are to follow the radius of the pawl retainer plate.

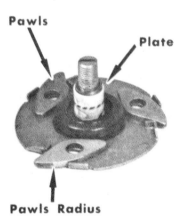

Pawls

Plate

Pawls Radius

Installing the starter pawls (© Kiekhaefer Mercury)

10. Install the sheave shaft spacer on the sheave shaft.

11. Install the wave washer retainer with the cupped end up.

12. Place the washer equalizer ring into the cup and set the wave washer and pawl retainer plate in position.

13. Be sure that the pawls extend through the slots in the sides and insert the sheave shaft so that the keyway goes through the spring retainer notch.

14. Insert the sheave shaft through the pawl retainer-plate assembly and sheave.

15. Insert the free end of the starter cable through the outlet in the starter housing and tie a temporary knot about one foot from the end of the cable.

16. Place the sheave assembly (sheave shaft up) into the starter housing.

17. Install the lockwasher and nut (left-hand thread) on the sheave shaft.

18. Untie the temporary knot and insert the cable through the starter handle end cap.

19. Install the cable into the starter handle as illustrated.

20. Pull the cable and end cap into the handle.

21. Turn the sheave shaft counterclockwise with a screwdriver until the handle is against the guide bushing. Turn an additional 1¼ turns to wind the spring to correct tension.

22. Tighten the nut on the sheave shaft while keeping the screwdriver in the slot to prevent the spring from unwinding.

23. Lock the nut in place with the lockwasher tabs (bend one up and one down).

24. Replace the cover and secure with a small screw.

25. Pull the cord several times to be sure that the mechanism operates correctly. Pull the cord out to full length to be sure that it will not stick.

INSTALLATION

1. Installation is the reverse of removal.

Powerhead

Specific repair procedures vary slightly between individual models but basic repair instructions are similar for all Mercury outboard powerheads. The powerhead consists of cylinder block and crankcase, crankshaft and center main bearing, connecting rod and piston, crankcase end caps, manifold covers, and cylinder block covers.

Cleanliness is of the utmost importance when working on the powerhead. All components must be inspected and cleaned before assembly. Refer often to the lubrication and torque charts.

2 CYLINDER MODELS
Powerhead

REMOVAL

1. Remove the front panel and side cowl.

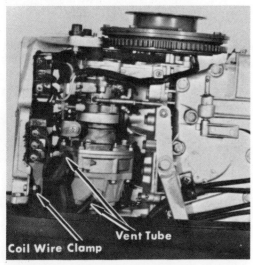

2-cylinder powerhead (starboard side) (© Kiekhaefer Mercury)

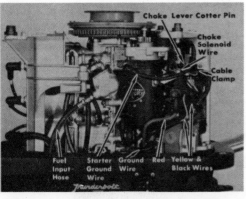

2-cylinder power head (port side) (© Kiekhaefer Mercury)

2. Pull the starter rope and tie the rope to hold it. Remove the rope handle.

3. Remove the 2 nuts holding the fuel line adaptor to the bottom cowl.

4. Remove the bolts securing the mounting bracket to the bottom cowl.

5. Remove the water discharge hose from the bottom cowl outlet.

6. Remove three screws and the driveshaft housing cover.

7. Remove the nuts holding the powerhead to the driveshaft housing.

8. Loosen the powerhead from the bottom cowl.

9. Remove the powerhead from the driveshaft housing.

INSTALLATION

1. Install new gaskets on the driveshaft housing and adaptor and install the powerhead on the bottom cowl and driveshaft housing. Torque to specifications.

2. Install the discharge hose, magneto actuator linkage mounting bracket, and fuel line adaptor.

3. Connect the shut-off switch wires and magneto ground wires to the terminal block.

4. Install the driveshaft cowling, top cowl, and side cowl.

Flywheel

REMOVAL

1. With the powerhead mounted on a stand, remove the flywheel nut and washer.

2. Attach a puller to the flywheel, using the screwholes in the top of the flywheel to secure the puller.

3. If the flywheel is exceptionally tight, tap on the center screw with a hammer.

4. Remove the flywheel key from the crankshaft.

INSTALLATION

1. With the stator in place on the powerhead, install the flywheel key on the crankshaft. Tap to seat.

2. Install the flywheel, aligning the key and keyway.

3. Install the washer and flywheel nut. Torque to specifications.

Flywheel Flexplate Replacement

1. Remove the flywheel.

2. Mark the inner hub with relation to the timing mark on the outer ring.

3. Remove the inner and outer hex-head cap screws. These screws have been installed with Loctite and are staked on the end. Be careful to apply an even amount of pressure.

4. Install a new flexplate on the outer ring and inner hub—making certain the previous matchmarks are aligned.

5. Apply Loctite to the $\frac{1}{4}$ x 28 x $\frac{5}{8}$

screw and install to the inner hub. Torque to 150–160 in. lbs.

6. Do the same to the ¼ x 28 x ⁹⁄₁₆ (¼ x 28 x ¹⁵⁄₁₆ on Merc 350) screws and install to the outer ring.

7. Stake all screws on the end with a center punch.

8. Install the flywheel and check the timing.

Upper and Lower End Cap Assembly

1. See "4 and 6 Cylinder Powerhead" for removal and installation procedures.

4 AND 6 CYLINDER MODELS

Powerhead

REMOVAL

1. Remove the front panel, wraparound cowl, top cowl, and trim cover.

2. Place the shift arm in Neutral.

3. Disconnect the vent tubes from the distributor cap and distributor housing (where applicable).

4. Disconnect large red wire from the solenoid. Disconnect the small yellow and black leads from the solenoid and detach the starter ground wire.

5. Remove the distributor wires.

6. Detach the wires from the rectifier.

7. Remove the choke solenoid wire from the choke solenoid.

8. Remove the clamp holding the wire harness.

9. Remove the choke lever cotter pin.

10. Remove the spark plugs.

11. Remove five nuts from the rear bracket and remove the bracket.

12. Remove the fuel input hose from the fuel pump.

13. Compress the clamp on the water discharge hose (on the port side of the powerhead) and remove the hose from the bottom cowl.

14. Detach the remaining wires.

15. Detach the clamp holding the coil wire from the front bracket (where applicable). Remove the primary coil wire from the coil.

16. Unscrew and remove the driveshaft cowl.

17. Remove the ground straps from the powerhead and bottom cowl.

18. Disconnect the shift link rod from the anchor bracket.

19. Remove eight nuts securing the powerhead to the driveshaft housing.

20. Loosen the powerhead from the bottom cowl.

21. Install a lifting ring and lift the powerhead from the bottom cowl. Install the powerhead on some sort of stand to avoid damage.

INSTALLATION

1. Install the powerhead-to-exhaust plate gasket. Be sure that the gasket surfaces are clean.

2. Using a hoist, lower the powerhead onto the bottom cowl.

3. Attach the powerhead to the driveshaft housing with eight nuts. Torque to specification.

4. Connect the shift link rod to the anchor bracket.

5. Install the ground straps between the powerhead and bottom cowl.

6. Connect the front and rear support brackets to the bottom cowl and powerhead.

7. Push the primary coil wire into the coil. Connect the coil ground wire to the front bracket and attach the coil wire clamp to the front bracket (where applicable).

NOTE: *Coat the surfaces of electrical connections with Liquid Neoprene.*

8. Attach all wires, noting the color code.

9. Attach the distributor wires to the switch box.

10. Install the water discharge hose to the bottom cowl and connect with a hose clamp.

11. Install the input fuel hose to the fuel pump.

12. Install the choke lever cotter pin.

13. If applicable, install the wire harness cable clamps.

14. Connect the vent tube to distributor cap and distributor housing (where applicable).

15. Install the spark plugs.

16. Install the driveshaft housing, cowl, top cowl, wraparound cowl and front panel.

Flywheel

REMOVAL

1. Remove the elastic stop-nut and washer which hold the flywheel to the crankshaft. Do not strike the crankshaft nut with a hammer to loosen or tighten.

Use an automotive flywheel holder to hold the flywheel.

2. Remove the magneto driver pulley by removing the screw and lockwasher. Detach the timing belt from the pulley.

3. Remove the flywheel with a puller.

4. If the flywheel is exceptionally tight, tap the shaft lightly to remove.

5. Remove the flywheel key from the crankshaft keyway.

INSTALLATION

1. With the stator in place on the powerhead, place the flywheel key on the crankshaft. Tap to seat.

2. Install the timing belt on the flywheel pulley first, then the magneto driven pulley, while installing the flywheel on the crankshaft. See "Electrical System" for timing and adjustments.

3. Place the flange on top of the driven pulley.

4. Install the washer and flywheel nut. Torque the nut to specification.

Flywheel Flexplate Replacement

MERC 500, 650, 800, 950, 1000, 1100, 1150, 1250, AND 1350

1. Perform steps 1–7 of the "Flywheel Flexplate Replacement" procedure under one- and two-cylinder models. Note that although the size of the screws differ, the torque remains the same.

2. Should it be necessary to replace the timing belt pulley, proceed as follows:

    a. Remove the pulley by splitting it with a chisel.

    b. Remove the dowel pin from the flywheel hub and replace.

    c. Press a new flange, pulley, and pulley hub onto the flywheel, making sure that the keyway is aligned with the dowel pin.

3. Install the flywheel on the powerhead and check the timing.

Upper and Lower End Cap Assemblies

REMOVAL

4 and 6 Cylinder Models and Merc 350—With Bearing in End Cap

1. Remove the hex-head screws which hold the end caps to the crankcase and the cylinder block.

2. Attach a puller with the screws securely attached to the end cap. Pull off the end cap.

3. Remove the ball bearing in the end cap.

4. Tap out the oil seal with a punch. Remove the O-ring and shims. It is wise to measure the shims with a micrometer at this point in case shim replacement is necessary.

4 and 6 Cylinder Models and Merc 400—With Bearing on Crankshaft

1. Upper and lower crankshaft ball bearings are pressed onto the crankshaft, providing a slip-fit in the end caps.

2. To remove the end caps, remove the hex-head screws which hold the end caps to the cylinder block and crankcase.

3. The bearings will remain on the crankshaft. To remove the upper or lower bearings from the crankshaft without disassembling the powerhead, use a screw-type jaw puller.

4. Remove the ball bearing from the crankshaft.

5. Remove the cap screws from the lower end cap and remove the end cap, bearing, and oil seals.

CAUTION: *Do not use a slide-hammer type puller. This type puller exerts force against the center main bearing and connecting rods and can damage the powerhead.*

NOTE: *New crankshafts are stocked as an assembly only, with upper and lower bearings installed.*

Cleaning and Inspection— All Models

1. Needle bearings should be replaced at overhaul, and when rust is present. Caged needle bearings should also be replaced at overhaul or when wet or rusty.

2. Clean and dry ball bearings before checking. Grasp the outer race firmly and attempt to move the inner race in or out. There should be no play. Lubricate the outer race with oil and spin it by hand. Never spin bearings by using compressed air. If the bearing sounds or feels rough, or catches, discard it. Bearings should have smooth action and no rust stains.

3. Inspect oil seals for leaking or damaged lips.

4. Always press in cartridge-type needle

bearings with the lettered side up. After installation, check to see that the bearings do not bind because of a tight fit. In particular, inspect roller bearings. These should be replaced at each overhaul.

INSTALLATION

4 and 6 Cylinder Models Through 1967 and 2 Cylinder Merc 350–400

1. Install new oil seals in the end caps, using a tool of appropriate diameter. An arbor press makes the best tool.

2. The oil seal should be pressed in from inside the end cap until flush with the inner surface. The lips should face down.

3. Install new ball bearings (if necessary).

4. Place the O-ring around the end cap. Install the upper and lower end caps temporarily on the crankcase with the original shims.

5. Tighten the nuts on the top and bottom.

6. Measure the end-play of the crankshaft, between the crankshaft ball bearing journal thrust face and the inner race of the ball bearings. Tap the crankshaft in either direction with a soft-faced mallet to fully seat the crankshaft and bearings. The measured end-play should be 0.008–0.012 in. If the end-play is excessive, add or remove shims to correct. Shims are available in 0.002 in., 0.003 in., 0.005 in., and 0.010 in. sizes.

7. After checking end-play, remove end caps and install the O-ring seals, lubricat-

ing with New Multipurpose Lubricant. NOTE: *It is extremely important that the shims be equally spaced on the upper and lower caps, to keep the rod journal centerlines in the centerline of the cylinder bore.*

8. Install the end caps once again.

4 and 6 Cylinder Models (1968 and later)

1. To install new bearings on the crankshaft without disassembling the powerhead, place the ball bearing on the crankshaft. Do not pound directly on the bearing.

2. Mercury recommends the use of a special tool to seat the bearing. However, in the absence of such a tool, the following method will suffice.

   a. Obtain one piece of flat steel that is large enough to cover the bearing.

   b. Obtain a piece of thick-walled pipe which will fit solidly on the outer edge of the bearing (or a piece of steel just large enough to cover the bearing).

   c. Drill holes in the steel plates large enough to fit over the crankshaft without damaging the threads.

   d. Install the pipe over the crankshaft to rest solidly on the outer rim of the bearing. Place the piece of steel cut to length, with just enough room to install a nut on the crankshaft threads. Using a wrench, turn the nut down until the bearing is fully seated.

3. A different procedure is used for checking crankshaft end-play. Using the original shims, temporarily install the

Measuring crankshaft end-play—up to and including 1967 (© Kiekhaefer Mercury)

Measuring crankshaft end-play—1968 and later (© Kiekhaefer Mercury)

upper and lower end caps on the crankshaft and secure them to the cylinder block with the end cap screws. Do not install the crankcase.

4. Tap the crankshaft in either direction with a mallet.

5. Using a feeler gauge, check the end-play between the inner face of the upper end cap and the top (first) counterweight of the crankshaft.

6. After the reading is obtained, tap the crankshaft in the other direction to seat the bearings. Make the same measurement at the lower end cap. Difference between the two readings is the amount of crankshaft end-play. This should be 0.004–0.008 in.

7. If the end-play is incorrect, add or remove shims to correct the end-play.

8. If necessary, correct the end-play and assemble the components.

Separating Crankcase and Cylinder Block—All Models

Disassembly

1. Remove the flywheel from the powerhead.

2. Remove the exhaust manifold cover plate and remove the cover and baffle plate.

3. Remove the cylinder block covers and intake deflectors.

NOTE: *These covers do not have to be removed unless cleaning of the exhaust and water cooling chambers is desired.*

4. Remove the upper end cap.

5. Remove all nuts securing the crankcase to the cylinder block.

6. Remove the lower end cap.

7. Separate the crankcase from the cylinder block by prying the two apart at the special recesses provided.

8. Remove the crankshaft, piston, and connecting rod assembly.

Cleaning and Inspection

1. Inspect the cylinder block for cracks and general condition.

2. Remove carbon and varnish with a fine wire wheel attached to an electric drill.

3. Finish hone the cylinder walls slightly to seat new rings.

4. On engines which display evidence of overheating, check the bore for an out-of-round condition, using an inside microme-

ter. If the bore exceeds 0.005–0.006 in. out-of-round, bore the cylinders 0.015 in. oversize and install oversize pistons. This operation should be done only by Kiekhaefer Mercury or a well-equipped machine shop with qualified personnel.

Finish Honing

1. Follow the manufacturer's directions for use of the hone and lubrication during honing.

Cylinder honing (© Kiekhaefer Mercury)

2. Start stroking at the smallest diameter. Maintain firm stone pressure against the cylinder walls.

3. Localize the stroking at the smallest diameter until the drill speed is constant throughout the length of the bore. Stroke at a rate of 30 complete cycles per minute to produce the best cross-hatch pattern. Expand the stone as necessary to compensate for stock removal and stone wear.

4. Use a coarse grit for roughing operation. The softer the material, the coarser the grit that can be used for roughing. Leave approximately 0.002 in. for finishing cast iron.

5. For finishing operation, finer grit stones are used to bring the cylinder to desired size and produce the desired finish.

6. For best results, a continuous flow of honing oil should be pumped into the

work. If this is not practical, apply oil generously and frequently with an oil can.

7. After honing, clean the cylinder bores with hot water and detergent. Scrub well and rinse with hot water. Bores should be swabbed several times with light engine oil and wiped with a clean dry cloth. Do not clean with kerosine or gasoline.

ASSEMBLY

1. Install the crankshaft, piston and connecting rod assembly, as detailed later.
2. Coat the joint face of the crankcase with gasket sealer for good metal-to-metal contact.
3. Set the crankcase over the cylinder block, insert the bolts, and attach nuts and washers. Do not tighten.
4. Install the center main bearing locking screws, with tab washer, through the respective hole in the crankcase, to hold the center main bearing.
5. Align the opening of the valve-type center main bearing with that of the crankcase fuel intake opening, so that they are evenly centered.
6. Start tightening with A and follow with B roller-type center main. (See illustration in "Tightening Sequences".)
7. Crimp the locktab washers after torquing to specification.
8. Install the end caps, being careful not to damage the oil seal. Coat the face of the O-ring with New Multipurpose Lubricant. Check crankshaft end-play.
9. Place the proper screws in the end cap, but do not tighten.
10. Tighten the crankcase bolts according to the appropriate illustration in the specifications section and to the proper torque figure.
11. Tighten the end cap screws evenly.
12. Rotate the crankshaft several times to be sure that all parts in the powerhead are free to move.
13. Install the intake port covers and cylinder block cover. Use new gaskets before installing.
14. The intake port covers have a beveled face toward the front of the intake passage toward the crankcase. Install the gasket on the manifold and baffle plate. Install the gasket for the outside cover.
15. Tighten the cylinder block covers and exhaust manifold screws, using the appropriate illustration in the specifications. Torque to the proper figure.

Power dome type piston (© Kiekhaefer Mercury)

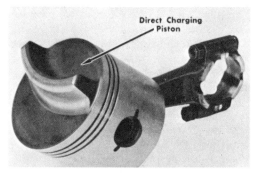

Direct charging type piston (© Kiekhaefer Mercury)

Pistons—All Models

REMOVAL

1. Perform steps 1–7 of "Separating the Crankcase and Cylinder Block" (disassembly).
2. Punch-mark or otherwise identify each piston and cylinder so that the piston can be returned to its original cylinder.
3. Remove the crankshaft and piston and connecting rod assembly from the cylinder block.
4. Remove the piston rings from the pistons using a piston ring expander.
5. Do not attempt to disassemble the lockrings and wrist pins from the piston. A special tool is needed to hold the wrist pin bearings in place.

CLEANING AND INSPECTION

1. Check the pistons for scoring and cracking.
2. Inspect the ring grooves for wear, burn, and distortion. It is recommended practice that when piston rings are removed, new ones be installed.
3. Before replacing piston rings, clean the grooves in the pistons with the broken portion of a piston ring. Varnish and car-

bon deposits should be removed from the top of the piston with a soft, wire brush.

4. To assure positive seat of piston rings, hone or de-glaze the cylinders when pistons are removed.

5. Remove burrs from the piston skirt by polishing with crocus cloth.

6. If the engine has been submerged, check the wrist pin and boss. In the event of submersion, it will probably be necessary to remove the wrist pin by removing the locktabs on each end and driving the wrist pin out with a soft drift.

NOTE: *Wrist pins are not sold separately.*

7. Pistons 0.015 in. oversize are available from Mercury for installation to overbored cylinders. It is recommended that cylinders be rebored 0.015 in. oversize if score marks exceed 0.0075 in. in depth.

INSTALLATION

1. Installation is the reverse of removal. A piston ring compressor should be used when installing piston and ring assemblies into the cylinder. Be sure that the crankshaft is installed correctly. If a piston ring compresser is not available, carefully compress the piston rings by hand.

Connecting Rods

REMOVAL FROM CRANKSHAFT

1. Remove the crankshaft and the piston and connecting rod assembly from the cylinder block as detailed above.

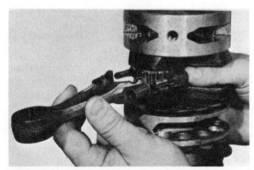

Removing and installing connecting rods (© Kiekhaefer Mercury)

2. Remove the connecting rod locknuts, allowing separation of the connecting rod from the rod cap.

NOTE: *Mark the front of the pistons and, immediately after removing the connecting rods from the crankshaft, re-match the rod and cap, observing the*

raised matchmarks on the side of the rod and cap. It is also good practice to number the connecting rods, so that they are returned to their original crankshaft journal.

3. Remove the connecting rods from the crankshaft.

CLEANING AND INSPECTION

1. Check for rust (explained under "Crankshaft").

2. Check rods for alignment by placing the rods on a flat surface. If light can be seen under any part of the machined surface, the rod is probably bent and should be replaced.

3. It is necessary that all bearings be kept separate and returned to the original connecting rod. This is especially true of the Merc 1250.

4. Do not attempt to clean Merc 1250 connecting rods by polishing.

5. Do not polish crankshaft journals.

INSTALLATION ON THE CRANKSHAFT

1. One at a time, open the matched connecting rod and cap.

2. Place a small amount of New Multipurpose Lubricant on each half of the connecting rod bearing race to hold the bearing in place. Do not mix bearings from different connecting rods.

3. Where applicable, place the bearing retainer race in the connecting rod.

4. Install the roller bearings around each side for assembly. Always count roller bearings to be sure that none have been lost. Never intermix new and old roller bearings in the same connecting rod.

5. Install the connecting rod cap so that the knob markings match perfectly.

6. Install the connecting rod nuts and torque to specification.

7. After torquing the nuts, rotate the

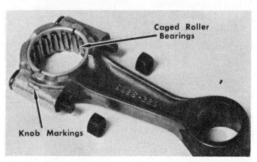

Connecting rod identification—caged roller bearings (© Kiekhaefer Mercury)

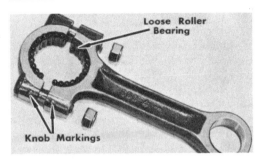

Connecting rod identification—loose roller bearings (© Kiekhaefer Mercury)

connecting rod to be sure that it rotates freely. If it rotates roughly, remove the rod and check the bearing race and rollers.

8. Repeat the procedure for the other rods.

9. Always recheck the matchmarks (knob markings) on the rod to assure a correct and perfect match.

Center Main Bearing—Reed Valve and Valve Cage

REMOVAL

1. Remove the crankshaft.

2. The reed-valve-type, center main bearing can be removed by extracting the 2 phillips head screws securing the assembly. Be careful not to bend or distort the reed valves or the reed valve stops.

3. Rematch the bearing halves immediately after removal.

4. Remove the reed valves and the reed valve stops by removing the cap screws.

CLEANING AND INSPECTION

1. Be sure that the inside diameter is not sprung.

Removing center main bearing—2-cylinder engines (© Kiekhaefer Mercury)

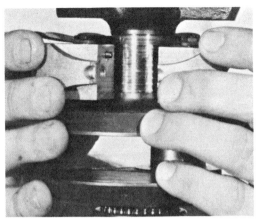

Removing center main bearing—4- and 6-cylinder engines (© Kiekhaefer Mercury)

2. Check the wear from the reed valves on face of the block.

3. Resurface the reed valve cage on a lapping plate after removing the locating pins.

4. Inspect for bent, chipped, or damaged reeds.

ADJUSTMENT

1. When replacing reed valves on the bearing, be sure that the left reed valve is set on the left side and the right reed on the right side. Right and left are determined by viewing from the point end of the valve stop.

2. Adjust the reeds on the center main bearing so that the reeds are set squarely over their respective openings and are at "no preload." This means that the reed valves should not adhere tightly to the seat, but have a slight opening, never more than 0.007 in.

3. Tighten the reed stop screws.

4. Check all reed valves for the proper opening. See the specifications section. Always check for proper opening. Excessive

Reed valve stop setting—2-cylinder engines (© Kiekhaefer Mercury)

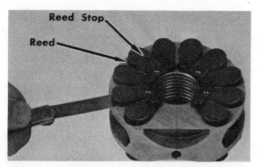

Measuring reed valve opening—4- and 6-cylinder engines (© Kiekhaefer Mercury)

opening can cause breakage and minimal opening can cause fuel starvation at high rpm.

INSTALLATION

1. Lubricate with New Multipurpose Lubricant.

2. When installing, align the locking screw holes in the crankcase cover and bearing.

3. Replace the bearing and reed valve gauge on the crankshaft. Tighten the two screws to assure a tight fit.

4. Recheck the reed valve clearance.

5. Install the crankshaft as detailed.

Center Main Bearing—All Models

REMOVAL

1. Bearing halves are machine-mated and should not be intermixed.

2. Remove the crankshaft.

3. Remove the screws which hold the bearing halves together.

4. Separate the bearing halves from the crankshaft. The rear half of the bearing has a dowel pin holding the inner race of the bearing. Tap lightly to remove.

5. Remove the lockring from the inner races.

6. Separate the inner races, being careful to catch all of the roller bearings.

CLEANING AND INSPECTION

1. Needle bearings should always be replaced at overhaul and whenever rust is present.

2. Inspect the oil seals for leaking or damaged lips.

ASSEMBLY

1. Lubricate the inner races of the bearing with New Multipurpose Lubricant.

2. Space the roller bearings equally

around the inner bearing races. Be sure that all the bearings are replaced.

3. Install the bearings and inner race over the crankshaft and install the snaprings around the races.

4. Rotate several times to be sure that the roller bearings do not bind.

5. Place the dowel in position and install the bearing halves on the inner race.

6. Install the bearing with the word "Top" uppermost. This will allow the internal bleed systems to function.

7. Install the screws and tighten securely.

Motor Leg and Water Pump

MERC 350, 400, AND 500

Gear Housing

REMOVAL

1. Drain the lubricant from the gear housing by removing the filler plug and vent plug. Do not loose the washers under the screw and plug.

2. After draining, replace the washers, screw, and plug.

3. Remove the propeller.

4. Remove the locknuts holding the gear housing to the driveshaft housing.

5. Remove the locknut from the center bottom side of the cavitation plate.

6. Remove the water pick-up or trim tab from under the trailing edge of the cavitation plate.

7. Remove the locknut from inside the trim tab cavity.

8. Separate the gear housing from the driveshaft housing.

INSTALLATION

1. If the water intake-to-powerhead tube was removed with the gear housing, coat the upper end of the tube with New Multipurpose Quicksilver Lubricant and slip it into the rubber seal in the bottom cowl. Insert it into the recess in the powerhead.

2. Lubricate the bottom end of the water tube.

3. Apply a heavy coat of Multipurpose Lubricant to the driveshaft splines.

4. Install the allen-head water pick-up or trim tab screw in the top of the gear housing.

5. Be sure that the shift control unit and lower unit are in Forward gear before installing gear housing.

6. Install the driveshaft into the driveshaft housing, aligning the water pump tube with the water pump body outlet. Align the driveshaft splines with the crankshaft. Slide these into place while joining the housings.

7. Be sure that the water pump tube enters the water pump body recess and rubber seal in the water pump cover.

8. Place the shift lever in Neutral, then in Forward, to be sure that the upper and lower shift shaft splines are properly aligned.

9. Rotate the propeller shaft to permit the driveshaft splines to enter the crankcase splines. The upper and lower shift shaft splines must also be aligned.

10. Install and tighten the locknuts.

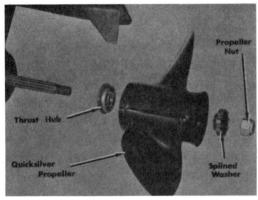

Propeller installation—Merc 350, 400, 500 (© Kiekhaefer Mercury)

11. Install the water pick-up or trim tab.

12. Lubricate the gear housing. See "Lubrication" section.

13. To install the propeller, install the backing washer, then place the thrust hub and washer into the propeller hub.

14. Lubricate the propeller shaft splines.

15. Align the propeller hub splines with the propeller shaft splines and install the propeller.

16. Replace the splined washer.

17. Replace the propeller nut and tighten.

Water Pump

REMOVAL

1. Remove the gear housing.

2. Position the gear housing in a vise

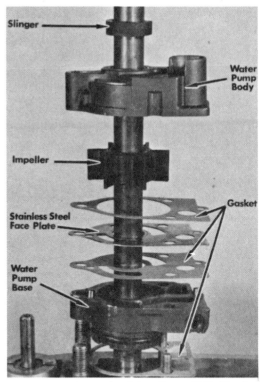

Water pump removal and installation (© Kiekhaefer Mercury)

(with soft jaws) and rest the skeg on a block of wood.

3. Remove the centrifugal slinger from the driveshaft.

4. Remove the water pump body assembly.

5. Remove the water pump insert, impeller, and impeller pin, along with the water pump body gasket, water pump face plate, and gasket face plate. Be sure to remove the oil seal.

6. Check the impeller and water pump insert carefully for wear or damage.

7. Remove the flushing screw, seal, and gasket to allow the water pump base to be removed.

8. The water pump base in the late-style gear housing has a threaded hole located next to the forward stud to aid removal. Install a 10 x 24 screw and turn in until the water pump base is forced away from the gear housing.

9. Remove the O-ring and oil seal from under the base plate assembly and watch for shims under the base plate.

10. The gear housing with water intake in the strut has an additional gasket located between the water pump base and the gear housing.

INSTALLATION

1. Install the seal in the water pump base assembly with the lips facing downward.

2. Late model four-cylinder gear housings use two water-pump base oil seals. The upper oil seal is installed with the lips facing down and the lower seal is installed with lips facing upward.

3. Install the water pump base assembly.

4. The gear housing with the water intake in the strut requires a gasket between the water pump base and the gear housing.

5. No play should exist between the bearing and water pump base assembly when the water pump base assembly is depressed. Shims may be added or removed as necessary. Place a feeler gauge between the gear housing and the water pump body. If gap exists, remove sufficient shims to reduce the gap to zero.

6. Install the water pump base-to-face plate gaskets. Replace the stainless steel face plate.

7. Gear housings with water intake in the trim tab must have the water intake tube installed in the water pump base before the stainless steel face plate.

8. Place a new drive pin on the driveshaft, holding it in place with New Multipurpose Lubricant.

9. If necessary, install a new impeller.

10. Install the stainless steel water pump cartridge in the water pump body and place the water pump body-to-face plate gasket on the water pump body.

11. Slide the water pump body assembly over the driveshaft and impeller.

12. Turn the driveshaft clockwise and press the body into place, at the same time seating the impeller. Be sure that the impeller drive pin is in position.

13. Replace the lockwashers and tighten the nuts.

14. Replace the driveshaft centrifugal slinger.

15. Check the backlash of the gears.

16. Install the gear housing.

4 AND 6 CYLINDER MODELS

Gear Housing

REMOVAL

1. The procedure is the same as for the gear housing removal for the Merc 350, 400, and 500. The size and number of bolts may vary. Additionally, remove the upper reverse locking cam and nylon spool sleeve after the housings have been separated.

INSTALLATION

1. The installation procedure is identical to that for gear housing installation on the Merc 350, 400, and 500. The only slight deviation is that the $7/32$ in. allen head screw in the driveshaft housing should be torqued to 180 in. lbs through the plastic plug hole in the driveshaft housing, after the water pick-up and trim tab are installed. Be sure to replace the plastic plug.

2. The propeller installation is also slightly different, in that there is a tab washer to be installed directly behind the propeller nut.

Water Pump

REMOVAL

1. See the procedure for water pump removal under the Merc 350, 400, and 500. Note that the water intake hose must be removed from the water pump.

INSTALLATION

1. Refer to the procedure for water pump installation under the Merc 350, 400, and 500.

2. Change step 3 to read as follows:

There should be no play between the bearing and water pump base assembly when the water pump base assembly is depressed. With a new gasket installed, place a feeler gauge between the gear housing and water pump body. If the gap is 0.010 in., remove 0.012 in. shim; if 0.005 in., remove 0.007 in. shim. This will allow for 0.002–0.003 in. compression of the gasket and produce a zero gap, which should not be altered.

3. Do not forget that the gear backlash should be 0.006–0.008 in.

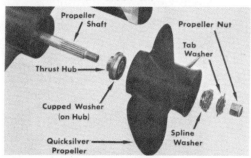

Propeller installation—Merc 650, 800 and all 4- and 6-cylinder engines (© Kiekhaefer Mercury)

4 · Outboard Marine Corporation (Evinrude and Johnson)

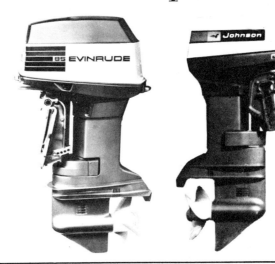

Introduction

Outboard Marine Corporation (OMC) designed and produced its first motor in 1909. Since the first motor, there have been many engineering and design changes to the basic concept. In the past few years, the compact V4 engine design has been introduced and that has been followed by the loop-charged engine.

OMC outboards are recognizable by their departure from inline engine design on larger models. The V4 profile is noticeably lower and much broader, while the inline twins and three-cylinder engines retain the conventional profile associated with inline engines.

There are many notable design features on OMC engines. Pressure-backed piston rings, which seal due to combustion pressure rather than spring tension, reduce friction and ring sticking. Instead of mixing dissimilar metals underwater (which tends to induce corrosion), compatible metals like stainless steel and aluminum are used. Water passages are coated with a baked-on varnish finish to resist corrosion. Propeller shafts and fittings which are exposed to salt water are stainless steel.

These service procedures have been compiled from Evinrude service manuals, since service procedures for Evinrude and Johnson outboards are virtually identical. Some relatively minor specifications may vary between manufacturers but, otherwise, specifications and service remain common to each.

Model Identification

Year	Model (hp)	No. of Cyls	Cubic Inch Displacement	Engine Type
1966–70	33	2	40.5	Inline
1966–72	40	2	43.9	Inline
1971–72	50	2	41.5	Inline
1968–69	55	3	49.7	Inline
1966–67	60	4	70.7	V4
1970–71	60	3	49.7	Inline
1968	65	4	70.7	V4
1972	65	3	49.7	Inline
1966–67	80	4	89.5	V4
1968–72	85	4	92.6	V4
1966–68	100	4	89.5	V4
1971–72	100	4	92.6	V4
1969–70	115	4	96.1	V4
1971–72	125	4	99.6	V4

1971 Evinrude 40 HP—2 cyl. (© Outboard Marine Corporation)

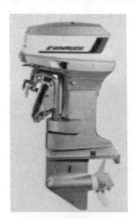

1971 Evinrude 50 HP—2 cyl. (© Outboard Marine Corporation)

1971 Evinrude 65 HP—2 cyl. (© Outboard Marine Corporation)

1971 Evinrude 125 HP—2 cyl. (© Outboard Marine Corporation)

1971 Johnson 40 HP—2 cyl. (© Outboard Marine Corporation)

1971 Johnson 50 HP—2 cyl. (© Outboard Marine Corporation)

1971 Johnson 65 HP—3 cyl. (© Outboard Marine Corporation)

1971 Johnson 125 HP—V4 (© Outboard Marine Corporation)

General Engine Specifications

Year	Model (hp)	HP (OBC) @ rpm	Full Throttle rpm Range	Bore (in.)	Stroke (in.)	Carburetion	Fuel/Oil Ratio
1966	33	33 @ 4500	4000–5000	3.0625	2.750	1—1 bbl	50/1
	40	40 @ 4500	4000–5000	3.188	2.750	1—1 bbl	50/1
	60	60 @ 4500	4000–5000	3.000	2.500	1—2 bbl	50/1
	80	80 @ 4500	4000–5000	3.375	2.500	1—2 bbl	50/1
	100	100 @ 5000	4500–5500	3.375	2.500	1—4 bbl	50/1
1967	33	33 @ 4500	4000–5000	3.0625	2.750	1—1 bbl	50/1
	40	40 @ 4500	4000–5000	3.188	2.750	1—1 bbl	50/1
	60	60 @ 4500	4000–5000	3.000	2.500	1—2 bbl	50/1
	80	80 @ 4500	4000–5000	3.375	2.50	1—2 bbl	50/1
	100	100 @ 5000	4000–5000①	3.375	2.50	1—4 bbl	50/1
1968	33	33 @ 4500	4000–5000	3.0625	2.750	1—1 bbl	50/1
	40	40 @ 4500	4000–5000	3.188	2.750	1—1 bbl	50/1
	55	55 @ 5000	4000–5000①	3.000	2.344	3—1 bbl	50/1
	65	65 @ 5000	4000–5000①	3.000	2.500	1—2 bbl	50/1
	85	85 @ 5000	4000–5000①	3.375	2.500	1—2 bbl	50/1
	100	100 @ 5000	4000–5000①	3.375	2.50	1—4 bbl	50/1
1969	33	33 @ 4500	4000–5000	3.0625	2.750	1—1 bbl	50/1
	40	40 @ 4500	4000–5000	3.188	2.750	1—1 bbl	50/1
	55	55 @ 5000	4000–5500	3.000	2.344	3—1 bbl	50/1
	85	85 @ 5000	4500–5500	3.375	2.588	2—1 bbl	50/1
	115	115 @ 5000	4500–5500	3.438	2.588	2—1 bbl	50/1

General Engine Specifications (cont.)

Year	Model (hp)	HP (OBC) @ rpm	Full Throttle rpm Range	Bore (in.)	Stroke (in.)	Carburetion	Fuel/Oil Ratio
1970	33	33 @ 4500	4000–5000	3.0625	2.750	1—1 bbl	50/1
	40	40 @ 4500	4000–5000	3.188	2.750	1—1 bbl	50/1
	60	60 @ 5000	4500–5500	3.000	2.344	3—1 bbl	50/1
	85	85 @ 5000	4500–5500	3.375	2.588	2—1 bbl	50/1
	115	115 @ 5000	4500–5500	3.348	2.588	2—1 bbl	50/1
1971	40	40 @ 4500	4000–5000	3.188	2.750	1—1 bbl	50/1
	50	50 @ 5500	5000–6000	3.0625	2.8125	2—1 bbl	50/1
	60	60 @ 5000	4500–5500	3.000	2.344	3—1 bbl	50/1
	85	85 @ 5000	4500–5500	3.375	2.594	2—1 bbl	50/1
	100	100 @ 5000	4500–5500	3.375	2.594	2—1 bbl	50/1
	125	125 @ 5000	4500–5500	3.500	2.594	2—1 bbl	50/1
1972	40	40 @ 4500	4000–5000	3.1875	2.750	1—1 bbl	50/1
	50	50 @ 5500	5000–6000	3.060	2.820	2—1 bbl	50/1
	65	65 @ 5000	4500–5500	3.000	2.340	3—1 bbl	50/1
	85	85 @ 5000	4500–5500	3.375	2.588	2—2 bbl	50/1
	100	100 @ 5000	4500–5500	3.375	2.588	2—2 bbl	50/1
	125	125 @ 5500	5000–6000	3.500	2.588	2—2 bbl	50/1

① 5500 rpm under limited conditions

Tune-Up Specifications

Year	Model (hp)	Spark Plugs Type AC	AL	Ch	Gap (in.)	Compression Pressure (psi)	Ignition Type	Breaker Point Gap (in.)	Sensor Air Gap (in.)
1966	33	M42K	A21X	J4J	0.030	①	Fly Mag	0.020	———
	40	M42K	A21X	J4J	0.030	①	Fly Mag	0.020	———
	60	M42K	A21X	J4J	0.030	①	Dist Mag	0.020	———
	80	M42K	A21X	J4J	0.030	①	Dist Mag②	0.020	———
	100	M42K	A21X	J4J	0.030	①	Batt Dist	0.020	———
1967	33	M42K	A21X	J4J	0.030	①	Fly Mag	0.020	———
	40	M42K	A21X	J4J	0.030	①	Fly Mag	0.020	———
	60	M42K	A21X	J4J	0.030	①	Batt Dist	0.020	———
	80	M42K	A21X	J4J	0.030	①	Batt Dist	0.020	———
	100	——	——	L19V	③	①	Trans Batt Dist	——	0.028
1968	33	M42K	A21X	J4J	0.030	①	Fly Mag	0.020	———
	40	M42K	A21X	J4J	0.030	①	Fly Mag	0.020	———
	55	V40FF	——	L19V	③	①	CD w/Points	0.010	———
	65	——	——	L19V	③	①	CD w/Points	0.010	———
	85	——	——	L19V	③	①	CD w/Points	0.010	———
	100	——	——	L19V	③	①	CD Breakerless	0.010	———
1969	33	M42K	A21X	J4J	0.030	①	Fly Mag	0.020	———
	40	M42K	A21X	J4J	0.030	①	Fly Mag	0.020	———
	55	V40FF	——	L19V	③	①	CD w/Points	0.010	———
	85	V40FF	——	L19V	③	①	CD w/Points	0.010	———
	115	V40FF	——	L19V	③	①	CD Breakerless	——	0.028

Tune-Up Specifications (cont.)

Year	Model (hp)	Spark Plugs			Gap (in.)	Compression Pressure (psi)	Ignition Type	Breaker Point Gap (in.)	Sensor Air Gap (in.)
		AC	AL	Ch					
1970	33	M42K	——	J4J	0.030	①	Fly Mag	0.020	——
	40	M42K	——	J4J	0.030	①	Fly Mag	0.020	——
	60	V40FF	——	L19V	③	①	CD w/Points	0.010	——
	85	V40FF	——	L19V	③	①	CD w/Points	0.010	——
	115	V40FF	——	L19V	③	①	CD Breakerless	——	0.028
1971	40	M42K	——	J4J	0.030	①	Fly Mag	0.020	——
	50	——	——	UL77V	③	①	CD Breakerless w/Magneto	——	0.028
	60	——	——	L77V	③	①	CD w/Points	0.010	——
	85	——	——	L77V	③	①	CD w/Points	0.010	——
	100	——	——	L77V	③	①	CD w/Points	0.010	——
	125	——	——	L77V	③	①	CD Breakerless	——	0.028

① All cylinders within 15 psi of each other
② May also be equipped with automotive-type battery distributor system
③ Surface gap plug—no gap adjustment
Fly Mag—Flywheel Magneto
Dist Mag—Distributor Magneto
Dist Mag②—Distributor magneto or automotive battery and distributor-type
Batt Dist—Automotive-type battery and distributor-type
CD w/Points—Capacitor discharge electronic system with breaker points
CDBreakerless—All electronic capacitor discharge without breaker points
CD Breakerless w/Magneto—Capacitor discharge with magneto using no breaker points
AC—AC
AL—Autolite
Ch—Champion
——Not available

Torque Specifications

Year	Model (hp)	Flywheel Nut (ft lbs)	Connecting Rod (ft lbs)	Cylinder Head ▲ (in. lbs)	Crankcase to Cylinder Block (in. lbs) Upper and Lower	Crankcase to Cylinder Block (in. lbs) Center	Spark Plugs (ft lbs)	Driveshaft Pinion Nut (ft lbs)	Crankcase Head (ft lbs) Upper	Crankcase Head (ft lbs) Lower
1966	33	100–105	29–31	168–192	150–170	162–168	20–21	—	—	—
	40	100–105	29–31	168–192	150–170	162–168	20–21	—	—	—
	60	70–85	29–31	168–192	144–168	162–168	20–21	—	—	—
	80	70–85	29–31	168–192	144–168	162–168	20–21	—	10–12	8–10
	100	70–85	29–31	168–192	144–168	162–168	20–21	70–80	10–12	8–10
1967	33	100–105	29–31	168–192	150–170	162–168	17–21	—	—	—
	40	100–105	29–31	168–192	150–170	162–168	17–21	—	—	—
	60	70–85	29–31	168–192	144–168	162–168	17–21	—	10–12	8–10
	80	70–85	29–31	168–192	144–168	162–168	17–21	—	10–12	8–10
	100	70–85	29–31	168–192	144–168	162–168	17–21	70–80	10–12	8–10
1968	33	100–105	29–31	168–192	150–170	162–168	17–21	—	—	—
	40	100–105	29–31	168–192	150–170	162–168	17–21	—	—	—
	55	70–85	29–31	168–192	144–168	144–168	17–21	—	—	—
	65	70–85	29–31	168–192	144–168	162–168	17–21	—	10–12	8–10
	85	70–85	29–31	168–192	144–168	162–168	17–21	—	10–12	8–10
	100	70–85	29–31	168–192	144–168	162–168	17–21	70–80	10–12	8–10
1969	33	100–105	29–31	162–192	150–170	102–168	17–21	—	—	—
	40	100–105	29–31	168–192	150–170	162–168	17–21	—	—	—
	55	70–85	29–31	168–192	144–168	144–168	17–21	—	—	—
	85	70–85	29–31	168–192	144–168	162–168	17–21	—	10–12	8–10
	115	70–85	29–31	168–192	144–168	162–168	17–21	40–45	10–12	8–10
1970	33	100–105	29–31	168–192	150–170	162–168	17–21	—	—	—
	40	100–105	29–31	168–192	150–170	162–168	17–21	—	—	—
	60	70–85	29–31	168–192	144–168	144–168	17–21	—	—	—
	85	70–85	27–31	168–192	144–168	162–168	17–21	—	10–12	8–10
	115	70–85	29–31	168–192	144–168	162–168	17–21	40–45	10–12	8–10
1971	40	100–105	29–31	168–192	150–170	162–168	17–21	—	—	—
	50	70–85	29–31	168–192	144–168	144–168	17–21	40–45	—	—
	60	40–85	29–31	168–192	144–168	144–168	17–21	40–45	—	—
	85	70–85	29–31	168–192	144–168	162–168	17–21	60–65	10–12	8–10
	100	70–85	29–31	168–192	144–168	162–168	17–21	60–65	10–12	8–10
	125	70–85	29–31	168–192	144–168	162–168	17–21	60–65	10–12	8–10

▲—Recheck torque on cylinder head screws after motor has been run, has reached operating temperature, and has cooled until it is comfortable to the touch.

NOTE: *Due to the extensive use of aluminum and white metal to resist corrosion, torque specifications must be adhered to strictly. When tightening two or more screws on the same part, do not tighten screws one at a time. To avoid distortion, tighten all screws to ⅓ specified torque, then ⅔ specified torque, and finally torque completely.*

Standard Screw Torque Chart

Standard Screw Size	Torque	
	In. Lbs	Ft Lbs
No. 6	7–10	——
No. 8	15–22	——
No. 10	25–35	2–3
No. 12	35–45	3–4
¼ in.	60–80	5–7
⁵⁄₁₆ in.	120–140	10–12
⅜ in.	220–240	18–20
⁷⁄₁₆ in.	340–360	28–30

NOTE: *Due to the extensive use of aluminum and white metal to resist corrosion, torque specifications must be adhered to strictly. When tightening two or more screws on the same part, do not tighten screws one at a time. To avoid distortion, tighten all screws to ⅓ specified torque, to ⅔ specified torque, then torque completely.*

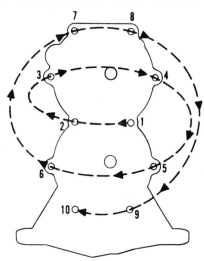

Cylinder head—1971 50 HP (© Outboard Marine Corporation)

Torque Sequences

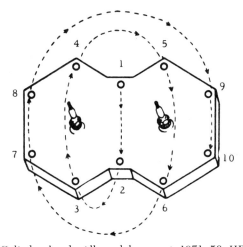

Cylinder head—All models except 1971 50 HP, 1968–69 55 HP and 1971 60 HP (© Outboard Marine Corporation)

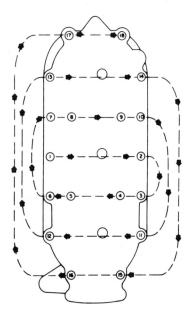

Cylinder head—1968–69 55 HP and 1971 60 HP (© Outboard Marine Corporation)

Crankshaft, Piston and Ring Specifications

Year	Model (hp)	Crankshaft (in.) Journal Diameter — Upper	Center	Lower	End-Play	Pistons (in.) Piston to Cylinder Clear.	Oversize(s)	Ring (in.) Ring to Groove Clearance	End-Gap
1966	33	1.2495–1.250	0.9995–1.000	0.9995–1.000	0.007(max)	0.003–0.0045	0.020, 0.040	0.0045–0.007	0.007–0.017
	40	1.2495–1.250	0.9995–1.000	0.9995–1.000	0.007(max)	0.003–0.0045	0.025	0.0045–0.007	0.007–0.017
	60	1.2653–1.2658	1.3748–1.3752	1.1810–1.1815	0.007(max)	0.0035–0.005	0.020, 0.040	0.0045–0.007	0.007–0.017
	80	1.2653–1.2658	1.3748–1.3752	1.1810–1.1815	0.007(max)	0.0045–0.006	0.020, 0.040	0.0045–0.007	0.007–0.017
	100	1.2653–1.2658	1.3748–1.3752	1.1810–1.1815	0.007(max)	0.0045–0.006	0.020, 0.040	0.0045–0.007	0.007–0.017
1967	33	1.2495–1.750	0.9995–1.000	0.9995–1.000	0.007–0.011	0.003–0.0045	0.020, 0.040	0.0045–0.007	0.007–0.017
	40	1.2495–1.250	0.9995–1.000	0.9995–1.000	0.003–0.011	0.003–0.0045	0.025	0.0045–0.007	0.007–0.017
	60	1.2653–1.2658	1.3748–1.3752	1.1810–1.1815	0.0019–0.0089	0.0035–0.005	0.020, 0.040	0.0045–0.007	0.007–0.017
	80	1.2653–1.2658	1.3748–1.3752	1.1810–1.1815	0.0019–0.0089	0.0025–0.004	0.020, 0.040	0.0045–0.007	0.007–0.017
	100	1.2653–1.2658	1.3748–1.3752	1.1810–1.1815	0.0019–0.0089	0.0025–0.004	0.020, 0.040	0.0045–0.007	0.007–0.017
1968	33	1.2495–1.250	0.9995–1.000	0.9995–1.000	0.007–0.011	0.003–0.0045	0.020, 0.040	0.0045–0.007	0.007–0.017
	40	1.2495–1.250	0.9995–1.000	0.9995–1.000	0.003–0.011	0.003–0.0045	0.025	0.0045–0.007	0.007–0.017
	55	1.4974–1.4979	1.3748–1.3752	1.1810–1.1815	0.003–0.011	0.004–0.0055	0.020	0.0045–0.007	0.007–0.017
	65	1.2653–1.2658	1.3748–1.3752	1.1810–1.1815	0.0019–0.0089	0.0035–0.005	0.020, 0.040	0.0045–0.007	0.007–0.017
	85	1.2653–1.2658	1.3748–1.3752	1.1810–1.1815	0.0019–0.0089	0.0025–0.004	0.020, 0.040	0.0045–0.007	0.007–0.017
	100	1.2653–1.2658	1.3748–1.3752	1.1810–1.1815	0.0019–0.0089	0.0025–0.004	0.020, 0.040	0.0045–0.004	0.007–0.017
1969	33	1.2495–1.250	0.9995–1.000	0.9995–1.000	0.003–0.011	0.003–0.0045	0.020, 0.040	0.0045–0.007	0.007–0.017
	40	1.2495–1.250	0.9995–1.000	0.9995–1.000	0.003–0.011	0.003–0.0045	0.025	0.002–0.0045	0.007–0.017
	55	1.4974–1.4979	1.3748–1.3752	1.1810–1.1815	0.005–0.0165	0.004–0.0055	0.020	0.001–0.0045	0.007–0.017
	85	1.4975–1.4980	1.3748–1.3752	1.1810–1.1815	0.003–0.011	0.004–0.0055	0.020, 0.040	0.0045–0.007	0.007–0.017
	115	1.4975–1.4980	1.3748–1.3752	1.1810–1.1815	0.003–0.011	0.004–0.0055	0.030	0.0045–0.007	0.007–0.017
1970	33	1.2495–1.250	0.9995–1.000	0.9995–1.000	0.003–0.011	0.003–0.0045	0.020, 0.040	0.0045–0.007	0.007–0.017
	40	1.2495–1.250	0.9995–1.000	0.9995–1.000	0.003–0.011	0.003–0.0045	0.025	0.002–0.0045	0.007–0.017
	60	1.4974–1.4979	1.3748–1.3752	1.1810–1.1815	0.0006–0.0156	0.0035–0.005	0.020, 0.030	0.0015–0.0045	0.007–0.017
	85	1.4975–1.4980	1.3748–1.3752	1.1810–1.1815	0.003–0.011	0.0025–0.004	0.020, 0.040	0.0045–0.007	0.007–0.017
	115	1.4975–1.4980	1.3748–1.3752	1.1810–1.1815	0.003–0.011	0.0035–0.005	0.030	0.0015–0.004	0.007–0.017
1971	40	1.2495–1.250	0.9995–1.000	0.9995–1.000	0.003–0.011	0.003–0.0045	0.030	0.0015–0.004	0.007–0.017
	50	1.4974–1.4979	1.3748–1.3752	1.1810–1.1815	0.0006–0.0156	0.0045–0.006	0.030	0.0015–0.004	0.007–0.017
	60	1.4974–1.4979	1.3748–1.3752	1.1810–1.1815	0.0006–0.0156	0.0035–0.005	0.020, 0.030	0.0015–0.004	0.007–0.017
	85	1.4975–1.4980	1.3748–1.3752	1.1810–1.1815	0.0006–0.0336	0.0025–0.004	0.020, 0.030	0.0045–0.007	0.007–0.017
	100	1.4975–1.4980	1.3748–1.3752	1.1810–1.1815	0.0006–0.0336	0.0025–0.004	0.020, 0.030	0.0045–0.007	0.007–0.017
	125	1.4975–1.4980	1.3748–1.3752	1.1810–1.1815	0.0006–0.0336	0.003–0.0045	0.020, 0.030	0.002–0.004	0.007–0.017

Wiring Diagrams

NOTE: *Wiring diagrams for models listed are basically similar. However, small production changes may have occurred which are not shown for a specific motor.*

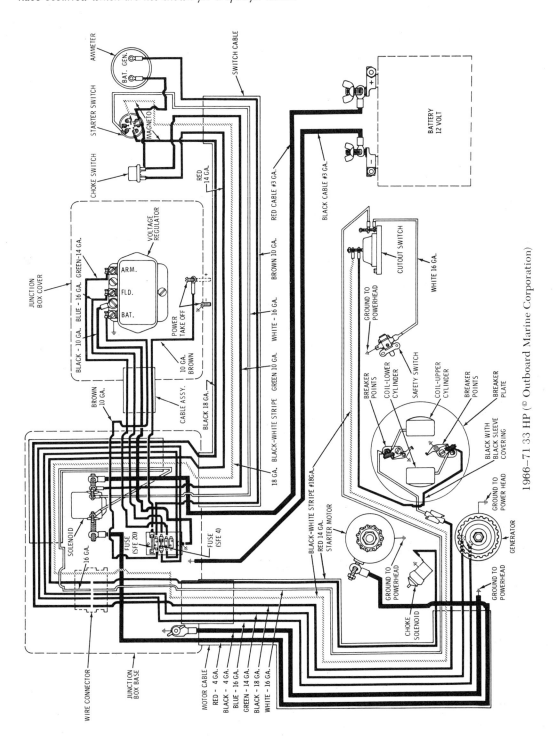

1966–71 33 HP (© Outboard Marine Corporation)

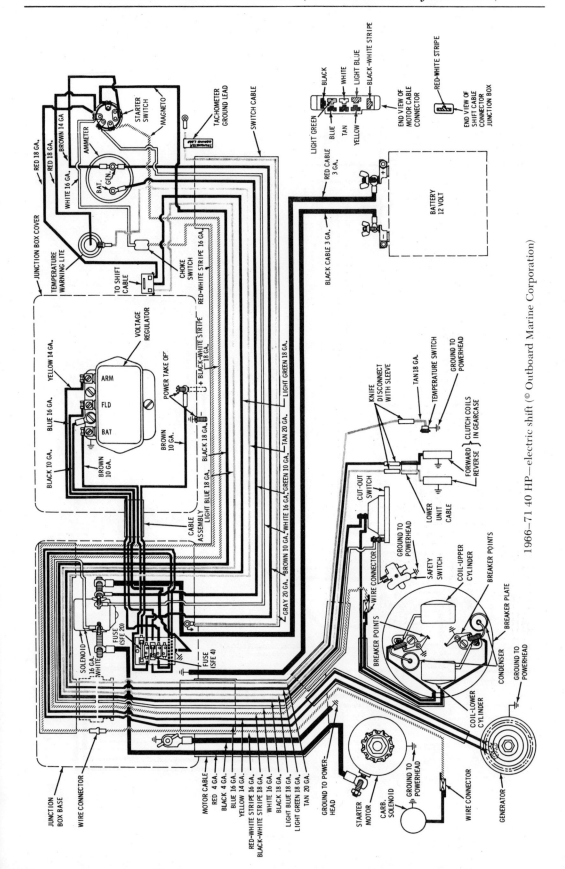

1966–71 40 HP—electric shift (© Outboard Marine Corporation)

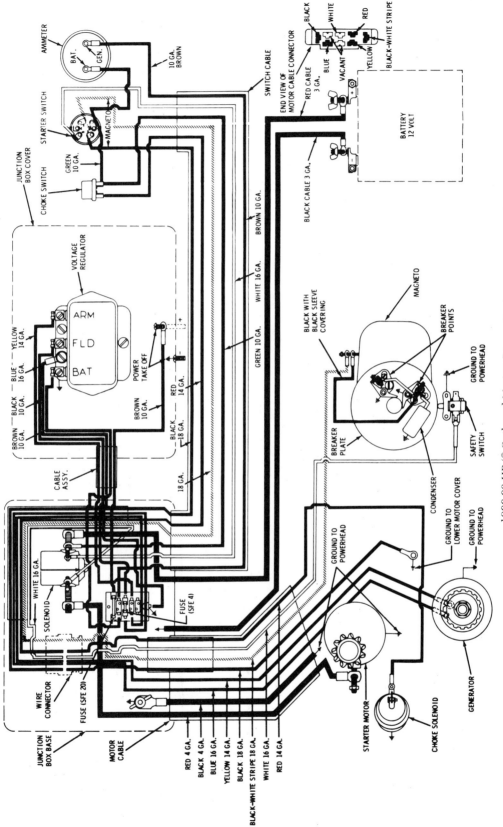

1966 60 HP (© Outboard Marine Corporation)

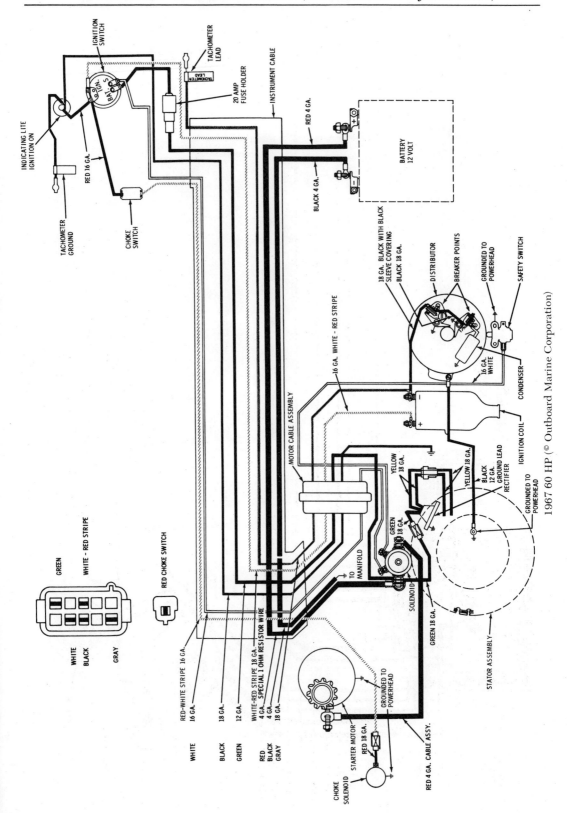

1967 60 HP (© Outboard Marine Corporation)

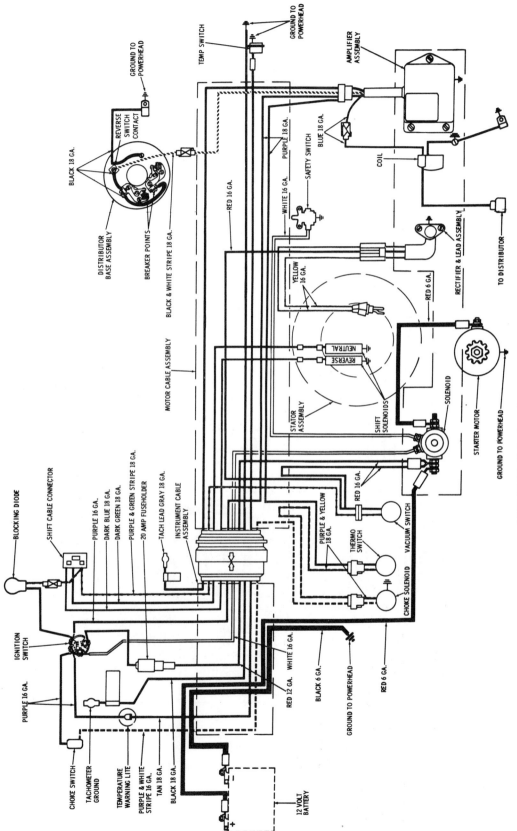

1969 55 HP (© Outboard Marine Corporation)

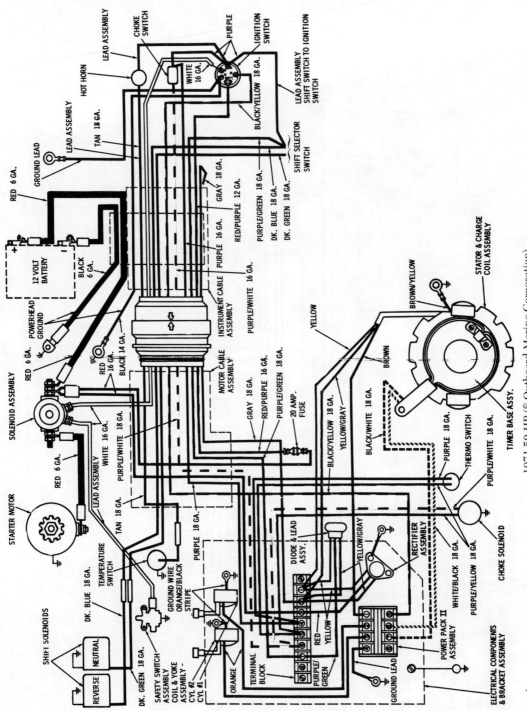

1971 50 HP (© Outboard Marine Corporation)

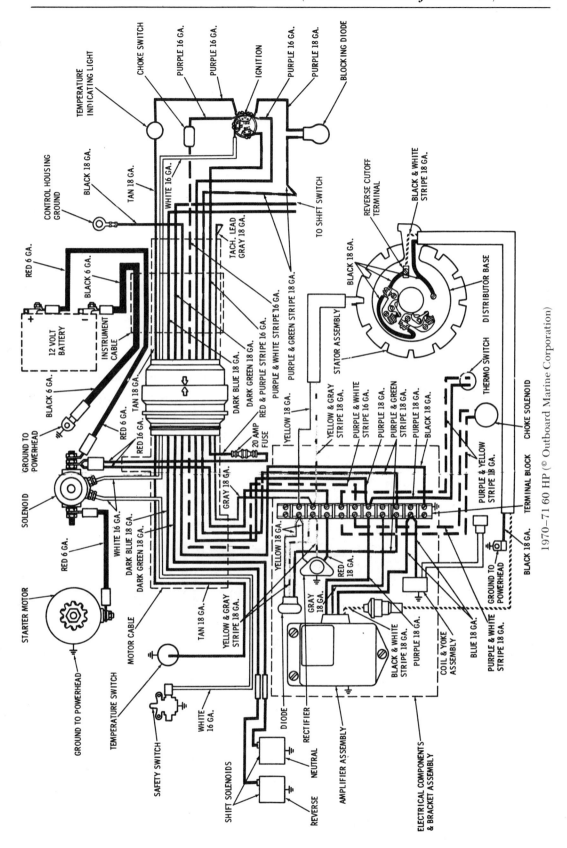

1970-71 60 HP (© Outboard Marine Corporation)

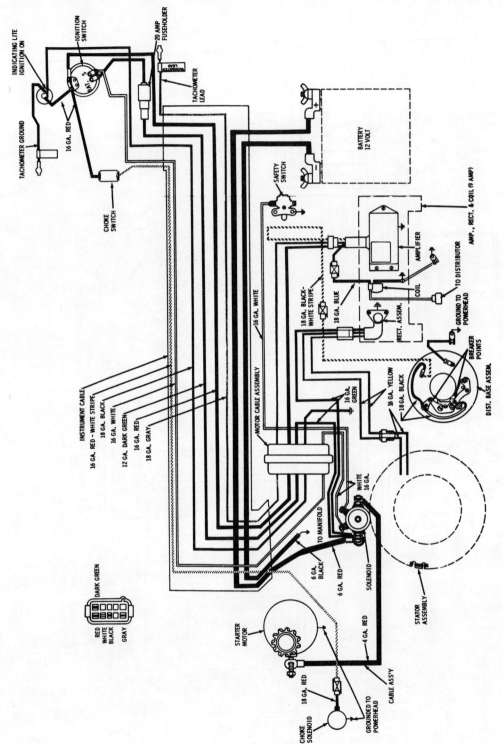

1968 65 HP (© Outboard Marine Corporation)

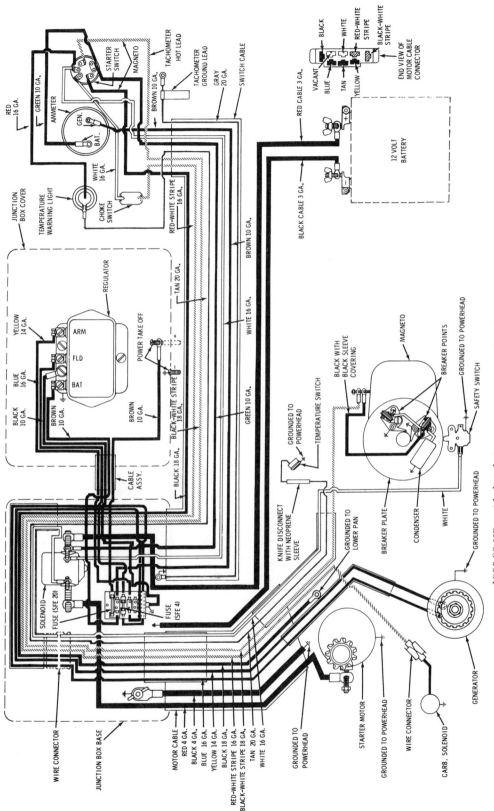

1966 80 HP—with distributor magneto ignition (© Outboard Marine Corporation)

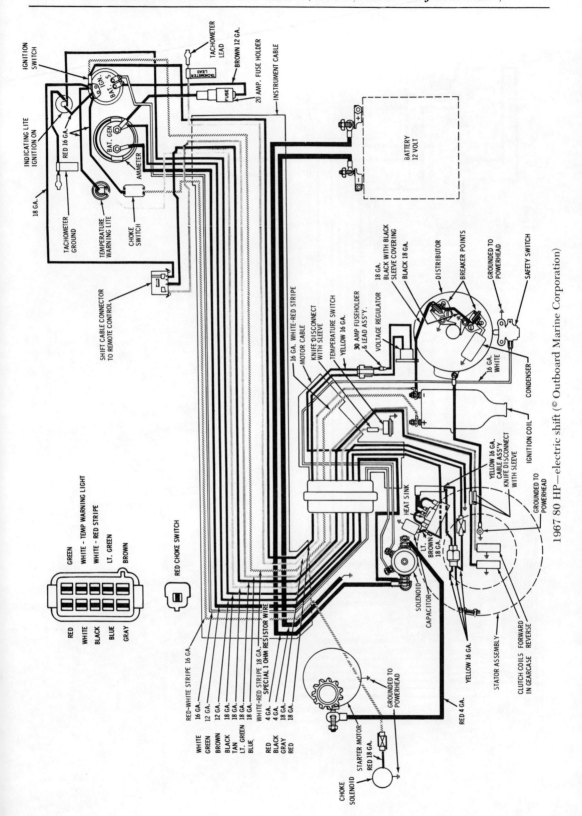

1967 80 HP—electric shift (© Outboard Marine Corporation)

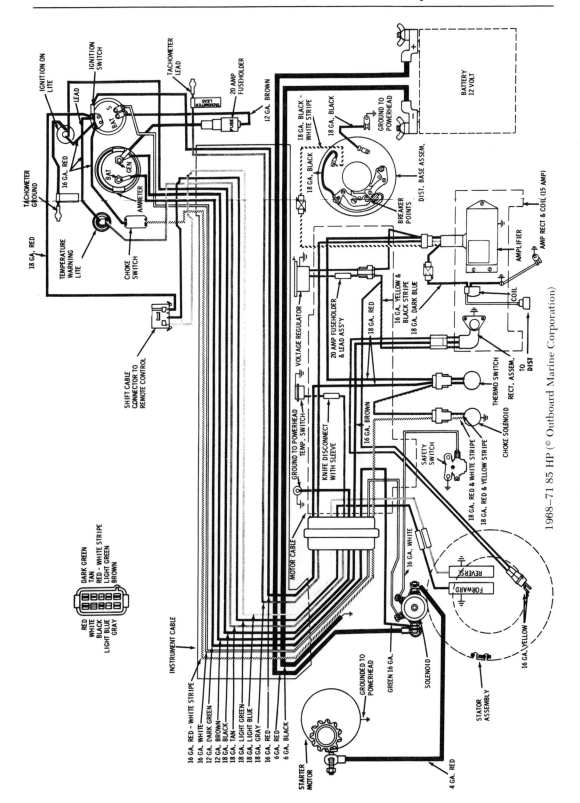

1968–71 85 HP (© Outboard Marine Corporation)

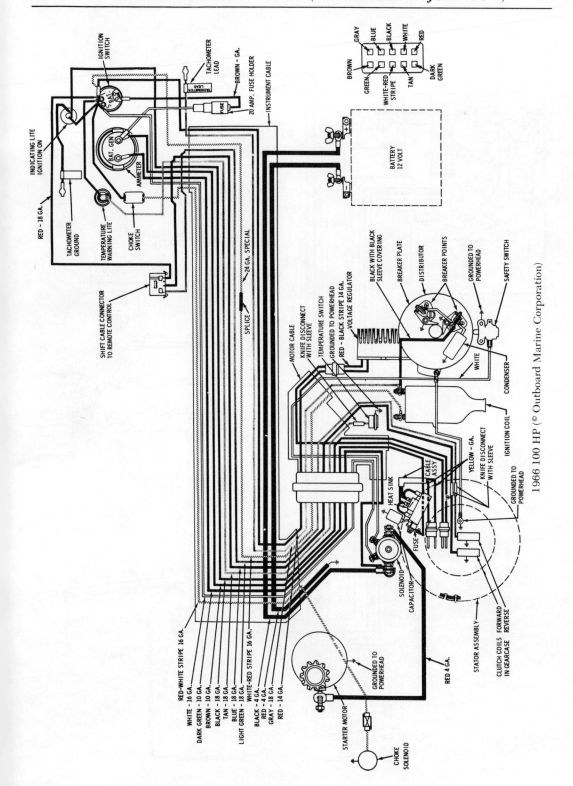

1966 100 HP (© Outboard Marine Corporation)

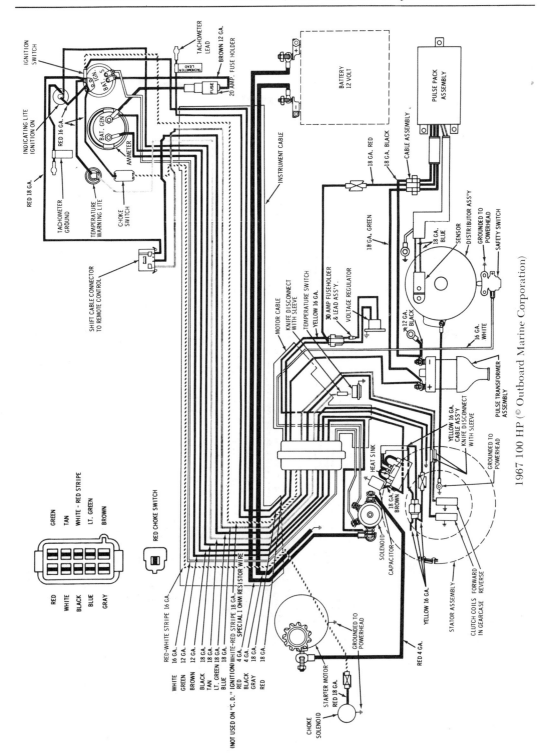

1967 100 HP (© Outboard Marine Corporation)

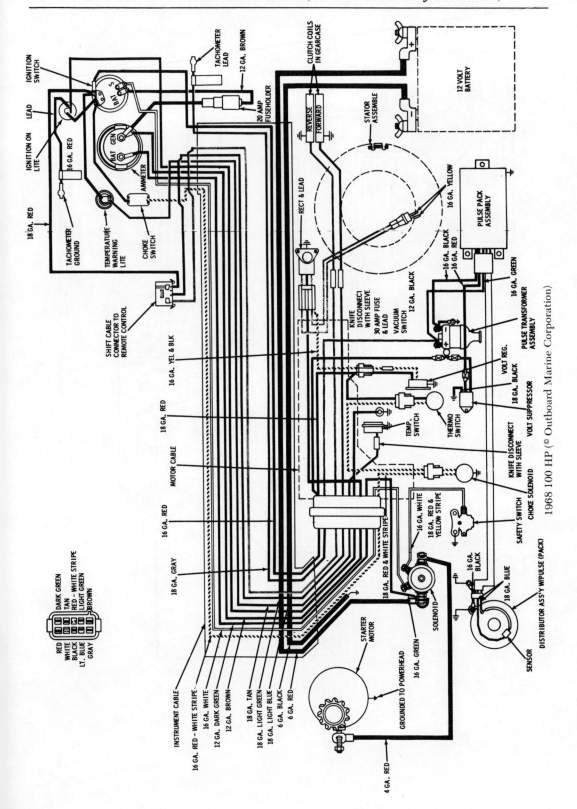

1968 100 HP (© Outboard Marine Corporation)

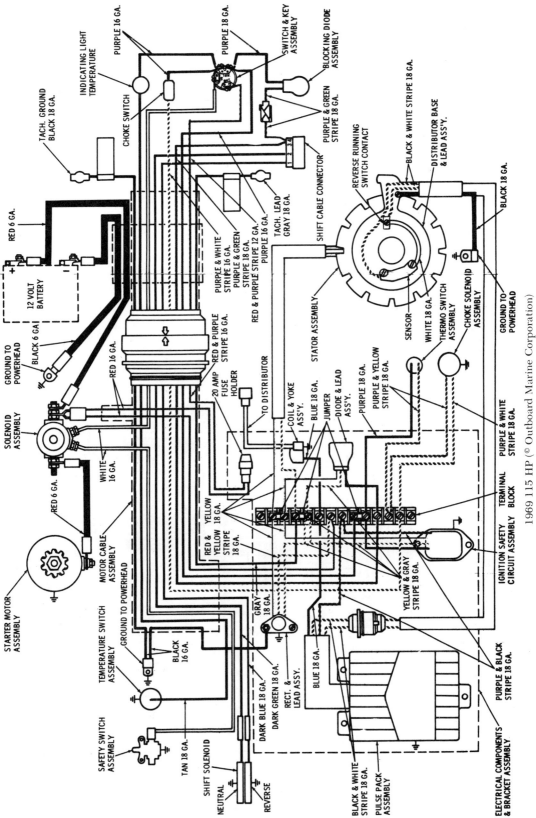

1969 115 HP (© Outboard Marine Corporation)

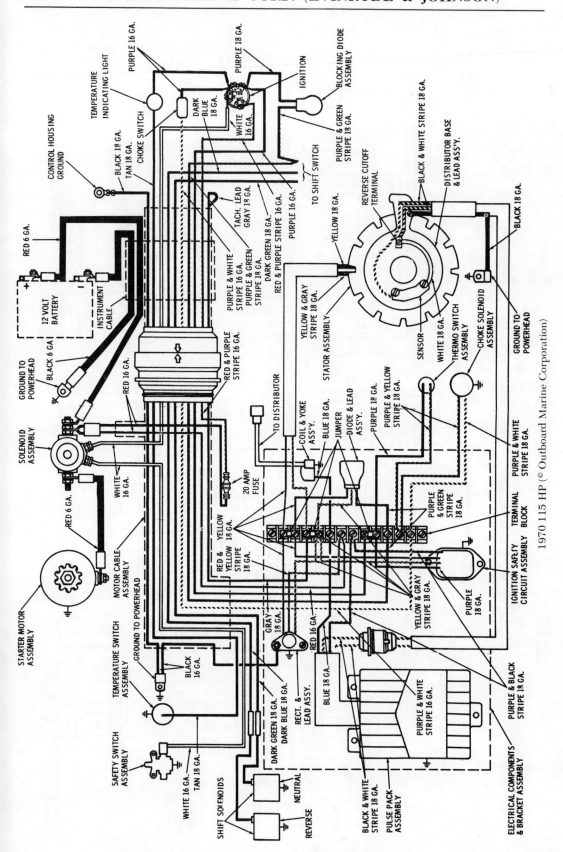

1970 115 HP (© Outboard Marine Corporation)

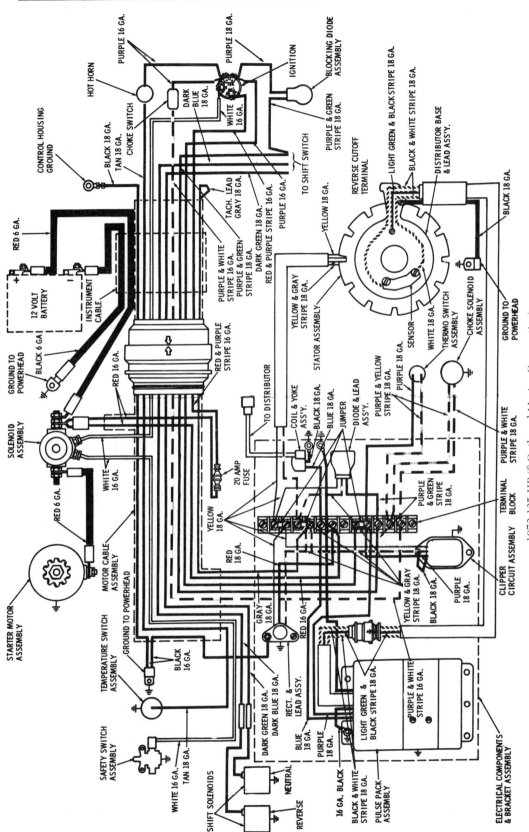

1972 125 HP (© Outboard Marine Corporation)

General Maintenance and Lubrication

GENERAL MAINTENANCE

Tune-Up And/Or Winterizing

The following procedure can be followed for a mid-season tune-up or for end-of-season winterizing.

1. Remove the exhaust covers and cylinder head(s). Slowly rotate the flywheel and visually inspect the pistons, rings, and cylinders for wear, free movement, or excessive carbon buildup.

NOTE: *Piston ring condition should be determined before continuing. Gum and varnish can be removed with an application of OMC Engine Cleaner.*

2. If pistons and rings are in satisfactory condition, remove all carbon and reinstall the exhaust covers.

3. Clean the carbon from the cylinder head and the top of the pistons. Replace the upper bearing crankshaft seal. Reinstall the cylinder head using a new gasket.

4. Remove all spark plugs and inspect each one. Clean all serviceable plugs and set each to the correct gap. Replace plugs as necessary. Install all spark plugs and torque to specification.

5. Inspect and test the ignition coil, sensor, points, and ignition wires (depending on equipment). Replace parts as necessary and set the point gap or sensor gap (depending on equipment).

6. Inspect all carburetors and the automatic choke.

7. Inspect the fuel pump and fuel lines. Replace any fuel lines which are cracked or rotted. Replace the fuel filter element and gasket.

8. Synchronize the carburetor linkage.

9. Inspect the electric shift operation (if equipped).

10. Check the condition of the propeller for nicks, scratches, bent blades, and correct pitch. Remove the propeller and lubricate the propeller shaft splines. If equipped, inspect the condition of the drive key and replace if necessary. Reinstall the propeller.

11. Drain and refill the gearcase and thoroughly lubricate all components of the motor.

12. Tighten all screws and nuts to the specified torque.

13. Tank-test or boat-test the motor and adjust the low-speed jets on the carburetor. Check the cooling system operation. After the motor has cooled until it is comfortable to the touch, retorque the cylinder head screws.

NOTE: *Steps 14 and 15 should only be performed when winterizing the motor.*

14. Run the engine at idle and disconnect the fuel line. Rapidly inject rust preventive oil through the carburetor throat(s) until the engine smokes profusely. This will lubricate the internal moving parts of the motor.

15. Fog the motor for storage using OMC Accessory Rust Preventive Oil. Store the motor in a clean, dry area in an upright position.

Battery Care

OMC outboards are designed to be operated with a 12 volt battery.

The battery should be kept fully charged at all times. Check the state of charge with a hydrometer approximately every two weeks. If the battery has been standing for thirty days or more, it should be recharged before placing it back in service. Refer to the introductory chapter of this book for further battery care.

NOTE: *An application of petroleum jelly will prevent corrosion on the battery terminals.*

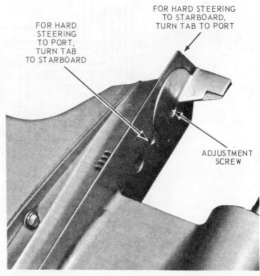

Trim tab adjustment (© Outboard Marine Corporation)

Trim Tab Adjustment

The trim tab is located on the lower unit, just below the cavitation plate and just above the propeller. A running adjustment may be necessary to achieve best steering results. Loosen the adjustment screw which is located in the center of the trim tab mounting plate. If the boat steers hard to starboard, turn the trim tab toward the port side. If the boat steers hard to port, turn the trim tab toward the starboard side. It may take several attempts to satisfactorily adjust the trim tab.

Propeller Selection

Next to the selection of a motor and boat, the most important decision to be made is what propeller to install on your motor. The standard propeller is usually satisfactory for general purposes and all-around use. However, it is wise to check and be sure that your motor is running in the recommended operating range (see specifications) with any propeller that is being used (see Chapter 1).

The following propellers are available from OMC as alternate or spare propellers.

Propeller Chart

HP	Year	Boat Size and Recommendation	Boat Speed (MPH)	Part No.	Material	No. of Blades	Diameter	Pitch
33, 40 (all years)		Heavy-duty Large Boats and Houseboats	1–20	376738	Al	3	11 in.	9 in.
		17½–20 ft all Loads	18–26	378581	Al	3	10⅜ in.	11½ in.
		16–18 ft all Loads	22–29	380637	Al	3	10½ in.	12 in.
		14–17 ft all Loads	24–32	384460	Al	3	10½ in.	13 in.
		13–15 ft Light Loads	26–35	378571	Al	3	10⅜ in.	14 in.
50	58–59	General Usage		278155	Al	3	12⅛ in.	14 in.
50 thru-hub exhaust only	through 71	Large Non-planing Boats	1–15	383160	Al	3	14 in.	9 in.
		Large Boats or Planing Houseboats	13–20	382761	Al	3	14 in.	11 in.
		Heavy-duty Large Boats	18–26	382762	Al	3	14 in.	13 in.
		15–18 ft Boats	24–30	382763	Al	3	13¾ in.	15 in.
		14–16 ft Boats	27–34	382764	Al	3	13¼ in.	17 in.
		14–16 ft Boats	27–34	384139	SST	3	13⅜ ni.	17 in.
		13–15 ft Boats	32–38	382765	Al	3	13 in.	19 in.
		13–15 ft Boats	32–38	384142	SST	3	13 in.	19 in.
		12–14 ft High-speed Boats	36–42	382766	Al	3	12¾ in.	21 in.
		12–14 ft High-speed Boats	36–42	384702	SST	3	12¾ in.	21 in.
		12–14 ft High-speed Boats	36–42	384140	Br	2	13¾ in.	21 in.
		12–14 ft Light, Fast Boats High Transom	36–42	384141 *	Br	2	13¾ in.	21 in.
55 and 60 thru-hub exhaust only	through 68	Barges, non-planing Houseboats	1–12	383160	Al	3	14 in.	9 in.
		Planing Houseboats Large Boats	10–17	382761	Al	3	14 in.	11 in.
		17–21 ft Large Boats	15–22	382762	Al	3	14 in.	13 in.
		15½–19 ft Boats	20–28	382763	Al	3	13¾ in.	15 in.
		15½–17 ft Boats	26–33	382764	Al	3	13¼ in.	17 in.
		15½–17 ft Boats	26–33	384139	SST	3	13⅜ in.	17 in.
		14–16 ft Boats	31–38	382765	Al	3	13 in.	19 in.
		14–16 ft Boats	31–38	384142	SST	3	13 in.	19 in.
		13–15 ft Fast Boats	36–45	382766	Al	3	12¾ in.	21 in.
		13–15 ft Fast Boats	36–48	384702	SST	3	12¾ in.	21 in.
		13–15 ft Fast Boats	36–45	384140	Br	2	13¾ in.	21 in.
		13–15 ft Fast Boats	36–45	384141	Br	2	13¾ in.	21 in.
		High Transom	43–55	384703	SST	3	12¾ in.	23 in.

Propeller Chart (cont.)

HP	Year	Boat Size and Recommendation	Boat Speed (MPH)	Part No.	Material	No. of Blades	Diameter	Pitch
55 and 60 thru-hub exhaust only	through 68	High-performance Boats High Transom	43–55	384138 *	Br	2	13¾ in.	23 in.
		High-Performance Boats High Transom	43–55	384136	Al	3	12¾ in.	23 in.
		High-Performance Boats						
60, 65, 75, 80, 85	all years through 68	General Usage		379260	Al	3	10 in.	9¼ in.
		Propeller Kit †		379448	Al	3	10 in.	9¼ in.
		General Usage		381446	Al	3	10 in.	11 in.
		General Usage		378039	Al	3	10 in.	12 in.
100	through 68	Barges, Work Boats	5–12	381296	Al	3	14¼ in.	10 in.
		Houseboats	12–19	382676	Al	3	14 in.	11 in.
		18–20 ft Planing Boats	16–23	382017	Al	3	14 in.	12 in.
		16–18 ft Boats	18–26	381442	Al	3	13 in.	14 in.
		14–17 ft Boats	22–30	381020	Al	3	12½ in.	16 in.
		13–16 ft Boats	27–35	381021	Al	3	12½ in.	18 in.
		12–15 ft Boats	38–46	381465	Br	2	13 in.	18 in.
		12–15 ft High Transom Boats	38–46	381464 *	Br	2	13 in.	18 in.
85 thru-hub exhaust only	through 69	Barge or Work Boat	1–8	383160	Al	3	14 in.	9 in.
		Non-planing Boats and Houseboats	6–18	382761	Al	3	14 in.	11 in.
		Large Boats and Planing Houseboats	15–27	382762	Al	3	14 in.	13 in.
		17½–20 ft Boats	24–35	382763	Al	3	13¾ in.	15 in.
		16–18 ft Boats	30–41	382764	Al	3	13¼ in.	17 in.
		16–18 ft Boats	30–41	384139	SST	3	13⅜ in.	17 in.
		14–17 ft Boats	36–46	382765	Al	3	13 in.	19 in.
		14–17 ft Boats	36–46	384142	SST	3	13 in.	19 in.
		13–16½ ft Boats	40–52	382766	Al	3	12¾ in.	21 in.
		13–16½ ft Boats	40–52	384702	SST	3	12¾ in.	21 in.
		13–16½ ft Boats	40–52	384140	Br	2	13¾ in.	21 in.
		13–16½ ft Boats	40–52	384141 *	Br	2	13¾ in.	21 in.
		High Transom	47–59	384138 *	Br	2	13¾ in.	23 in.
		High-Performance	47–59	384703	SST	3	12¾ in.	23 in.
		Boats	47–59	384136	Al	3	12¾ in.	23 in.
100 thru-hub exhaust only	through 71	Barges or Work Boats	1–12	382761	Al	3	14 in.	11 in.
		Non-planing Boats and Large Houseboats	10–22	382762	Al	3	14 in.	13 in.
		Large Boats and Planing Houseboats	18–32	382763	Al	3	13¾ in.	15 in.
		17½–19 ft Boats	27–38	382764	Al	3	13¼ in.	17 in.
		17½–19 ft Boats	27–38	384139	SST	3	13⅜ in.	17 in.
		15½–18 ft Boats	33–45	382765	Al	3	13 in.	19 in.
		15½–18 ft Boats	33–45	384142	SST	3	13 in.	19 in.
		13½–16½ ft Boats	42–52	382766	Al	3	12¾ in.	21 in.
		13½–16½ ft Boats	42–52	384702	SST	3	12¾ in.	21 in.
		13½–16½ ft Boats	42–52	384140	Br	2	13¾ in.	21 in.
		13½–16½ ft Light, Fast Boats	42–52	384141 *	Br	2	13¾ in.	21 in.
		High-Performance Boats	50–62	384138 *	Br	2	13¾ in.	23 in.
		High-Performance Boats	50–62	384703	SST	3	12¾ in.	23 in.
		High-Performance Boats	50–62	384136	Al	3	12¾ in.	23 in.

Propeller Chart (cont.)

HP	Year	Boat Size and Recommendation	Boat Speed (MPH)	Part No.	Material	No. of Blades	Diameter	Pitch
115 thru-hub exhaust only	through 69	Barges or Work Boats	1–12	382761	Al	3	14 in.	11 in.
		Non-Planing Boats and Large Houseboats	10–22	382762	Al	3	14 in.	13 in.
		Large Boats and Planing Houseboats	18–32	382763	Al	3	13¾ in.	15 in.
		17½–20 ft Boats	27–38	382764	Al	3	13¼ in.	17 in.
		17½–20 ft Boats	27–38	384139	SST	3	13⅜ in.	17 in.
		16–18 ft Boats	33–45	382765	Al	3	13 in.	19 in.
		16–18 ft Boats	33–45	384142	SST	3	13 in.	19 in.
		14–17 ft Boats	42–52	382766	Al	3	12¾ in.	21 in.
		14–17 ft Boats	42–52	384702	SST	3	12¾ in.	21 in.
		14–17 ft Boats	42–52	384140	Br	2	13¾ in.	21 in.
		14–17 ft Boats	42–52	384141 *	Br	2	13¾ in.	21 in.
		High-Performance Boats	46–62	384138 *	Br	2	13¾ in.	23 in.
		High-Performance Boats	46–62	384703	SST	3	12¾ in.	23 in.
		High-Performance Boats	46–62	384136	Al	3	12¾ in.	23 in.
125 thru-hub exhaust only	through 71	Barges or Work Boats	1–12	382761	Al	3	14 in.	11 in.
		Non-planing Boats and Large Houseboats	10–22	382762	Al	3	14 in.	13 in.
		Large Boats and Planing Houseboats	18–32	382763	Al	3	13¾ in.	15 in.
		19–22 ft Boats	27–38	382764	Al	3	13¼ in.	17 in.
		19–22 ft Boats	27–38	384139	SST	3	13⅜ in.	17 in.
		17–19 ft Boats	33–45	382765	Al	3	13 in.	19 in.
		17–19 ft Boats	33–45	384142	SST	3	13 in.	19 in.
		15–18 ft Boats	42–52	382766	Al	3	12¾ in.	21 in.
		15–18 ft Boats	42–52	384702	SST	3	12¾ in.	21 in.
		15–18 ft Boats	42–52	384140	Br	2	13¾ in.	21 in.
		15–18 ft Boats	42–52	384141 *	Br	2	13¾ in.	21 in.
		High-Performance Boats	46–62	384136	Al	3	12¾ in.	23 in.
		High-Performance Boats	46–62	384138 *	Br	2	13¾ in.	23 in.
		High-Performance Boats	46–62	384703	SST	3	12¾ in.	23 in.

*—Cupped propellers
†—Kit includes propeller, cotter pin, drive pin, and propeller nut
Al—Aluminum
Br—Bronze
SST—Stainless steel, Teflon-S® coated

Lubrication and Fuel

FUELS

Fuel Recommendations

Use any regular grade of automotive gasoline in your motor. Higher octane fuels may be used but will generally offer no advantages over regular grade gasoline. When operating your motor in any country other than the United States or Canada, use any gasoline that will perform satisfactorily in an automotive engine.

OMC (Johnson or Evinrude) outboard motor oil is recommended. A reputable outboard 50/1 lubricant can be used, as long as it is BIA (Boating Industry Association) certified for service TC-W (two-cycle, water-cooled). Any outboard lubricant which meets the above conditions will perform satisfactorily. Automotive oils should not be used except in extreme emergencies. Should an emergency of this type arise, use only SAE 30 oil with a container marked "Service ML-MM" or "Service MM." Avoid the use of oils marked as "ML" or multiviscosity oils as 10W-30. It should be recognized that automotive oils are formulated for use in automotive engines and outboard oils are designed specifically for two-cycle, water-cooled outboards.

NOTE: *Additive compounds, such as "tune-up" compounds, "tonics," "friction reducing" compounds, etc., are unnecessary and are not recommended for use in OMC outboards. OMC engine cleaner or OMC rust preventive oil are recommended as additives.*

LUBRICATION

Gear Housing

Refer to the following chart for the frequency of lubrication and for the recommended type of lubricant.

1. Remove the plugs and gasket assemblies marked "Oil Level" and "Oil Drain" from the starboard side of the gear housing.

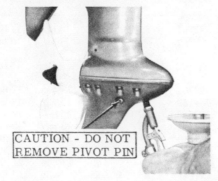

Lubricating the gear housing (© Outboard Marine Corporation)

2. With the propeller shaft in a normal running position, allow the oil to drain from the gear housing.

3. Fill the gear housing with the recommended lubricant until grease appears at the oil level hole.

4. Install the oil level plug before removing the lubricant filler tube from the oil drain hole. This allows the oil drain plug to be installed without lubricant loss.

TYPES OF LUBRICANT

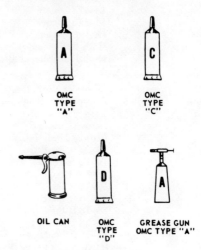

(© Outboard Marine Corporation)

Lubrication Points—1966–70 33 HP and 1971 40 HP

Lubrication Point	Lubricant	Frequency (Period of Operation)	
		Fresh Water	Salt Water #
1. Cam Follower Linkage and Locking Lever	OMC Type A	60 days	30 days
2. Throttle Shaft Bearings	SAE 90 Oil	60 days	30 days
3. Magneto Linkage	OMC Type A	60 days	30 days
4. Throttle Shaft Gears and Bushings	OMC Type A	60 days	30 days
5. Choke Linkage	OMC Type A	60 days	30 days
6. Starter Pinion Gear Shaft (Electric only)	SAE 10 Oil	60 days	30 days
7. Tilt-Lock Pin and Clamp Screws	OMC Type A	60 days	30 days
8. Gearcase	OMC Type C	Check level after first 10 hours of operation and every 50 hours of operation thereafter. Add lubricant if necessary.	Same as Fresh Water
		Drain and refill every 100 hours of operation or once each season, whichever occurs first.	Same as Fresh Water
9. Swivel Bracket Fittings	OMC Type A	60 days	30 days
10. Gearshift Lever Shaft and Lockout	OMC Type A	60 days	30 days

Some areas may require more frequent lubrication.

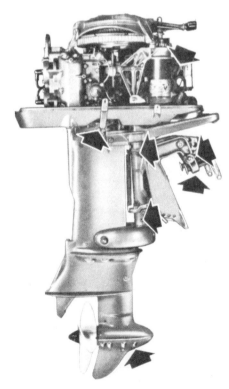 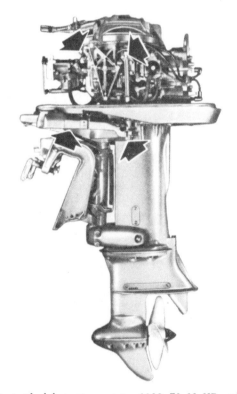

Starboard-side lubrication points—1966–70 33 HP and 1971 40 HP (© Outboard Marine Corporation)

Port-side lubrication points—1966–70 33 HP and 1971 40 HP (© Outboard Marine Corporation)

Lubrication Points—1966–70 40 HP

Lubrication Point	Lubricant	Frequency (Period of Operation)	
		Fresh Water	Salt Water #
1. Gearcase	OMC Type C	Check level after first 10 hours of operation and every 50 hours of operation thereafter. Add lubricant if necessary.	Same as Fresh Water
		Drain and refill every 100 hours of operation or once each season, whichever occurs first.	Same as Fresh Water
2. Locking Lever	OMC Type A	60 days	30 days
3. Cam Follower, Carburetor and Magneto Linkage	OMC Type A	60 days	30 days
4. Clamp Screws	OMC Type A	60 days	30 days
5. Throttle Shaft Bearing	SAE 90 Oil	60 days	30 days
6. Throttle Shaft Bushing	OMC Type A	60 days	30 days
7. Swivel Bracket Fitting	OMC Type A	60 days	30 days
8. Stern Bracket and Tilt-Lock	OMC Type A	60 days	30 days
9. Starter Pinion Gear Shaft	SAE 10 Oil	60 days	30 days

\# Some areas may require more frequent lubrication.

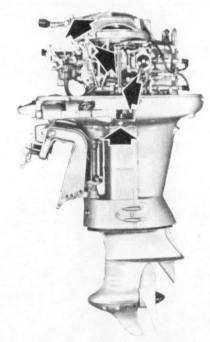

Starboard-side lubrication points—1971 40 HP (© Outboard Marine Corporation)

Port-side lubrication points—1971 40 HP (© Outboard Marine Corporation)

Lubrication Points—1971 50 HP, 1968–69 55 HP, and 1971 60 HP

Lubrication Point	Lubricant	Frequency (Period of Operation)	
		Fresh Water	Salt Water #
1. Starter Pinion Gear Shaft	SAE 10 Oil	60 days	30 days
2. Cam Follower, Roller Shaft	OMC Type A	60 days	30 days
3. Throttle Arm and Distributor Linkage	OMC Type A	60 days	30 days
4. Safety Switch Cam on Distributor Base	OMC Type A	60 days	30 days
5. Throttle and Choke Shaft Springs and Linkage	OMC Type A	60 days	30 days
6. Gearcase	OMC Type C	Check level after first 10 hours of operation and every 50 hours of operation thereafter. Add lubricant if necessary.	Same as Fresh Water
		Drain and refill every 100 hours of operation or once each season, whichever occurs first.	Same as Fresh Water
7. Swivel Bracket and Tilt-Lock Lever	OMC Type A	60 days	30 days
8. Ignition—Reverse Cutoff Spring	OMC Type D	At time of ignition service.	
9. Distributor Cap High Tension Terminals. Fill towers ⅓ full.	OMC Type D	At time of ignition service.	

Some areas may require more frequent lubrication.

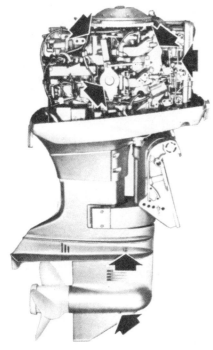

DRAIN AND REFILL

Starboard-side lubrication points—1971 50 HP, 1968–69 55 HP and 1971 60 HP (© Outboard Marine Corporation)

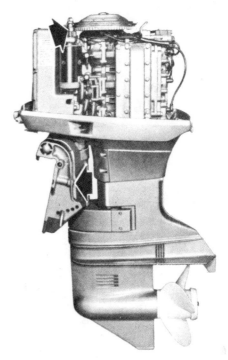

Port-side lubrication points—1971 50 HP, 1968–69 55 HP and 1971 60 HP (© Outboard Marine Corporation)

Lubrication Points—1966–67 60 HP and 1968 65 HP

Lubrication Point	Lubricant	Frequency (Period of Operation)	
		Fresh Water	Salt Water #
1. Gearcase	OMC Type C Lubricant	Check level after first 10 hours of operation and every 50 hours of operation thereafter. Add lubricant if necessary.	Same as Fresh Water
		Drain and refill every 100 hours of operation or once each season, whichever occurs first.	Same as Fresh Water
2. Starter Pinion Gear Shaft	SAE 10 Oil	60 days	30 days
3. Carburetor and Magneto Linkage	OMC Type A	60 days	30 days
4. Tilt and Trailing Lever	OMC Type A	60 days	30 days
5. Safety Switch Cam	OMC Type A	60 days	30 days
6. Throttle Shaft Gears	OMC Type A	60 days	30 days
7. Throttle and Shift Shaft Bearings	SAE 90 Oil	60 days	30 days
8. Gearshift Lever Shaft and Lockout	OMC Type A	60 days	30 days
9. Swivel Bracket Fitting	OMC Type A	60 days	30 days

Some areas may require more frequent lubrication.

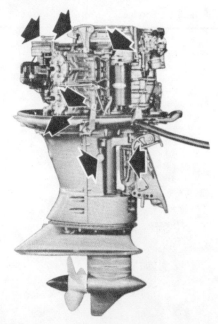

Starboard-side lubrication points—1966–67 60 HP and 1968 65 HP (© Outboard Marine Corporation)

Port-side lubrication points—1966–67 60 HP and 1968 65 HP (© Outboard Marine Corporation)

Lubrication Points—1966–67 80 HP, 1968 85 HP and 1966–68 100 HP

Lubrication Point	Lubricant	Frequency (Period of Operation)	
		Fresh Water	Salt Water #
1. Gearcase	OMC Type C Lubricant	Check level after first 10 hours of operation and every 50 hours of operation thereafter. Add lubricant if necessary.	Same as Fresh Water
		Drain and refill every 100 hours of operation or once each season, whichever occurs first.	Same as Fresh Water
2. Choke Linkage	OMC Type A	60 days	30 days
3. Carburetor and Magneto Linkage or Carburetor and Distributor Linkage	OMC Type A	60 days	30 days
4. Tilt and Trailing Lever	OMC Type A	60 days	30 days
5. Safety Switch Cam	OMC Type A	60 days	30 days
6. Throttle Shaft Gears	OMC Type A	60 days	30 days
7. Throttle and Shift Shaft Bearings	SAE 90 Oil	60 days	30 days
8. Gearshift Lever Shaft and Lockout	OMC Type A	60 days	30 days
9. Swivel Bracket Fitting	OMC Type A	60 days	30 days
10. Starter Pinion Gear Shaft	SAE 10 Oil	60 days	30 days

Some areas may require more frequent lubrication.

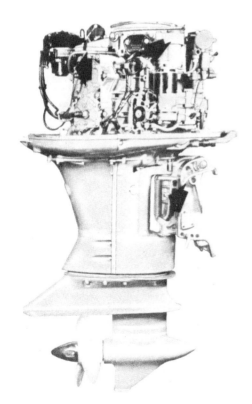

Starboard-side lubrication points—1966–67 80 HP and 1968 85 HP (© Outboard Marine Corporation)

Port-side lubrication points—1966–67 80 HP and 1968 85 HP (© Outboard Marine Corporation)

Lubrication Points—1969–71 85 HP, 1971 100 HP, 1969–70 115 HP, and 1971 125 HP

Lubrication Point	Lubricant	Frequency (Period of Operation)	
		Fresh Water	Salt Water #
1. Stern Bracket Tilt-Lock	OMC Type A	60 days	30 days
2. Carburetor Linkage	OMC Type A	60 days	30 days
3. Cover Latches, Front and Rear	OMC Type A	60 days	30 days
4. Choke and Low-Speed Adjustment Linkage	OMC Type A	60 days	30 days
5. Gearcase	OMC Type C	Check level after first 10 hours of operation and every 50 hours of operation thereafter. Add lubricant if necessary.	Same as Fresh Water
		Drain and refill every 100 hours of operation or once each season, whichever occurs first.	Same as Fresh Water
6. Control Lever Bearing	OMC Type A	60 days	30 days
7. Control Shaft Bushing			
8. Safety Switch Cam	OMC Type A	60 days	30 days
9. Swivel Bracket	OMC Type A	60 days	30 days
10. Starter Pinion Gear Shaft	SAE 10 Oil	60 days	30 days
11. Ignition—Reverse Cutoff Spring	OMC Type D	At time of ignition service.	
12. Distributor cap high tension terminals. Fill towers ⅓ full.	OMC Type D	At time of ignition service.	

Some areas may require more frequent lubrication.

Starboard-side lubrication points—1969–71 85 HP, 1971 100 HP, 1969–70 115 HP and 1971 125 HP (© Outboard Marine Corporation)

Port-side lubrication points—1969–71 85 HP, 1971 100 HP, 1969–70 115 HP and 1971 125 HP (© Outboard Marine Corporation)

Fuel System

CARBURETOR AND INTAKE MANIFOLD

Removal

1966–71 33 HP AND 1971 40 HP

These models use a single-barrel, float-feed-type carburetor with an adjustable high and low-speed jet. The carburetor has a manual choke.

1. Disconnect the fuel line at the carburetor and remove the throttle link by disconnecting the lever pin at the throttle arm.

2. Remove the starter motor if equipped.

3. Remove the two nuts and lockwashers attaching the carburetor to the intake manifold. Disconnect the solenoid lead at the screw terminal.

4. Remove the carburetor and gasket from the intake manifold.

5. Remove the cotter pin from the bottom end of the starter lever lockout rod. Remove the rod from the throttle lever.

6. Remove the cutout switch hose from the intake manifold. Remove the screws attaching the intake manifold to the powerhead. Remove the intake manifold from the powerhead.

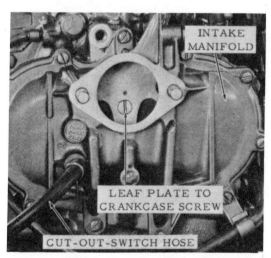

Intake manifold with carburetor removed—33 HP and 1971 40 HP (© Outboard Marine Corporation)

7. Remove the screw attaching the leaf plate to the crankcase and remove the leaf valve assembly and gasket.

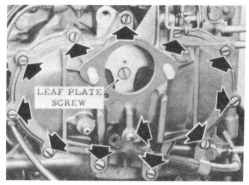

Intake manifold showing leaf plate screw (© Outboard Marine Corporation)

1966–70 40 HP

These carburetors are single-barrel, float-feed types with a fixed, high-speed jet and an adjustable low-speed jet.

1. Remove the manual starter and ring gear guard, if equipped.

2. Remove the heat tube shield and heat exchanger tubing (automatic choke models only).

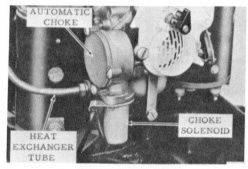

Removing the heat exchanger tubing (© Outboard Marine Corporation)

3. Disconnect the leads from the starter, generator, and choke solenoid. Remove the starter and generator.

4. Disconnect the fuel hose at the carburetor. Disconnect the cam follower link from the throttle arm.

5. Remove the two nuts and lockwashers attaching the carburetor to the intake manifold. Remove the carburetor and gasket from the intake manifold.

6. Perform steps 6 and 7 of the preceding procedure.

1971 50 HP

These motors use two single-barrel carburetors with a fixed, high-speed jet and an adjustable low-speed jet.

1. The carburetors and air silencer can be removed as an assembly to permit service of the leaf valve assembly without disturbing the carburetor linkage.

2. Disconnect the fuel line from the fuel pump.

3. Remove the cotter pin holding the low-speed adjustment link and disconnect it from the low-speed shaft and arm.

4. Disconnect the choke link by pulling it from the retainer.

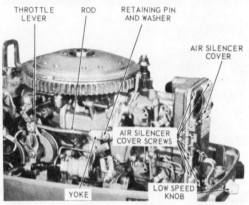

1971 50 HP carburetor linkage and air silencer (© Outboard Marine Corporation)

5. Remove the drain hose at the bottom of the intake manifold.

6. Remove the hose from the pump to the crankcase.

7. Remove the screws from the air silencer cover and remove the cover.

8. Disconnect the choke solenoid spring.

9. Remove the four carburetor mounting nuts and lockwashers.

10. Remove the carburetor and air silencer assembly. Discard the gaskets.

11. Unbolt and remove the choke solenoid.

12. Remove the intake manifold and leaf valve assembly. Do not remove the four leaf plate screws.

1968–69 55 HP AND 1970–71 50 HP

These motors use three single-barrel, float-feed-type carburetors with a fixed, high-speed jet and an adjustable low-speed jet.

1. Disconnect the three fuel hoses at the fuel pump.

2. Remove the screw holding the low-speed adjustment lever and remove the lever.

1971 50 HP intake manifold and leaf plate screws (© Outboard Marine Corporation)

3. Remove the air silencer cover screws and disconnect the drain hose.

4. Disconnect the choke, throttle, and low-speed linkages by pulling them from

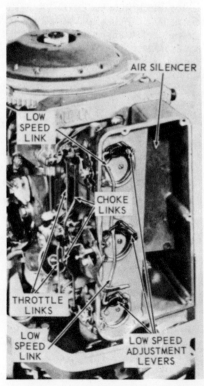

Carburetor linkage on 1968–69 55 HP and 1970–71 50 HP (© Outboard Marine Corporation)

Starboard-side view of carburetor and powerhead on 1968–69 55 HP and 1970–71 50 HP (© Outboard Marine Corporation)

the top and bottom carburetor lever retainers.

5. Remove the six screws retaining the air silencer cover and remove the cover and fuel pump as an assembly.

6. Disconnect the choke solenoid spring and remove the three screws and rear ring guard.

7. Disconnect the fuel hoses between the carburetors.

8. Unbolt and remove the carburetors. Discard the gaskets.

9. Disconnect the leads from the choke solenoid.

10. Remove the choke solenoid.

11. Unscrew and remove the intake manifold and leaf valve assembly.

12. Remove the leaf plate and base assembly.

1966–67 60 HP AND 1968 65 HP
1966–67 80 HP AND 1968 85 HP

These models use a two-barrel, downdraft-type carburetor with adjustable low-speed needles.

1. Remove the cotter pin and washer to disconnect the throttle rod from the throttle cam yoke.

2. Disconnect the solenoid wire.

Carburetor attaching screws (© Outboard Marine Corporation)

3. Disconnect the fuel pump hoses and mark them to ensure correct assembly.

4. Remove the carburetor and gasket from the manifold.

5. Remove the fuel pump from the intake manifold.

6. Remove the intake manifold and leaf plate assembly from the crankcase. Be careful not to damage the leaf plate. To ease removal of the intake manifold, remove the starboard silencer assembly from the lower front motor cover.

1969–71 85 HP, 1971 100 HP, 1969–70 115 HP, AND 1971 125 HP

These models use two two-barrel, side-draft, float-feed-type carburetors with adjustable low-speed jets.

1. Disconnect the fuel hoses from the fuel pump.

2. Remove the low-speed adjustment arm.

Removing the low-speed adjustment arm (© Outboard Marine Corporation)

3. Remove the screws attaching the air silencer cover.

4. Remove the low-speed links and bellcrank assembly and the four low-speed adjustment arms. The low-speed arms are removed by prying them loose with a screwdriver, using the air silencer base as leverage.

NOTE: *The low-speed links are not interchangeable.*

5. Disconnect the air silencer-to-manifold hose.

6. Remove the retaining ring and choke solenoid ring from the upper choke arm. Remove the screws holding the choke solenoid yoke to the air silencer base.

7. Remove the air silencer and fuel pump as an assembly.

8. Disconnect the fuel hoses between the carburetors.

9. Remove the throttle and choke linkage and the choke-to-throttle linkage from the choke and throttle shaft arm.

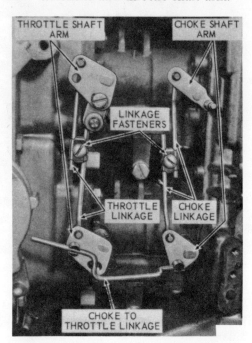

Throttle and choke linkage (© Outboard Marine Corporation)

10. Remove the carburetor nuts, lockwashers, and carburetors.

11. Remove the intake manifold retaining screws and remove the intake manifold.

12. Remove the four leaf plate assemblies from the intake manifold.

1966–68 100 HP

The carburetors on these models are four-barrel sidedraft types with straight-in manifolds to each cylinder. The high-speed jets are fixed and the low-speed jets are linked together for simultaneous adjustment.

1. Disconnect the throttle linkage by removing the anchor yoke pin.

2. Remove the throttle cam and bushings from the carburetor body.

3. Remove the air intake shield.

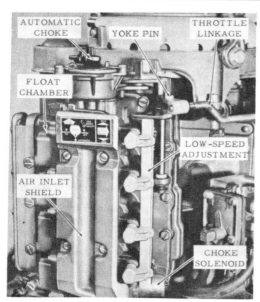

Carburetor and linkage—1966–68 100 HP (© Outboard Marine Corporation)

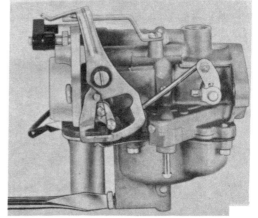

Removing the drain plug (© Outboard Marine Corporation)

4. Drain the carburetor by removing the plugs from the four float chambers.

5. Disconnect the fuel line and bowl vent hose at the carburetor.

6. Disconnect the solenoid wire at the terminal.

7. Disconnect the heat exchanger tube at the automatic choke housing.

8. Remove the ten screws holding the carburetor and leaf plate to the manifold. Remove the carburetor and leaf plate assembly, being careful not to damage the leaf plate.

Carburetor Overhaul

SINGLE-BARREL TYPES

1. Drain the carburetor by removing the screw plug in the bottom of the float chamber.

2. Remove the screw(s) in the adjusting needles to permit removal of the adjusting knob(s).

3. Remove the control panel from the carburetor.

4. If the carburetor is equipped with a fixed, high-speed jet, remove this from the carburetor body. This should be done carefully to avoid damaging the jet.

5. Remove the low-speed needle packing nut and low-speed needle valve from the carburetor. To remove the needle, temporarily replace the adjusting knob.

6. If the carburetor is equipped with

an adjustable high-speed jet, remove the packing nut and remove it in the same manner as used for the low-speed jet.

7. Remove all needle valve packing and washers, being careful of the threads.

8. Remove the float chamber and gasket from the carburetor body.

9. Remove the nylon hinge pin and remove the float and float arm.

10. Remove the float valve, float valve seat, and gasket from the carburetor body Unscrew the high-speed nozzle.

11. Scribe the choke cover to assure correct assembly. Remove the automatic choke cover (if equipped). Remove the choke solenoid and plunger. Do not remove the choke housing.

12. Clean all parts, except the cork float. in carburetor solvent and blow dry with compressed air or air-dry. Do not dry parts with a cloth. Flush all passages in

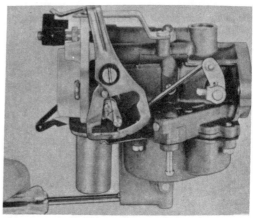

Removing the fixed, high-speed jet (© Outboard Marine Corporation)

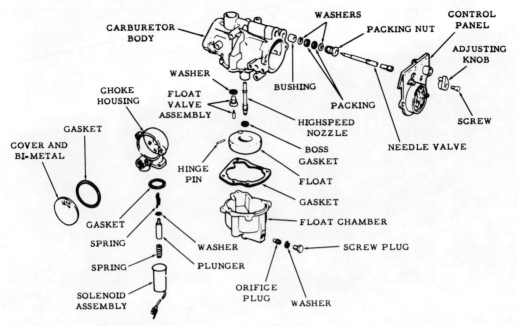

Exploded view of single-barrel carburetor (© Outboard Marine Corporation)

the carburetor with solvent to be sure all gum and varnish is removed. Do not attempt to clean the small passages in the carburetor with pieces of wire or the like.

13. Inspect the float and arm for wear or damage. If the float is oil-soaked, discard it and install a new one.

14. Inspect the intake needle valve for wear or grooves. If any are found, replace the float valve assembly.

15. Check the needle valve seat for nicks, scratches, or wear. The valve seat and needle are a matched set; if either is worn, both parts must be replaced.

16. Check the throttle and choke shafts for excessive play. These are staked in place at assembly and, while replacement of these shafts is possible, carburetor body replacement is recommended.

17. Check the core plugs for leakage. If leakage is slight, a sharp rap with a hammer and flat punch will normally correct the situation. If leakage persists, drill a 1/8 in. hole in the plug and carefully pry the plug out. Apply a drop of sealant to the new plug and flatten the new plug to a tight fit.

18. Inspect the leaf valves, which must be free of all gum and varnish. The leaves must be perfectly flat and free from distortion. Under no circumstances should the leaves be repaired or flexed by hand.

19. Assemble the carburetor in a clean area, using new gaskets and O-rings.

20. Install the high-speed nozzle and new carburetor boss gasket in the float chamber. Replace the float valve, seat and gasket, float, and hinge pin.

21. Turn the carburetor body upside down so that the weight of the float closes the needle. The top of the float should be even with the rim of the casting.

22. Reassemble the float chamber to the carburetor body.

23. If so equipped, install the high-speed orifice plug and screw plug.

24. Install the packing and packing washers, followed by the low-speed needle. Install the low-speed needle, turning it in carefully until it lightly contacts the seat. Do not overtighten. Back the needle out 7/8 of a turn.

25. Install the packing nut and tighten it until the needle can just be turned using finger pressure.

26. If the carburetor is equipped with an adjustable high-speed jet, perform steps 24 and 25 to replace the high-speed adjustable jet.

27. If so equipped, replace the non-adjustable high-speed jet.

28. Check the choke for free operation and be sure that the valves move freely.

29. Assemble the automatic choke. Be

sure that the choke plunger moves freely.

30. The importance of keeping the leaf valves free cannot be overemphasized. The leaf is so designed that it maintains constant contact with the leaf plate and will spring away under predetermined pressure.

31. Replace the control panel assembly and the adjusting knobs.

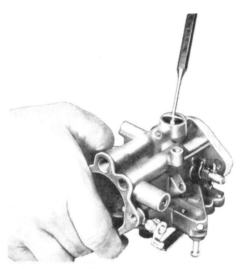

Removing Core Plug

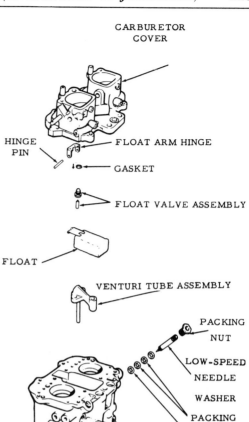

CARBURETOR COVER

HINGE PIN — FLOAT ARM HINGE

GASKET

FLOAT VALVE ASSEMBLY

FLOAT

VENTURI TUBE ASSEMBLY

PACKING

NUT

LOW-SPEED NEEDLE

WASHER

PACKING

WASHER

CARBURETOR BODY

Exploded view of two-barrel carburetor (© Outboard Marine Corporation)

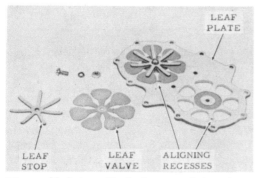

LEAF PLATE

LEAF STOP

LEAF VALVE

ALIGNING RECESSES

Disassembled view of leaf valves—single-barrel carburetor (© Outboard Marine Corporation)

Two-Barrel Types

1. Remove the plugs from the carburetor body and drain the carburetor.

2. Remove the orifice plugs using the proper size screwdriver.

3. Remove the fixed, high-speed jet with the proper size screwdriver.

4. Remove the air intake screens.

5. Remove the choke solenoid from the

Removing the drain plugs—two-barrel carburetor (© Outboard Marine Corporation)

carburetor body. Remove the lever and bellcrank.

6. The threaded ends of the choke and throttle shafts are staked in position. If these are in need of replacement, it is best to replace the entire carburetor body. Under normal conditions, replacement of the throttle and choke shafts is not necessary.

7. Separate the carburetor and cover.

8. Remove the nylon hinge pin, float, and float arm.

9. Remove the float valve, float valve seat, and gasket assembly.

10. Remove the low-speed packing nuts and low-speed needle valves from the carburetor. The needles can be more easily removed by placing the adjustment knobs on the needles upside down.

11. Remove the needle valve packing and washers, being careful to avoid damaging the threads.

12. Disassemble the leaf block assemblies. Special caution should be observed: do not damage or interchange the leaf valves. The leaf valves must be absolutely flat to maintain a good seal.

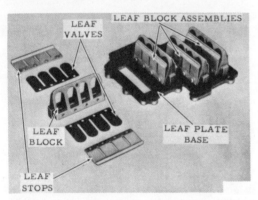

Disassembled view of leaf valves—one two-barrel model (© Outboard Marine Corporation)

13. Perform the inspection (steps 13–21 of the preceding procedure). In addition, check the space between the leaf and the leaf stop. The gap should be 0.023–0.039 in. If not, bend the leaf stop to achieve this dimension.

14. Install new packing and washers in the body.

15. Install the low-speed needles, turning them in carefully with finger pressure to seat them lightly. Do not overtighten. Back the needles out $1\frac{1}{4}$ turns.

16. Install the packing nuts and washers, and tighten these until the needles can just be turned with finger pressure.

17. Check the operation of the choke, to be sure that the valves correctly shut off the air flow. Install the float valve seat and gasket, float valve, float, and hinge pin.

18. Be sure that the float is properly adjusted. Invert the carburetor cover and position it so that the weight of the float

forces the needle closed. With the float arm straight, the float should be parallel with the casting and about $\frac{1}{4}$ in. away from it.

19. Attach the carburetor cover to the carburetor body.

20. Check the choke for free operation.

21. Attach the choke arm to the choke shaft and install the choke solenoid and spring.

22. Adjust the position of the choke solenoid so that the choke valves close when the choke plunger bottoms out. The closed end of the solenoid should be approximately flush with the boss. With the choke knob pulled all the way out, the choke shaft should have $\frac{1}{16}$ in. free movement.

Choke solenoid adjustment (© Outboard Marine Corporation)

23. Each leaf valve must lie perfectly flat. They are in constant contact with the leaf block and spring away from the block under predetermined pressure. The travel of the leaf is limited by the leaf stop. Attach the leaf valve and leaf stop to the leaf block and adjust the leaf stop as outlined previously.

24. Attach the four leaf block assemblies to the leaf plate base with a new gasket. Tighten the screws evenly to avoid distortion.

FOUR-BARREL TYPES

1. Remove the float chamber and plug assembly.

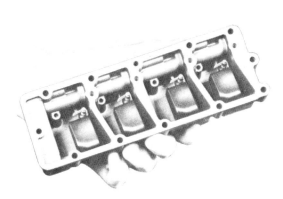

Removing float chamber—four-barrel carburetor (© Outboard Marine Corporation)

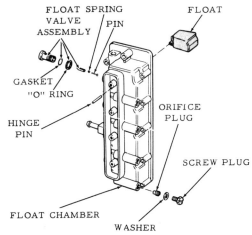

Four-barrel carburetor float and needle valve (© Outboard Marine Corporation)

2. Lift out the floats, needles, pins, and springs and then unscrew the needle valve seats. Keep each set together until reassembly since the needle and seat form a matched set.

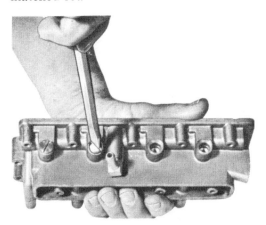

Removing needle valve seats (© Outboard Marine Corporation)

Removing the high-speed tube assemblies (© Outboard Marine Corporation)

3. Remove the orifice plugs using the proper size screwdriver.

4. Remove the high-speed tube assemblies and gaskets between the float chamber and carburetor body.

5. Before disassembling the automatic choke assembly, scribe a mark along the lean side of the indexed quadrant to serve as a reference to the original setting.

6. Remove the automatic choke cover, choke knob, and washers.

7. Disconnect the choke solenoid spring from the choke arm and remove the choke solenoid from the carburetor body.

8. The threaded ends of the throttle and choke shaft are staked in place at assembly and, in normal service, require no

attention. Should these develop excessive play from wear, they can be replaced, although it is best to replace the entire body casting.

9. Remove the friction springs, low-speed adjusting knobs, and the control knob adjusting link. The low-speed knobs are fitted to the low-speed needles by means of friction splines. A screwdriver will pry them off.

10. With the low-speed needle knobs temporarily installed, turn the low-speed needles counterclockwise to remove. Do not lose the retaining ring spring or washers.

11. Disassemble the leaf block assemblies. Do not damage or interchange the

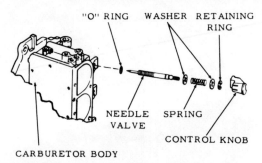

Low-speed needle assembly (© Outboard Marine Corporation)

leaves. It is advisable to clean and inspect the leaf assemblies and reassemble them immediately.

12. Perform the inspection procedure (steps 13–21) of the procedure under "Carburetor Overhaul, Single Barrel Types."

13. Pay particular attention to the leaf valves because they must lie perfectly flat and may not be warped.

14. Replace the high-speed orifice plugs, washers, and screw plugs.

15. Install a new carburetor gasket between the carburetor body and the float chamber. Attach the high-speed tube assemblies to the carburetor body.

16. Install the intake needle valve seats in the float chamber.

17. Install the intake needles with the spring and pins, and install the floats on the hinge pins. Be sure that the floats do not bind on the hinges.

18. Turn the float chamber upside down so that the weight of the floats closes the needle valves.

19. Scribe a line (in pencil) 5/16 in. from the inner gasket surface and parallel to the gasket surface. From the point where this line touches the gasket surface, measure down 9/16 in. This is the correct float level setting. Do not compress the spring. The weight of the float should close the needle valve. To adjust the float level, bend the tang as close to the hinge pin as possible.

20. Install the float chamber on the carburetor body.

21. Replace the low-speed jet O-ring in the carburetor body.

22. Place the spring, washers, and retaining rings on the low-speed needle.

23. Install the low-speed needle and tighten it until it just contacts the needle seat and back it out 1/2 turn. Do not overtighten.

24. Reassemble the automatic choke as-

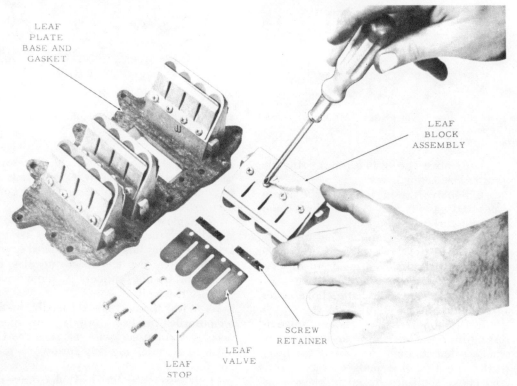

Leaf valve assembly—four-barrel carburetor (© Outboard Marine Corporation)

sembly, being sure that the choke spring is properly installed. Check the choke for free operation. The spring must hold the choke valves closed, when the choke is in the "on" position and hold the valves open when the choke is in the "off" position.

25. Install the choke solenoid and spring. Adjust the position of the choke solenoid so that the choke valves close when the plunger bottoms. The closed end of the solenoid should extend ⅝ in. beyond the boss.

26. Check the operation of the throttle to be sure that all throttle plates are completely closed.

27. The importance of keeping the leaf valves free of distortion cannot be overemphasized. Any leaf which shows signs of distortion should be replaced. The leaf is designed to lay flat against the leaf block and to spring away from the leaf block under a predetermined pressure. The leaf travel is limited by the leaf stop.

28. Attach the leaf valves and leaf stop to the leaf blocks and examine each leaf carefully. They must lie flat with no turned-up edges.

29. Attach the four leaf block assemblies to the leaf plate base, using a new gasket. Tighten the screws evenly to avoid distortion of the leaf plates.

Installation

1966–71 33 HP and 1971 40 HP

1. Attach the leaf plate assembly to the crankcase with a new gasket.

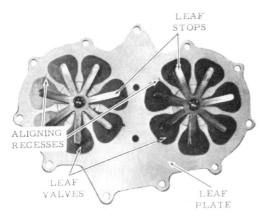

Leaf plate assembly—33 HP and 1971 40 HP (© Outboard Marine Corporation)

2. Install the intake manifold using a new gasket.

3. Place a new gasket in position on the intake manifold studs.

4. Install the carburetor and tighten the retaining nuts.

5. Connect the fuel line to the carburetor.

1966–70 40 HP

1. Attach the leaf plate assembly to the crankcase with a new gasket.

2. Install the intake manifold, using a new gasket.

3. Connect the cutout switch hose to the intake manifold.

4. Install the carburetor on the intake manifold with a new gasket.

5. Connect the fuel hose at the carburetor.

6. Connect the cam follower link to the throttle arm.

7. If removed, install the starter and generator. Connect the leads to the starter, generator, and choke solenoid.

8. Install the heat exchanger tubing and heat shield.

9. If applicable, install the starter and ring gear guard.

1971 50 HP

1. Install the carburetors on the studs of the intake manifold using a new gasket.

2. Connect the fuel hose between the carburetors.

3. Connect the throttle and choke linkage.

4. Connect the choke solenoid spring.

5. If removed, install the air silencer and connect the fuel hoses to the fuel pump and filter.

6. Install the low-speed adjusting arms and link.

7. Adjust the carburetor low-speed needles to ⅝ turn open.

8. Connect the drain hose and install the air silencer cover.

9. Install the low-speed needle adjustment lever in the horizontal position to the port side and secure it to the low-speed link with a cotter pin.

1968–69 55 HP and 1970–71 50 HP

1. Install the spring in the solenoid plunger 2½–3½ turns.

2. Install the solenoid on the intake manifold and connect the leads.

3. Install the leaf valve and plate assembly on the intake manifold.

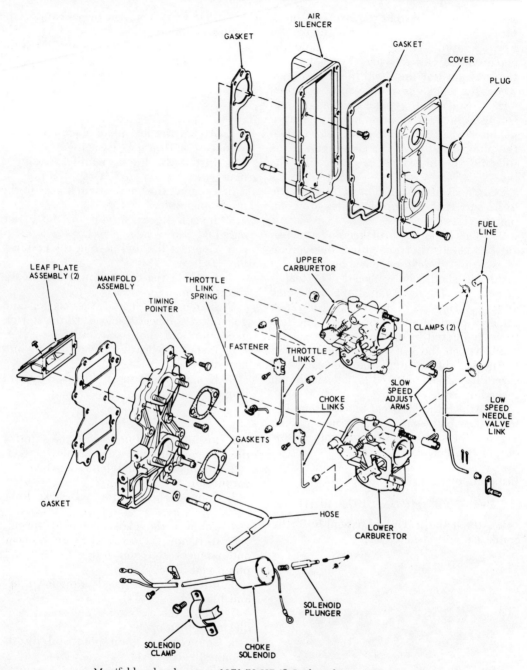

Manifold and carburetor—1971 50 HP (© Outboard Marine Corporation)

4. Place a new gasket on the studs of the intake manifold and install the carburetor on the studs.

5. Connect the fuel hoses between the carburetors and connect the choke and throttle linkages.

6. Connect the choke solenoid spring and install the ring gear guard.

7. Install the air silencer.

8. Connect the fuel hoses to the fuel pump and filter.

9. Adjust the carburetors as described under "Carburetor Adjustments."

10. Connect the drain hose and install the air silencer cover.

11. Install the low-speed needle adjustment lever in the horizontal position facing the port side and secure with a screw.

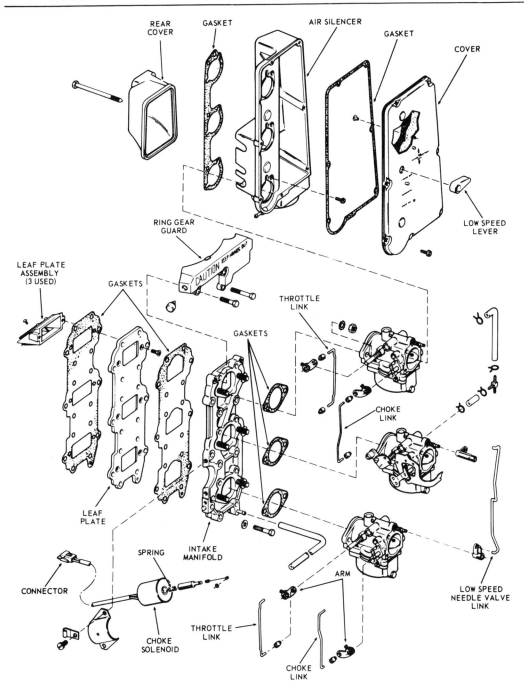

Exploded view of carburetor and manifold—1968–69 55 HP and 1970–71 55 HP (© Outboard Marine Corporation)

1966–67 60 HP AND 1968 65 HP
1966–67 80 HP AND 1968 85 HP

1. Install the intake manifold and leaf plate assembly, using a new gasket.

2. Attach the fuel line to the carburetor connection and install the carburetor on the intake manifold.

3. Install the fuel pump on the intake manifold and install the fuel pump hoses.

4. Connect the solenoid wire to the terminal on the solenoid.

5. Attach the throttle control rod.

6. Check the throttle cam adjustment and check the synchronization of the linkage as described under "Carburetor Adjustments."

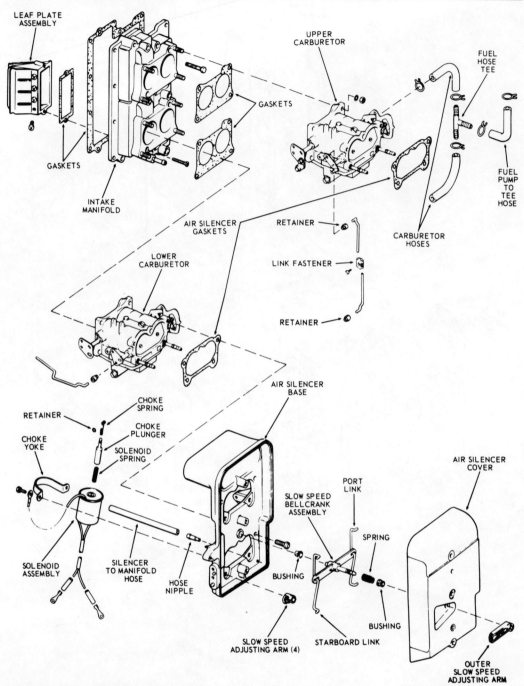

Carburetors and manifolds used on 1969–71 85 HP, 1971 100 HP, 1969–70 115 HP, and 1971 125 HP
(© Outboard Marine Corporation)

1969–71 85 HP, 1971 100 HP, 1969–70 115 HP AND 1971 125 HP

1. Install the leaf plate assembly on the intake manifold.

2. Install the intake manifold and leaf plate on the powerhead, with a new gasket.

3. Install the carburetors on the intake manifold studs, using new gaskets.

4. Connect the fuel hoses between the carburetors.

5. Connect the throttle and choke linkages.

6. Install the air silencer base and con-

nect the fuel lines to the fuel filter and fuel pump.

7. Snap on the low-speed needle adjustment arms, facing outward.

1966–68 100 HP

1. Install the carburetor and leaf plate assembly to the motor and tighten the retaining screws.

2. Install the throttle cam and bushings on the carburetor body.

3. Connect the throttle linkage to the throttle cam with the anchor yoke pin and cotter pin.

4. Install the heat exchanger tube to the automatic choke housing.

5. Connect the solenoid wire at the terminal.

6. Attach the fuel chamber and float chamber vent hoses to the carburetor.

7. Install the air intake shield.

Float Level Adjustments—All Models

Float adjustment on 1966–70 33 HP and 1966–71 40 HP models. Turn the carburetor upside down so that the weight of the float closes the needle. The top of the float should be even with the rim of the casting. (© Outboard Marine Corporation)

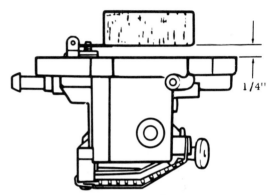

Float adjustment 1966–67 60 HP, 1968 65 HP, 1966–67 80 HP, and 1968 85 HP models. Turn the carburetor cover upside down so the weight of the float closes the needle. With the float arm straight, the float should be parallel with the face of the casting and 1/4 in. above it. (© Outboard Marine Corporation)

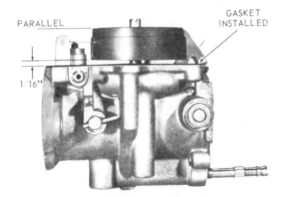

Float adjustment on 1971 50 HP, 1968 55 HP, and 1970–71 60 HP models. Turn the carburetor upside down so the weight of the float closes the needle. The top of the float should be parallel to the top of the gasket surface and 1/16 in. above it. (© Outboard Marine Corporation)

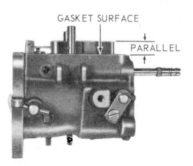

Float level adjustment on 1969–71 85 HP, 1971 100 HP, 1969–70 115 HP, and 1971 125 HP models. Turn the carburetor upside down so the weight of the float closes the needle. The float should be parallel to the gasket surface. (© Outboard Marine Corporation)

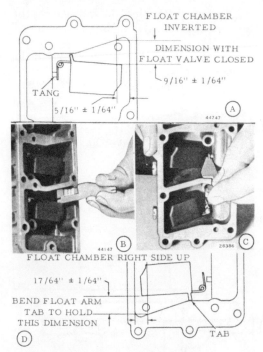

High- and low-speed needle adjustments 33 HP and 1971 40 HP (© Outboard Marine Corporation)

Float level adjustment on 1966–68 100 HP models. Turn the chamber upside down so the weight of floats closes the needles. Scribe a pencil line 5/16 in. from the gasket surface and parallel to it. Where this line touches the top gasket surface, measure down 9/16 in. to correct float level setting. (© Outboard Marine Corporation)

Synchronizing Throttle and Distributor or Ignition Linkage—All Models

See this procedure in the "Electrical System."

Carburetor Adjustments

1966–70 33 HP AND 1971 40 HP

High-Speed Needle

1. Seat the high and low-speed needles until they just contact the seats. Do not overtighten.

2. Back the high-speed needle out 3/4 turn and back out the low-speed needle 1 1/4 turns (1966 33 HP). On 1967 33 HP models, back the high-speed needle out 3/4 turn and back the low-speed needle out 1 turn. On 1968–70 33 HP and 1971 40 HP models, back the high-speed needle out 3/8 turn and the low-speed needle 1 1/4 turns.

3. Start the engine and allow it to reach operating temperature. Run the engine in a test tank or on the boat for at least five minutes at half throttle.

4. Using a tachometer, adjust the high-speed needle until the best rpm is reached.

Low-Speed Needle

NOTE: *The high-speed needle must be adjusted before the low-speed needle is adjusted.*

1. With the motor at operating temperature, run it in gear at about 700–750 rpm. Adjust the low-speed knob until the highest rpm is attained with the smoothest performance. Allow fifteen seconds for the motor to respond to the adjustment.

2. Adjustment of the high-speed needle must be done again after the low-speed needle is adjusted.

3. Loosen the center screw but do not disturb the position of the needle. Position the knob so that the knob is pointing straight up, leaving enough clearance so that the knob will turn without binding.

4. Loosen the center screw in the needle valve without disturbing the position of the needle. With the high-speed knob in the straight-up position, place the arm on the needle so it can be attached to the link on the high-speed knob. Tighten the center screw on the needle valve arm after replacing the link.

5. Adjust the idle screw to obtain 550 rpm (for 1966 33 hp) or 650 rpm (for 1967–70 33 hp and 1971 40 hp) in Forward gear.

Throttle Cam

1. If the throttle does not close, either the throttle return spring is too weak and should be replaced, or else the throttle or linkage is binding.

2. Advance the throttle control to the point where the mark on the throttle cam

Throttle cam adjustment—33 HP and 1971 40 HP (© Outboard Marine Corporation)

is just opposite the projection on the intake manifold. At this point, the throttle valve should be closed.

3. If the throttle valve is not closed, advance the throttle control until the mark on the cam is aligned with the raised projection on the intake manifold.

4. Loosen the throttle arm clamp screw and rotate the eccentric cam until the cam follower roller just touches the cam and begins to open the throttle valve. Tighten the clamp screw and check to see that the throttle valve just begins to open after the cam mark passes the mark on the intake manifold.

5. To adjust the Cruise-Throttle, move the armature base by hand to full spark advance, without touching the throttle control. Adjust the control rod collar for 1/32 in. clearance from the pivot pin.

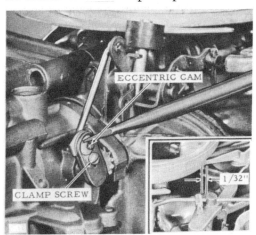

Adjusting the Cruise Throttle—33 HP and 1971 40 HP (© Outboard Marine Corporation)

1966–70 40 HP

Low Speed

1. Loosen, but do not remove, the screw in the center of the low-speed adjusting knob. Pull the knob out so that it will turn past the stop on the left of the knob.

2. Tighten the center screw. Turn the knob clockwise until the needle just contacts the seat. Do not overtighten.

3. Turn the low-speed knob counterclockwise 7/8 turn.

4. Warm the engine for at least five minutes at half throttle in a test tank or on the boat.

5. With the motor at operating temperature, run at fast idle in gear (700–750 rpm).

6. Adjust the low-speed knob until the highest rpm with the smoothest performance is obtained. Allow fifteen seconds for the motor to respond to adjustment.

7. Loosen the center screw. Do not disturb the position of the needle and position the knob so that it is pointing straight up and replace it on the needle. Leave enough clearance so that it can move without binding. Tighten the center screw.

8. Adjust the idle stop so the motor will idle at 650 rpm in gear.

Throttle Cam

1. Follow the procedure for 1966–70 33 hp and 1971 40 hp motors.

Throttle cam adjustment—1966–70 40 HP (© Outboard Marine Corporation)

Automatic Choke

1. The automatic choke may require adjustment for a leaner mixture in warm climates or for a richer mixture in colder climates. Proper adjustment of the choke will

assure easy starting and will improve overall operation at low speeds during the warm-up cycle.

2. Before you disturb the original factory setting, scribe a mark to serve as a reference to the original setting.

3. Loosen the setscrews and adjust the quadrant two or three notches leaner or richer. The actual amount of adjustment will vary depending on conditions and will also vary from one motor to another.

4. Do not attempt to check the automatic choke operation until the motor has cooled to room temperature (70° F.). Usually motor temperature is normalized after the motor has stood for one hour with the cover off or for two hours with the cover on.

1971 50 HP

Throttle and Choke Linkage

1. Loosen the throttle link screw and hold the throttles closed with finger pressure on the upper and lower throttle links.

2. Tighten the link screw while holding the throttles closed.

3. Repeat the procedure for the choke valves.

Synchronizing throttle and choke linkage—1971 50 HP (© Outboard Marine Corporation)

Throttle Cam

1. The scribe mark on the throttle cam should align with the center of the cam follower roller.

2. With the scribe mark aligned as above, loosen the throttle arm screw.

Move the arm to close the throttle valve and tighten the screw.

3. Move the throttle lever to full throttle position. A clearance of 0–0.020 in. is allowed between the cam and roller with the throttle linkage held open manually.

Throttle linkage clearance—1971 50 HP (© Outboard Marine Corporation)

Low Speed

1. Turn each low-speed needle in until they seat lightly. Do not overtighten.

2. Back each low-speed needle out ⅝ turn.

3. Allow the motor to reach operating temperature by running it at one-third throttle for several minutes.

4. With the motor at operating temperature, run at approximately 750–800 rpm in gear. Adjust the low-speed needles one at a time until the highest rpm and smoothest performance is obtained. Allow sufficient time for the motor to respond to adjustment.

5. Pull off the levers and connect the linkages. Do not disturb the position of the needles. Position the levers so that they are pointing straight out to the port side and install them on the needles.

6. Adjust the idle screw to obtain a maximum of 700 rpm in Reverse gear.

7. Install the silencer and cover.

1968–69 55 HP

Throttle and Choke Linkage

1. See the preceding "Throttle and Choke Linkage Adjustment" procedure.

Throttle Cam

1. See the preceding "Throttle Cam Adjustment" procedure.

Low Speed

1. The procedure is the same as for the 1971 50 hp model. The adjusting levers should be installed pointing to starboard. Adjust the idle screw to obtain 600–650 rpm in gear.

1970–71 60 HP

Throttle and Choke Linkage

1. The procedure is the same as that for the 1971 50 hp model.

Throttle Cam

1. Refer to the procedure for 1971 50 hp models.

Low Speed

1. Turn each low-speed needle in until it just contacts the seat lightly.
2. Allow the motor to reach operating temperature by running it at half-throttle for several minutes.
3. With the motor at operating temperature, run the motor at approximately 650–700 rpm in gear. Adjust no. 2 and 3 carburetor (bottom and lower) low-speed needles until the highest rpm and smoothest performance are obtained.
4. Run the rpm up to 1000–1200 and adjust the top carburetor in the same manner. Allow ample time for the motor to respond to the adjustment.
5. Remove the adjusting levers and connect the linkages. Do not disturb the position of the needles.
6. Install the levers so that they are pointing to starboard.
7. Adjust the idle screw so that approximately 650 rpm is obtained in gear.
8. Adjust the wide-open throttle stop screw so that the throttle valves go fully open without any strain.

1966–67 60 HP AND 1968 65 HP

Throttle Cam

1. Refer to the procedure for 1971 50 hp models.

Low Speed

1. Remove the low-speed adjusting knobs and replace them upside down on

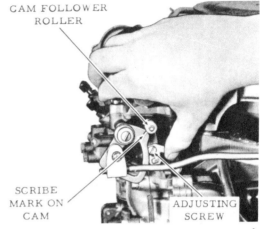

CAM FOLLOWER ROLLER

SCRIBE MARK ON CAM

ADJUSTING SCREW

Throttle cam adjustment—1966–67 60 HP and 1968 65 HP (© Outboard Marine Corporation)

the needles so they will clear the stops on the carburetor.
2. Turn in each needle valve gently, until they just contact the needle valve seat. Do not overtighten.
3. Back the needles out as follows: $1\frac{1}{4}$ turns for 1966 60 hp, $\frac{3}{4}$ turn for 1967 60 hp and $\frac{5}{8}$ turn for 1968 65 hp.
4. Start the motor and allow it to reach operating temperature by running it at half-throttle for five minutes in gear.

NOTE: *Since it is almost impossible to detect minor speed changes on the V4 engine, a tachometer must be used to obtain proper adjustment.*

5. With the motor in gear, retard the throttle to approximately 700–750 rpm.
6. Slowly lean one low-speed needle valve by turning it clockwise until the motor hesitates slightly. Enrich the needle valve by turning it counterclockwise to the point where the highest rpm reading and smoothest performance are obtained.
7. Repeat the adjustment on the second low-speed needle.
8. Snap the throttle wide open and note the response. If the motor hesitates, repeat the above steps until the motor responds without hesitation.
9. Without disturbing the position of the needles, replace the adjusting knobs in the normal position.
10. Adjust the idle screw to obtain 600–650 rpm in gear.

1966–67 80 HP AND 1968 85 HP

Throttle Cam

1. Refer to the procedure for 1971 50 hp models.

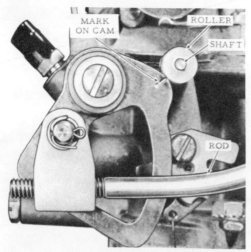

Throttle cam adjustment 1966–67 80 HP and 1968 85 HP (© Outboard Marine Corporation)

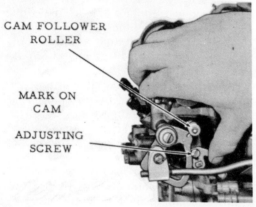

Throttle cam follower adjustment—1966–67 80 HP and 1968 85 HP (© Outboard Marine Corporation)

Low Speed

1. The procedure is the same as the preceding procedure. Back out the low-speed needles as follows: ¾ turn for 1966–67 80 hp models and 1 turn for 1968 85 hp models.

Automatic Choke

1. This procedure is identical to that for 1966–70 40 hp models.

1969–71 85 HP, 1971 100 HP, 1969–70 115 HP, AND 1971 125 HP

Throttle and Choke Linkage

1. Loosen the upper and lower carburetor-throttle rod screws and allow the spring on the throttle shafts to close the

throttle valves. The cam roller must touch the cam on this adjustment.

2. Tighten the setscrew.

3. Repeat the same procedure for the choke valves by manually closing the choke valves.

NOTE: *If the spring is removed from the solenoid plunger, twist it onto the plunger 2½ to 3½ turns.*

4. Attach the solenoid to the air silencer base.

Throttle Cam

1. Refer to the procedure for 1971 50 hp models.

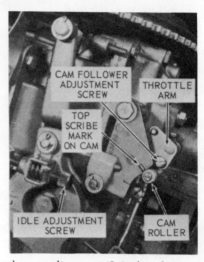

Throttle cam adjustment (© Outboard Marine Corporation)

Low Speed

1. Turn in each low-speed needle until it lightly contacts the needle valve seat. Do not overtighten.

2. Back each low-speed needle out, counterclockwise, ⅞ turn.

3. Allow the motor to reach operating temperature by running the motor at half-throttle for several minutes in gear.

4. With the motor at operating temperature, run the motor in gear at approximately 700–750 rpm. Adjust one low-speed needle at a time to obtain the highest rpm and smoothest performance. Allow ample time for the motor to respond to adjustment. The final adjustment must be within ¾ to 1 turn open.

5. Do not disturb the position of the needles and press the low-speed adjusting arms on the needles, making sure that each arm points outward.

6. Adjust the idle screw so that the motor will idle at 600–650 rpm in gear.

1966–68 100 HP

Throttle Cam

1. Check the pick-up position of the throttle with respect to the cam. The roller should begin to open the throttle as the center of the roller shaft aligns with the mark on the cam.

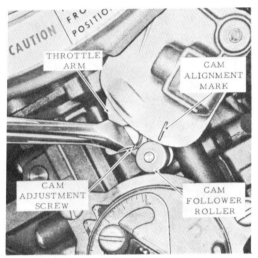

Throttle cam adjustment—1966–68 100 HP (© Outboard Marine Corporation)

2. If the adjustment is incorrect, loosen the screw.

3. Push the throttle arm to the closed position and, while holding the cam follower roller in contact with the cam and correctly aligned with the mark, tighten the screw.

4. Recheck the adjustment. The cam follower should just begin to move as the mark on the cam passes the centerline of the cam follower roller.

Automatic Choke

1. Refer to the procedure for 1966–70 40 hp models.

Low Speed

1. Before attempting this adjustment, time the engine and synchronize the carburetor and distributor linkage.

2. Center the low-speed control knob link and remove all four knobs.

3. Gently turn each low-speed needle in until they just contact the needle valve seats. Do not overtighten. Back each nee-

dle valve out ½ turn counterclockwise. Replace the four knobs, but do not disturb the position of the needles.

4. Start the motor and allow it to reach operating temperature by running it at half-throttle for several minutes, in gear. With the motor in gear, run it at full throttle briefly to clear out the motor.

5. Keep the motor in gear and idle the motor at approximately 650 rpm.

6. Since it is almost impossible to detect minor changes in engine speed on the V4, a tachometer should be used to obtain proper adjustment.

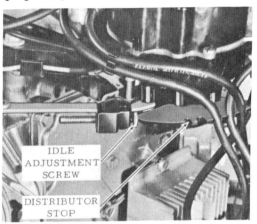

Idle adjustment screw—1966–68 100 HP (© Outboard Marine Corporation)

7. If the motor hesitates or begins to load up at 650 rpm, adjust the control rod link upward or downward one, two, or three notches (upward if too lean and downward if too rich). Allow fifteen seconds for the motor to respond to each adjustment.

NOTE: *It is better that the motor run too rich than too lean.*

8. With the motor in gear, run it at 3500–4000 rpm to clear the cylinders. Again, bring the motor to 650 rpm and repeat the adjustment if necessary.

9. Set the idle adjustment screw so that the motor idles at 650 rpm.

FUEL PUMP AND FUEL FILTER

**All 33 HP, All 40 HP, 1971
50 HP, 1968–69 55 HP, 1970–71
60 HP, 1969–71 85 HP, 1971
100 HP, 1969–70 115 HP
and 1971 125 HP**

Before servicing the fuel pump, remove and clean the fuel filter and install a new filter element. Remove the fuel line from the fuel tank and blow through all passages and lines with compressed air. Restriction or clogging may be the cause of inadequate fuel delivery and this could cure it, eliminating unnecessary replacement of the fuel pump. If the trouble still exists, the fuel pump is probably malfunctioning and should be replaced.

REMOVAL

1. Disconnect the hoses from the filter and pump assembly.
2. Remove the screws which attach the pump and filter assembly to the powerhead or air silencer and remove the fuel pump and filter.

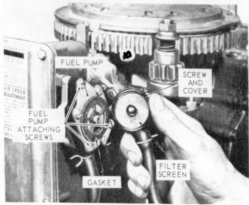

Fuel pump and filter (© Outboard Marine Corporation)

CLEANING AND INSPECTION

1. The fuel pump components are not serviceable. If a malfunction exists, replace the complete pump.
2. Inspect the filter for sediment accumulation. The filter can be removed by unscrewing the filter cap and removing the cap.
3. Clean all parts of the filter assembly and fuel connectors in solvent and blow dry with air or air-dry. Do not dry parts with a cloth as particles of lint may stick to the components and clog the passages. Dissolve any gum deposits or varnish with OMC Accessory Engine Cleaner.

NOTE: *It is recommended that a new filter element be installed whenever the filter and fuel pump are serviced.*

INSTALLATION

1. Reassemble the fuel filter in reverse order of disassembly.

2. Attach the fuel pump and filter to the powerhead or air silencer and connect the fuel hoses.

1966–67 60 HP, 1968 65 HP, 1966–67 80 HP, 1968 85 HP and 1966–68 100 HP

Before beginning fuel pump repair, remove the fuel filter and install a new one. Check the edge of the fuel filter bowl for chipping. If any chips are found, replace the bowl and gasket. Remove the fuel hose from the fuel tank and blow through all passages and lines with compressed air. If clogged lines are the cause of poor fuel delivery, this could possibly eliminate unnecessary replacement of the fuel pump. If this does not cure the difficulty, the fuel pump valves may be stuck or the pump diaphragm may be ruptured.

REMOVAL

1. Disconnect the fuel intake and outlet hoses from the intake manifold and disconnect the crankcase suction hoses.
2. Color-code or matchmark the hoses for correct assembly.
3. Remove the screws attaching the fuel pump to the powerhead.

DISASSEMBLY

1. Carefully note the positions of the components to facilitate correct assembly. Take all precautions to avoid getting dirt into the parts as very small pieces of dirt can cause the pump to malfunction.
2. Remove the screws attaching the cover and elbow to the pump body. All parts of the pump, except the valves and retainer, can be lifted out.
3. Remove the screws attaching the valve retainer to the pump body.
4. Remove the valve retainer and lift out the valves.

CLEANING AND INSPECTION

1. Refer to the inspection procedure under the preceding type of fuel pump.
2. Inspect the diaphragm carefully for cracks.
3. Replace all gaskets and any worn or damaged parts.

ASSEMBLY

1. Place the gasket into the pump body.
2. Install the valves as shown in the exploded view.

3. Install the valve retainer.

4. To facilitate assembly of the valve and springs, use a straightedge to hold down the parts under the diaphragm while installing the screws.

INSTALLATION

1. Attach the assembled fuel pump to the powerhead.

2. Connect the fuel hoses and crankcase suction hose.

3. If leakage at the core plugs occurs, follow the corrective procedures for core plugs listed under "Carburetor Overhaul for One-Barrel Types."

OIL DRAIN VALVE—1966–70 33 HP, 1966–71 40 HP, 1966–67 80 HP and 1968 85 HP

Ordinarily, the oil drain valve requires little or no attention. However, when servicing the motor, remove and clean the drain valve. Inspect the flame arrestor screens and clean these.

If either gum or varnish is present in the crankcase during servicing, clean the drain valve and screens with OMC Accessory Engine Cleaner.

Be sure that the leaf valve seats against the leaf plate and that the screens are not clogged. Assemble the leaf valves and oil drain and install them. Check the space between the leaf and leaf stop, which should be 0.023–0.039 in. Adjust the leaf stops by bending to achieve this dimension.

FUEL TANK

NOTE: *All fuel tanks, hoses, primer bulbs, fuel level indicators, and the upper housing and valves are serviced in the same manner, but 1969–70 85 hp, 1969 115 hp, 1971 100 hp and 1971 125 hp models must use a fuel hose with a yellow band.*

Upper Housing and Level Indicator

INSPECTION AND REPAIR

1. The fuel level indicator is mounted in the upper housing. The entire upper housing assembly can be removed by removing the attaching screws and lifting the assembly from the tank. Be careful not to damage the float or screen on the end of the fuel line.

2. Check for free movement of the indi-

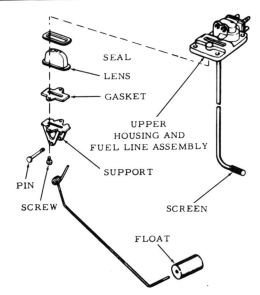

Exploded view of level indicator and float (© Outboard Marine Corporation)

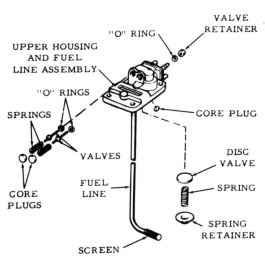

Exploded view of upper housing (© Outboard Marine Corporation)

cator on the indicator pin. Remove the pin from the indicator support by compressing the free end and pulling it out.

3. Be sure that the float arm is straight and that the float is not oil-soaked.

4. Remove the screws holding the indicator support to the upper housing.

5. Lift out the lens and clean it with thinner.

6. The release valves must seat tightly to prevent fumes from escaping, but must open a clear passage for air to enter when the fuel hose is connected. The release valves are best cleaned by removing the core plugs and disassembling.

7. Replace the O-rings to be sure of a good fit.

8. The air intake disc valve must seat tightly to prevent fumes from escaping, but must allow air to enter. The disc valve spring retainer is staked in place and may be removed by filing off the burrs. Restake the new one in place with a small punch.

Hose and Primer Bulb

CLAMPS

1. To release the clamps, grip the clamps with pliers and bend the overlapping hook backward.

2. To install the clamps, grip the clamps with pliers and apply slight pressure to the hook on the top side with a screwdriver. Squeeze the clamps with pliers until the hooks interlock.

Connector Housings

Installation of the O-ring in the fuel hose connectors requires the use of two fabricated tools; one to hold the plunger down and one to remove the O-ring. Both of these instruments are illustrated and can be made from 16 gauge ($1/16$ in. diameter) wire. Form a small hook on the bottom of the longer tool with about a $1/16$ in. radius. Be sure there are no burrs on the ends to scratch the O-ring seats or plungers.

Tools to be fabricated (see text) (© Outboard Marine Corporation)

O-RING REMOVAL

1. Place the connector housing in a vise between two wood blocks.

2. Push the plunger down with the straight instrument.

3. Insert the hooked instrument between the O-ring and its seat with the hook in a horizontal position.

4. Twist the hook to grasp the O-ring.

5. Carefully (to avoid scratching the plunger) pull the O-ring out of the housing.

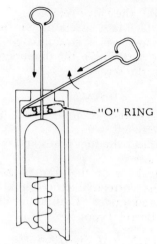

Removing the O-ring (© Outboard Marine Corporation)

O-RING INSTALLATION

1. Place a drop of oil on the O-ring.

2. Place the O-ring on the face of the connector.

3. Push the plunger down with the straight instrument.

4. Pinch the O-ring together with the fingers and gently push it into position.

Fuel Hose

When assembling the fuel hose, check for cracks in the primer bulb or in the hose. The primer bulb must be installed so that the fuel flows from the shorter length to the longer length. Fuel flow through the primer bulb is indicated by an arrow.

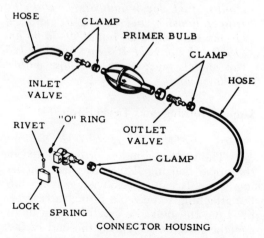

Exploded view of primer bulb and hose (© Outboard Marine Corporation)

Electrical System

IGNITION

OMC outboards use several different types of ignition systems. For service reasons, all motors using a common type of ignition system have been grouped together. For quick reference, refer to the following chart which contains a type number, type of ignition system, and the models using the particular system.

NOTE: *The type number is an editorial designation and is not to be considered a manufacturer's designation.*

Ignition Identification

Type Number	Ignition Type	Models
1	Flywheel Magneto	1966–70 33 hp 1966–71 40 hp
2	Capacitor Discharge (Breaker-less) w/magneto	1971 50 hp
3	Battery Distributor	1966 100 hp 1967 60 hp 1967 80 hp
4	Transistorized Battery Distributor	1967 100 hp
5	Distributor Magneto	1966 60 hp 1966 80 hp
6	Capacitor Discharge w/Breaker Points	1968–69 55 hp 1970–71 60 hp 1968 65 hp 1968–71 85 hp 1971 100 hp
7	Capacitor Discharge (Breaker-less)	1968 100 hp 1969–70 115 hp 1971 125 hp

TYPE 1

These ignition systems are composed of a flywheel and a magneto connected to the spark plugs. The magneto is a self-contained, electrical generating unit, consisting of an armature plate with two ignition coil and lamination assemblies, condensers, and breaker assemblies. A permanent magnet is cast into the flywheel.

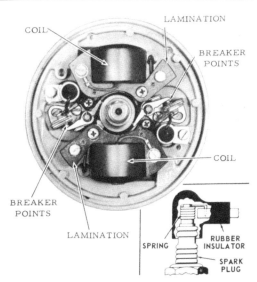

Magneto breaker plate—1966–70 33 HP and 1966–71 40 HP (© Outboard Marine Corporation)

Magneto

REMOVAL

1. Remove the starter from the powerhead by removing the locking lever screw and spring. Remove the screws attaching the starter assembly and remove the starter.
2. Twist the leads off the spark plugs counterclockwise.
3. Disconnect the lead from the vacuum cut out switch.
4. Remove the flywheel nut (an automotive flywheel holder may be necessary) and remove the screws from the flywheel.
5. Using a puller, pull the flywheel from the crankshaft.
6. Disconnect the leads from the stop switch by lifting the tabs on the connectors and pulling the connector apart.
7. Remove the armature link spring and washer.
8. Remove the screws attaching the magneto armature plate to the powerhead and remove the magneto from the powerhead.

DISASSEMBLY

1. All components can be removed from the armature plate by removing the attaching screws. Pull the spark plug leads from the coil and lamination assemblies.

INSPECTION

1. Inspect spark plugs for cracked insulators, worn electrodes, and fouling condi-

tions. Replace any plugs that are in questionable condition. Before installing the spark plugs, be sure the seat is clean. Screw the plugs in and tighten to the specified torque.

2. Inspect the breaker points for dirt, pitting, or wear. Replace any points that are in questionable condition. If the points need cleaning, use alcohol or trichloroethylene. Never subject the points to oil or grease. Even the oil from your hands can affect the performance of the points.

3. The condenser can be checked by following the instructions in the introductory chapter of this book, after the magneto has been partially reassembled and installed.

Assembly

1. Reassemble the magneto in the reverse order of disassembly.

2. Correct location of the coil and lamination assemblies is dependent on the machined mounting surfaces on the armature plate. The coil lamination heels should be flush with the machined surfaces.

3. Alignment of the magneto coils is simplified by the use of a coil locating ring. The locating ring is ⅝ in. thick and has an inside diameter of 4.472 in., and is machined to fit over the four bosses.

4. Reconnect all leads and be sure that the connections are clean and tight.

5. Be sure that a new oiler wick is installed under the forward coil.

Installation

1. If the flywheel key was removed, install it to the crankshaft keyway with the outer edge in a vertical position.

2. Apply a coating of OMC Type A lubricant to the magneto support and retaining ring and install to the powerhead. Be sure that the lip on the retaining ring faces up.

3. Align the screw holes in the magneto support ring to correspond with those in the magneto.

4. Place the retainer washer over the crankshaft as shown. Align the slots in the washer with the threaded holes in the retaining ring. Do not add oil to the wick.

5. Place the magneto over the crankshaft, being careful not to damage the breaker arms on the cam or to bend the cam follower.

6. Install the armature link and spring.

7. Check the breaker point setting as described below.

8. Clean any oil from the flywheel and crankshaft tapers.

9. Install the flywheel. Tighten the flywheel nut to the specified torque.

10. Install the starter.

11. Install the locking lever and locking lever spring.

12. Connect the spark plug leads making sure there is a good contact.

Breaker Point Adjustment

1. To adjust the breaker points, the magneto must be assembled on the motor and the flywheel must be removed.

2. Disconnect all leads from the breaker point assemblies.

3. To check the timing and point gap, it is best to use a special timing tool which is available from Evinrude or Johnson dealers for a nominal price (a few dollars) and a simple test light which is illustrated in the introductory chapter of this book.

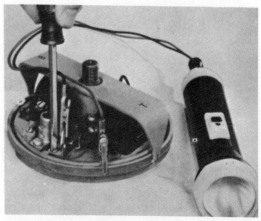

Breaker point adjustment on 33 HP and 40 HP magneto models (© Outboard Marine Corporation)

4. Connect the test light between the breaker plate and the forward breaker point screw terminal.

5. Advance the breaker plate to the full-throttle position against the stop. Place the timing fixture on the crankshaft with the end marked "T" aligned with the first projection on the armature plate. Rotate the crankshaft in a clockwise direction only.

6. Move the timing fixture slowly back and forth until the instant at which the points close is determined, as shown by the test light. The points should open

when the mark on the tool is midway between the two projections on the armature plate.

7. If the timing is incorrect, align the timing tool and the first timing mark and adjust the points until the light indicates a closed circuit.

8. If a test light or timing tool is not available, set the point gap to specification with the breaker arm on the high lobe of the cam (fully open).

9. Rotate the crankshaft 180° (clockwise) and repeat the procedure for the other set of points.

10. Reattach all leads and install the flywheel. Tighten the flywheel nut to the specified torque and install the starter ratchet.

VACUUM CUTOUT AND SAFETY SWITCH

If the throttle suddenly closes while the motor is operating in Neutral, crankcase suction may become abnormally high, causing erratic carburetor operation. The function of the cutout switch is to short out the breaker point on the low cylinder, preventing the bottom spark plug from firing and thus reducing motor speed.

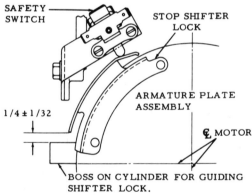

THE SAFETY SWITCH SHOULD BE ADJUSTED TO MAKE CONTACT WHEN THE SHIFTER LOCK STOP ON THE ARMATURE PLATE ASSEMBLY IS PLACED IN THE PROPER DIMENSIONAL RELATIONSHIP WITH THE SHIFTER LOCK GUIDE BOX ON THE CYLINDER, AS SHOWN ABOVE.

Adjusting the safety switch (© Outboard Marine Corporation)

The safety switch should be adjusted on its bracket to open the circuit when the plunger is on the midpoint of the slope of the shifter lock-stop. A test light will indicate a closed circuit when the plunger is below the cam slope.

If the vacuum switch is not functioning, check the manifold vacuum hose for leaks and check the hole in the intake manifold with a no. 76 drill, to be sure that it is open. To test the operation of the switch, connect a test light to the switch terminal and to ground. Alternate suction and pressure at the switch hose connector will indicate switch operation.

If the switch operation is faulty or erratic, disassemble the switch and replace parts as required. Reinstall the switch and test operation again.

TYPE 2

The capacitor discharge ignition on 1971 50 horsepower models consists of five basic components; a stator and charge coil assembly located under the flywheel, a flywheel and ring gear assembly, a timer base and sensor located under the flywheel, a power pack located on the starboard side of the powerhead, and two ignition coils and spark plugs located on the rear of the powerhead.

WARNING: *DO NOT ATTEMPT TO OPEN THE POWER PACK ASSEMBLY, AS THIS WILL VOID THE WARRANTY.*

Precautions

1. Always observe correct polarity.

2. Do not attempt to open the power pack as this will void the warranty.

3. Do not pull on the high-tension leads at the ignition coils.

4. Do not open or close the plug-in connector while the engine is running.

5. Do not set the spark advance to anything but specification.

6. Do not hold spark plug wires in your hand while checking spark advance. Use insulated pliers for this purpose or a severe shock will result.

7. Do not attempt any tests except those listed.

8. Do not connect any tachometer or timing light unless it is a type which will accept the higher output of the CD system.

9. Do not connect any voltage source, other than the type specified.

10. Make sure all wiring is properly connected so that it will not rub against metal edges.

11. Do not disturb any electrical connections while the ignition switch is turned on.

Troubleshooting the CD System

1. A malfunction in the system will result in the engine running roughly or failing to run at all.

2. Engine missing may be caused by improper fuel or a maladjusted carburetor. Be sure that this is not the cause before proceeding.

3. Check for spark by removing the high-tension lead from the spark plug and removing the spark plug. Connect the high-tension lead and the spark plug, and lay the spark plug on the powerhead. DO NOT HOLD IT IN YOUR HAND. Be sure that you are not standing in water, then crank the engine. DO NOT TOUCH THE ENGINE WHILE CRANKING. If spark is apparent, proceed to the following checks. If weak or erratic spark is evident, have a dealer check your CD system on special test equipment.

4. Check all wiring associated with the system for any loose or corroded terminals or wires.

5. Check the timing. The motor has a full timing grid and pointer on the flywheel. Normally, the timing will not require resetting unless the pointer is damaged, removed, or any major powerhead component is replaced. If the spark advance stop screw has been disturbed or the power pack has been replaced, timing should be checked and adjusted as necessary.

Stator and Timer Base

REMOVAL

1. Remove the flywheel nut, using an automotive-type flywheel holder to hold the flywheel.

2. Remove the flywheel using a puller.

3. Disconnect the stator leads (yellow and yellow/gray) at the terminal board. Remove the stator.

4. Remove the retaining clips and screws from the timer assembly. These clips engage a nylon ring which fits around the timer base.

INSTALLATION

1. The timer base has a cast-in brass bushing which rotates with a very close tolerance on the upper bearing and seal assembly as the spark is advanced or retarded.

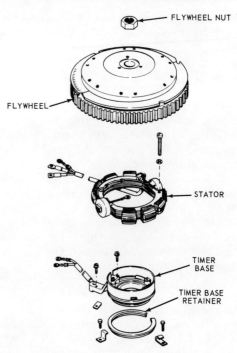

CD magneto and timer base assembly (© Outboard Marine Corporation)

2. Check for dirt which may prevent the timer base from rotating properly.

3. Oil and assemble the nylon retainer to the timer base and attach the assembly to the crankcase.

4. If the flywheel key has been removed, install it on the crankshaft with the outer edge parallel to the centerline of the crankshaft.

5. Install the stator and torque the screws evenly.

6. Clean the crankshaft and flywheel tapers of any traces of oil or grease.

7. Replace the flywheel and torque the nut to specification.

8. Check and adjust the timing.

TIMING POINTER ADJUSTMENT

The performance of the engine depends largely on accurate adjustment of the ignition timing and carburetor synchronization. If major powerhead components have been replaced, check the timing as follows.

1. Disconnect the spark plug leads and remove the spark plugs.

2. Obtain a timing plunger (available commercially from any well-stocked snowmobile or marine supplier). This is a simple device consisting of a body which screws into the spark plug port and houses

Timing grid and adjustable pointer (© Outboard Marine Corporation)

Idle-speed adjustment screw—1971 50 HP (© Outboard Marine Corporation)

a plunger which will move when contacted by the piston.

3. Screw the timing plunger into the top spark plug port.

4. Turn the flywheel clockwise until the plunger moves upward as far as possible and begins to move down. The point where the plunger reaches its peak is TDC.

5. Lightly pencil a mark on the flywheel rim opposite the timing pointer. If the pencil mark on the flywheel and the cast-in TDC mark are in alignment the timing is correct. If not, turn the flywheel to align the midpoint pencil mark with the timing pointer. Without moving the flywheel further, move the pointer to align with the cast-in TDC mark on the flywheel and tighten the screw to lock the pointer.

Synchronizing Carburetor and Throttle Linkage

1. The mark on the throttle cam must align with the center of the cam roller follower just as the roller makes contact with the cam.

2. Adjust the throttle cam as described under "Fuel System."

3. Connect a good quality timing light to the upper cylinder.

4. Start the motor and adjust the idle-speed adjustment screw to give 3° ±1° advanced timing.

5. Stop the motor and adjust the throttle cam yoke to align the embossed mark on

Throttle cam adjustment—1971 50 HP (© Outboard Marine Corporation)

the throttle cam with the center of the throttle cam roller.

Safety Switch

1. The safety switch is not adjustable. The switch is normally open and must close to permit starting. A test light should show that the switch is closed when it is on the throttle lever ramp.

TYPE 3

This type of battery ignition system is similar to an automotive-type ignition. It consists of a battery, ignition coil, distributor, and spark plugs. The distributor cam and pulley are driven by a timing belt which synchronizes the distributor with the crankshaft.

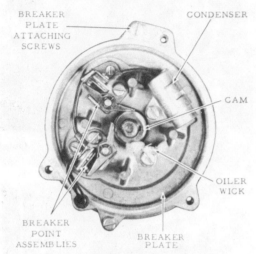

Battery ignition distributor with cap removed (© Outboard Marine Corporation)

Distributor

REMOVAL

1. Remove the spark plug wires by twisting them in a counterclockwise direction.
2. Remove the distributor cap.
3. Disconnect the control shaft linkage and the safety switch lead. Do not lose the carbon rotor brush and spring from the center cavity of the distributor cap.
4. Remove the rotor from the distributor shaft. Disconnect the breaker point lead at the ignition coil.
5. Remove the ignition coil and ring gear cover.
6. Remove the mounting bracket screws and slide the distributor bracket forward. Lift the belt off the pulley.
7. Remove the distributor bracket and bearing assembly from the motor.

DISASSEMBLY

1. Back the distributor shaft nut off one full turn and use two screwdrivers to pry off the cam. Remove the key from the distributor shaft.

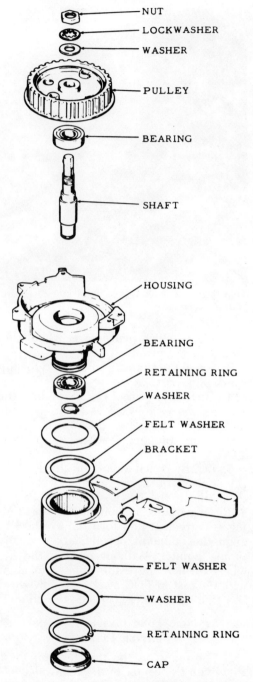

Exploded view of battery ignition distributor (© Outboard Marine Corporation)

2. Remove the nut, lockwasher, and flat washer that are attaching the pulley to the distributor shaft.
3. Remove the cap from the bottom of the distributor housing and sleeve assembly. Remove the snap-ring and separate the distributor housing from the bracket to

expose the large needle bearing pressed into the distributor bracket.

4. It is necessary to remove the snap-ring before attempting to remove the bearings. The distributor shaft bearings are easily damaged if the shaft is pressed from the housing. Do not attempt to remove the shaft unless it is certain that the bearings are in need of cleaning or replacement. Rotate the shaft slowly by hand and check for any roughness; move it from side to side. The shaft should rotate freely without any play. If it is necessary to replace the bearings, press them out with an arbor press and a suitable support.

5. Most testing of the distributor can be done without disassembling the condenser, breaker points, etc., from the breaker plate. If necessary, remove all components from the breaker plate and unscrew the spark plug leads from the distributor cap in a counterclockwise direction.

INSPECTION

1. Perform the inspection procedure listed for the Type 1 ignition system.

2. In addition, check the distributor cap for worn contacts or carbon leak paths.

ASSEMBLY

1. Assemble the bearings and shaft to the distributor housing. Press the top bearing on the shaft, using an arbor press and press against the inner race only.

2. Press the top bearing and shaft into the distributor housing. Press only against the outer race. Press the bottom bearing into place using press plates so that pressure is applied to the inner and outer races of both bearings.

3. Replace the pulley, washers, and nut. Use a new flat washer over the pulley to assure proper tightening.

4. Start the cam (with the top up) over the shaft and ball assembly, and place the key in the keyway. Use a deep $9/16$ in. socket to seat the cam squarely on the shaft.

5. Reassemble the distributor housing and bracket using new felt washers. Replace the retaining ring and housing cap. Attach the distributor to the motor, leaving the screws loose enough to permit belt adjustment.

6. Install the belt in position over the pulley. Check the timing and belt tension as described under "Belt Timing."

7. Attach the breaker plate assembly and check the breaker point adjustment as described later.

8. Replace the rotor, distributor cap, and linkage. Be sure that the correct rotor (part no. 580338) is used. Do not replace with that rotor (part no. 580260) which is a magneto rotor.

9. Check the synchronization of the linkage as described later.

NEW TIMING BELT INSTALLATION

1. Remove the ignition coil and flywheel ring gear cover.

2. Remove the distributor cap, rotor, and breaker plate.

3. Remove the flywheel and alternator stator.

4. Lift off the old belt and place the new belt in position.

5. Check the timing and belt tension as described below.

6. Install the ring gear cover.

7. Install the breaker points and check the point gap. Install the rotor, distributor cap, and linkage.

Adjustments

BELT TIMING

1. Rotate the flywheel so that the timing marks on the flywheel cover and ring gear or flywheel and cylinder block are aligned. NOTE: *Rotate the flywheel clockwise only, to prevent damaging the water pump impeller. Remove the spark plugs to relieve compression in the power-head.*

2. With the timing marks on the flywheel aligned, the timing marks on the distributor pulley and bracket should be in line. If not, loosen the distributor bracket mounting screws and release the belt tension.

3. Rotate the distributor pulley until the timing marks are aligned.

4. Adjust the distributor bracket for the proper amount of slack in the belt. The belt tension is correct when the belt can be deflected $1/4$–$3/8$ in. using light thumb pressure near the center of the belt.

5. Tighten the distributor bracket mounting screws.

BREAKER POINTS

1. Inspect the points to be sure the gap is approximately 0.020 in.

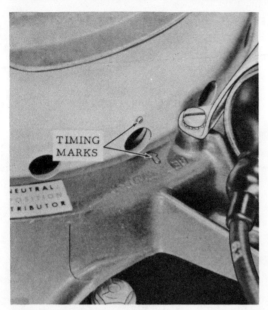

Timing marks—flywheel and ring gear cover (© Outboard Marine Corporation)

Timing marks—flywheel and cylinder block (© Outboard Marine Corporation)

2. Disconnect the breaker point lead and connect it to a test light. Ground the test light on the distributor breaker plate.

3. Rotate the distributor housing to the fully advanced position where the boss on the housing strikes the rubber stop on the distributor bracket.

4. The housing must be held in this position throughout the breaker point adjustment.

5. Rotate the flywheel (clockwise only) so that the mark on the distributor pulley aligns with synchronizing mark on the distributor housing.

6. The breaker point arm opposite the condenser should be on the high lobe of the cam.

7. Slightly loosen the breaker point lockscrew and turn the breaker point adjusting screw so that the points close, causing the light to come on, indicating a closed circuit.

8. Tighten the point lockscrew and recheck the adjustment. The points should open the instant the mark on the pulley passes the distributor mark.

9. Rotate the flywheel 90° so that the mark on the pulley aligns with the second mark on the distributor breaker plate. Repeat the adjustment for the second set of points. Care should be taken to be sure that the points break 90° apart, to assure even firing.

10. Check the belt timing and synchronize the linkage. Replace the lead at the ignition coil and replace the distributor cap.

SYNCHRONIZING CARBURETOR AND DISTRIBUTOR LINKAGE

1. By hand, move the distributor to the full-advance position.

2. The inside surface of the control arm shaft should be parallel with the edge of the diamond-shaped projection on the control shaft bracket (viewed from above).

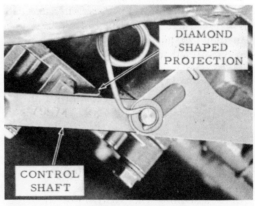

Alignment of control shaft arm in full-advance position (© Outboard Marine Corporation)

3. If the control arm shaft is not in the correct position, loosen the linkage screws and make the adjustment while holding the distributor at full advance.

4. Retighten the screws. Check the

pick-up position of the throttle with the cam. The roller should begin to open the throttle as the center of the roller shaft aligns with the mark on the cam.

5. If this adjustment is incorrect, make the adjustment as described in "Fuel System."

6. Hold the control shaft against its stop in the full-throttle position and check that the throttle arm is against its stop on the carburetor.

7. The linkage is correctly synchronized when the throttle arm and throttle control shaft reach their full-advance positions at the same time.

SAFETY SWITCH

1. Loosen the adjustment screws and set the switch to close at the midpoint on the cam slope.

2. A click will be heard when the switch closes. After the adjustment is made, tighten the screws.

3. The switch is normally open and must close to permit starting. A test light will reveal the switch closing.

TYPE 4

The capacitor discharge ignition system used on the 1967 100 horsepower model, consists of three major components: a pulse transformer; a sensor, and a pulse pack assembly. The pulse transformer replaces the conventional ignition coil while the sensor, located within the distributor, replaces the conventional breaker points and condenser. The pulse pack which is completely sealed in epoxy is located on a bracket on the lower rear motor cover.

WARNING: *DO NOT ATTEMPT TO OPEN THE PULSE PACK AS THIS WILL VOID THE WARRANTY.*

Precautions

1. Follow the precautions outlined under the section for the Type 2 capacitor discharge system.

Troubleshooting the CD System

1. A malfunction in the system will result in either the engine missing or failure of the engine to run at all.

2. An engine miss may be caused by improper fuel or an improperly adjusted carburetor. Be sure that the fuel system is not at fault before investigating the CD system.

3. Check all of the wiring associated with the CD system to be sure there is a clean, tight connection. Be sure that all wires are in good condition; that they are not cracked or oil-soaked.

4. Check the timing. The engine timing should not change during engine operation but if the seal is broken on the adjustment screw or if the electronic pack has been replaced, the timing should be checked.

5. Check the spark plugs. If the center electrode is worn to a point where it is below the ceramic, the plug should be replaced. Any plugs with cracked insulators should always be replaced. If the plugs are fouled in any way, determine this condition and remedy it before returning the motor to service.

6. Check the pulse transformer terminal studs to determine if any have come loose. Check for any cracks or carbon leak paths. If any of the above are located, replace the unit. Remove the pulse transformer-to-distributor cap lead at the distributor and hold the lead approximately $3/8$ in. from the engine block with insulated pliers.

WARNING: *There is extremely high voltage in this system. Do not touch the engine or the wiring, and do not stand in water when conducting any cranking tests on the engine.*

7. A good pulse transformer will easily produce a spark that will jump a $3/8$ in. gap when the motor is cranked. If the spark is weak or erratic, replace the unit to determine whether it is the cause of trouble.

8. Check the pulse pack. Connect a low-reading ammeter between the terminals of the red wire. The reading should be 0.4–0.5 amp with the ignition key turned on (do not crank the engine).

Remove the green lead from the positive terminal of the pulse transformer and connect a no. 57 bulb to the disconnected green lead and the negative terminal of the pulse transformer. Crank the engine and observe the bulb. A flickering glow of the bulb at each firing impulse indicates that the sensor unit and pulse pack are operating satisfactorily.

9. If a light is observed in step 8 and no spark is observed in steps 7 and 8, the pulse transformer is defective and should be replaced.

10. Check the distributor cap and rotor for any cracks or carbon leak paths.

11. Turn on the ignition switch and bridge the sensor and trigger wheel with a feeler gauge. If sparks are observed at the transformer high-tension lead, the sensor is good.

12. Remove the leads from the sensor and check each terminal to ground with an ohmmeter. The reading should be infinity. If resistance is found, replace the sensor.

13. Connect an ohmmeter between two sensor terminals. Reading should be 4–6 ohms.

Distributor

REMOVAL

1. Remove the spark plug leads.

2. Remove the distributor cap from the breaker plate, being careful not to lose the carbon brush and spring from inside the cap.

3. Disconnect the control shaft linkage and the safety switch lead.

4. Remove the rotor from the distributor shaft and disconnect the leads to the ignition coil.

5. Use two screwdrivers to carefully pry the sensor rotor from the distributor shaft. Remove the key from the distributor shaft.

6. Remove the nut, lockwasher, and flat washer, holding the distributor pulley to the shaft.

7. Remove the distributor plate assembly by removing the two screws which attach it to the distributor housing.

8. Remove the ring gear cover.

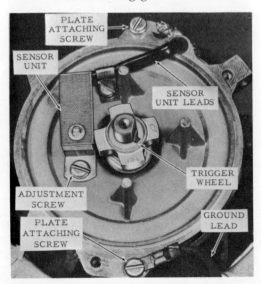

1967 100 HP distributor with cover removed (© Outboard Marine Corporation)

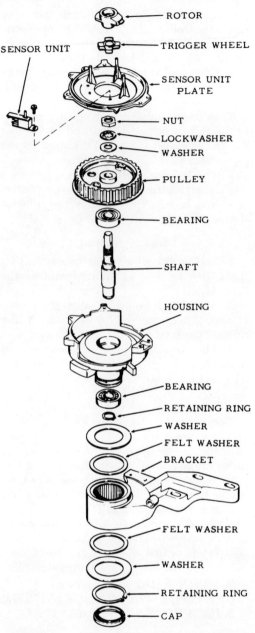

1967 100 HP distributor (© Outboard Marine Corporation)

DISASSEMBLY

1. Remove the three bracket mounting screws and slide the distributor bracket forward to release the belt tension.

2. Lift the belt from the pulley.

3. The distributor bracket and bearing assembly can now be removed from the motor.

4. Perform steps 3 and 4 of the Type 3 distributor disassembly procedure.

5. Most testing of the distributor can be done without removing the sensor unit from the plate. If parts replacement is necessary, all components can be removed from the plate. The spark plug leads can be unscrewed from the cap counterclockwise.

INSPECTION

1. Inspect the unit as listed under the procedures for the Type 1 ignition system.

2. In addition, inspect the distributor cap for cracks or carbon leak paths.

3. The bearings are shielded ball bearings. They should be trouble-free under normal service but, if there is any reason to suspect that water (especially salt water) has entered the bearings (for whatever reason), they should be washed in clean gasoline and allowed to air-dry. Do not spin the bearings with compressed air. Repack them with high-speed, high-melting-point grease.

ASSEMBLY

1. This procedure is the same as the Type 3 Distributor Assembly given previously.

Adjustments

ENGINE TIMING

1. Connect a good quality timing light to no. 1 cylinder and start the engine. Set the engine speed to 500 rpm in gear.

2. The timing marks on the distributor housing and pulley should align. If not, check for a worn distributor shaft, damaged keyways, or incorrect sensor gap adjustment (see "Sensor Gap Adjustment" following).

3. With the timing light still connected to no. 1 cylinder, run the engine to 4500 rpm in gear. The timing mark on the flywheel must fall within the square timing mark at the rear of the ring gear cover. NOTE: *There are two ring gear timing marks on some models. If the front ring gear timing mark is used, connect the light to no. 3 cylinder.*

4. If necessary, move the sealed adjustment screw to obtain the proper timing. Reseal the adjustment screw to prevent further adjustment.

SENSOR GAP

1. With the trigger wheel lobe aligned with the sensor, the air gap should be

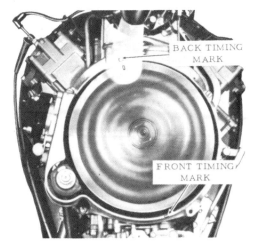

1967 100 HP timing marks (© Outboard Marine Corporation)

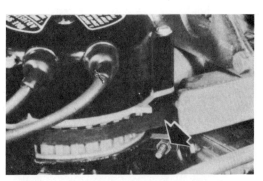

1967 100 HP sealed adjustment screw (© Outboard Marine Corporation)

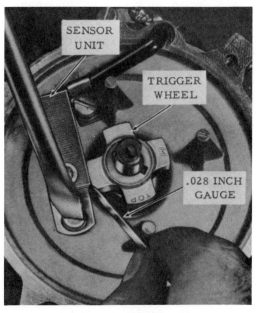

1967 100 HP sensor gap adjustment (© Outboard Marine Corporation)

0.028 in., measured with a feeler gauge.

2. If necessary, adjust by loosening the sensor retaining screw and placing a feeler gauge (0.028 in. thick) between the sensor and trigger wheel lobe.

3. Move the sensor in or out to obtain the proper gap. Tighten the adjusting screw.

NOTE: *Erratic engine operation is sometimes caused by a sensor which is loose and moving around during engine operation.*

New Timing Belt Installation

1. Refer to this procedure in the section on the Type 3 ignition.

Belt Tension

1. Refer to this procedure in the section on the Type 3 ignition.

Synchronizing Carburetor and Distributor Linkage

1. Refer to this procedure in the section on the Type 3 ignition.

Safety Switch

1. Refer to this procedure in the section on the Type 3 ignition.

TYPE 5

An ignition system consisting of a distributor-type magneto, high-tension leads, and spark plugs is used on 1966 60 horsepower models and 1966 80 horsepower models. Some 1966 80 horsepower models are equipped with an automotive battery ignition system consisting of a battery, ignition coil, distributor, high-tension leads, and spark plugs. Since both of these ignition systems are covered as Type 5 ignitions, refer to the specific service procedures for the equipment installed on your motor.

Distributor / Magneto (Single Assembly)

Removal

1. Disconnect the safety switch lead and the ignition lead.

2. Twist the spark plug leads (counterclockwise) off the spark plugs. Unscrew the leads from the distributor cap.

3. Remove the linkage screws.

4. Loosen the bracket mounting screws and slide the bracket forward to release belt tension.

5. Lift the belt off the pulley.

6. Remove the magneto and bracket assembly from the motor.

Disassembly

1. Remove the nut, lockwasher, and flat washer from the distributor shaft.

2. Lift off the magneto pulley, magneto cam, and distributor shaft key.

3. Unscrew the breaker plate from the magneto housing. Remove the breaker plate assembly. If necessary, remove the breaker plate components.

4. Separate the bearing bracket and magneto housing, noting the position of the washers.

5. Remove the distributor cap and gasket from the housing and remove the rotor from the shaft. Do not lose the carbon brush and spring from inside the distributor cap.

6. Disconnect the primary leads of the coil from the insulated terminal and retainer screw spring.

7. Remove the retainer springs and lift the coil from the housing.

8. The distributor shaft bearings are easily damaged if the shaft is pressed from the housing. Before removing the shaft, be

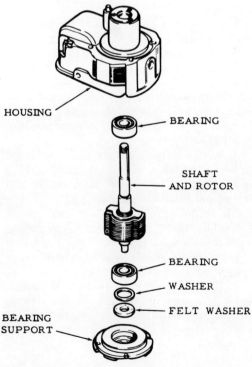

Rotor shaft and bearing assembly from distributor / magneto (© Outboard Marine Corporation)

sure that the bearings are in need of replacement or cleaning. Check for wear or dirt in the bearings by slowly rotating the bearings by hand. Move the shaft from side to side and check for any side-play. There should be no play and the bearings should rotate smoothly and evenly. If cleaning of the bearings is necessary, use an arbor press to remove them and repack them with high-melting-point grease.

INSPECTION

1. Refer to the inspection procedures listed in the section for the Type 1 ignition system.

ASSEMBLY

1. Assemble the bearings and shaft to the magneto housing, using an arbor press to assemble the bearings to the shaft. Press the shaft with the upper bearing into the magneto housing. Place the bearing washer and felt washer into the recess in the bearing support and press the support into place over the lower bearing. Attach the bearing support to the magneto housing, first tightening the flat-head screws to assure correct shaft alignment.

2. Install the coil with the insulators into the housing. The coil must be positioned so that the core laminations butt against the field laminations without air gap. Connect the primary leads to the ground screw and to the insulated screw terminal.

3. Install the rotor on the shaft and install the carbon brush and spring in the distributor cap (if removed). Install the distributor cap.

4. Assemble the magneto housing and breaker plate to the bearing bracket, making sure that the felt and steel washers are in place.

5. Install the key and cam to the shaft. If the components of the breaker plate were removed, install these.

6. Replace the pulley and attach with washers and nut.

INSTALLATION

1. Install the magneto bearing bracket to the motor. Leave the screws loose enough to permit belt adjustment.

2. Adjust the breaker points as described later.

3. Install the belt over the magneto and pulley, and adjust the magneto and flywheel timing.

4. Connect the safety switch and ground leads.

5. Install the spark plug leads.

6. Connect the throttle arm to the magneto linkage and adjust as described later.

7. Check the safety switch adjustment.

NEW TIMING BELT INSTALLATION

1. Remove the rewind starter and release the belt tension by loosening the screws holding the magneto bracket to the powerhead.

2. Cut away the old belt.

3. Install the new belt (without removing the flywheel) by carefully threading the belt between the flywheel and carburetor. Check the magneto timing and belt tension.

4. Tighten the magneto bracket screws and replace the rewind starter. Check the linkage adjustment.

Distributor

REMOVAL

1. Disconnect the safety switch lead and the breaker point lead.

2. Twist the spark plug leads (counterclockwise) off the spark plugs. Unscrew the leads from the distributor cap.

3. Remove the linkage screws.

4. Remove the distributor cap; do not lose the carbon brush and spring from the cap.

5. Remove the rotor from the distributor shaft.

6. Remove the breaker plate from the distributor housing.

7. Loosen the bracket mounting screws and slide the distributor forward to release the belt tension.

8. Lift the belt off the pulley and remove the distributor bracket and bearing assembly from the motor.

DISASSEMBLY AND INSPECTION

1. This distributor is disassembled, inspected, and assembled in the same manner as used for the Type 3 ignition distributor.

INSTALLATION

1. Install the distributor to the motor, leaving the screws loose enough to permit adjustment.

2. Place the belt over the pulley. Check the timing and belt tension.

3. Install the breaker plate assembly and check the breaker point gap.

4. Install the rotor, distributor cap, and linkage. Be sure that the proper rotor (part no. 580388) is used. Do not confuse this rotor with the magneto rotor (part no. 580260).

5. Check the safety switch adjustment and connect the throttle arm to the distributor linkage and adjust it.

New Timing Belt Installation

1. Remove the ignition coil and flywheel ring gear cover.

2. Remove the distributor rotor, cap, and breaker plate.

3. Remove the flywheel and stator assembly.

4. Lift off the old belt and install a new belt. Replace the alternator stator and flywheel. Check the distributor timing and belt tension.

5. Install the breaker plate and check the point gap adjustment. Replace the rotor distributor cap and linkage.

Adjustments

Belt Timing—Magneto Models

1. Rotate the pulley so that the timing mark aligns with the center of the safety switch plunger.

2. Rotate the flywheel so that the timing marks on the flywheel, starter housing, and by-pass cover are aligned. Rotate the flywheel clockwise only.

Timing marks on magneto pulley (© Outboard Marine Corporation)

3. With the flywheel timing marks aligned, the timing mark on the magneto pulley and the safety switch plunger should be aligned. If not, loosen the magneto bracket mounting screws and rotate the pulley until the marks are aligned.

Flywheel timing marks on 1966 60 and 80 HP (© Outboard Marine Corporation)

4. Adjust the magneto bearing bracket to obtain proper belt tension. The belt tension is correct when the belt can be deflected 1/4–3/8 in. under light thumb pressure at the middle of the belt.

5. Tighten the adjustment screws and check the linkage synchronization.

Belt Timing—Distributor Models

1. This procedure is identical to the Type 3 ignition procedure.

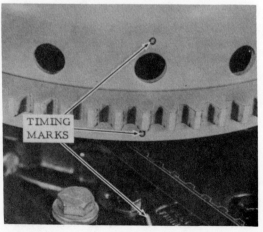

Timing marks—distributor model 1966 80 HP (© Outboard Marine Corporation)

BREAKER POINTS

1. The timing belt must be loosened to permit it to turn freely.

2. Remove the pulley cover or the distributor cap and inspect the points, making sure that they are set at approximately 0.020 in.

3. Disconnect the breaker point lead and connect it to a test light. Ground the test light on the breaker plate.

4. Rotate the pulley so that the mark on the pulley aligns with the mark on the breaker plate. The breaker arm nearest the condenser should be on the high lobe of the cam.

Adjusting breaker points—1966 60 and 80 HP (© Outboard Marine Corporation)

5. Turn the point adjusting screw so that the points close and the test light indicates a closed circuit.

6. Check the adjustment by rotating the pulley slightly in both directions. The points should be closed at the instant when the marks are aligned.

7. Rotate the pulley 90° and repeat the adjustment on the second set of points. Be sure that the points break 90° apart, since this will ensure even firing.

8. Check the belt timing and install the breaker point lead. Replace the pulley cover or distributor cap. Check the linkage synchronization.

SYNCHRONIZING THE CARBURETOR-TO-DISTRIBUTOR (OR MAGNETO) LINKAGE

1. Check the distributor or magneto timing.

2. By hand, move the distributor (or magneto) to the full-advance position. On magneto models, the motor should be in Forward gear.

3. The inside surface of the throttle control shaft should be parallel to the edge of the triangular projection on the control shaft bracket.

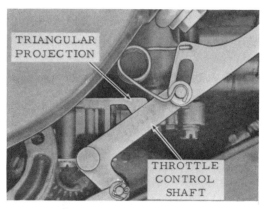

Synchronizing carburetor linkage—1966 60 and 80 HP (© Outboard Marine Corporation)

4. If the throttle control shaft is not correctly positioned, loosen the linkage screws and make the adjustment while holding the distributor (or magneto) in full-advance. Tighten the linkage screws.

5. Position the throttle cam so that the scribe mark is aligned with the center of the cam follower roller.

6. Loosen the clamp screw and move the throttle arm to its limit to close the throttle valves. Be sure that the mark on the roller is contacting the cam and that the scribe mark is aligned with the center of the roller shaft.

7. With the distributor (or magneto) in the full-advance position, loosen the cotter

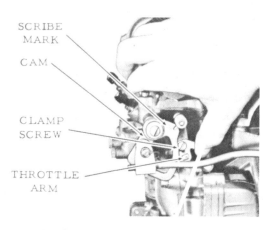

Throttle adjustment—1966 60 and 80 HP (© Outboard Marine Corporation)

pin on the throttle control rod and adjust it so that the throttle control arm and throttle shaft reach their fully opened position at the same time. Install the cotter pin.

SAFETY SWITCH

1. Refer to this procedure in the section for the Type 3 ignition.

TYPE 6

This system is a capacitor discharge system using breaker points. It consists of three major components: an ignition coil, two sets of breaker points, and an amplifier assembly which is completely sealed and mounted on the rear of the powerhead.

WARNING: *DO NOT ATTEMPT TO OPEN THE AMPLIFIER AS THIS WILL VOID THE WARRANTY.*

Precautions

1. Before proceeding further, refer to the precautions listed in the section for the Type 2 ignition system.

Troubleshooting the CD System

The procedures listed here are simple checks which can be made and will quite often locate the trouble. For more complicated testing, have a dealer go over your motor with special test equipment.

1. Check for spark. Remove the spark plugs, one at a time, and attach the spark plug lead to it. Lay the spark plug on the powerhead to ground it. *During this test, while cranking the engine, do not touch the powerhead or any part of the motor, and do not stand in water.* Crank the engine briefly and observe the spark at the plug. If sparking does not occur, proceed with the following steps.

2. Check the wiring. Check all wiring associated with the system for any loose or corroded terminals or plug-in connections. Check for cracked or oil-soaked wires. Be sure that correct battery polarity is observed.

3. Check all spark plugs for wear at the center electrode. If the center electrode is worn to the point where it is below the ceramic, it should be replaced. Any spark plugs having cracked insulators should naturally be replaced. If the plugs are fouled, determine the cause and correct it before returning the motor to service.

4. Have the amplifier and coil checked by an Evinrude or Johnson dealer.

5. Synchronize the carburetor and distributor linkage.

6. Check the engine timing as described later.

Distributor

DISASSEMBLY

1. Remove the flywheel.

2. Disconnect the stator leads at the connector and remove the stator.

3. Lift off the distributor cap, wave washer, and rotor. This will expose the breaker assemblies and anti-reverse mechanism.

4. The breaker base is held in place by retaining clips and screws. The clips engage a nylon ring which fits around the breaker base.

INSPECTION

1. Inspect the distributor using the same procedures as those used for the Type 1 ignition system.

ASSEMBLY

1. The breaker base has a cast-in brass bushing which rotates, with a very close

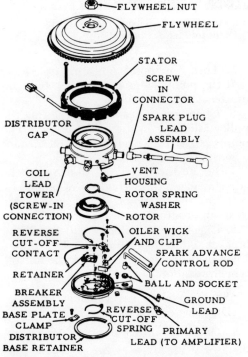

Breaker type CD ignition CD distributor (© Outboard Marine Corporation)

tolerance, on the crankcase head as the throttle is moved. Check carefully for damage which may impair the ability of the ring to rotate.

2. Install a new anti-reverse spring. Lubricate with Shell EP 2 grease and assemble the nylon ring to the breaker base.

3. Install the assembly on the crankcase head with the retainer clips and screws.

4. Install both sets of points. Adjust the points gap to 0.010 in. with the rubbing block on the high lobe of the cam.

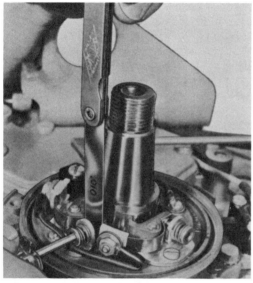

Adjusting the points—breaker type CD ignition
(© Outboard Marine Corporation)

5. Install the distributor cap, wave washer, and rotor.

6. Obtain the full-advance position of the distributor by aligning the boss on the distributor cap with the boss on the breaker base control arm. Make necessary adjustments by turning the screw.

7. Replace the distributor cap and install the alternator stator. Dip the stator screws in Loctite before installing.

8. Install the flywheel.

9. Check the timing and adjust as necessary.

Adjustments

ENGINE TIMING

1968 65 and 85 HP

1. The timing of the engine should not change; however, if the spark advance screw has been disturbed or if the amplifier replaced, check the timing.

2. Connect a good quality timing light to no. 1 cylinder and set the engine speed to full throttle in gear.

3. The timing mark on the flywheel must fall within the square timing mark on the lift bracket. If necessary, move the spark advance screw to obtain this setting.

Flywheel timing marks—1968 65 and 85 HP
(© Outboard Marine Corporation)

NOTE: *There are two flywheel timing marks. The straight mark is the mark for the port cylinders (1 and 3) and the triangular mark is the mark for the starboard cylinders (2 and 4). The starboard cylinders are fired by the forward set of points.*

1971 85 and 100 HP

1. The breaker points must be set to specification and the timing pointer must be set to TDC. (The procedure for setting the timing pointer is explained in the section for 1971 50 hp, Type 2 ignition systems.)

2. Connect a good quality timing light to no. 1 cylinder and run the engine to 4500 rpm in gear.

3. The 28° timing mark on the flywheel must fall in line with the timing pointer. If necessary to adjust the timing, stop the motor and move the full-advance adjustment screw to obtain the proper setting. One turn counterclockwise advances the timing about 1°, while one turn clockwise retards the timing about 1°.

Timing pointer and grid—1971 85 and 100 HP
(© Outboard Marine Corporation)

Spark advance adjustment screw—1971 85 and
100 HP (© Outboard Marine Corporation)

1968–69 55 HP

1. Connect a good quality timing light to no. 1 cylinder.

2. Set the engine speed to full throttle, in gear.

3. The straight timing light on the fly-

Flywheel timing marks—1968–69 55 HP (© Outboard Marine Corporation)

wheel must align with the square timing mark on the ring gear guard.

4. If necessary, move the advance stop adjustment screw to obtain the proper setting.

NOTE: *There are two flywheel timing marks. The straight mark is used for 1968–69 55 hp models. The triangular mark is not used.*

1970–71 60—With Timing Grid on the Ring Gear Guard

1. Connect a good quality timing light to no. 1 cylinder and run the engine at 4300–4600 rpm in gear.

2. The straight timing mark on the flywheel must align with the 22° mark on the ring gear guard. Move the advance stop screw to obtain this adjustment.

NOTE: *There are two flywheel timing marks. Use the straight timing mark; the triangular mark is not used.*

Timing marks on ring gear guard—1970–71 60 HP (© Outboard Marine Corporation)

1970–71 60 HP—With Timing Grid on the Flywheel

1. Use the previous procedure, but align the 22° mark on the flywheel timing grid with the timing pointer.

2. Be sure that the timing pointer is aligned with the TDC mark on the flywheel if the timing is not correct. Timing pointer alignment is detailed in the section for the 1971 50 hp, Type 2 ignition system.

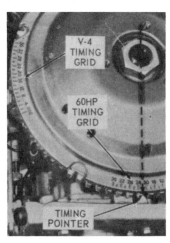

Timing marks on flywheel—1970–71 60 HP (© Outboard Marine Corporation)

1969–70 85 HP

1. Set the breaker points to specifications.

2. Connect a good quality timing light to no. 1 cylinder and run the engine at 4500 rpm in gear.

3. The timing mark on the flywheel must align with the mark on the lift bracket.

4. Move the adjustment screw to obtain the proper setting.

Timing marks—1969–70 85 HP (© Outboard Marine Corporation)

SYNCHRONIZING CARBURETOR AND DISTRIBUTOR LINKAGE

1968 65 and 85 HP

1. With the distributor in the full-advance position, the mark on the distributor base plate arm should align with the mark on the distributor cap.

2. The mark on the throttle cam must align with the center of the roller just as the roller makes contact with the cam.

Linkage adjustment—1968 65 and 85 HP (© Outboard Marine Corporation)

3. With the control shaft at full throttle, the throttle shaft arm must be against its stop. Make necessary adjustments by turning the throttle cam yoke on the throttle control rod.

1971 85 and 100 HP

1. Adjust the throttle cam (see "Fuel System").

2. Connect a timing light to no. 1 cylinder and adjust the idle-speed adjustment screw to 5° BTDC.

3. Stop the motor and adjust the throttle cam yoke to align the upper embossed mark on the throttle cam with the center of the cam roller.

4. Open the throttle to WOT. The upper carburetor roll pin will be against its stop. Move the full-throttle adjustment screw to prevent strain on the throttle shaft. A 0.003 in. feeler gauge should just pull out with light drag.

5. Recheck the timing.

1968–69 55 HP

1. See this adjustment in the section for 1968 65 and 85 hp motors.

Wide-open throttle adjustment (© Outboard Marine Corporation)

1970–71 60 HP

1. See this adjustment in the section for 1968 65 and 85 hp motors. If the throttle cam yoke has been removed from the throttle rod, install the throttle rod so that the end of the throttle link is $4^{31}/_{32}$ in. from the face of the yoke.

1969–70 85 HP

1. Remove the flywheel and adjust the throttle cam.

2. The center of the cam follower roller must align with the mark on the throttle cam just as the throttle begins to open.

3. Align the marks on the distributor base plate and distributor cap.

4. Adjust the spark advance stop screw.

Spark advance adjustment screw—1969–70 85 HP (© Outboard Marine Corporation)

5. Adjust the throttle cam yoke with the throttle lever held against its stop on the crankcase.

6. The marks on the distributor base and cap must remain aligned.

7. Replace the flywheel and check the timing.

8. If the timing is incorrect, a complete readjustment of the advance stop screw is required.

SAFETY SWITCH

1. Loosen the adjustment screw and connect a test light between the switch lead and ground.

2. Set the starting circuit switch to close on the flat of the cam. A click will be audible when the switch closes.

3. Tighten the adjustment screw. The switch is normally open and must close to permit starting.

TYPE 7

This capacitor discharge system consists of three major components: a coil; a sensor, and a pulse pack assembly.

WARNING: *DO NOT ATTEMPT TO OPEN THE PULSE PACK OR THE WARRANTY WILL BE VOIDED.*

Precautions

1. The same precautions as apply to the Type 2 CD system apply here.

NOTE: *Due to the sophistication and complexity of this unit, it is recommended that it be referred to a dealer who is equipped with the necessary special test equipment to properly evaluate the unit's performance.*

Distributor

DISASSEMBLY

1. Remove the flywheel.

2. Disconnect the stator leads and remove the stator.

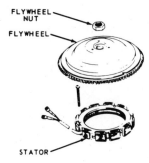

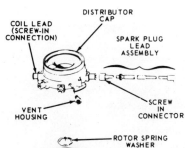

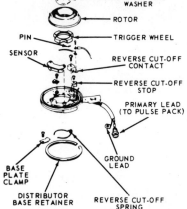

Breaker-less CD ignition distributor (© Outboard Marine Corporation)

3. Lift off the distributor cap, wave washer, and rotor.

4. Remove the sensor rotor. This will expose the sensor and anti-reverse mechanism.

5. The distributor base is retained by clamps and screws. The clamps engage a nylon ring which fits around the distributor base.

INSPECTION

1. Inspect the spark plugs for worn electrodes or cracked insulators.

2. Before installing the spark plugs, be sure that the seats are clean. Tighten plugs to the specified torque.

3. Inspect the distributor cap for arcing, cracks, and carbon leak paths.

4. Be sure that the ventilating screens in the distributor cap are sufficiently clean to assure proper ventilation.

ASSEMBLY

1. The distributor base has a cast-in brass bushing which rotates with a very close tolerance to the upper crankcase. Be sure that this is not dirty or chipped.

2. Install the reverse cutout spring over the top of the crankshaft with the flat side down.

3. Lubricate and assemble the retainer to the distributor base and install this to the crankcase.

4. Install the sensor assembly.

5. Check each sensor lead to ground with an ohmmeter. On the high ohms scale, the reading should be infinity for each terminal.

6. Connect an ohmmeter to the two sensor terminals. On the low ohms scale, the reading should be between four and six ohms.

7. Check the air gap at the sensor. With a sensor lobe aligned with the sensor, the gap should be 0.028 in. Adjust by loosening the sensor retaining screws and placing a feeler gauge between the lobe and sensor.

8. Install the rotor, wave washer, and distributor cap. Install the stator after dipping the retaining screws in Loctite.

9. If the flywheel key was removed, assemble to the crankshaft with the outer edge parallel to the centerline of the crankshaft.

10. Install the flywheel.

Adjustments

SYNCHRONIZING CARBURETOR AND DISTRIBUTOR LINKAGE

1969–70 115 HP

1. See this adjustment under the Type 6 ignition system, in the section for 1969–70 85 hp motors.

1968 100 HP

1. See this adjustment under Type 6 ignition system, in the section which covers 1968 65 and 85 hp motors.

1971 125 HP

1. See this adjustment under the Type 6 ignition system, in the 1971 85 and 100 hp section.

Timing Pointer Adjustment— 1971 125 HP

1. Disconnect the spark plug leads and remove the spark plugs.

2. Temporarily set the pointer midway in its adjusting slot.

3. Obtain a timing plunger tool from any well-stocked marine or snowmobile supplier. Install this tool in the spark plug hole (no. 1 cylinder).

4. Turn the flywheel clockwise until the plunger moves upward and just starts down (this indicates that the piston is at TDC).

5. Make a pencil mark on the flywheel rim at TDC as indicated by the plunger and timing pointer. If the pencil mark and cast-in TDC mark coincide, the pointer alignment is correct.

6. If these marks do not coincide, turn the flywheel to align the pencil mark with the pointer. (Do not move the flywheel.)

7. Loosen the pointer adjustment screw and align the pointer with the cast-in TDC mark on the flywheel. Tighten the adjustment screw.

SAFETY SWITCH

1. See this adjustment in the section on the Type 6 ignition system.

STARTER MOTOR

Maintenance operations on the starter motor are generally limited to periodic inspection for tight mountings. Unless it is certain that the starter motor is defective, do not remove it for overhaul. In general, starter motor removal procedures are alike

Timing pointer alignment at TDC—1971 125 HP (© Outboard Marine Corporation)

among OMC models. The following procedure can be used for all models, noting minor variations among models.

Removal

1. Disconnect and tag the lead(s) from the starter motor.

2. Depending on equipment, either detach the starter and mounting bracket from the crankcase or remove the thrubolts from the starter.

3. If the former method is chosen, remove the starter and bracket, and separate the motor from the bracket.

4. If the latter method (step 2) is chosen, the starter can now be dropped from the starter drive housing. If it is necessary to remove the starter drive housing, remove the ring gear cover, loosen the screw, and remove the starter drive housing.

Installation

1. Installation is the reverse of removal.

AUTOMATIC REWIND STARTER

The manual starter engages the powerhead flywheel, by means of three pawls, when the rope handle is pulled. A coil spring is wound as the handle is pulled and then unwinds, pulling the rope back.

NOTE: *Do not release the handle at the end of each pull, allowing it to snap back. Serious damage can occur.*

Removal

1. Disconnect the locking lever assembly by removing the screw holding the locking lever to the starter housing.

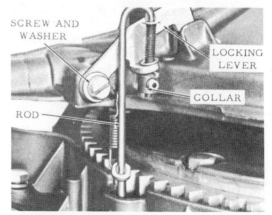

Manual starter locking mechanism (© Outboard Marine Corporation)

2. Remove the attaching screws and lift the mechanism from the powerhead.

Disassembly

1. Pull out the rope and tie a knot in the end of it.

2. Pry the rope from the handle.

3. Remove the handle, release the knot and, very gently, ease the starter drum back until the spring is fully unwound. It is an excellent idea to wear safety glasses and heavy gloves when overhauling rewind starters of this type.

4. Remove the starter spindle screw, washer, and pawl retainers.

5. Remove the spindle, spring washer, friction ring, pawls, and nylon bushing.

6. Jar the housing (bottom side down) on the workbench to dislodge the spring and pulley.

Bottom view of manual starter (© Outboard Marine Corporation)

Inspection

1. Wash the metal components in solvent and allow them to air-dry.

2. Inspect the spring for broken end loops or weak tension.

3. Examine the pawls for wear.

4. Inspect the rope and discard it if it is frayed or worn. A new rope should be cut to 73¾ in. from nylon stock.

5. Examine the pulley and housing eye for sharp edges which could cut the rope.

Assembly

1. Be sure to wear heavy gloves when assembling the mechanism.

2. Attach an end of the spring to the pin on the drum and carefully wind the spring in a counterclockwise direction.

3. When the spring is wound tight, very carefully release the spring about one turn or until the loop in the spring aligns with the hole drilled in the edge of the pulley. Slide a pin through the pulley and spring loop.

4. Install the pulley and spring into the starter housing and be sure that the outside spring loop is on top of its appropriate stud in the housing.

5. Press down on the pulley so that the stud moves into the spring loop, forcing the pin out.

6. Tie a knot in one end of the rope. Be sure that the rope is 73¾ in. long. With an open flame, burn each end of the nylon rope to prevent it from fraying.

7. Lubricate the spindle and install it in the pulley.

8. Turn the starter pulley counterclockwise to be sure that the starter spring is fully wound. Allow it to unwind one turn so that the pulley rope hole aligns with the housing rope hole.

9. Insert the rope through the pulley and pull it through the starter housing. Tug hard on the end of the rope to seat the knot in the pulley.

10. Tie a knot in the rope and allow the pulley to rewind.

11. Install the bushing in the pulley. Install the pawls and lock them in place. Attach the friction spring, spring washer, and spindle.

12. Install the spindle washer and screw.

13. Attach a piece of wire to the end of the rope and thread it into the handle and pull it through. It may need some lubrication.

14. Attach the rope to the handle and untie the knot. Allow the rope to wind up on the pulley.

15. Activate the mechanism to be sure that it works properly. The pawls should pivot out to engage the flywheel ratchet and return to their original positions.

Installation

1. Align the starter with the powerhead and attach it with three screws.

2. Attach the locking lever with the screw and washer.

Lock-Out Adjustment

1. Set the gearshift lever in Neutral.
2. Loosen the collar screw.
3. With the gearshift in Neutral, turn the speed control grip until the magneto stop butts against the shifter lock.
4. Push the lock link collar against the locking lever far enough to cause the ends of the locking lever to clear the stop lugs on the starter pulley.
5. Tighten the collar screw to hold the collar on the control rod.

Powerhead

REMOVAL

1966–70 33 HP and 1966–71 40 HP

1. Remove the carburetor, manifold, leaf valves, fuel pump and filter, and fuel hoses.
2. Remove the manual starter.
3. If equipped with an electric starter, remove the starter motor.
4. Remove the flywheel magneto, cutout switch, and safety switch.
5. Remove the port and starboard starter mounting brackets.
6. Remove the armature plate support and retaining ring.
7. Remove the throttle control lever and the lifting lever from the lower motor cover.
8. Remove the shifter lock spring and shifter lock.
9. Remove the screws and nuts attaching the powerhead to the exhaust housing.

1968–69 55 HP and 1970–71 60 HP

1. Remove the carburetor, leaf plate assembly, fuel pump, fuel filter, and fuel hoses.
2. Remove the flywheel.
3. Remove the stator, distributor, and safety switch.
4. Remove the electric starter and push the red cable and grommet through the crankcase web.
5. Disconnect the wiring connectors and remove the wiring from the clamps.
6. Remove the amplifier, complete with the wiring intact.
7. Remove the throttle control lever and throttle cam.

33 HP and 40 HP powerhead attaching screws (© Outboard Marine Corporation)

8. Remove the screws attaching the crankcase front bracket to the lower motor cover.
9. Remove the front and rear exhaust cover screws. Remove the nut and washer from the aft stud in the powerhead.
10. Remove the screws attaching the powerhead and the adaptor assembly.
11. Remove the powerhead from the adaptor.

1971 50 HP

1. Remove the front and rear exhaust cover screws.
2. Slide back the insulating sleeve on the shift cable wires so that the terminals between the shift cable and the motor cover are exposed. Disconnect the cables.
3. Remove the aft nut and washer from the stud in the powerhead.
4. Remove the nuts attaching the powerhead to the exhaust housing and adaptor assembly.

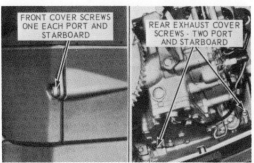

Front and rear exhaust cover removal (© Outboard Marine Corporation)

5. Lift the powerhead and lower motor cover assembly from the adaptor.

6. Remove the lower motor cover.

7. Remove the starter.

8. Remove the carburetors.

9. Remove the flywheel, stator, and timer base, and remove the electrical components bracket.

10. Remove the throttle and timer advance linkage.

11. Remove the choke solenoid.

1966–67 60 HP and 1968 65 HP
1966–67 80 HP and 1968 85 HP

1. Disconnect the throttle linkage at the throttle cam and control shaft.

2. Remove the throttle control shaft and linkage.

3. Disconnect all electrical connections from the motor and identify all leads as to their correct location.

4. Remove the lower front motor cover and the rear exhaust housing cover with the rear lower motor cover.

5. Remove the carburetor, leaf valve assembly, fuel pump, and fuel lines. Remove the heat exchanger tube (if equipped).

6. Remove the lifting bracket.

7. Remove the flywheel.

8. Remove the distributor and starter motor (with Bendix drive).

9. Disconnect the thermostat hoses.

10. Remove the nuts and screws which attach the powerhead to the exhaust housing. Lift the powerhead from the exhaust housing and place it on a bench. The powerhead should be supported by four bosses on the cylinders.

1969–71 85 HP, 1971 100 HP,
1969–70 115 HP and 1971 125 HP

1. Remove the flywheel nut using an automotive-type flywheel holder. Loosen the lift bracket screws and remove the flywheel.

2. Disconnect the distributor linkage at the spark advance lever and remove the choke control link.

3. Disconnect all electrical connections and tag each for proper assembly.

4. Remove the ignition coil and unscrew the high-tension lead from the distributor cap (if applicable).

5. Remove the alternator stator, distributor cap, wave washer, rotor, and distributor base assembly.

6. Remove the starter motor and Bendix drive.

7. Remove the air silencer and carburetors, fuel pump, and fuel hoses, and then remove the lower throttle link and choke link from the throttle and choke arms.

8. Remove the electrical bracket.

9. Remove the rear exhaust housing cover.

10. Remove the port and starboard motor cover mount screws.

11. Disconnect the thermostat hoses and ground strap.

12. Remove the throttle lever and throttle cam, leaving the throttle link connected to the cam.

13. Remove the cylinder heads and by-pass covers.

14. Remove the nuts and screws which attach the powerhead to the exhaust housing. Remove the powerhead and place it on a bench so the crankshaft is horizontal and so the weight of the motor is supported by the bosses on the four cylinders.

1966–68 100 HP

1. Disconnect the throttle linkage at the throttle cam.

2. Disconnect the distributor link from the control shaft ball joint and remove the throttle control shaft with the linkage from the powerhead.

3. Disconnect all electrical connections and tag each for proper assembly.

4. Remove the diode, pulse transformer, voltage regulator, and starter solenoid.

5. Disconnect the carburetor drain hose and remove the carburetor, leaf valve assembly, fuel pump, and fuel hoses.

6. Loosen the lift bracket screws.

7. Using an automotive, flywheel-holding tool, remove the flywheel nut. Remove the flywheel using a puller.

8. Remove the stator and distributor.

9. Remove the starter motor and Bendix drive.

10. Remove the rear lower motor cover with the exhaust cover and pulse pack. Remove the lower front motor cover.

11. Disconnect the thermostat hoses and remove the by-pass covers and cylinder heads.

12. Remove the nuts and screws which attach the powerhead to the lower unit. Lift the powerhead from the exhaust hous-

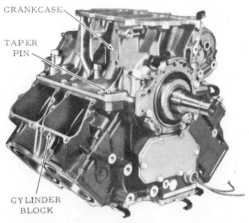

CRANKCASE

TAPER
PIN

CYLINDER
BLOCK

Powerhead on the bench for disassembly (© Outboard Marine Corporation)

ing and place it on a bench with the crankshaft in a horizontal position and the weight of the powerhead supported on the bosses of the four cylinders.

Disassembly

OMC powerheads are one of three types: a two-cylinder inline, a three-cylinder inline, and a V4. A typical disassembly procedure for two- and three-cylinder inline engines and for V4 engine is given. Small differences may exist between models of any type, but service procedures are basically alike.

2 and 3 Cylinder Inline

1. Remove the lift bracket, cylinder head, and cylinder head gasket. Remove the lower main bearing seal housing (if equipped).

2. Remove the bypass covers and gaskets.

3. Remove the inner and outer exhaust covers and gaskets. If pitting is encountered on the inner exhaust plate, install a new plate at assembly.

4. Loosen the clamps and remove the oil return hose from the crankcase.

5. Drive the taper pins from the back to the front of the crankcase.

6. Remove the large and small screws attaching the crankcase to the cylinder block. Tap the top end of the crankshaft with a rubber mallet or rawhide mallet to break the seal between crankcase and cylinder block.

7. Lift the crankcase from the cylinder block.

8. Remove the oil drain valve from the crankcase for cleaning and inspection.

9. Remove the connecting rod caps and needle bearings.

NOTE: *The connecting rod caps and connecting rods are matched assemblies. Mark each connecting rod cap, connecting rod, piston, cylinder, and bearing component to assure correct mating when they are assembled.*

10. Remove the snap-ring from the end of the crankshaft and remove the seal components.

11. Lift the crankshaft from the cylinder block and lay it on a clean cloth to avoid damage. Lift the retaining ring out of the groove and remove the center main needle bearing.

12. Some two-cylinder motors of larger horsepower are equipped with upper and lower bearings on the crankshaft. The top main bearing and seal assembly (with O-ring) slides off. The bottom main bearing can be removed, if necessary, with a bearing puller.

13. Reinstall the matched caps on the connecting rods and remove the matched caps and connecting rods from the cylinders.

14. Remove the rings from the pistons. Do not try and save the rings; new rings should be installed at each overhaul.

15. It is possible to remove the pistons from the connecting rods. However, the better procedure is to replace the connecting rod, piston, and bearing assembly if this is necessary.

V4

1. If necessary, remove the intake manifold.

2. Drive the two taper pins out of the crankcase and cylinder block assembly. Drive these from the back of the crankcase toward the front.

3. Remove the large and small screws attaching the crankcase to the cylinder block.

4. Remove the hex screws from the upper crankcase head.

5. Remove the hex screws from the lower crankcase head.

6. Remove the retaining ring and carbon seal from the lower end of the crankshaft. Remove the remaining seal components.

7. Loosen (but do not remove entirely)

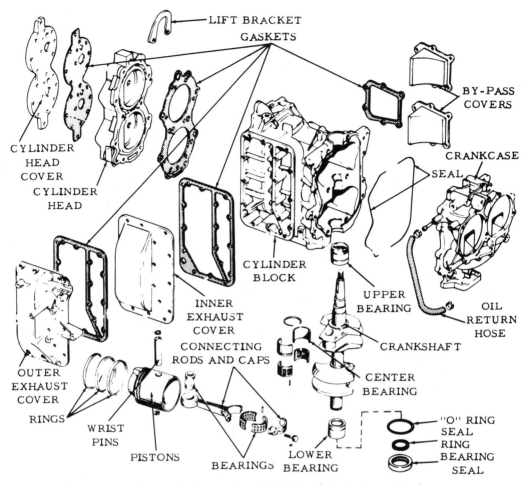

Typical two-cylinder powerhead (© Outboard Marine Corporation)

Removing the taper pins—V4 (© Outboard Marine Corporation)

the screws holding the lower bearing retainer plate to the lower crankcase head. Tap the crankshaft with a rawhide mallet

to break the seal between the crankcase and cylinder block. Remove the crankcase from the cylinder block.

8. Match-mark each connecting rod, connecting rod cap, piston, cylinder, and bearing assembly, so that they can be replaced in their original positions.

9. Remove the connecting rod caps and the needle bearing assemblies. A $5/16$ in., twelve point, deep socket is required for this.

10. Lift the crankshaft and crankcase heads from the cylinder block and place them on a clean cloth on the bench to avoid damage.

11. Reinstall the connecting rod caps on the connecting rods and remove the connecting rods and pistons.

12. Lift the upper crankcase heads from the crankshaft. To remove the seal, insert a punch through the bottom of the bearing to engage the seal. Drive the seal out. Do

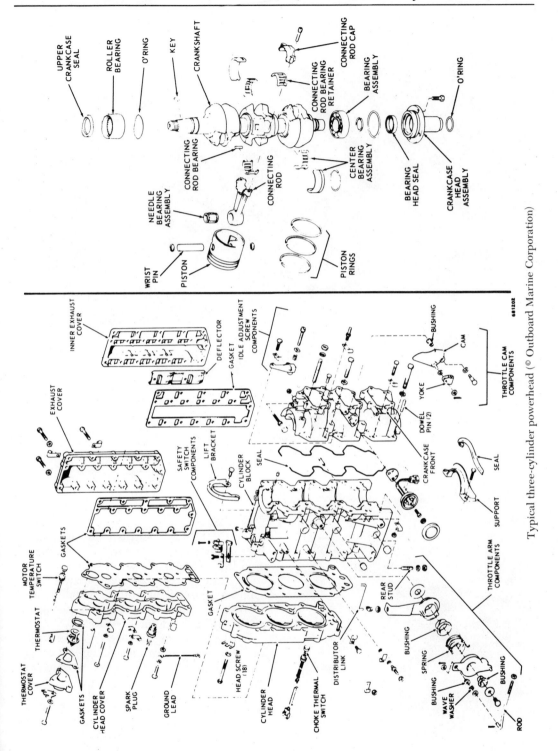

Typical three-cylinder powerhead (© Outboard Marine Corporation)

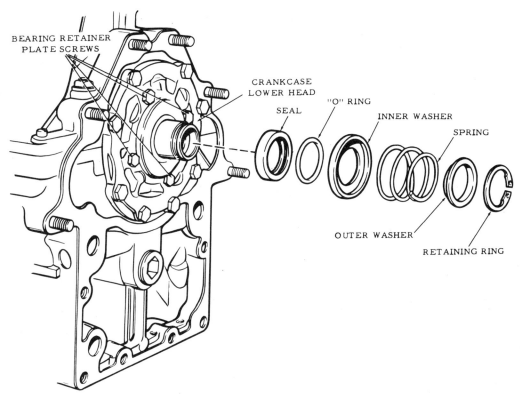

Carbon seal on V4 powerhead (© Outboard Marine Corporation)

Crankshaft removal—V4 (© Outboard Marine Corporation)

Removing crankshaft head seal—V4 (© Outboard Marine Corporation)

not reuse the seal. To remove the bearing, press it out from the top side of the crankcase head with an arbor press.

13. Remove the screws which attach the lower crankcase head to the lower bearing retainer plate and remove the lower crankcase head from the crankshaft. Remove the retaining ring under the bearing with snap-ring pliers.

14. Inspect the ball bearing at the lower end of the crankshaft and replace it if

damaged. It can be removed by using a puller.

15. The center journal needle bearing may be removed by lifting the retaining ring and sliding it to one side. This will separate the halves of the bearing.

16. Remove the piston rings from the pistons. Do not try to save the rings; install new rings at each powerhead overhaul.

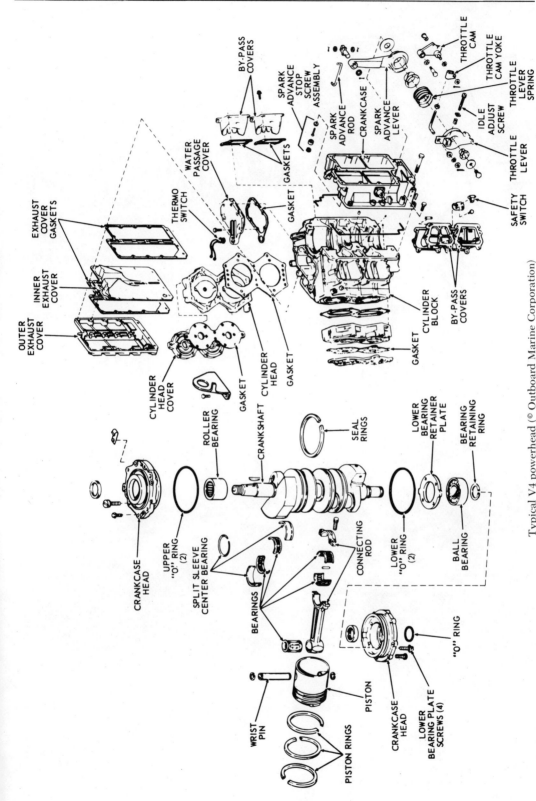

Typical V4 powerhead (© Outboard Marine Corporation)

17. It is possible to remove the pistons from the connecting rods. However, the better practice is to install a new piston and a new connecting rod and bearing assembly, should it become necessary.

CLEANING AND INSPECTION— ALL MODELS

Cylinder Block and Crankcase

1. Check all cylinder walls for wear and check cylinder ports for carbon accumulation. Cylinder walls wear depending on lubrication and operating conditions. The major portion of wear is above the ports and the area covered by ring travel.

2. Check the cylinders for out-of-round. If wear is greater than 0.003 in., replace the cylinder block or have the block rebored and install oversize pistons (see specifications).

3. Carbon accumulation on the walls of the exhaust ports restricts the flow of exhaust gases and has a large effect on the motor's performance. Carefully scrape the carbon from the cylinder heads and exhaust ports with a scraper or blunt instrument. Avoid getting carbon in the water jackets.

4. Before installing the pistons in the cylinders, break the glaze on the cylinder walls with a cylinder hone. A few up-and-down motions of the hone should remove the glaze. Do not scratch the cylinder walls.

Gasket Surfaces

1. Remove all traces of dried cement with trichloroethylene. Check all gasket faces for straightness.

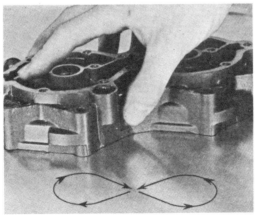

Finishing the cylinder head gasket surface (© Outboard Marine Corporation)

2. To check for flatness, use a straight-edge or lay a sheet of no. 120 emery paper on a sheet of plate glass. Place the part to be surfaced on the emery cloth and move it back and forth slowly as indicated in the illustration. Be sure to exert even pressure. If the surface is warped, the high spots will take on a dull polish while the low spots will retain the original finish. Continue surfacing until the entire area has a dull polish. Finish surfacing with no. 180 emery cloth in the same manner.

Seal Rings

1. Check the crankshaft seal rings for excessive wear. They should fit snugly in the crankcase and cylinder block and should provide a tight seal.

Bearings

1. Keep the bearings free of dirt and oil when servicing.

2. Wash all bearings in solvent until they are clean and free of dirt and sludge. Air-dry the bearings; do not spin them to dry, as this will cause irreparable harm.

3. Bearings rust easily and should be lubricated immediately with light, clean oil.

4. Discard any bearings showing any of the following:
   a. Rusted balls, rollers, or races;
   b. Fractured rings;
   c. Worn or abraded surfaces;
   d. Badly discolored balls, rollers, or races (this is usually due to inadequate lubrication).

Seals

1. Replace the upper crankcase head seal. Seat the new seal with the lip facing in and flush with the top of the crankcase head.

2. Replace the lower crankcase head seal.

Pistons

1. Check the pistons for roundness, scoring, or wear. The pistons skirts must be perfectly round to prevent exhaust gases from entering the compression chamber.

2. Carefully remove all carbon deposits.

3. Scrape carbon from the ring grooves, using a piece of an old ring. Do not damage the ring grooves or the lower ring lands.

4. Remove carbon from inside the piston head.

5. Before installing new piston rings check the piston ring gap by installing the ring in its bore and seating it squarely with the bottom of a piston. Check the ring groove clearance with a feeler gauge.

Checking ring gap (© Outboard Marine Corporation)

Checking ring-to-groove clearance (© Outboard Marine Corporation)

Assembly

2 AND 3 CYLINDER INLINE

1. Proceed slowly and do not force parts unless press-fits are specified. Do not test-assemble parts. Be sure that all parts are clean and free of dirt and grit. Use new gaskets and seals throughout.

2. Install the piston rings on each piston and be sure they fit freely. The ring gaps are staggered to prevent loss of compression. The ring grooves are pinned to locate the gaps.

3. Coat the cylinders and pistons with oil and install the piston and connecting rod assemblies, with the intake side of the piston deflector toward the intake port. Avoid the use of automotive-type ring compressors as these frequently damage the pistons and rings through improper alignment of the rings.

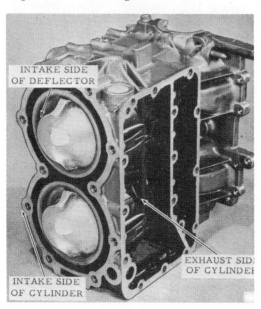

Piston positioning in the cylinder—two-cylinder (© Outboard Marine Corporation)

4. Replace the main journal bearings on the crankshaft and place the O-rings in position on the upper and lower bearings.

5. Remove the rod caps from the connecting rods. Apply a coat of OMC Needle Bearing Grease to the connecting rod bearing area. Place the retainer half and seven roller bearings on each rod.

6. Place the crankshaft in position on the cylinder block and align the dowel pins with the main bearings.

7. Apply OMC Needle Bearing Grease to the crankpins and install two roller bearings and the remaining seven roller bearings in each retainer.

8. Install the connecting rod caps. These are not interchangeable between rods, nor may they be turned endwise. Small raised dots are provided to assist in matching the sides of the rod and cap.

9. Tighten the connecting rod screws to the specified torque.

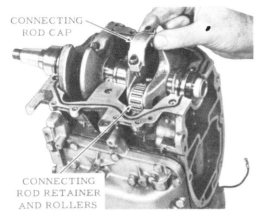

CONNECTING ROD CAP

CONNECTING ROD RETAINER AND ROLLERS

Installing connecting rod caps (© Outboard Marine Corporation)

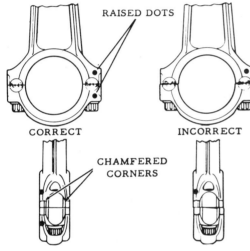

RAISED DOTS

CORRECT   INCORRECT

CHAMFERED CORNERS

Correct connecting rod cap alignment (© Outboard Marine Corporation)

10. The crankcase face is grooved for proper installation of a new seal. The seal should be seated in the groove and cut somewhat longer than is necessary, to obtain a good seal against both ends of the crankcase. Run a fine bead of Sealer 1000 in the groove, before installing the seal. After the sealer has set, trim the ends of the seal, leaving approximately $1/32$ in. on each end for a good butt.

11. Apply a thin line of Sealer 1000 to the crankcase face.

12. Install the crankcase on the cylinder block and install the screws finger-tight. Install the crankcase taper pins, driving them in carefully with a hammer.

13. Rotate the crankshaft and check for binding between the crankshaft and bearings or the connecting rods and bearings.

14. Torque all crankcase screws to the specified torque.

15. Install the cylinder head and lifting bracket. Tighten the cylinder head bolts to the specified torque in the sequence illustrated in the specifications.

NOTE: *Retorque the cylinder head screws after the motor has cooled to the point where it is comfortable to the touch.*

16. Replace the inner and outer exhaust covers. Install all screws finger-tight before torquing.

17. Install the by-pass covers. The upper by-pass cover has tapped holes for mounting the fuel pump.

18. Install the oil return hose on the crankcase and tighten the clamps.

19. The oil drain valve ordinarily requires little service; however, if the motor is serviced, remove and clean the oil drain valve and screen. If gum or varnish is found in the crankcase, it is likely there will be similar substances in the drain valve. Be sure that the leaf seats squarely against the leaf plate.

V4

1. Steps no. 1 and 2 of the preceding procedure apply.

2. On certain models, seal rings must be selectively fitted to the crankshaft grooves with a minimum side clearance of 0.0015 in. and a maximum clearance of 0.0025 in. For models which do not require this seal ring procedure, proceed to step 12.

3. Crankshaft replacements do not require this fitting since seal rings come with the crankshaft as an assembly. When a seal ring has been broken during repairs, measure the diameter with a micrometer and install a new ring of the same thickness. Three different thicknesses of seal rings are available.

4. If there is no means of identifying the seal rings, use the following procedure.

5. Obtain the set of three seal rings from a dealer for each groove.

6. Starting with the ring groove nearest the top, roll the largest size ring into the groove. If it will not fit into the groove, or if it appears at all tight, select the middel size ring and repeat the procedure.

7. Select the ring which appeared to fit correctly and install it in the groove.

8. A final clearance check should be

Measuring crankshaft tolerance (© Outboard Marine Corporation)

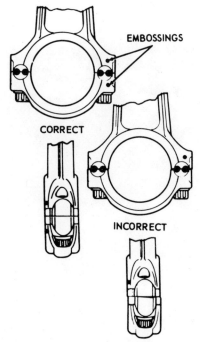

Correct connecting rod cap alignment—V4 (© Outboard Marine Corporation)

made after installation to be sure that a clearance of 0.0015–0.0025 in. exists. This can be done with a feeler gauge.

9. Should less than 0.0015 in. clearance exist, replace the seal ring with the next size smaller.

10. Repeat the steps (6–9) for each groove.

11. Liberally lubricate each ring and groove with oil.

12. Install a new lower seal in the crankcase head (if applicable).

13. Place the lower bearing retainer plate over the lower end of the crankshaft. Press the ball bearing onto the lower journal with an arbor press. Oil the bearing and install the retaining ring.

14. Install the O-ring and gasket on the lower crankcase head and install the crankcase head with the lug cavity aligned with the lug on the bearing retainer plate.

15. Install the retainer plate screws, using new O-rings or screws if necessary.

16. Draw the screws tight and back off two turns to provide a slight degree of end-play which will ease crankcase installation.

17. Oil and install the center main bearing on the center journal of the crankshaft and position the dowel pin hole in the bearing toward the cylinder block.

18. Install the upper crankcase head, O-rings, seal, and bearing assembly on the crankshaft. Remove the connecting rod caps.

19. Install the crankshaft and align the center main bearing with the dowel pin in the cylinder block. When installing the crankshaft, the pistons must be as close to the bottom of the cylinders as possible.

20. Perform steps 5–11 of the preceding procedure.

21. Place the crankcase in position on

the cylinder block being careful to avoid damaging the crankcase head gasket and O-rings. Rotate the crankcase heads to their proper positions.

22. Install the upper and lower crankcase head screws finger-tight.

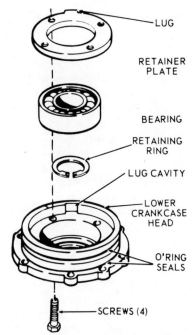

Lower crankcase head assembly—V4 (© Outboard Marine Corporation)

23. Drive the crankcase taper pins in with a hammer and punch.

24. Install the crankcase screws finger-tight. One of the eight smaller screws is shorter than the rest and holds the starter mounting bracket to the crankcase. This screw should be left loose for installation of the starter.

25. Rotate the crankshaft and check for any binding.

26. Tighten all screws to the specified torque, beginning with the center main crankcase screws.

27. Install a new carbon seal and replace any parts of this assembly which are damaged or worn.

INSTALLATION

In all cases, installation is the reverse of removal. Note the following procedures:

1. Be sure that the gasket surfaces of the powerhead and exhaust housing are clean. Install a new gasket.

2. Install the powerhead, being careful not to damage the splines on the crankshaft and driveshaft. Rotate the powerhead slightly as it is lowered onto the exhaust housing, to engage the splines.

CAUTION: *In no case, should the driveshaft be caused to rotate counterclockwise as this will damage the water pump impeller.*

3. Inspect the flywheel and crankshaft tapers to be sure that they are free of dirt, burrs, and oil. They must be perfectly dry and clean.

4. Torque all nuts to specification.

5. Perform all necessary adjustments (see "Fuel System" and "Electrical System").

6. Test the motor on the boat or in a test tank and check carefully for leaks.

7. Retorque the cylinder head nuts after the motor has cooled so it is comfortable to the touch.

BREAK-IN PROCEDURE

Following an engine overhaul, the break-in procedure specified in the owners manual should be followed to allow all parts to seat properly.

Motor Leg and Water Pump

OMC outboards use three basic types of lower unit: a standard, manual shift gear-

case; an electric shift gearcase, and an electric-hydraulic shift-type gearcase.

CAUTION: *Lower units—especially the electric shift and the electric-hydraulic shift—are very sensitive. They should be repaired by qualified mechanics with the necessary special tools and equipment. Due to the complexity of OMC lower units, no overhaul procedures of the gearcase are given. It is suggested that this be left to a dealer who is equipped with the special equipment necessary for these operations.*

Service procedures are divided according to the application of the lower unit. All lower units under one application listing have basically similar service procedures, although minor differences may be noted on individual models.

1966–70 33 HP AND 1966–71 40 HP

Manual Shift Gearcase Removal

1. It is possible to remove the upper and lower gearcase assembly without removing the powerhead. If disassembly of the exhaust housing is required, the powerhead must be removed.

2. Disconnect the spark plug wires and drain the gearcase.

3. Remove the rear exhaust cover.

4. Remove the inner and outer exhaust housing cover plates.

5. Remove the shift-rod connector lower screw.

6. Remove the gearcase from the ex-

Remove the lower shift rod connector (© Outboard Marine Corporation)

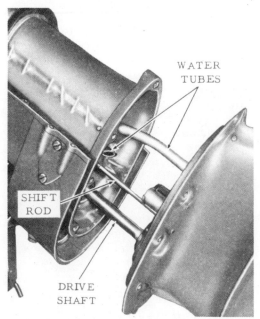

Removing the gearcase (© Outboard Marine Corporation)

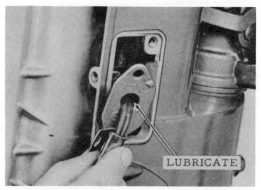

Removing the rear exhaust housing plate (© Outboard Marine Corporation)

4. Remove the upper and lower gearcase assembly from the exhaust housing or gearcase extension (long leg models).

Water Pump Replacement

1. Remove the three screws which attach the water pump impeller housing to the upper gearcase.
2. Lift off the driveshaft and impeller housing assembly.
3. Remove the seals, O-ring, and grommets.

haust housing or gearcase extension (long leg models).

Electric Shift Gearcase Removal

1. Disconnect the spark plug wires and drain the gearcase.
2. Slide back the insulating sleeve on the shift cable. Disconnect the terminals between the shift cable and motor cable.

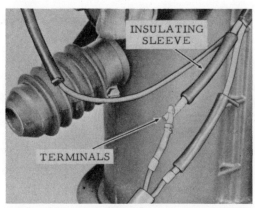

Disconnecting the electric shift cable terminals (© Outboard Marine Corporation)

3. Remove the rear exhaust cover and exhaust housing plate. Remove the screws from the inner exhaust housing plate and clamp. Lubricate the cable sleeve and remove the grommet.

Impeller housing and plate (© Outboard Marine Corporation)

4. Inspect the water pump assembly for damaged vanes, a scored pump housing, or a scored impeller housing plate. Replace all damaged or worn parts.

5. Apply Sealer 1000 to the gearcase and position the impeller plate on the gear housing.

6. Install new seals, O-rings, and grommets in the impeller housing.

7. Oil the impeller and driveshaft. Install the driveshaft through the impeller housing from the top.

8. Install the impeller on the driveshaft.

9. Install the driveshaft with the impeller and housing on the gearcase. Rotate the driveshaft to engage the pinion gear splines.

10. Install the impeller key, lubricate the impeller, and position the impeller over the key.

11. Install the impeller housing over the impeller and rotate the driveshaft clockwise to position the impeller blades for clockwise rotation.

12. Install the screws holding the impeller housing to the gearcase. Apply sealer to the screws.

Adjustments

GEARSHIFT

1. Place the shift handle in Neutral and be sure the propeller rotates freely. The shift lever pin must be centered in the Neutral detent.

2. Move the shift handle to Forward gear and rotate the propeller until it contacts the shifter dog on Forward gear.

3. Note the point of engagement and the point where the shift lever pin rides in the Forward gear detent.

4. Repeat the procedure for Reverse gear. The shift lever pin should stop an equal distance from the Forward and Reverse detents.

5. To adjust the gearshift, ground the spark plug wires.

6. Loosen the shift handle clamp and adjustment screws.

7. Adjust the shift handle as required and recheck the adjustment after tightening the screws.

1966–67 60 HP, 1968 65 HP, 1966–67 80 HP, 1968 85 HP, AND 1966–68 100 HP

Gearcase Removal

1. It is possible to remove the upper and lower gearcase without removing the powerhead. If the exhaust housing is to be removed, the powerhead must be removed.

2. Disconnect the spark plug wires.

3. Drain the gearcase.

4. Slide back the insulating sleeve on the shift cable and detach the terminals between the shift cable and the motor cable.

5. Remove the rear outer exhaust cover and lower motor cover as an assembly. Remove the shift cable at the clamp below the powerhead.

6. Remove the screws and nuts which attach the gearcase and extension to the

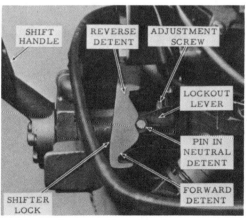

Shift lever adjustment (© Outboard Marine Corporation)

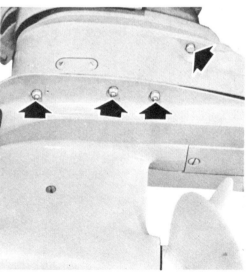

Gearcase attaching screws (© Outboard Marine Corporation)

exhaust housing. Remove the gearcase and extension housing.

Water Pump Replacement

1. Remove the driveshaft O-ring.
2. Remove the water pump housing.
3. Remove the impeller and key.
4. Remove the impeller plate and gasket from the gearcase extension.
5. Inspect the water pump impeller, pump housing, and impeller housing plate, and replace any of them if scored, damaged, or pitted.
6. Apply sealer to both sides of the water housing plate gasket and install it on the extension. Install the plate with the short hex-head screw in the aft corner of the plate.

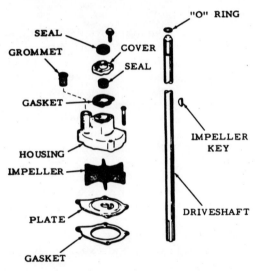

Exploded view of water pump—heavy-duty-type illustrated (© Outboard Marine Corporation)

7. Install the impeller over the key in the driveshaft with either side up if installing a new impeller.
8. Install the pump housing seal. Lubricate the impeller blades and rotate the driveshaft clockwise while sliding the housing over the impeller.
9. Slide the extension tube over the driveshaft with the marked end facing up.
10. Install a new O-ring in the groove below the splines on the driveshaft.

Gearcase to Exhaust Housing Installation

1. Assemble the stern bracket and shock absorbers. Attach these to the front exhaust cover.

2. Install the upper and lower thrust washers in their original locations. Place the outer exhaust housing in position in the front exhaust cover.
3. Install the screws through the front exhaust cover to the rubber mount on the outer exhaust housing.
4. Install the adaptor assembly on the water tubes with the new seals, gaskets, and grommets in position. Tighten the screws at each rubber mount and the screws to the outer exhaust housing. Be sure that the water tube grommets are installed.

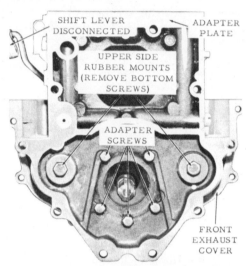

Powerhead adaptor attaching screws (© Outboard Marine Corporation)

5. Install the powerhead.
6. Apply sealer to both sides of a new gasket and place it on the gearcase extension. Align the gearcase and exhaust housing. Be sure that the water tubes enter the pump grommets. Turn the flywheel clockwise to align the driveshaft and crankshaft splines.
7. Install the screws which attach the gearcase to the extension.
8. Install the shift cable on the powerhead with the thermostat screw and clamp. Connect the leads and slide the insulating sleeve over the connections.
9. Install the rear exhaust and lower motor covers. Install the exhaust relief boot.
10. Fill the gearcase with OMC Type C lubricant.
11. Connect the spark plug wires.
12. Touch up any scratches on the lower

unit with a spray enamel of a matching color.

1971 50 HP, 1970–71 60 HP, IN 1968–69 55 HP, 1969–71 85 HP, 1970 115 HP, 1971 100 HP, AND 1971 125 HP

Gearcase Removal

1. Disconnect the spark plug wires.
2. Drain the lubricant from the gearcase.
3. Slide back the insulating sleeve on the shift cable wires and disconnect the terminals between the shift cable and motor cable.
4. Lubricate the cable sleeve and push it through the hole in the exhaust housing adaptor when removing the gearcase.
5. Match-mark the gearcase and trim tab so that the trim tab can be installed in its original position. Remove the trim tab.
6. Using a ½ in. socket with a short extension, remove the screw from the trim tab cavity.
7. Using a ⅝ in. thin-wall socket, remove the countersunk screw.
8. Remove the port and starboard attaching screws.
9. Remove the gearcase and cable from the exhaust housing. Do not damage the shift cable or lose the plastic water tube guides.

Water Pump Replacement

1. Remove the water pump cover and seal assembly.
2. Remove the screws and slide the impeller housing off the driveshaft.
3. Remove the impeller drive key and impeller plate.
4. Inspect the water pump impeller, pump housing, and impeller plate for damage, pitting, or scoring.
5. Apply sealer to the bottom edge of the impeller plate and install the plate, aligning the holes in the plate and gearcase. Install the impeller drive key.
6. Install a new seal in the impeller housing and attach the cover to the impeller housing, but do not tighten the screws.
7. Install the water tube guides in the pump housing cover.

8. Install the impeller over the key in the driveshaft.
9. Install the pump housing. Lubricate the impeller and rotate the driveshaft clockwise while sliding the housing over the impeller.
10. Secure the pump housing with screws that have been dipped in sealer. Tighten the pump cover screws.
11. Route the shift cable around the water pump and up through the hole in the impeller housing.

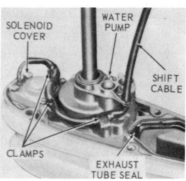

Shift cable routing and clamps (© Outboard Marine Corporation)

Gearcase Installation

1. Install a new O-ring on the driveshaft. Apply a light coating of sealer to the splines.
2. Install the plastic water tube guides in the water pump housing.
3. Lubricate the upper end of the shift cable sleeve.
4. Insert a length of wire with the terminals through the shift cable hole in the adaptor and attach to the gearcase terminals.
5. Carefully install the gearcase, making sure that the water tube guides feed the water tubes into the pump grommets while pulling the shift cable through the exhaust housing and adaptor assembly.
6. Dip the gearcase attaching screws into sealer and install them.
7. Install the trim tab, aligning the match-marks made at removal.
8. Install the powerhead.
9. Install the front and rear exhaust covers.
10. Connect the shift cable leads.
11. Touch up the finish with spray enamel in a matching color.
12. Adjust the trim tab.

Appendix

Safety Afloat

BOATING SAFETY COURSES

As an aid to boating safety, wise boatmen know the value of becoming involved in a voluntary education program so that they will better understand their responsibilities on the water. The Coast Guard Auxiliary offers any boatman the opportunity to obtain instruction in seamanship, smallcraft handling, and safety practices aloft. Qualified members of the Coast Guard Auxiliary present each of the following courses:

1. Outboard Motorboat Handling—primarily for outboard operators with the emphasis on safety. Covers the fundamental rules of boat handling, equipment requirements, and common-sense courtesy.

2. Safe Boating—provides instruction in the elements of seamanship, navigation, rules of the road, and boating safety for outboards and inboards.

3. Basic Seamanship and Smallboat Handling—provides a practical and comprehensive study of boating, seamanship, navigation, piloting (charts and compass), rules of the road, safe motorboat operation, and accident prevention. Those who successfully complete this course are awarded the U.S. Coast Guard Auxiliary Basic Smallboat Seamanship Certificate.

To obtain information on any of the above courses, write to the director of the Auxiliary located in your district (see list of U.S. Coast Guard Districts) or contact any member of the Coast Guard Auxiliary Flotilla nearest you.

In addition to the above courses, U.S. Power Squadrons and the American National Red Cross offer free courses for any boater.

Troubleshooting Emergencies Afloat

SAFETY PRECAUTIONS

Wise boatmen take a tip from professional sailors who know the value of being prepared for emergencies. By studying the following sections, and familiarizing yourself and at least one other person with them, your reactions in an emergency situation will be fast and may save a life. Before venturing into any waters, it is wise to check the following items. Remember, that it is not necessary to be on the open seas, to encounter an emergency. Many boating accidents occur each year on protected waters, inland waterways, and lakes or rivers.

1. Check the weather.
2. Advise someone of your destination.
3. Check your fuel supply and be sure that you carry enough fuel for a round trip.
4. Be sure that you have lifesaving equipment for all hands.

SAFE LOAD CAPACITIES

The Outboard Boating Club of America has calculated weight capacity specifications as a guide for small craft operators. Most manufacturers display this information on a plate somewhere on their boats. These are recommended weight capacities for cruising in good weather and calm water. It is still the responsibility of the operator to exercise caution and sound judgment regarding the capacity of his craft. In the absence of capacity plates, the following formulae will help to determine the capacity of boats of more or less standard design.

CAPACITY (NUMBER OF PERSONS)

The number of persons that your boat can carry in good weather conditions without crowding can be calculated as follows:

L = Length Overall (feet)
B = Maximum Width (feet)

$$\frac{L \times B}{15} = \text{——number of persons}$$

(to the nearest whole number).

CAPACITY (WEIGHT)

The weight capacity of your boat, taking into account the weight of people, engine, fuel, and gear can be calculated as follows:

L = Length Overall (feet)
B = Maximum Width (feet)
De = Minimum Effective Depth of Boat (feet). "De" should be measured at the lowest point that water can enter. This takes into account low transom cutouts or acceptable engine wells.

$$7.5 \times L \times B \times De = \text{——pounds for persons, engines, fuel, and gear.}$$

MINIMUM NECESSARY EQUIPMENT

The states and the Federal Government have established minimum equipment requirements, which, by law, must be carried at all times. The following chart sets down additional equipment which is recommended for various classes of boats and various types of waters. "D" designates items which are desirable and "E" indicates essential items. Common sense and experience will dictate any changes to this recommended equipment list.

Item	Class A (to 16')			Class I (16'–26')			Class 2 (26'–40')		
	Open waters	Semi-protected	Protected	Open waters	Semi-protected	Protected	Open waters	Semi-protected	Protected
Anchor(s)	E	E	E	E	E	E	E	E	E
Anchor cable (line, chain, etc.)	E	E	E	E	E	E	E	E	E
Bailing device (pump, etc.)	E	E	E	E	E	E	E	E	E
Boat hook	—	—	—	D	D	D	E	E	E
Bucket (fire fighting/bailing)	E	E	E	E	E	E	E	E	E
Coast pilot	—	—	—	D	D	—	D	D	—
Compass	E	E	D	E	E	D	E	E	E
Course protractor or parallel rules	D	D	—	E	E	D	E	E	E
Deviation table	D	D	—	E	E	D	E	E	E
Distress signals	E	E	E	E	E	E	E	E	E
Dividers	D	D	—	E	E	D	E	E	E
Emergency rations	E	—	—	E	—	—	E	—	—
Emergency drinking water	E	D	—	E	D	—	E	D	—
Fenders	D	D	D	D	D	D	D	D	D

Item	Class A (to 16')			Class I (16'–26')			Class 2 (26'–40')		
	Open waters	Semi-protected	Protected	Open waters	Semi-protected	Protected	Open waters	Semi-protected	Protected
First-aid kit and manual (10- to 20-unit)	E	E	E	E	E	E	E	E	E
Flashlight	E	E	E	E	E	E	E	E	E
Heaving line	—	—	—	—	—	—	D	D	D
Lantern, kerosine	—	—	—	—	—	—	D	D	D
Light list	D	D	—	E	E	D	E	E	E
Local chart(s)	E	D	—	E	E	E	E	E	E
Megaphone or loud hailer	—	—	—	—	—	—	D	D	D
Mooring lines	E	E	E	E	E	E	E	E	E
Motor oil and grease (extra supply)	—	—	—	D	D	D	D	D	D
Nails, screws, bolts, etc.	D	D	D	D	D	D	D	D	D
Oars, spare	E	E	E	E	E	E	—	—	—
Radar, reflector, collapsible	D	D	—	D	D	—	D	D	—
Radio direction finder	—	—	—	D	—	—	D	—	—
Radio, telephone	D	—	—	D	D	—	D	D	—
Ring buoy(s) (additional)	D	D	D	D	D	D	D	D	D
RPM table	—	—	—	D	D	D	D	D	D
Sounding device, (lead line, etc.)	D	D	—	D	D	D	E	E	E
Spare batteries	D	D	D	D	D	D	D	D	D
Spare parts	E	D	—	E	E	D	E	E	D
Tables, current	—	—	—	—	—	—	—	D	D
Tables, tide	—	—	—	—	—	—	—	D	D
Tools	E	D	—	E	E	D	E	E	D

COAST GUARD COURTESY EXAMINATIONS

You are required by law to carry certain equipment on board at all times, while underway, depending on the class of your boat and method of power. While there is no obligation, any boat owner or operator may request a free Courtesy Motorboat Examination from the Coast Guard Auxiliary or U.S. Coast Guard. If your boat is properly equipped, you will receive the Auxiliary's Official Courtesy Motorboat

Examination decal. If your boat is improperly equipped, you will be so advised.

NOTE: *If you are advised that your boat is improperly equipped, NO report is made to any law enforcement agency. You are advised of deficiencies so that they can be corrected.*

WEATHER AND STORM SIGNALS

Wise boatmen are always aware of the weather, since, for the most part, you are at the mercy of the prevailing conditions when on the open seas or large bodies of water. Before venturing onto any body of water, it is wise to check the weather and sea condition as well as the forecast for your area. Weather forecasts are available from the U.S. Weather Bureau Office in your area, as well as from radio stations and newspapers. On the Great Lakes, Atlantic, Gulf, and Pacific coasts, all Coast Guard stations and some yacht clubs fly storm signals. Small craft warnings, in particular, should never be ignored. Remember, also, that many areas of the country, and especially coastal areas, are subject to sudden squalls and the dreaded "northeasters" even in the presence of optimistic forecast. These squalls and northeast storms can arise suddenly; all small craft should seek the nearest shelter at the first sign of foul weather. It is poor practice to try to weather a storm when shelter is available. If it is impossible to reach shelter, however, the best practice is to keep the bow into the wind. Under no circumstances should you allow the craft to become broadside to large waves.

Storm Signals

The storm signals following are descriptive of the type of weather indicated. All boatmen should become familiar with their meaning and the location (in your area) from which they are flown.

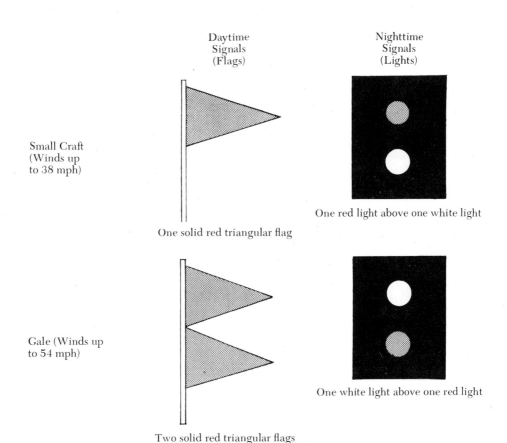

Daytime
Signals
(Flags)

Nighttime
Signals
(Lights)

Small Craft
(Winds up
to 38 mph)

One red light above one white light

One solid red triangular flag

Gale (Winds up
to 54 mph)

One white light above one red light

Two solid red triangular flags

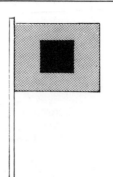

Whole Gale
(Winds up to
72 mph)

Two red lights, one above the other

One square red flag with a center black square

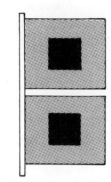

Hurricane
(Winds 72
mph and up)

Two red lights with a white light in between

Two square red flags with a center black square in each flag

NOTE: *This table includes general statements about the weather and can be very useful. However, the latest Weather Bureau forecast should be used whenever available. These forecasts are available on scheduled marine radiotelephone broadcasts, commercial radio stations, and from Weather Bureau Offices.*

Wind Barometer Chart

Wind Direction	Barometer Reduced to Sea Level	Character of Weather
SW to NW	30.10 to 30.20 and rising rapidly	Fair followed within 2 days by rain.
SW to NW	30.20 and above and stationary	Continued fair with no decided temperature change.
SW to NW	30.20 and above and falling slowly	Slowly rising temperature and fair for 2 days.
S to SE	30.10 to 30.20 and falling slowly	Rain within 24 hours.
S to SE	30.10 to 30.20 and falling rapidly	Wind increasing in force, with rain within 12 to 24 hours.
SE to NE	30.10 to 30.20 and falling slowly	Rain in 12 to 18 hours.
SE to NE	30.10 to 30.20 and falling rapidly	Increasing wind and rain within 12 hours.
E to NE	30.10 and above and falling slowly	In summer, with light winds, rain may not fall for several days. In winter, rain in 24 hours.

Wind Barometer Chart (cont.)

Wind Direction	Barometer Reduced to Sea Level	Character of Weather
E to NE	30.10 and above and falling fast	In summer, rain probably in 12 hours. In winter, rain or snow with increasing winds will often set in when the barometer begins to fall and the wind set in NE.
SE to NE	30.00 or below and falling slowly	Rain will continue 1 or 2 days.
SE to NE	30.00 or below and falling rapidly	Rain with high wind, followed within 36 hours by clearing and, in winter, colder.
S to SW	30.00 or below and rising slowly	Clearing in a few hours and fair for several days.
S to E	29.80 or below and falling rapidly	Severe storm imminent, followed in 24 hours by clearing and, in winter, colder.
E to N	29.80 or below and falling rapidly	Severe NE gale and heavy rain; winter, heavy snow and cold wave.
Going to W	29.80 or below and rising rapidly	Clearing and colder.

Beaufort Wind Scale

Wind Force	Wind Velocity (Knots)	Water Condition	Wind Condition
1	1–3	Ripples	Light air
2	4–6	Small wavelets	Light breeze
3	7–10	Wavelets crest	Gentle breeze
4	11–16	Small waves	Moderate breeze
5	17–21	Moderate waves	Fresh breeze
6	22–27	Many whitecaps	Strong breeze
7	28–33	Foam flies	Moderate gale
8	34–40	——	Fresh gale
9	41–47	——	Strong gale
10	48–55	——	Whole gale
11	56–66	——	Storm
12	66 and up	——	Hurricane

NOTE: *This is a traditional scale used to estimate wind force from wind and water conditions.*

DISTRESS PROCEDURES

Distress Signals

Searching for a vessel in distress is a time-consuming procedure when there is insufficient information on which to base the search. Your chances of receiving assistance is greatly increased if you know the recognized distress signals and have the proper equipment.

Radiotelephones are the best piece of equipment for communicating distress, and should be carried by all vessels which are used for off-shore cruising. Pleasure craft, merchant vessels, Coast Guard ships, and monitoring stations listen on 2182 kilocycles, which is a calling and distress frequency. Occasionally, 2638 or 2738 kilocycles may not be busy and may bring assistance sooner. However, in an emergency, you may use any frequency available. In an extreme emergency, the spoken word MAYDAY (international code word for needing emergency assistance) stands a good chance of being heard in most areas. The spoken word MAYDAY should not be used unless immediate assistance is required.

Many search craft today are also equipped with radar; however, wood and plastic boats do not make good radar targets. A radar reflector of the small collapsible type positioned high on the craft will infinitely increase your chances of radar detection.

The latest distress signal for small craft on waters of the United States is the act of standing as high as possible on the craft and SLOWLY RAISING AND LOWERING THE ARMS OUTSTRETCHED TO EACH SIDE. This is a distinctive signal, not likely to be mistaken for a greeting. It is important to remember that when in need of emergency assistance, any signal that will attract attention is acceptable. However, your chances are enhanced by using any of the recognized distress signals, which are shown following.

Recognized Distress Signals

Signal	Inland Rules	Great Lakes Rules	Western Rivers	International Rules[*]
A gun or other explosive fired at intervals of about a minute	Yes (day and night)	Yes (day and night)	Yes (day and night)	Yes
A continuous sounding with any fog-signal apparatus	Yes (day and night)	Yes (day and night)	Yes (day and night)	Yes
Rockets or shells, throwing red stars fired one at a time at short intervals				Yes
Signal made by radiotelegraphy or by any other signaling methods consisting of the group ···−−−··· (SOS) in Morse Code				Yes
A signal sent by radiotelephony consisting of the spoken word "Mayday"				Yes
The International Code signal of distress indicated by N.C.			Yes (day)	Yes
A signal consisting of a square flag having above or below it a ball or anything resembling a ball		Yes (day)	Yes (day)	Yes
Flames on the vessel (as from a burning tar barrel, oil barrel, etc.)	Yes (night)	Yes (night)	Yes (night)	Yes
A rocket parachute flare showing a red light				Yes
Rockets or shells, bursting in the air with a loud report and throwing stars of any color or description, fired one at a time at short intervals			Yes (day and night)	
A continuous sounding with steam whistle			Yes (day and night)	
Rockets or shells, throwing stars of any color or description fired one at a time at short intervals	Yes (day and night)			

[*] International rules do not distinguish between day and night use of signals.

Reporting Emergencies

In general, the search and rescue responsibilities of the U.S. Coast Guard include conducting harbor checks, searches for missing craft, effecting emergency repairs, towing to the nearest port of safe anchorage, and furnishing emergency medical assistance or evacuation, depending on circumstances.

To assist the Coast Guard in search and rescue operations, remember the following points.

1. When requesting assistance by radio, provide information listed on the form shown on p. 283.

```
┌─────────────────────────────────────────────────────────────┐
│              DISTRESS INFORMATION SHEET                       │
│                                                               │
│  When requesting assistance from the Coast Guard furnish the  │
│              following information after establishing          │
│                     communications                            │
│                                                               │
│              SPEAK SLOWLY AND CLEARLY                          │
│                                                               │
│  _____ This is _____    │
│  (Coast Guard Station being called)  (Your boat's name and    │
│                                         radio call sign)      │
│  I am _____ in position _____  │
│     (Nature of distress—Disabled, sinking,        (Latitude   │
│            grounded, etc.)                          and        │
│                                                               │
│  _____  │
│  longitude bearing (True or Magnetic) and distance from a     │
│             prominent point of land)                          │
│  I have _____ persons aboard. I am in _____   │
│        (Number)                     (Immediate or no          │
│                                      immediate danger)        │
│  My boat is _____, _____, _____, _____     │
│          (Length and type) (Type of rig) (Color of hull)      │
│                                          (Color of topside)   │
│  I request _____ assistance.│
│          (Source of assistance—Coast Guard or commercial)     │
│  I will standby _____               OVER          │
│               (Radio frequency)                               │
└─────────────────────────────────────────────────────────────┘
```

2. Advise someone of your itinerary, and at the first opportunity, notify those concerned of any change in plans.

3. Do not use MAYDAY in voice distress communications unless immediate assistance is required.

Man Overboard

The following procedures are recommended in the event of a man overboard.

1. Keep calm. Do not panic or allow others to panic.

2. Swing the stern of the boat away from the man. This reduces the danger of his being injured by a propeller.

3. Throw the man a lifesaving device as soon as possible. A ring buoy is best, since these are easiest to handle in the water. However, speed may be essential, and any device is better than none.

4. Keep the man in view at all times. If another person is available, have him act as a lookout. At night, direct the best possible light on the man in the water.

5. Maneuver to approach the man from downwind or into the sea. The particular maneuver that you use to approach the man will depend on circumstances (physical condition of the man in the water, availability of assistance, maneuvering room, etc.).

6. If capable assistance is available, it might be best to have that person put on a life jacket and go into the water to assist the person overboard. The person entering the water should not do so without attaching himself to the craft with a line.

7. Assist the man in boarding the boat. In small boats, the best way to take a person aboard from the water is over the stern. This will avoid capsizing and shipping water on small craft, which are sensitive to weight distribution. Common sense dictates that the propeller should be stopped or the engine shut off.

Fire Afloat

Fire on the water is a terrifying experience. In a real sense the person is trapped. He has a choice of staying with a burning boat or jumping into unfamiliar surroundings. Either prospect is less than pleasant. The first thought should be to stay calm and assess the situation. More can be done in the first few minutes, than in the next few hours.

Fire extinguishers such as dry chemical, carbon dioxide, and foam are most effective on oil or grease fires, when the extinguisher is directed at the base of the flames. Vaporizing liquids (chlorobromomethane and carbon tetrachloride) should not be used in confined areas, because of the danger to health. Burning items such as wood, mattresses, and rags should be extinguished by water. (Throwing them over the side is as good a method as any.)

If the fire occurs in a relatively closed space, it can be confined by closing all hatches, doors, vents, and ports to cut off the oxygen supply.

Maneuvering the craft can also be a great aid in controlling fires. Reducing speed will help to minimize the fanning effect of the wind. To help in preventing the spread of the fire, keep the fire downwind by maneuvering the boat according to the position of the fire and direction of wind.

The following steps should be taken (not necessarily in order) in the event of fire.

1. Apply the extinguishing agent by:
   a. Fire extinguisher,
   b. Discharging the fixed smothering system, or
   c. Applying water to wood or similar materials.
2. If practical, burning materials should be thrown over the side.
3. Reduce the air supply by:
   a. Maneuvering the craft to reduce the effect of wind, and
   b. Closing hatches, ports, vents, and doors if the fire is in an area where this will be effective.
4. Make preparations for abandoning the craft:
   a. Put on lifesaving devices;
   b. Signal for assistance by radio or other means.

Capsizing

Many ships and boats involved in accidents have continued to float for long periods of time. If your boat capsizes, do not leave it. There are many reasons for this school of thought. Generally, a damaged boat can be sighted more easily than a swimmer in the water.

NOTE: *Information pertaining to Minimum Necessary Equipment, Weather and Storm Signals, Wind Barometer Chart, and Distress Procedures is taken from the Recreational Boating Guide, CG-340, United States Coast Guard. This pamphlet is for sale from the Superintendent of Documents, United States Government Printing Office at 40 cents per copy.*

General Conversion Table

Multiply by	To Convert	to	
2.54	Inches	Centimeters	0.3937
30.48	Feet	Centimeters	0.0328
0.914	Yards	Meters	1.094
1.609	Miles	Kilometers	0.621
0.645	Square Inches	Square cm	0.155
0.836	Square Yards	Square meters	1.196
16.39	Cubic Inches	Cubic cm	0.061
28.3	Cubic Feet	Liters	0.0353
1.152	Knots/Hour	MPH	0.8684
2.113	Liters	US Pints	0.473
1.057	Liters	US Quarts	1.06
0.21998	Liters	Imp. Gallons	4.54
0.2642	Liters	US Gallons	3.785
0.4536	Pounds	Kilograms	2.2045
0.068	PSI	Atmospheres	14.7
To Obtain	From		Multiply by

NOTE: 1 cm = 10 mm; 1 mm = 0.0394 in.
1 Imp. Gallon = 1.2 US Gallons = 4.5459 liters
1 US Gallon = 0.833 Imp. Gallon = 3.78543 liters

Conversion—Common Fractions to Decimals and Millimeters

INCHES			INCHES			INCHES		
Common Fractions	Decimal Fractions	Millimeters (approx.)	Common Fractions	Decimal Fractions	Millimeters (approx.)	Common Fractions	Decimal Fractions	Millimeters (approx.)
1/128	0.008	0.20	11/32	0.344	8.73	43/64	0.672	17.07
1/64	0.016	0.40	23/64	0.359	9.13	11/16	0.688	17.46
1/32	0.031	0.79	3/8	0.375	9.53	45/64	0.703	17.86
3/64	0.047	1.19	25/64	0.391	9.92	23/32	0.719	18.26
1/16	0.063	1.59	13/32	0.406	10.32	47/64	0.734	18.65
5/64	0.078	1.98	27/64	0.422	10.72	3/4	0.750	19.05
3/32	0.094	2.38	7/16	0.438	11.11	49/64	0.766	19.45
7/64	0.109	2.78	29/64	0.453	11.51	25/32	0.781	19.84
1/8	0.125	3.18	15/32	0.469	11.91	51/64	0.797	20.24
9/64	0.141	3.57	31/64	0.484	12.30	13/16	0.813	20.64
5/32	0.156	3.97	1/2	0.500	12.70	53/64	0.828	21.03
11/64	0.172	4.37	33/64	0.516	13.10	27/32	0.844	21.43
3/16	0.188	4.76	17/32	0.531	13.49	55/64	0.859	21.83
13/64	0.203	5.16	35/64	0.547	13.89	7/8	0.875	22.23
7/32	0.219	5.56	9/16	0.563	14.29	57/64	0.891	22.62
15/64	0.234	5.95	37/64	0.578	14.68	29/32	0.906	23.02
1/4	0.250	6.35	19/32	0.594	15.08	59/64	0.922	23.42
17/64	0.266	6.75	39/64	0.609	15.48	15/16	0.938	23.81
9/32	0.281	7.14	5/8	0.625	15.88	61/64	0.953	24.21
19/64	0.297	7.54	41/64	0.641	16.27	31/32	0.969	24.61
5/16	0.313	7.94	21/32	0.656	16.67	63/64	0.984	25.00
21/64	0.328	8.33						